CONTESTING INDONESIA

A volume in the series

Cornell Modern Indonesia Project

Edited by Eric Tagliacozzo and Thomas B. Pepinsky

A list of titles in this series is available at cornellpress.cornell.edu.

CONTESTING INDONESIA

Islamist, Separatist, and Communal Violence since 1945

Kirsten E. Schulze

SOUTHEAST ASIA PROGRAM PUBLICATIONS
AN IMPRINT OF CORNELL UNIVERSITY PRESS   ITHACA AND LONDON

Southeast Asia Program Publications Editorial Board

Mahinder Kingra (ex officio)
Thak Chaloemtiarana
Chiara Formichi
Tamara Loos
Andrew Willford

Copyright © 2024 by Cornell University

All rights reserved. Except for brief quotations in a review, this book, or parts thereof, must not be reproduced in any form without permission in writing from the publisher. For information, address Cornell University Press, Sage House, 512 East State Street, Ithaca, New York 14850. Visit our website at cornellpress.cornell.edu.

First published 2024 by Cornell University Press

Library of Congress Cataloging-in-Publication Data

Names: Schulze, Kirsten E., author.
Title: Contesting Indonesia : Islamist, separatist, and communal violence since 1945 / Kirsten E. Schulze.
Description: Ithaca : Cornell University Press, 2024. | Series: Cornell modern Indonesia project | Includes bibliographical references and index.
Identifiers: LCCN 2024011137 (print) | LCCN 2024011138 (ebook) | ISBN 9781501777660 (hardcover) | ISBN 9781501777677 (paperback) | ISBN 9781501777684 (epub) | ISBN 9781501777691 (pdf)
Subjects: LCSH: Political violence—Indonesia. | Nationalism—Indonesia. | Communalism—Indonesia. | Islam and politics—Indonesia. | Indonesia—Politics and government—20th century. | Indonesia—Politics and government—21st century.
Classification: LCC HN710.Z9 V528 2024 (print) | LCC HN710.Z9 (ebook) | DDC 303.609598—dc23/eng/20240424
LC record available at https://lccn.loc.gov/2024011137
LC ebook record available at https://lccn.loc.gov/2024011138

To my father—Horst Dieter Schulze—you were my anchor.
And to my daughter—Hannah Rowena Alexandra
Schulze—you are the light of my life.

Contents

Acknowledgments	ix
Note on Orthography and Transliteration	xi
Abbreviations	xii
Introduction: Violence and the Indonesian National Imaginary	1
1. The Darul Islam Rebellions, 1947–1965	24
2. Jemaah Islamiyah's Jihad and Quest for an Islamic State, 1993–2019	54
3. The East Timor Conflict, 1975–1999	84
4. The Aceh Conflict, 1976–2005	123
5. The Poso Conflict, 1998–2007	155
6. The Ambon Conflict, 1999–2005	189
Conclusion: National Imaginaries at War	227
Notes	237
Index	295

Acknowledgments

This book is the result of over twenty years of research in Indonesia. It could not have been written without the many Indonesians who so generously shared their time, hospitality, experiences, and personal stories with me. I would like to start by thanking all of those who agreed to be interviewed or had informal conversations with me—Indonesian policymakers, generals, soldiers in the field, police officers, humanitarian aid workers, journalists, clerics, and members of political organizations, religious organizations, armed movements, and resistance movements. You showed me your world. You helped me understand how you felt about Indonesia, what being Indonesian meant to you, and what motivated you to engage in violence to defend your community, your religion, your political vision, or the state. This book could not have been written without you; the mistakes are all mine.

I would like to extend further gratitude to Khariroh Maknunah for transcribing the audio files of Abdullah Sungkar's sermons for me and to everyone who accompanied me along parts of my journey, on some of my research trips, or even just to meet someone they thought I ought to meet: Theodor Hanf, Hendro Purnomo, Merry Nikijuluw, Yusran Laitupa, Nasir Abas, Julie Chernov Hwang, Taufik Andrie, and Machmudi Hariono, better known as Yusuf. You ensured that my research trips were not just educational but also a lot of fun! Terima kasih also to the Center for Strategic and International Studies (CSIS) in Jakarta, and especially to Clara Juwono and Rizal Sukma for providing me with temporary office space and assistance when I first embarked on this research. I could not have had a better home away from home.

A very special thanks to those who helped me while I was stuck in lockdown in London: Lela Madjiah who assisted me with research in Jakarta, chasing up the missing bits and pieces, transcribing old audio files, and translating some of my almost illegible documents in old Indonesian spelling. Al Chaidar who generously shared some of his Negara Islam Indonesia documents with me. Frega Wenas Inkiriwang and Desra Percaya who helped me get books from Indonesia. And Paul Horsler who organized for documents to be sent to my home from the London School of Economics (LSE) library pamphlets collection.

My heartfelt appreciation also goes to my "sounding boards" while writing particular chapters—sorry I drove you crazy!—and to those who read either parts or the full manuscript: Joseph Liow, John Sidel, Julie Chernov Hwang, Amy

Freedman, Jeff Malaihollo, Carool Kersten, Aboeprijadi Santoso, Nezar Patria, Greg Fealy, Nasir Abas, Kiki Syahnakri, Lela Madjiah, Jacky Manuputty, Sidney Jones, Ed Aspinall, Damien Kingsbury, the two anonymous reviewers, and my editor Sarah Grossman. You kept me sane and your valuable feedback kept me on track.

Moreover, I am deeply grateful to all those who contributed to the funding of my research over the years: the British Academy, the German Bishops Conference, the Nuffield Foundation, the Arts and Humanities Research Board, the LSE Suntory and Toyota International Research Centres for Economic and Related Disciplines, the LSE Saw Swee Hock Southeast Asia Centre, and my own LSE Department of International History.

Last, but certainly not least, I would like to thank my daughter Hannah, my parents, and my friends for supporting me through the ups and downs of the writing process. I am sorry if I did not get the work-life balance right all the time.

Note on Orthography and Transliteration

The Indonesian words in this book have been standardized to the new orthography, except for direct quotes using the old spelling and some personal names. Arabic words appear in their Indonesian transliteration, hence syariah, not shariah, and mujahidin, not mujahideen.

Abbreviations

ABRI	Angkatan Bersenjata Republik Indonesia (The Armed Forces of Indonesia). Comprised army, navy, air force, and police.
AGAM	Angkatan Gerakan Aceh Merdeka (Armed Forces of the Free Aceh Movement). Name adopted around 1998. Changed to TNA in 2002.
AM	Aceh Merdeka (Free Aceh Movement), name used from 1976 to 1998. Thereafter, it changed to GAM.
APODETI	Associação Popular Democrática Timorense (Timorese Popular Democratic Association). Timorese political party established in 1974.
ASDT	Associação Social Democrática Timor (Timorese Social Democratic Association). Timorese political party established in 1974.
ASNLF	Aceh Sumatra National Liberation Front. Also known as AM and GAM. Established in 1976.
BAKIN	Badan Koordinasi Intelijen Negara (State Intelligence Coordination Agency).
BBM	Bugis, Butonese, and Makassar. Migrants from Sulawesi to Maluku and other parts of the archipelago after Indonesian independence.
Brimob	Brigade Mobil (Police mobile brigade).
CMI	Crisis Management Initiative. Finnish nongovernmental organization established in 2000 to assist with conflict resolution through dialogue. Also known as the Martti Ahtisaari Peace Foundation.
COHA	Cessation of Hostilities Agreement. Agreement between the Indonesian Government and the Free Aceh Movement in December 2002.
CRRN	Conselho Revolucionário da Resistência Nacional (Revolutionary Council of National Resistance). Established in East Timor in 1981.
DDII	Dewan Dakwah Islamiyah Indonesia (Indonesian Islamic Propagation Council). Established in 1967 by Mohammad Natsir.

DI	Darul Islam (Abode of Islam). Led the 1947–1965 Darul Islam rebellions. Known as Darul Islam movement after 1965.
DOM	Daerah operasi militer (military operations area).
DPR	Dewan Perwakilan Rakyat (People's Representative Assembly). Indonesian parliament.
DPRD	Dewan Perwakilan Rakyat Daerah (Regional People's Representative Assembly). Regional Indonesian parliament.
EMOI	ExxonMobil Oil Indonesia.
FALINTIL	Forças Armadas de Libertação de Timor Leste (Armed Forces for the Liberation of East Timor). Military wing of FRETILIN.
FKM	Front Kedaulatan Maluku (Maluku Sovereignty Front). Established in 2000.
FPI	Front Pembelaan Islam (Islamic Defenders Front). Established in 1998 by Muhammad Rizieq Shihab.
FRETILIN	Frente Revolucionária do Timor Leste Independente (Revolutionary Front for an Independent East Timor). Established in 1974.
GAM	Gerakan Aceh Merdeka. Free Aceh Movement. Established as AM and ASNLF in 1976. Renamed GAM around 1998.
GKST	Gereja Kristen Sulawesi Tengah (Central Sulawesi Christian Church).
GPI	Gerakan Pemuda Islam (Muslim Youth Movement).
GPM	Gereja Protestant Maluku (Malukan Protestant Church).
HMI	Himpunan Mahasiswa Islam (Muslim Student Association).
ICMI	Ikatan Cendekiawan Muslim se-Indonesia (Indonesian Muslim Intellectuals Association). Established in December 1990.
JI	Jemaah Islamiyah (Islamic Community). Jihadi organization established in 1993 after a split in DI.
KAMMI	Kesatuan Aksi Mahasiswa Muslim Indonesia (Action Front for Indonesian Muslim Students).
KISDI	Komite Indonesia Untuk Solidaritas dengan Dunia Islam (Indonesian Committee for Solidarity with the Islamic World).
KMI	Korps Mubaligh Indonesia (Lay Preachers Corps).
KNIL	Koninklijk Nederlands-Indisch Leger (Royal Netherlands East Indies Army). Established in 1814.
Kodam	Komando Daerah Militer (Regional Military Command).

Kodim	Komando Distrik Militer (District Military Command).
KOMPAK	Komite Aksi Penanggulangan Akibat Krisis (Action Committee for Tackling the Consequences of the Crisis). Established in 1997 by DDII in the context of the Asian financial crisis to help ordinary Muslims.
Kopassus	Komando Pasukan Khusus (Special Forces Command).
KOPKAMTIB	Komando Operasi Pemulihan Keamanan dan Ketertiban (Operational Command for the Restoration of Security and Order).
KRIYT	Kesatuan Rakyat Indonesia Yang Tertindas (Association of the Oppressed Indonesian People).
MPR	Majles Permusyawartan Rakyat (People's Consultative Assembly).
MUI	Majelis Ulama Indonesia (Indonesian Ulama Council).
NAD	Nanggroe Aceh Darussalam. Name of the province of Aceh from 2001 to 2009.
NASAKOM	Nationalisme, Agama, Kommunisme (nationalism, religion, communism). Concept devised by Sukarno and implemented during the Guided Democracy period from 1959 to 1965.
NICA	Netherlands Indies Civil Authorities. Established April 1944.
NII	Negara Islam Indonesia (Indonesian Islamic State). Name of the state established by Kartosuwirjo. Name of the Islamist movement after 1965. Often used interchangeably with DI.
NKRI	Negara Kesatuan Republik Indonesia (Unitary State of the Republic of Indonesia).
NU	Nahdlatul Ulama (Awakening of the Muslim Scholars). Traditionalist Muslim mass organization established in 1926 on Java.
Parmusi	Partai Muslimin Indonesia (Indonesian Muslim Party). Established in 1968. Ceased to exist in 1973.
PDI	Partai Demokrasi Indonesia (Indonesian Democratic Party). Established in 1973.
PDI-P	Partai Demokrasi Indonesia Perjuangan (Indonesian Democratic Party of Struggle). Established in 1999 by Megawati Sukarnoputri.
Permesta	Piagam Perjuangan Semesta Alam (Universal Struggle Charter). Led antigovernment rebellion from 1957 to 1961.
Persis	Persatuan Islam (Islamic Organization). Established in 1923.
PKI	Partai Komunis Indonesia (Indonesian Communist Party). Established in 1914. Disbanded in 1965.

PPI	Pasukan Pro-Integrasi (Pro-Integration Forces). Established in 1999 in East Timor. Led by Joao da Silva Tavares.
PPP	Partai Persatuan Pembangunan (United Development Party). Formed by the New Order in 1973 by amalgamating all Muslim parties.
PRRI	Pemerintah Revolusioner Republik Indonesia. Revolutionary Government of the Republic of Indonesia. Established in Sumatra in 1958. Part of the PRRI/Permesta rebellion from 1957 to 1961.
PSII	Partai Sarekat Islam Indonesia (Indonesian Islamic Union Party). Originally founded in 1930 first as PSI then PSII. Re-established in 1947. Ceased to exist in 1973.
PUPJI	Pedoman Umum Perjuangan Al Jemaah Al Islamiyah (General Guidelines for the Struggle of Jemaah Islamiyah).
PUSA	Persatuan Ulama-ulama Seluruh Aceh (All-Aceh Ulama Association). Established in 1939 to oust the Dutch from Aceh's territory.
RADIS	Radio Dakwah Islamiyah Surakarta (Islamic Propagation Radio Surakarta). Pirate radio station run by Abdullah Sungkar and Abu Bakar Ba'asyir.
RIS	Republik Indonesia Serikat (United States of Indonesia).
RMS	Republik Maluku Selatan (Republic of South Maluku). Declared April 1950. Followed by the RMS rebellion from 1950 to 1963. The RMS Movement has been based in the Netherlands since 1950.
RPII	Republik Persatuan Islam Indonesia (United Islamic Republic of Indonesia).
SARA	Suku, Agama, Ras, Antar-Golongan (ethnic, religious, race, intergroup). Acronym designating divisive issues that could lead to social conflict.
SI	Sarekat Islam (Islamic Association). Evolved from Sarekat Dagang Islam, the Muslim Traders Association. Established in 1912.
TASTOS	Total Amniah Sistem dan Total Solution (Total Security System and Total Solution). JI's security system devised by Para Wijayanto.
TII	Tentara Islam Indonesia (Indonesian Islamic Army). Army of the Indonesian Islamic State under Kartosuwirjo.
TNA	Tentara Negara Aceh (Army of the State of Aceh). Formerly AGAM. Renamed in 2002.

TNI	Tentara Nasional Indonesia (Indonesian National Military).
UDT	União Democratica Timorense (Timorese Democratic Union). Timorese political party established in 1974.
UNAMET	United Nations Mission in East Timor. Operational June to September 1999.
VOC	Vereenigde Oost-Indische Companie. Dutch United East India Company. Established in 1602. Went bankrupt in 1799.
Wanra	Perlawanan rakyat (civil defense groups).
YonGab	Batalyon Gabungan (Combined Battalion). Comprised army, navy, and air force special forces.

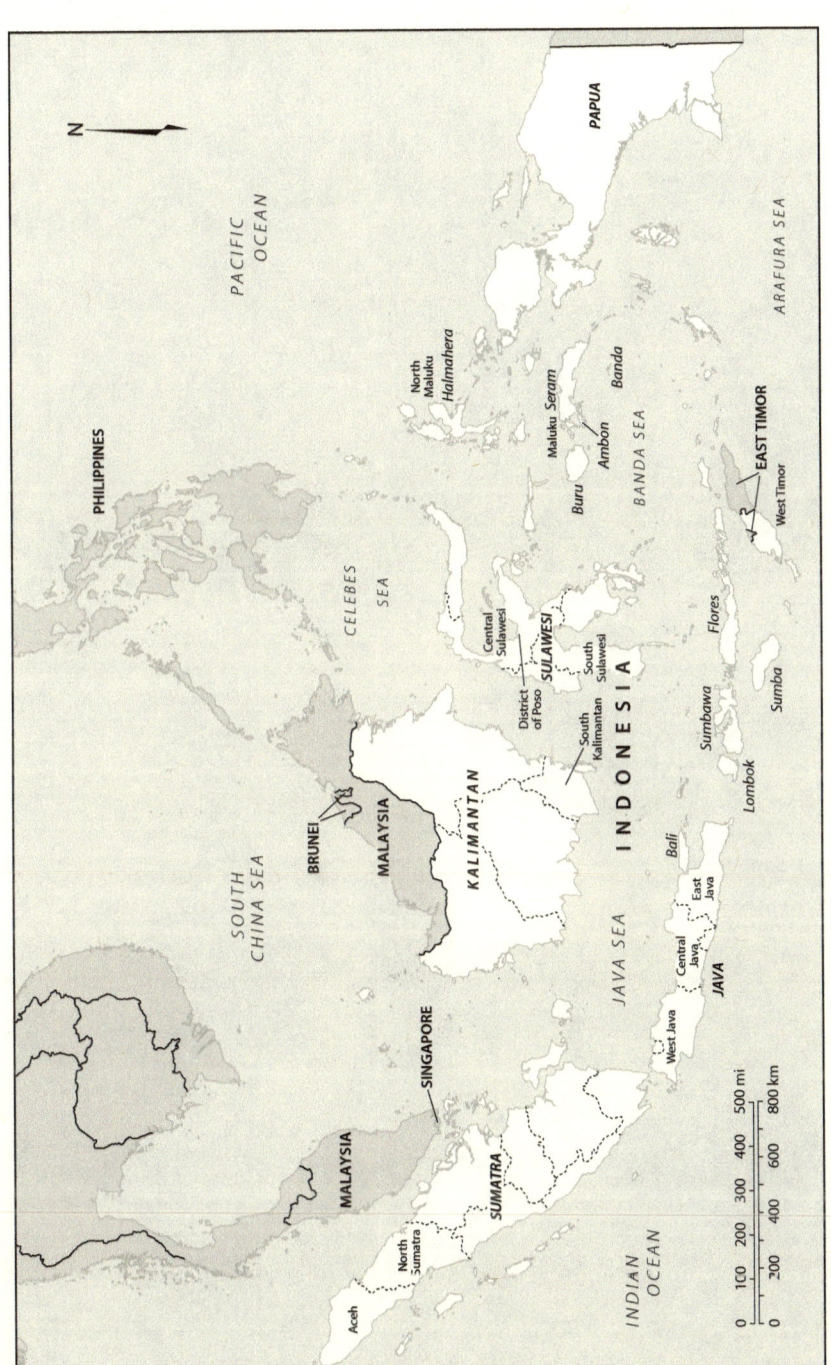

MAP 1. Map of Indonesia. Drawn by Bill Nelson.

CONTESTING INDONESIA

Introduction

VIOLENCE AND THE INDONESIAN NATIONAL IMAGINARY

From October through December 2016, Islamists gathered in the center of Jakarta demanding the arrest of the city's ethnic Chinese Christian governor, Ahok, on the grounds of blasphemy. These demonstrations brought together a variety of Muslim groups ranging from traditionalists to salafis, who sought to advance their shared agenda of Islamizing the Indonesian state. The divide over the role of Islam in politics and society was also present in the 2019 Indonesian elections that pitted those who favored a pluralist Indonesia against those who preferred an Islamist one.[1] Several days after the election results were announced, on May 27, the former military commander of the Free Aceh Movement (GAM), Muzakir Manaf, called for a referendum to decide whether the province of Aceh would remain part of Indonesia.[2] Disappointed with the continued nonimplementation of crucial aspects of the 2005 Memorandum of Understanding that had brought the Aceh conflict to an end, he declared that it was time for "the Acehnese people and nation to stand on their own feet" and that it would be better for Aceh to follow in East Timor's footsteps, meaning separation from Indonesia and independence.[3] Several months later, in August 2019, protests erupted in the Indonesian province of Papua after a video circulated that showed soldiers and civilians in the city of Surabaya calling Papuan students "monkeys." At one of these protests Victor Yeimo, the spokesman for the National Committee for West Papua, stated that "if you see us as animals, at least let us live in peace in the jungle and give us back our independence."[4]

These events in 2016 and 2019 show that what constitutes "Indonesia" remains contested in terms of both its political character and its boundaries more than seven decades after nationalist leaders Sukarno and Mohammed Hatta declared the country's independence in August 1945. Indeed, during these seven decades Islamists and separatists have repeatedly, periodically, and in some cases continuously challenged the Indonesian state, its ideological foundations, the boundaries of its territory, and its conceptualization of the nation.

The first violent confrontation between nationalists who envisaged Indonesia as a pluralist country based on the philosophy of Pancasila and Islamists who sought a state based on *syariat Islam* (Islamic law) came in the form of the 1947–1965 Darul Islam (DI) rebellions, which erupted while Indonesia was still in the midst of its war of independence against the Dutch.[5] The rebellions spread from Java to South Sulawesi, Aceh, and South Kalimantan and continued throughout Sukarno's presidency.[6] The first violent separatist challenge was launched less than a year after the transfer of sovereignty from the Dutch to the Indonesian government in December 1949. In April 1950, Malukan secessionists on the island of Ambon declared the establishment of the Republic of South Maluku (RMS). In response, Jakarta sent the Indonesian military to put down this rebellion. While they managed to defeat the RMS in Ambon in November 1950, a drawn-out guerrilla war between Malukan fighters and Indonesian forces continued on the neighboring island of Seram until 1963, when RMS president Chris Soumokil was finally captured. In the meantime, in March 1957 the Universal Struggle Charter (Piagam Perjuangan Semesta Alam, Permesta) rebellion erupted in Sulawesi. In February 1958, Permesta was joined by the alternative Revolutionary Government of the Republic of Indonesia (Pemerintah Revolusioner Republik Indonesia, PRRI) based in Sumatra. Both rebellions were a reaction to the centralization of Indonesia, Javanese dominance, and economic stagnation in the outer regions. While the Indonesian military fought the PRRI-Permesta rebellion until 1961, they also launched a covert operation to ensure the integration into Indonesia of Irian (West New Guinea), which the Dutch were due to withdraw from in 1962. This marked the beginning of the Papua conflict (see table 1).

President Suharto's New Order, from 1967 to 1998, was similarly challenged. The Revolutionary Front for an Independent East Timor (FRETILIN) militarily resisted for almost three decades after the territory's forced incorporation into Indonesia in 1975. In 1976, on the other side of the archipelago, a small independence movement emerged in the province of Aceh, which was later known as GAM. This movement was formed around a core of former Acehnese Darul Islam fighters under the leadership of Hasan di Tiro, who declared Aceh's independence from Indonesia. This insurgency, too, continued for the next three decades.

TABLE 1. Islamist, separatist, communal, and anticentrist violence in Indonesia since 1947

VIOLENCE	GEOGRAPHIC AREA	DATE	TYPOLOGY
Darul Islam rebellions	Java	1947–1962	Islamist
Republic of South Maluku rebellion	Ambon and Seram	1950–1963	Separatist anticentrist ethnoreligious
Darul Islam rebellion	South Sulawesi	1952–1965	Islamist anticentrist
Darul Islam rebellion	Aceh	1953–1959/1962	Islamist anticentrist anti-Javanese
Darul Islam rebellion	South Kalimantan	1954–1963	Islamist anticentrist
PRRI-Permesta rebellion	Sumatra and Sulawesi	1957–1961	Anticentrist
Papua conflict	Papua	1962–present	Separatist ethnic
East Timor conflict	East Timor	1975–1999	Separatist ethnic
Aceh conflict	Aceh	1976–2005	Separatist ethnic anti-Javanese
Sanggau-Ledo conflict	West Kalimantan	1997	Communal ethnic anti-Madurese
Poso conflict	Central Sulawesi	1998–2007	Communal ethnoreligious
Ambon conflict	Maluku	1999–2005	Communal ethnoreligious
Sambas conflict	West Kalimantan	1999	Communal ethnic anti-Madurese
North Maluku conflict	North Maluku	1999–2000	Communal ethnoreligious
Sampit conflict	Central Kalimantan	2001	Communal ethnic anti-Madurese

The Islamist challenge during the New Order came largely in the form of civil disobedience rather than violence and was a response to the New Order's policy of imposing Pancasila as the sole ideological foundation of all organizations as well as the mistreatment of Muslims by the security forces in what became known as the 1984 Tanjung Priok and 1989 Talangsari massacres. Among the "disobedient" were Abdullah Sungkar and Abu Bakar Ba'asyir, who, among other things, refused to raise the Indonesian flag at their *pesantren* (Islamic boarding school). They also denounced Pancasila in their sermons and through their pirate radio station, Radio Dakwah Islamiyah Surakarta (RADIS). In 1985, Sungkar and Ba'asyir, having previously been arrested and released, fled to Malaysia to escape treason charges. It was only after the fall of Suharto in 1998 that they returned to Indonesia, bringing with them the organization they had established in 1993—Jemaah Islamiyah (JI). Like Darul Islam, JI sought to establish an Islamic state; some parts of the organization pursued this goal through education and *dakwah* (Islamic outreach) while others, convinced that the Indonesian government had been sufficiently weakened by the 1997 Asian financial crisis, embarked upon a campaign of violence that they believed would bring the Indonesian government to the point of collapse.

The fall of Suharto in May 1998 was preceded by paroxysms of religious and communal violence in various locations across Indonesia from 1995 onwards, including West Kalimantan, Tasikmalaya, Banjarmasin, Sampan, Situbondo, and Pekalongan. In the month of Suharto's resignation, the capital city, Jakarta, was wracked by riots. Civil unrest also occurred in Medan and Solo. Seven months later the first in a series of large-scale communal conflicts erupted in Poso in December 1998, followed by two further communal conflicts in Ambon and Sambas in January 1999.

These large-scale communal conflicts in Ambon, Poso, and Sambas do not, at first glance, look like they were challenging the Indonesian state, its ideological foundations, the boundaries of its territory, and its conceptualization of the nation. However, a closer examination reveals that most of the communities involved in these conflicts felt as alienated from the Indonesian state as the separatists and Islamists did and similarly questioned what it meant to be Indonesian. Some even advanced alternative visions of what constituted "Indonesia" or expressed support for seceding from Indonesia. It is this contestation of Indonesia that is the subject of this book.

This Book

This book looks at Islamist, separatist, and communal violence across Indonesian history since 1945. At the heart of this enquiry is the question why Islamist, separatist, and communal conflict only erupted in some areas of Indonesia despite the fact that all of Indonesia experienced Sukarno's rule, Suharto's New Order, the fall of Suharto, and the uncertainties as well as opportunities created by Indonesia's democratization and decentralization. It is interested in *where* the violence is located, not just in a geographic sense but above all in a conceptual sense. Islamist, separatist, and communal violence is thus explored in relation to the notion of the national imaginary as well as in relation to the concept of belonging, asking *what is Indonesia?* and *what does it mean to be Indonesian?*

Islamist, separatist, and communal violence has, of course, fluctuated both in intensity and location since 1945, and not all such violence can be covered in one book. Nor does all communal conflict during that time period relate to the Indonesian national imaginary. This book thus only examines select case studies of conflict, prioritizing depth over breadth. Islamist violence is explored by looking at the 1947–1965 Darul Islam rebellions and Jemaah Islamiyah's quest for an Islamic state from 1993 to 2019. This is followed by two studies of separatism: Aceh and East Timor. Aceh was selected as it was an integral part of Indonesia when Sukarno declared independence. In fact, as the only part of the Netherlands Indies not to be reoccupied after the Second World War, it became the springboard for Indonesia's liberation struggle. Its separatist insurgency only started in 1976, challenging Indonesia for the next three decades until an autonomy agreement was reached in 2005. Aceh as a case study is also interesting as it had joined the Darul Islam rebellions from 1953 to 1959 and thus links directly to the Islamist violence examined in this book. In contrast, East Timor was forcibly integrated into Indonesia in 1975. For over two decades until the independence referendum in 1999, Jakarta tried to make East Timor Indonesian. In both Aceh and East Timor armed independence movements sought territorial and political separation. The remaining two studies are communal conflicts that erupted right after the fall of Suharto and that had both religious (Christian-Muslim) and ethnic dynamics. The 1998–2007 Poso conflict was chosen as it also had an Islamist dimension that linked it to Jemaah Islamiyah. The 1999–2005 Ambon conflict was chosen as it also had a separatist dimension derived from the earlier RMS insurgency in the 1950s.

In its exploration of Islamist, separatist, and communal violence in Indonesia this book examines the violence in relation to the national imaginary and belonging. It also analyzes the causes, phases, and dynamics of the conflicts. And finally, it looks at the differing degrees of violence and strategies applied by both state and nonstate actors. Here it asks why Indonesia's response to the Darul Islam rebellions was so much harsher than its response to the bombing campaign of JI. Why did the East Timor conflict see so many more casualties than the Aceh conflict? And why were more troops sent to the communal conflict in Ambon than to Poso? This book advances three interlinked arguments explaining Islamist, separatist, and communal violence in Indonesia. The first posits that violence erupted particularly in those regions of Indonesia that were on the periphery of the national imaginary—geographically, ideologically, ethnically, religiously, and developmentally. Indonesian Islamists found themselves on the religious periphery of a state defined as pluralist. They challenged this national imaginary militarily, seeking to replace it with their alternative national imaginary, namely an Indonesian Islamic state. Aceh and East Timor found themselves on the geographic periphery as well as the religious and ethnic periphery, with GAM seeking to establish an independent state based on Acehnese nationalism and a more strictly Muslim identity while FRETILIN sought an independent East Timor based on Timorese nationalism and a Catholic identity. Ambon and Poso saw themselves as ethnically and developmentally marginalized. Christians in those areas also saw themselves on the religious periphery, especially when Suharto started courting Muslims in the 1990s. Interestingly, two completely different national imaginaries emerged in these two conflicts. The Ambon conflict saw the reemergence of a largely Christian Ambonese separatism while Muslims in Poso mobilized in favor of an Islamic state.

The second argument asserts that violence by nonstate actors was greatest and most protracted where there was a developed alternative national imaginary backed by an alternative historical narrative. This can be seen most obviously in Aceh and East Timor, which both could point to a separate history preceding their violent incorporation into the Netherlands Indies and Indonesia respectively. However, it is also evident in Ambon and to a lesser extent in Poso, where local Christians had a different colonial experience compared not only to that of other parts of Indonesia but also to that of local Muslims.

The third argument contends that violence by the state was greatest where the alternative national imaginary had a distinct territorial dimension. This can be seen in Aceh and East Timor as separatist conflicts, but this also explains why many more troops poured into Ambon compared to Poso, as Jakarta believed that it needed to send troops to Ambon to defend the unity and integrity of the Indonesian state. The territorial dimension further illuminates the difference in state responses to the Islamists. In simplistic terms, Darul Islam had territory, JI did not.

Indonesia's National Imaginary and Belonging

Drawing upon Benedict Anderson's notion of "imagined community" and Eric Hobsbawm and Terence Ranger's notion of "invented tradition," the national imaginary will be defined here as how the nation is conceived—culturally, religiously, politically, ideologically, geographically—and constructed by a state, government, or political movement as a conscious, deliberate exercise in which traditions, rituals, and symbols are selected, shaped, and projected.[7]

So, what then does Indonesia's national imaginary look like? What is this national imaginary that is being violently contested? The starting point of Indonesia's nationalist leader and first president, Sukarno, for discussing the Indonesian nation, as exemplified by his numerous speeches, was always the 350 years of colonial exploitation by the Netherlands. This became the core of the national narrative that was both constructed and discursive, being framed as a single, shared colonial experience in opposition to the Dutch. It was a narrative of subjugation and hardship but also of resistance, providing the first nationalist heroes in Indonesia's pantheon such as Imam Bondjol, Prince Diponegoro, Kapitan Pattimura, and Cut Nyak Dien. Indonesian nationalism was thus what Antony Reid labelled an "anti-imperial nationalism."[8]

The Netherlands Indies served to anchor the national narrative not just historically but also geographically. What is particularly interesting here is that there was not just one notion of what Thongchai Winichakul in his work on Siam refers to as the "geo-body" of the nation, by which he means "the territoriality which created nationhood spatially."[9] Taking a closer look at just one single speech by Sukarno exemplifies this. In "The Birth of Pancasila," a speech given to the Committee for Preparatory Work for Independence in June 1945, Sukarno advanced *four* different geographic imaginaries for the future Indonesian state. The first is in line with the territorial expanse of the Netherlands Indies and is conceptualized as from the "tip of Sumatra to Irian." However, as Sukarno made clear, this is a minimal conceptualization, a baseline. "The idea of unity *never included less* than 'from Sabang to Merauke,' from Ulusiau to Kupang."[10] The second geographic imaginary is *tanah air* (homeland, literally "land water"), which according to Sukarno is the unity that was created by Allah "who created the map of the world" where united territories are so obvious that even a small child can see that the Indonesian archipelago—land and water—constitutes one unit. The third is that Indonesia sits between the Pacific Ocean and the Indian Ocean, between the continent of Asia and the continent of Australia. The fourth is a historic one, that Indonesia is "everything that had already been established in the era of Sri Wijaya and Majapahit."[11]

The second, third, and fourth concepts set the borders of Indonesia's geographic imaginary beyond the baseline, encompassing a much greater territorial expanse from Langkasuka in Thailand in the west to the island of Timor in the east. This greater territorial conceptualization provided the ideational backdrop for Sukarno's 1963–1966 Konfrontasi campaign as well as Suharto's 1975 invasion and incorporation of Portuguese Timor, even if the military operations themselves were articulated in security terms. Indeed, in the minds of many Indonesians, neither constituted a crossing of international boundaries, in the sense that both territories lay in the realm of Indonesia's geographic imaginary.

Sukarno's Indonesia was a revolutionary state driven by the determination to stay nonaligned as encapsulated by its *bebas-aktif* (independent-active) foreign policy and domestic policies that sought to elevate the "average" Indonesian as represented by Marhaenism. Its national imaginary was also projected through the philosophy of Pancasila ("five principles"), which Sukarno formulated during his time of internal exile on the island of Flores in the 1930s, where he spent "incalculable hours under my private tree pondering," digging "way down into the soil of our traditions" where he "came up with five beautiful pearls."[12]

These five principles, as he explained in his speech on the birth of Pancasila, were Indonesian nationalism based on the *nationale Staat* (nation-state) and the notion of *Charaktergemeinschaft* (a community derived from sharing the same character); internationalism, which he equated with humanitarianism; democracy, derived from *musyawarah* (consultation); social justice; and belief in One God.[13] These five principles, he asserted, could be "compressed into one term—*gotong royong*," meaning "toiling together, sweating hard together. Acts of service by all for the interest of all."[14]

Pancasila defined the space for Islam in Sukarno's national imaginary. As a religion Islam was placed on the same level as the other official religions: Protestantism, Catholicism, Hinduism, Buddhism, and eventually Confucianism. Politically, Sukarno initially stated that Indonesia's Muslims could form political parties and could work toward an Islamic state like other political parties pursued their aims. A sentence making *syariat Islam* obligatory for all Muslims—derived from the Jakarta Charter and often equated with it—even made it into the preamble of the draft constitution. Its unilateral removal, however, just before the constitution was promulgated in August 1945, gave a clear indication of the direction Sukarno wanted to go. This was confirmed by his January 1953 speech given in Amuntai, South Kalimantan, which ruled out the possibility of an Islamic state in Indonesia.

The year 1959 initiated changes in the Indonesian national imaginary with the introduction of Guided Democracy, which shifted the balance of power toward the president, the army, and the Indonesian Communist Party (Partai Komunis Indonesia, PKI). This opened space for emphasizing the socialist origins of Indonesian nationalism and articulating a more socialist revolutionary national imaginary.[15] Laying out his new political manifesto, aptly titled "The Rediscovery of Our Revolution," Sukarno highlighted how Indonesia had departed from the principles of the revolution and the principles of Pancasila by going down the road of "liberal politics, in which the votes of the majority of the people are exploited, black-marketed and corrupted" and "a liberal economy wherein various groups wantonly grab riches through sacrificing the interests of the People."[16] Sukarno then called for "re-orientation, re-ordering, re-tooling, re-shaping, re-making."[17] This included stepping up efforts to "eradicate imperialism," "the greatest evil of our world."[18] It also included "Indonesian socialism," which in its more concrete steps included land reform and nationalizing foreign property.[19]

Sukarno's "socialism à la Indonesia," which he defined as "adjusted to conditions prevailing in Indonesia, adjusted to Indonesia's nature, to the people of Indonesia, to the customs, the psychology and culture of the Indonesian people," drew upon some of his earlier ideas.[20] One of these was an adaptation of an article he published in 1926 on "Nationalism, Islamism, and Marxism."[21] In this article he argued that unifying these three forces would take "us in the direction of greatness and independence."[22] What John Sidel referred to as the "promise of NASAKOM" when discussing the period from 1926 to 1945, now became actualized as an ideology that sat alongside Pancasila.[23] Interesting here is that in its new guise of NASAKOM—***nasionalisme*** (nationalism), *agama* (religion), ***komunisme*** (communism)—the Islam of the earlier idea was replaced by the more generic *agama*, reflecting both the equal status that all monotheistic religions in Indonesia had under Pancasila and Sukarno's circumscription of political Islam.

The Indonesian national imaginary shifted again with the rise to power of Suharto, who formally became Indonesia's second president in March 1968. His so-called New Order recast the Indonesian national imaginary as a bulwark against communism, cleansing Indonesian nationalism of its socialist origins. The "events" of 1965 that propelled him to power became the founding narrative of the New Order, which, much like Sukarno's national narrative of the 350 years of shared colonial oppression, was constructed and discursive. Suharto dedicated a significant portion of his autobiography to these events, starting his account with how he heard of "the abduction of several senior Army officers," followed by hearing the broadcast of the 30th September Movement led by Lieutenant Colonel Untung.[24] He quickly concluded that the PKI had staged a coup and that "the state and Pancasila [were] being placed in danger."[25] He thus had no choice but "to temporarily take command and leadership of the Army."[26] Suharto designated the 30th September Movement (G30S/PKI) as "counterrevolutionary," stating that it needed to "be completely crushed" so that the "Unitary State of the Republic of Indonesia, founded on Pancasila, will retain its glory."[27] This crushing needed to be a "single concerted effort" by the people joining with the army, seeking justice for the brutal torture and killing of the abducted generals whose bodies had been dumped in a well in Lubang Buaya.[28] He emphasized that the army's actions and his own were "to help the people defend themselves and rid their own environment of the roots of evil."[29] The violent purges, arrests, and internal exile of communists and alleged communists that followed in 1965 and 1966 also redefined what it meant to be Indonesian.[30]

While the New Order broke with Sukarno's socialist ideas, there was clear continuity with Sukarno's policies with respect to controlling political Islam, despite its initial use of Muslim organizations in the fight against communism. Masyumi, banned in 1960, remained banned and, in 1973, Suharto forcibly merged the remaining Muslim political parties into an apolitical Muslim bloc. In 1985, he even legislated the adoption of Pancasila as the foundational principle of every political, social, and cultural organization. Under Suharto Indonesia became a developmentalist state with a national imaginary that was capitalist, modern, productive, and prosperous. At the same time, Pancasila became more rigid, shifting from being a foundational philosophy to being a state ideology. It also became explicitly tied to the unity and integrity of the state—Negara Kesatuan Republik Indonesia (NKRI)—a term that became highly ideologized.

In the late New Order, Indonesia's national imaginary shifted again, this time toward a more Islamic one as the aging Suharto started to court Indonesian Muslims as a counterbalance to the increasingly critical military. The personal image he projected was a pious one. He loosened the restrictions on the overt display of Islam in state institutions, allowing for the wearing of the *jilbab* (headscarf) in schools and government offices as well as opening up the finance sector to Islamic banking and insurance. Most importantly, in 1990 he established the Indonesian Muslim Intellectuals Association (Ikatan Cendekiawan Muslim se-Indonesia, ICMI), which was headed by his vice president, Bacharuddin Jusuf Habibie. ICMI, according to Carool Kersten, stood out "as an affirmation of the increased significance of Muslim technocrats, professionals, and intellectuals ... in Indonesian public life" as well as how political Islam reinvented itself.[31] One of ICMI's aims was achieving "proportionality" for Muslims in the bureaucracy across all of Indonesia. This meant that as Muslims comprised more than 90 percent of Indonesia's population, more than 90 percent of bureaucratic positions, even in Christian- or Hindu-dominant areas, should be occupied by Muslims. By 1993, Suharto's cabinet was overwhelmingly staffed with ICMI members and Indonesia's national imaginary had been recast as a moderate, modernist, middle-class Islamic one, relegating non-Muslims to a lower place in the hierarchy of belonging. The anxieties this created among Christians in Eastern Indonesia were directly connected to the rise of religious tensions in East Timor in the mid-1990s and to the outbreak of the Christian-Muslim conflicts in Poso and Ambon only months after Suharto resigned.

Suharto fell from power in May 1998 after a year of protests against corruption, collusion, and nepotism, their connection to the 1997 Asian financial crisis, and its fallout. He was brought down by student demonstrations, the unwillingness of the military to support him, and especially the greed of his children, as well as by the burgeoning Indonesian middle class, which included those very Muslims he had been courting. He was succeeded by his vice president, Habibie, who became Indonesia's third president as well as the first president of the *reformasi* era. Habibie occupied an awkward place in that most Indonesians saw him as merely a placeholder and a continuation of the New Order. In contrast, he saw himself as a reformer. Interestingly, his reforms did not take Indonesia in a more Islamic direction as his ties to ICMI might have suggested, but in a more democratic one. As he later recounted in his memoirs, his Indonesian national imaginary was that of "an independent, free, cultured, democratic system of government," in accordance with "the spirit of the 1945 constitution" while embracing modern technology.[32] It was a decentralized Indonesia, home to "a new Indonesian society" that was based on "openness and respect for human rights," led by a government "that is clean and works responsibly."[33] He was also less committed to the more expansive Indonesian geo-body of the New Order, in particular to holding on to East Timor at all costs.

Looking at the whole period from Sukarno to Habibe, Indonesian nationalism was clearly conceived and constructed as a civic nationalism that aimed at being ethnically and religiously inclusive and diverse. However, as R. E. Elson in his history of the "idea" of Indonesia has demonstrated, there was tension from the start between the ethnic Javanese elements and civic Indonesian ideas, not least because many of the early nationalists were Javanese.[34] This is clearly reflected in Indonesia's national symbols and how nationalist ideas were expressed. Indonesia's red-and-white flag was based on the flag of the Majapahit Empire.[35] The red represented courage and the white purity, but the red and white also, according to Sukarno, represented "the mystical offering of the Javanese" of red porridge and white porridge, and it was, according to Indonesian nationalist ideologue Muhammad Yamin, grounded in 6,000 years of Javanese history.[36] Indonesia's official national motto, *Bhinneka Tunggal Ika* (unity in diversity), originated from an Old Javanese phrase meaning "out of many, one." The depiction of the Garuda on Indonesia's coat of arms was based on the *elang Jawa*, the Javanese eagle. And, in his autobiography Sukarno recounts how his protocol officer in the early days of the Indonesian Republic when drawing up regulations would borrow "high Javanese protocol as our guide."[37] During Suharto's New Order even laws drew upon Javanese customs, most notably Law No. 5/1979 on village governance, which legislated the standardization of the Javanese *desa* (village) model. The implementation of this law, which was presented in terms of uniformization, increasing participation at the local level, and making village governance more effective, resulted in the weakening or outright destruction of the traditional *adat* (customary law) institutions in the outer islands.[38] It also resulted in the loss of moral authority of the traditional community leaders as they were replaced by "modern" civil servants. Indonesia's civic nationalism in its notions, assumptions, symbols, and legislation was thus at times "ethnic" in its application and was often perceived as "Javanization" by non-Javanese Indonesians.

There was also tension between the national narrative of the single colonial experience and the actual colonial encounters as well as their recollections in local history, which differed by region as well as by religion. For example, the colonial experience of Ambon, where the first Dutch arrived in 1599 and whose Christian population became the backbone of the colonial military, diverged greatly from the colonial experience of Aceh, which was only invaded in 1873, whose Muslim population was labelled as fanatic, and whose relationship with the Dutch remained confrontational right up to the Second World War. Not surprisingly this too has become an area of contestation.

While the state, of course, seeks to have a monopoly on the national imaginary, this is rarely the case in practice. This book shows that how the nation, the state, and their geography are imagined from the periphery compared to from the center differs greatly. Indeed, it is on the periphery of the national imaginary projected by the state that the construction of alternative national imaginaries takes place, often being conceived ethnically or religiously. This "imagining" ranges from recasting the existing state—Indonesia—all the way to advancing ideas of separate states, altering both boundaries and identity. It is also in this space that much of Indonesia's political violence is located.

Important for the analysis of political violence in response to the national imaginary projected by the state is the relationship between the state and its citizens, between the government and the people. Here this book draws upon the notion of "belonging." Ernest Gellner asserted that belonging requires "reciprocal relations," and Rogers Brubaker, as well as Andrew Geddes and Adrian Favell, concluded that citizenship does not automatically equate to belonging.[39] Particularly useful for looking at how belonging is conceived by the "center"—the Indonesian state—is Michael Skey's notion of "hierarchies of belonging" in which some are deemed to belong more to the nation than others.[40] This also holds true when belonging is articulated from the "periphery."

When these frameworks are applied to the case studies in this book, it is apparent that Jakarta did not view all of its citizens as equal and as equally loyal. Indeed, once some groups were tarnished with disloyalty the stigma remained. During the three decades of conflict in Aceh the Indonesian security forces as well as the civil service periodically introduced loyalty tests, sent people to re-education camps, held public loyalty oath-swearing ceremonies, and even introduced new "red-and-white" identity cards. As in Aceh, in East Timor raising the "red-and-white" national flag became symbolic of the Indonesianization efforts by the military. In Ambon, six decades after the separatist RMS rebellion, the new bridge that was constructed to span Ambon Bay was tellingly named Jembatan Merah Putih (Red-and-White Bridge) to remind the Ambonese where their loyalty should be. Raising or not raising the national flag also became a key indicator of loyalty for assessing Islamic boarding schools.

From the periphery loyalty to the center and belonging were, not surprisingly, conditional. Many Acehnese and Ambonese struggled with the question of what it meant to be Indonesian. East Timorese may have been open to becoming Indonesian, but the way Indonesia incorporated the territory had the opposite effect.

From an ethnic perspective belonging fully was conditional upon equality with the Javanese. From a Christian perspective belonging fully meant equality with Muslims before the law, including the right to build houses of worship and hold religious services. For Islamists, belonging fully was conditional upon implementing *syariah* instead of man-made laws. Indeed, it was the conclusion that being Indonesian and being properly Muslim were irreconcilable that prompted more than 800 Indonesians to travel to Syria between 2013 and 2017 to join the Islamic State, tearing up and burning their passports once they arrived there.[41]

Framing, Narratives, and Historiography

Violence in Indonesia has attracted a considerable amount of scholarly attention. However, the literature has generally analyzed this violence in a fragmented manner across both the history and geography of Indonesia. Thus, Islamist violence, separatist insurgencies, and communal conflicts have, by and large, been treated as separate topics with separate scholarly debates that do not necessarily speak to each other. Examining the literature on Islamist violence shows this fragmentation quite clearly alongside distinct clustering. The first cluster revolves around the Darul Islam rebellions. Here the core debate is between those who see the rebellions as the product of non-Islamic factors and those who see them as Islamic in origin and nature. Representative of the former, Karl Jackson asserted that the decisions to join the rebellion were determined by personal relationships and the traditional system of authority.[42] Kees van Dijk as well as Solahudin saw the rebellions as driven by the relationship between the irregular guerrilla forces and the republican army, the expansion of central government control, changes in landownership, and government policies in general.[43] George McTurnan Kahin attributed them to the "dislocation of the traditional system of agrarian credit during the Japanese occupation."[44] In contrast, Pinardi's comprehensive overview of Sekarmadji Marijan Kartosuwirjo's movement afforded Islam a central role, as did C.A.O. van Nieuwenhuijze, Hiroko Horikoshi, Holk Dengel, Chiara Formichi, Herdi Sahrasad and Al Chaidar, and Kevin Fogg, who saw them as the product of "Indonesia as a closed community" that turned toward totalitarian revivalism, the failure of Islamic political parties to achieve an Islamic state, the charismatic leadership of Kartosuwirjo, and the attempt to realize "a dream inspired by Islamic teachings."[45] This book concurs with this school of thought.

The second cluster in the literature on Indonesian Islamism focuses on Jemaah Islamiyah (JI) with the scholarly debate revolving around how to evaluate

JI's international links. Globalists and security experts such as Rohan Gunaratna, Zachary Abuza, Maria Ressa, and Bilveer Singh defined JI in relation to Al-Qaeda. They asserted that JI was "incorporated as an associate group of al-Qaeda," that it was "the regional affiliate of al-Qaeda," that it was Al-Qaeda's network in the region, and that it "played a catalytic role in synergising regional terrorism, especially in close collaboration with the Al Qaeda."[46] Taking a more nuanced approach, Ken Conboy as well as Quinton Temby acknowledged the divisions within JI regarding its relationship with Al-Qaeda.[47]

This globalist framing of JI was challenged by Natasha Hamilton-Hart, John Sidel, and Greg Fealy and Carlyle A. Thayer, who criticized the globalists for their ignorance of complex local factors and oversimplified analytical frameworks.[48] Emphasizing the importance of the Indonesian context, Sidney Jones, Solahudin, and Julie Chernov Hwang, as well as Andrée Feillard and Rémy Madinier, have argued that JI is the product of Indonesian history, most notably the Darul Islam rebellions and the repression during the New Order.[49] They also cautioned against seeing JI as a homogenous organization, emphasizing the importance of understanding the internal debates and divisions within JI.[50] This book aligns with this Indonesianist position.

The third, still-emerging, cluster concerns local jihad in Indonesia. Here Islamist violence has been studied in the context of Indonesia's transition from authoritarianism to democracy. For instance, Sidel asserted that Islamism rose in the late New Order as a response to the "unprecedented social and political prominence of members of Indonesia's small Christian minority" and particularly the assertiveness of the new evangelical and charismatic churches in the 1990s that, in Muslim eyes, constituted aggressive Christianization.[51] This period also saw the rise of jihad in the context of Christian-Muslim communal conflict in Ambon and Poso. The initial focus of the research in this area was on the highly visible Laskar Jihad, with Noorhaidi Hasan examining Laskar Jihad's rise out of the Indonesian salafi movement, Birgit Bräuchler looking at its cyberwarfare, and Mohamed Shoelhi exploring how Laskar Jihad became the scapegoat in the Ambon conflict.[52] Research has also been published on the involvement of the more clandestine jihadi groups—JI and KOMPAK—with Dave McRae's as well as Muhammad Tito Karnavian's excellent books on local Muslim radicalization and the role of the Javanese mujahidin in the Poso conflict, Scott Atran's examination of the motivations for jihad of Poso Muslims, Julie Chernov Hwang, Rizal Panggabean, and Ihsan Ali Fauzi's analysis of disengagement from jihadism in Poso, Badrus Sholeh's account of jihad in Ambon, the work by Julie Chernov Hwang and myself on the recruitment of locals into jihad, and my own comparative analysis of the involvement of JI and Mujahidin KOMPAK in the Ambon and Poso jihads.[53]

While the academic literature on Islamist violence in Indonesia revolves around core academic debates, the literature on separatist insurgencies has been far more ideologically cast, with a divide between Indonesian historiography—often written by participants in these conflicts—and Western accounts. Narratives advanced by official Indonesian histories such as the five volumes of the *History of the TNI* (*Sejarah TNI*) lay the blame on intellectual actors peddling dangerous ideas such as Christiaan Soumokil in the 1950 RMS rebellion, or Hasan di Tiro in the 1976–2005 Aceh conflict.[54] Ideology is also woven through the Indonesian narrative on the 1975 invasion and incorporation of Portuguese Timor as exemplified by the writings of Indonesian generals Wiranto, Kiki Syahnakri, and Tono Suratman.[55] According to their accounts, Indonesia intervened, at the request of the prointegration groups and with the support of the United States, against FRETILIN, which had communist leanings.[56] It also intervened to bring stability and development.[57] The counternarratives advanced by those associated with the RMS, FRETILIN, or GAM are equally politicized, as exemplified by the writings of Hasan di Tiro, José Ramos-Horta, Xanana Gusmão, and Constancio Pinto.[58] In fact, all three independence movements tell a very similar story of illegal incorporation of their territory into Indonesia and brutal Indonesian violence against the steadfast and heroic local population.

Ideology has also not been absent from Western narratives and analyses of separatist struggles in Indonesia, most notably in the literature on East Timor. For instance, Stephen McCloskey framed East Timor's struggle for independence within the context of "Third World expropriation by developed countries," with Indonesia after its occupation of Portuguese Timor assuming "the aggressive colonial practices normally associated with Western imperialism."[59] The neocolonial paradigm was also used by Hamish McDonald and Richard Tanter, while Carmel Budiarjo linked both the Indonesian invasion of East Timor and the violence in this conflict to the "three decades of Suharto's stranglehold on power," and John Martinkus and John G. Taylor pointed to the role of Indonesian intelligence as the driving force.[60] The Western literature on East Timor written before the 1999 referendum collectively pushes back against Indonesia labeling FRETILIN as communist. This differs from the literature published after the referendum by authors such as Don Greenlees and Robert Garran, showing how the debate on the nature of FRETILIN has evolved.[61] Moreover, with the shadow of the Indonesian occupation removed, authors such as Douglas Kammen were able to caution that viewing the violence in East Timor as caused purely by Indonesian outsiders obscures the "violence produced by local (indigenous) actors by competing Timorese polities."[62] A final focus in the literature on East Timor has been on the role that Australia played in the run-up to the invasion, during the occupation, and in the referendum as examined by James Dunn, David Connery, and Bruce J. Watson.[63]

The literature on the RMS rebellion, too, has seen the rebellion as a response to Jakarta's policies. Here Richard Chauvel argued that the struggle by the RMS was the result of the dilemma posed by Indonesian nationalism "for those Ambonese who had acquired position, status and vested interest within the colonial regime," but also of Ambonese Christian fears associated with living in a predominantly Muslim Indonesia "rather than a Christian-ruled Netherlands Indies."[64] The latter reason was also emphasized by John Ruhulessin and Pieter Manoppo.[65] Ben van Kaam saw the RMS rebellion as a "reaction against the Indonesian struggle for liberation experienced by a section of the Moluccan population which largely identified with the colonial ruler," Fridus Steiljen described it as "a reaction to the collapse of the United States of Indonesia and an extreme effort to safeguard the interests of the Malukans," and Ernst Utrecht viewed the RMS through the lens of "colonization, de-colonization, and neo-colonization."[66] A particularly interesting memoir is that of Harold L. B. Lovestrand, an American missionary who recounts the RMS struggle as told to him by Soumokil while they were both in prison.[67]

Meanwhile, scholarly explanations of the origins of the Aceh conflict, which unlike the RMS and East Timor insurgencies cannot be solely assigned to either the Sukarno or the Suharto period, can broadly be divided into those who see the conflict primarily as a product of the New Order and those who see it as dating back to the period of Indonesian independence. Exemplifying the former, Geoffrey Robinson argued that "the New Order regime itself was largely responsible for the serious and protracted violence in Aceh" while Neta S. Pane asserted that during the New Order the Acehnese became foreigners in their own country.[68] Similarly, Tim Kell pointed to "the exploitation of Aceh's resources for the benefit of the central government; economic stagnation in the province itself; governmental and political over-centralization which has served to disenfranchise the people of the region; and social changes which have led to the mass of Acehnese losing their traditional social and political leaders."[69] Rizal Sukma, too, suggested that Jakarta's misrule and the determination to exploit Aceh's natural gas reserves played a role in perpetuating the conflict.[70] The Indonesian military also received considerable attention, with Damien Kingsbury and Lesley McCulloch stating that "the military was never comfortable with the pursuit of a peaceful, political solution to the conflict" as the exploitation of Aceh was too lucrative for the military, whereas Elizabeth Drexler saw the conflict as a product of how the Indonesian state has sustained itself through anxieties and insecurities.[71]

Dating the root causes of the Aceh conflict back to the time of the establishment of the Indonesian Republic, Edward Aspinall argued that "attempts by the postcolonial state to integrate Aceh's population into Indonesia by way of various nation-building processes . . . generated grievances that gave secessionism its force."[72] A similar argument was advanced by Rodd McGibbon and in my own work, while M. Isa Suleiman placed it in the colonial context.[73]

As can be seen there is little, if any, connection between the literature on Islamist violence and separatist insurgencies on how the causes of the conflict with the state, the violent contestation of Indonesia, are framed. How communal conflict is discussed is equally disconnected. Unlike the Islamist and separatist violence in Indonesia, which challenged the state through drawn-out insurgencies that often regenerated themselves generationally, communal violence in Indonesia has been more sporadic and sometimes periodic in nature. While there have been outbreaks of violence between ethnically or religiously different communities throughout Indonesian history, the literature on communal violence focused particularly on the conflicts that erupted shortly after the fall of Suharto in Poso (Central Sulawesi), Ambon (Maluku), Sambas (West Kalimantan), Halmahera (North Maluku), and Sampit (Central Kalimantan). Much of the scholarly debate has revolved around the causes of this violence as well as the roles played by national elites, local politicians, and the military.

The most common framework for analyzing these conflicts has been that of Indonesia's transition from authoritarianism, its processes of democratization and decentralization, and the associated opportunities for political, socioeconomic, and demographic change at a regional and local level. For instance, Harold Crouch argued that the violence was part of a drawn-out struggle in Jakarta between the old elites associated with the New Order regime and the reformist challengers as a result of the "scramble between factions and groups to secure positions in whatever regime was to emerge in the New Order's wake."[74] Jacques Bertrand contended that it was this period of institutional change that gave rise to ethnic conflict as these periods constituted "critical junctures," which allowed for the contestation and renegotiation of the relationship between ethnic groups and the Indonesian state.[75] The idea of renegotiating or reshaping sociopolitical and economic constellations was also advanced by Jamie Davidson's book on communal violence in West Kalimantan—but only with respect to the Malays who became involved in what hitherto had been Dayak-Madurese violence "with an ethnopolitical movement of their own to gain a share of the monopoly Dayaks had on indigeneity."[76] Gerry van Klinken skillfully demonstrated how it was political opportunities such as local elections that determined the timing of the eruption of the conflict as a whole or the start of new phases of violence in Ambon, Poso, North Maluku, and Central Kalimantan, as that was when social movements stood the best chance of making significant advances.[77] This was echoed by Lorraine Aragon, as well as by Martin van Bruinessen, who connected the violence to the "struggles for redistribution of economic and political resources in post-Suharto Indonesia."[78]

Looking at this period of transition from authoritarianism to democracy, contemporaneous analyses paid particular attention to the role of the military in the communal conflicts. One school of thought popular with civil society and human rights activists at the time posited that the military had instigated the violence in order to show that it was still needed, to protect its economic interests, to expand its territorial structure, or simply to profit from the violence. In this vein, Ingrid Wessel argued that the violence after the fall of Suharto had "to be assessed as the resistance of the New Order forces, especially the Suharto clan and the military."[79] Similarly, Liem Soei Liong claimed that "unrest and bloody incidents are deliberately created in certain regions," a view also advanced by Thamrin Tomagola in his work on Ambon and by George Aditjondro in his work on Poso.[80] While Wessel's suggestion is analytically sound, Liong's, Tomagola's, and above all Aditjondro's analyses often remained unsubstantiated and, at times, bordered on conspiracy theories.

A different kind of military involvement was highlighted by Nancy Lee Peluso in her analysis of the 1997 Dayak-Madurese violence in West Kalimantan, namely the role that the military played in the "strategic construction of violent ethnic identities to mobilize people."[81] This was echoed by Davidson, who contended that the violence was the unintended by-product of the Indonesian army's counterinsurgency campaign that "gained an internal logic" and became routinized.[82] An alternative argument on security and the role of the military that focuses on the "absence" rather than the "presence" of the military was advanced by Yukhi Tajima, who argued that "during authoritarian breakdowns, spikes in communal violence result from temporary mismatches that emerge between formal and informal institutions of security as the coercive grip of the state loosens."[83] This explains why small, seemingly trivial arguments escalated into full-scale conflict, as such a mismatch hindered "the military from intervening locally."[84]

While the fall of Suharto and the transition to a more democratic and decentralized Indonesia explained some of the timing of the violence and framed it as competition over political posts and economic resources as well as the possibility of renegotiating local and national relationships, these explanations fell short of addressing historically rooted causes, grievances, and patterns of violence. As Aragon pointed out in her work on Poso, "the accumulated resentments and subtle realignments of ethnic, religious, and economic consciousness that have developed over long periods of time in numerous Indonesian provinces" are important.[85] The literature here can be divided into three broad historical time frames: Suharto's New Order, the Sukarno era, and the colonial period.

Bertrand attributed the violence to the New Order's "institutionalization of the requisites of unity and the policies designed to preserve the vision of national unity."[86] Angel Rabasa and Peter Chalk pointed to Suharto's transmigration policy, which had created "tensions between ethnic groups and between the indigenous inhabitants and immigrants from Java and elsewhere," while Wessel, commenting on communal violence in the late New Order in West Kalimantan, Tasikmalaya, Banjarmasin, Sampan, Situbondo, and Pekalongan, contended that the New Order's development policy produced uneven development and with it social, economic, and ethnic tensions.[87] This was also argued by Mary Somers Heidhues and Freek Colombijn, while Elson contended that the state-sponsored violence during the New Order was grounded in the regime's "fear of the people."[88] It was this violence that at the same time legitimated the use of violence and produced counterviolence.

Situating the roots of the post-1997 violence in Indonesia in the early Sukarno period, Tim Lindsay argued that both the pattern of violence and the state's attitude toward violence can be traced back to the Indonesian Revolution, the "1945 Constitution and the political ideas that formed it," and the fact that the legal system was excluded from "a role in resolving disputes between the state and its citizens."[89] So violence became the preferred option for both.[90]

Stepping back even further in the history of the archipelago, Henk Schulte Nordholt suggested that the roots of the Indonesian violence that erupted in 1998 go back to the colonial period, in particular the "regime of fear" that the Indonesians inherited from the Dutch.[91] Tying the broader phenomenon of religious violence, including that in Ambon and Poso, to a different aspect of colonial policy, Sidel argued that this violence was rooted in the "transplanting" to Indonesia of the "pattern of linkages between religious denominations, school networks, associational activities, and political parties described in the Netherlands as 'pillarization' (*verzuiling*) redubbed as one of diverse competing streams or currents (*aliran*) in the nation's political and social life."[92]

These political, socioeconomic, historical, and institutional explanations were challenged by Sumanto Al Qurtuby in his book on the Ambon conflict, where he argued that it was above all a religious conflict in which theology underwrote both violence and reconciliation.[93] They were also challenged by Christopher R. Duncan who, in his work on the violence in North Maluku, asserted that "elite agendas and machinations were not as central to conflicts as many observers would have us think," that "the political fault lines in provincial towns, so often the subject of political analysis, were not always relevant to people trying to kill each other in the country-side," that "instigation could only succeed if the idea of violence itself found resonance with the masses," and that focusing "on high politics removes any meaning in the violence for those who perpetrated it, suffered through it, or in some cases both."[94] A similar emphasis on the experience of the victims "as narrated by the victims themselves" was advocated by Hilmar Farid.[95]

What this discussion of the literature on Islamist, separatist, and communal violence in Indonesia clearly shows is that there is not one body of literature but several, that these only tangentially connect, and that the scholarly debates do not speak to each other. This is a gap this book seeks to fill by analyzing Islamist, separatist, and communal violence in Indonesia through a single framework, namely that of the national imaginary, and by exploring this violence from a comparative perspective.

Methodology and Sources

This book approaches the analysis of Islamist, separatist, and communal violence through the *longue durée*. It is based on extensive fieldwork and empirical research between 1998 and 2023. Fieldwork was conducted in East Timor and West Kalimantan in 1999, in Aceh from 2001 to 2005, in Ambon from 2000 to 2017, in Central Sulawesi in 2003 and 2017, and in Java continuously since December 1998. In all of these areas in-depth interviews and, in many instances, several repeat interviews, were conducted with religious leaders, politicians, members of the Indonesian security forces, Indonesian and international NGOs, journalists, academics, community leaders, and members of jihadi, separatist, and communally based militant groups. Interviewees were given the option to remain anonymous, use an alias, or use their names. There were also numerous off-the-record discussions that informed the research. This book is thus the product of a long-term and intensive research effort that offers a broader perspective across time and place than any other study.

In total 474 interviews were conducted over a period of twenty years, which has made it possible to record, collect, and assemble a series of local oral histories of the Islamist, separatist, and communal violence in Indonesia. This is particularly important as Indonesian history has largely been written from "the center" with official narratives, which dominated history teaching during both the Sukarno and Suharto periods, serving to underwrite the nation-building and state-building process. They were written in accordance with the national imaginary advanced by the government. This book is thus not only a book on Islamist, separatist and communal violence in Indonesia; it is also a book on Indonesian history examined through narratives from "the periphery."

It is important to note that the interviews conducted cover both the conflict and postconflict periods. This has allowed for a close reading of the dynamics of the violence as well as direct exposure to the narratives during the conflict.

At times, research was complicated by the ongoing violence, as access to some areas was restricted and moving from one side in the conflict to the other could be difficult. This is where further research after the conflict became very useful, to access those areas not previously reachable, but also to observe how narratives shifted once the violence had subsided. The exploration of sensitive issues was both hindered and eased by ongoing conflict. For instance, participation by local civilians in communal violence was often played down after the conflict was over. In comparison, members of the security forces, as well as jihadis, were more at ease explaining their aims, strategies, and tactics. Thus, the combination of interviews both during the conflicts and after the violence has enabled a more nuanced and comprehensive analysis. It also sets this book apart from most of the literature discussed above, especially on the communal conflicts, which were researched either during the conflict or after rather than both.

In addition to the fieldwork and oral histories, this book also draws upon a range of written primary sources. These include archival documents from Indonesian, American, British, Dutch, and Australian archives as well as Indonesian presidential speeches, decrees, instructions, and laws. These are supplemented by national and local Indonesian newspapers and magazines as well as websites. Of particular importance to the analysis of Islamist, separatist, and communal violence are the writings and publications by the RMS, FRETILIN, GAM, and the Maluku Sovereignty Front (FKM) as well as jihadi writings, publications, and sermons associated with Darul Islam, Jemaah Islamiyah, Mujahidin KOMPAK, and Laskar Jihad. Memoirs and firsthand accounts by members of the Indonesian security forces, humanitarian observers, peace mediators, and members of both separatist and Islamist organizations, as well as reports by Indonesian and international NGOs, were also utilized to give a more comprehensive and nuanced picture.

The Structure of the Book

This book comprises six chapters. The first two chapters cover Islamist violence in Indonesia. Chapter 1 looks at the 1947–1965 Darul Islam (DI) rebellions. It explores the root causes of these rebellions as well as their ideological underpinnings and aims. This is followed by an analysis of the conceptualization of the struggle and Islamist national imaginaries advanced, constructed, and projected by DI's key leaders: Sekarmadji Marijan Kartosuwirjo, Abdul Kahar Muzakkar, Daud Beureueh, and Ibnu Hajar. It also examines how the Indonesian state responded to this ideological challenge and how military strategy and tactics evolved.

Chapter 2 focuses on the rise of Jemaah Islamiyah and the Islamist violence from 1999 to 2009. It explores the root causes of this violence and its ideological underpinnings. This is followed by an analysis of the narratives and Islamist national imaginaries advanced by JI's founders, Abdullah Sungkar and Abu Bakar Ba'asyir, by JI's general guidelines (PUPJI), and by JI's *mantiqis* (regions). This chapter then examines the revived JI under the amirship of Para Wijayanto from 2008 to his arrest in 2019 before concluding with a more general reflection on Muslim belonging and the persistence of Islamist violence in Indonesia.

The next two chapters deal with separatist violence. Chapter 3 looks at the origins and dynamics of the East Timor conflict from the Indonesian invasion in December 1975 to the postreferendum violence in September 1999. It explores where Portuguese Timor fit into the Indonesian national imaginary and analyzes the strategies, tactics, and targets of the Indonesian military and the Timorese resistance. This chapter also examines Indonesia's efforts to "Indonesianize" East Timor as well as the competing narratives on the conflict. It concludes with a discussion of belonging and why the integration of East Timor ultimately failed.

Chapter 4 shifts to the 1976–2005 Aceh conflict, starting by exploring its origins as well as Acehnese grievances during Sukarno's rule and Suharto's New Order. It then examines the Free Aceh Movement (GAM), GAM's narrative, and GAM's national imaginary. This is followed by an analysis of the conflict and how the competing national imaginaries shaped the military side of the conflict, framing goals, influencing strategies, and above all determining target selection, before concluding with a reflection on belonging in Aceh.

The final two chapters are on communal violence. Chapter 5 focuses on the 1998–2007 Poso conflict. It explores its root causes, examining Christian-Muslim relations, in-migration, Islamization, and the opportunity structure for violence provided by *reformasi*. The chapter then analyzes the phases and dynamics of the conflict as well as Christian and Muslim combatants, and their aims, strategies, and national imaginaries. It concludes with a discussion on feelings of alienation from the Indonesian state.

Chapter 6 looks at the 1999–2005 Ambon conflict. It examines the history of intercommunal relations since the colonial period, the RMS (Republic of South Maluku) rebellion, and the impact of the New Order policies as well as the causes and triggers for the conflict and particular phases of the violence. Muslim and Christian combatants and their motivations, ideologies, sense of belonging to the Indonesian state, and what it means to be Indonesian are also explored. Taking the chapters on Poso and Ambon together, it is interesting that in Poso it was the Muslims who embraced an alternative national imaginary while in Ambon it was the Christians. It is equally interesting to see how these two communal conflicts intersect with and connect to both the separatist and Islamist dynamics in Indonesia discussed in the earlier chapters of this book.

This book concludes with a broader, comparative discussion on the interplay between Indonesia's national imaginary, alternative national imaginaries, and violence. It also discusses the role that territory has played as well as how belonging has been complicated by conditionality on the periphery and the focus on loyalty by the center.

1
THE DARUL ISLAM REBELLIONS, 1947–1965

Islam has been an integral part of identity in the Indonesian Archipelago since the thirteenth century. With Dutch colonial expansion, Islam also framed the increasing anticolonial violence as exemplified by the 1803–1837 Padri War, the 1825–1830 Java War, the 1873–1904 Aceh War, and the 1888 Banten Jihad. Not only was Islam used to mobilize the population, but the resistance itself was conceptualized as *perang sabil*, holy war, jihad against the foreign infidels as well as against local *adat* (customary) leaders who were favored by the Dutch.[1] The emergence of Indonesian nationalism in the early twentieth century, too, placed Islam at the heart of many of the debates on how to achieve independence and what form the future state should take. When this debate swung in favour of the "secular" nationalists, paving the way for Pancasila to become the foundational philosophy of the newly independent Republic of Indonesia, it split the Islamic nationalists into those who continued to engage politically in order to change the nature of the state, and those who disengaged from formal politics. It is the latter who are important for the genealogy of this chapter, as it is from their ranks that the first Indonesian militant Islamists were drawn.

This chapter looks at the 1947–1965 Darul Islam (DI) rebellions,[2] exploring their causes, their aims, their ideological underpinnings, and their evolution. It examines how Sekarmadji Marijan Kartosuwirjo conceptualized the Islamic struggle in the 1930s and 1940s and how he constructed his Islamist national imaginary. This chapter then analyses how and why South Sulawesi under Abdul Kahar Muzakkar, Aceh under Daud Beureueh, and South Kalimantan under Ibnu Hajar joined the DI rebellions. It also looks at the military strategies used by DI and examines how the Indonesian state responded to this ideological challenge.

This chapter demonstrates that the roots of the Darul Islam rebellions lie in Islam having been part and parcel of Indonesian nationalism in the early twentieth century. This provided the Islamist national imaginary with as much legitimacy as the "secular" one. This chapter further contends that how Indonesia was conceptualized as a state based on a man-made philosophy (Pancasila), rather than one based on the laws of Allah (*syariat Islam*), was at the heart of the Islamist violence. With respect to the Indonesian state's responses, this chapter posits that the considerable death toll in the DI rebellions was the result not just of the rebellion's lengthy persistence and the tactics adopted by all sides, but also of the fact that Kartosuwirjo's Islamic national imaginary directly challenged the narrative advanced by the Indonesian army, in particular the Siliwangi Division, on who had saved Indonesia from being stillborn.

The Roots of the Darul Islam Rebellions

Modern Indonesian nationalism started to emerge at the beginning of the twentieth century with the 1901 *Ethische Politiek* (ethical policy) and its tenets of "association" and "emancipation." Association saw the "talented youth" of the indigenous elites channelled into the colonial civil service, while emancipation sought the disassociation of Muslims from the "backwardness" of Islam but also from political expressions of Islam.[3] The latter had been identified as a threat by Dutch scholar Christiaan Snouk Hurgronje who, in his role as adviser on native affairs, recommended restricting Islam to the mosque and making it "exclusively cultural-spiritual."[4] Key to both association and emancipation was opening up the Dutch education system to select natives. It is with this access to Western education and the proliferation of Western ideas that the conventional narrative of the emergence of Indonesian nationalism begins. This narrative highlights the protonationalist cultural organizations set up by Dutch-educated elites such as Budi Utomo (1908) in Java, the Minangkabausche Bond (1910) in Sumatra, and Jong Minahasa (1918) in North Sulawesi, and culminates in the rise of largely Western-educated Indonesian nationalist leaders such as Sukarno and Mohammad Hatta who then challenged the colonizers on their own terms.[5]

This narrative served not only to create a linear history from the Netherlands Indies to Sukarno's Indonesian Republic but also to legitimize the "secular" nationalists, downplaying the role Islam had played in the emergence of Indonesian nationalism. It disregards that Islam was an integral part of the broader emerging Indonesian nationalist movement, not least as it served as a "signifier of nativeness."[6] Indeed, Islam played a key role as the "carrier of the national consciousness," and it served as a "catalyst" and "amplifier."[7] It was a unifying force across most of the archipelago.[8] Indeed, as Deliar Noer, Michael Laffan, Azyumardi Azra, and John Sidel have shown, Indonesian nationalism actually started with Muslim nationalism, its "seeds" sown in the Jawi communities in Mecca and Cairo, nurtured by a "distinctly cosmopolitan discursive, textual and associational infrastructure," and ideas travelling back to the Netherlands Indies through Malay-Indonesian-Middle Eastern networks, most notably Sufis and hajjis.[9] The Muslim reformist-modernist engagement with Western colonialism, in particular, influenced the Muslim thinking in the Netherlands Indies through the concepts of *watan* (homeland) and *umma* (community). These became embedded in the emerging Indonesian nationalism as early as 1906 as exemplified by the periodical *Al-Imam*, which conceptualized the broader Malay-speaking community as *umatul bangsa Melayu* (community of Malay nations) that sought the independence of their various lands.[10]

The first Indonesian nationalist organization was Sarekat Islam (SI), which was established as Sarekat Dagang Islam Surakarta in early 1912 by batik trader Hadji Samanhudi with the aim of fostering "solidarity and mutual help among all Muslims."[11] While it had started as a movement to protect Javanese merchants against the Chinese competition, it became a more diverse organization as its membership grew. By the end of 1912 not only had "almost all native and Muslim males in the city" joined Sarekat Islam, but it had expanded to all parts of Java and Madura, where it attracted the support of Indonesian youths, intellectuals, peasants, and members of the burgeoning labor movement.[12] In August of that year, Hadji Omar Said Tjokroaminoto, head of the Sarekat Islam branch in Surabaya and editor in chief of *Oetoesan Hindia*, joined the leadership, becoming Samanhudi's deputy.[13] Tjokroaminoto transformed Sarekat Islam into a political organization that became Indonesia's first large-scale, Indies-wide nationalist movement, its Islamic framework transcending ethnic divisions.[14] Over the next decade it also housed several different ideological strands under its umbrella: pan-Islamism, Islamic nationalism, Islamic socialism, and communism. What tied them all together was Sarekat Islam's increasingly anticolonialist stance, which was first noted by observers at SI's third national congress in September 1918 in Surabaya.[15]

A year later, in 1919, Sarekat Islam started to rupture, as its different ideological strands had radicalized within the ongoing Indonesian nationalist debates. The communists decided to go their own way, taking whole SI branches with them such as the Semarang branch.[16] According to Justus M. van der Kroef, this was the beginning of Sarekat Islam's decline, as its success had lain in its all-inclusive nature.[17] By the mid-1920s Islamic nationalism as an idea and ideology also started to be eclipsed by "secular" Indonesian nationalism.[18] Both developments took their toll on SI's membership, which dropped from more than two million in 1922 to less than one million in 1928.[19]

The now smaller Sarekat Islam, under the leadership of Tjokroaminoto, who had succeeded Samanhudi in 1914, became more cohesively Islamic nationalist, advocating Islam as the basis for the future Indonesian state. It also became a political party, Partai Sarekat Islam, renamed Partai Sarekat Islam Indonesia (PSII) in 1930.[20] In 1940, the PSII fractured over the issue of whether or not to cooperate with the colonial administration, and a rival second PSII was established that fiercely criticized the Dutch as Westerners, colonialists, and infidels.[21] It was this noncooperative, uncompromising Islamic nationalism that later underwrote the Darul Islam rebellions.

Sarekat Islam in its various forms, however, was not the only Islamic organization within the broader Indonesian nationalist movement. An often-overlooked role was played by the Indonesian reformist movement Muhammadiyah established in 1912 and the traditionalist Nahdlatul Ulama (NU) established in 1926. Similar to Sarekat Islam, they favored an Islamic basis for governance. They were joined in 1923 by Persatuan Islam (Persis), which was more pan-Islamic, and in 1925 by the Jong Islamieten Bond, which was modernist, seeking to combat Western colonial domination by purifying Islam while "adopting those achievements of Western civilization that had given the West its technical superiority."[22] In 1943, Masyumi (Majlis Syuro Muslimin Indonesia), which had been set up by the Japanese after their occupation of the Netherlands Indies in order to unify all Muslim organizations in support of Japan's Greater Asia Co-Prosperity Sphere, joined the fray.[23] In its emancipated form after the Japanese surrender, the "new" Masyumi advocated the establishment of an Indonesian Islamic state based on *syariah*. These various Muslim organizations not only were an integral part of the Indonesian nationalist movement; they also provided several prominent leaders such as Abdul Wahid Hasjim, who served as Indonesia's first minister of religious affairs; Agus Salim, who served as Indonesia's third foreign minister; Mohammad Roem, who served as Indonesia's fourth interior minister and fourth foreign minister; and Mohammad Natsir, who served as Indonesia's fifth prime minister. Even Kartosuwirjo had been asked by Amir Sjarifuddin to become second vice-minister of defense, an offer he rejected.[24]

The Japanese surrender in August 1945, according to Harry J. Benda, left Java "more truly Islamic" and "closer to the ideas of the *santri* (pious) civilization than had existed in March 1942," and Indonesia's Islamic nationalists in a strengthened position.[25] Yet, in the scramble to declare Indonesian independence before the Netherlands could reoccupy the Indies, the Islamic nationalists failed to realise their vision of an Islamic state. Even the compromise solution, known as the Jakarta Charter, which proposed inserting into the preamble of the Indonesian constitution that Muslims were obliged to follow Islamic law, was cut the day after the declaration of independence when the constitution was to come into force.[26] This removal of concessions to the Islamic nationalists, however, was not the cause for the Darul Islam rebellions. For Kartosuwirjo the Jakarta Charter would never have been enough. Instead, the roots of the Darul Islam rebellions can be found in the role Islam played in the emergence of Indonesian nationalism, which provided Kartosuwirjo with an ideological foundation and narrative that was as legitimate as that of the "secular" nationalists.

Conceptualizing the Struggle

In order to understand how the Darul Islam rebellions emerged out of Islamic nationalism, it is important to examine how their leader, Kartosuwirjo, conceptualized the struggle for an Islamic state in Indonesia in the 1930s and 1940s. Kartosuwirjo was a self-declared Islamic nationalist, whose ideology was rooted in Partai Sarekat Islam, which he had joined in 1927.[27] In the literature Kartosuwirjo is described as having had a secular education. He only started to engage in religious learning in his teens and his views were limited by his lack of fluency in Arabic.[28] Pinardi even went as far as asserting that Kartosuwirjo had acquired his knowledge of Islam mostly from Dutch publications.[29] The literature also tends to depict Kartosuwirjo's Islam as traditionalist, infused with mysticism, and colored by his association with rural Islamic leaders of West Java such as Kiyai Jusuf Tauziri and his father-in-law, Kiyai Ardiwiwastra.[30] He "carried two *pusaka* (magical heirlooms), a *kris* and a sword," which were believed to guarantee victory in battle.[31] In addition, many of his rural Muslim supporters saw him as the *ratu adil* (just king).[32] Noer believed that this mysticism placed Kartosuwirjo beyond the acceptability of the modernist Islamic community.[33]

This may not, however, be a completely accurate reading. Kartosuwirjo's first religion teacher, Notodihardjo, was not only a Sarekat Islam activist, but also a member of Muhammadiyah.[34] Others who influenced him deeply were Tjokroaminoto and Agus Salim. Thus, the guidance Kartosuwirjo received during his formative years placed him firmly on the track of a modernist Islam and a highly political Islamism. Kartosuwirjo never really left this track, as exemplified by the fact that he became an active member in both the PSII and later Masyumi, holding several leadership positions in these organizations. It is true that he added to this modernism some more traditionalist teachings and mysticism. However, according to Dengel, Kartosuwirjo did not actually believe he was the *ratu adil*, although he did not mind if the population connected his name to this mythology and had messianic expectations about him.³⁵ Thus the picture that emerges of Kartosuwirjo's Islam is not one that is purely traditionalist-mystical. Indeed, when looking at his many writings and particularly his ideas on what constitutes an Islamic state, it is the modernist ideology of Sarekat Islam that prevails, as Kartosuwirjo adopted a political rather than religious reading of the concepts at the heart of his ideology: *iman* (faith), *fitnah* (strife), *hijrah* (migration), jihad (struggle), and *darul Islam* (abode of Islam). His writings should thus, above all, be considered a political *tafsir* (exegesis) of the Quran.

Following the blueprint of the Prophet Muhammad's first Islamic state in Medina, these concepts became central to conceptualizing the struggle for an Islamic state in Indonesia. *Iman* for Kartosuwirjo was not raising the level of religiosity among Indonesian Muslims—this he left to the ulama (clerics)—but raising their political consciousness so they would become Islamic nationalists. He advocated this Islamic nationalism at the political meetings and conferences he regularly attended, but the main vehicle was Sarekat Islam's newspaper *Fadjar Asia*, which he started to work for in 1927, advancing quickly from proofreader to reporter, editor, and deputy editor in chief.³⁶

Kartosuwirjo saw the struggle for an Islamic state as revolving around two core concepts: *hijrah* and jihad. Both were the result of the *fitnah* prevailing in the Netherlands Indies; both were pathways to establishing a true Islamic state.³⁷ In his articles he advocated the superiority of Islamic nationalism over secular nationalism. Interestingly, Kartosuwirjo defined Islamic nationalism both in local Indonesian as well as in broader, global terms, with the former being the first step to the latter. He explained that as Muslims were the majority of the Indonesian population, Islam should be the national religion, and Indonesian nationalism should be solely based on Islamic values.³⁸ Referring to a hadith in which the Prophet declared that love for the "motherland is part of faith," he stated that "Muslims who do not love their homeland are not real Muslims but fake Muslims."³⁹ Islam should play a role in Indonesian politics as it laid out the "rules for the present world and for the afterlife"; it could not simply "be confined within the fences of *pesantren*."⁴⁰ Indeed, it was the duty of Indonesia's Muslims "to give priority to issues of the occupied land, particularly our religion, Islam, which is our most effective weapon."⁴¹ At the same time, Kartosuwirjo also wrote that Islamic nationalism "is borderless, does not discriminate against skin colour or language . . . but . . . only recognizes the boundaries set by Allah." He pointed to the hajj pilgrimage as an example of Islamic internationalism and emphasized that in the Quran it was written that "mankind is not but one community." He encouraged Muslims to not let their aspirations "remain a dream" but to realize this "dream and act on it," including nationalism and internationalism in Islam, "which are the duty of every Muslim."[42]

While Islamic internationalism was important to Kartosuwirjo in the late 1920s, not least because the 1924 abolition of the Ottoman Caliphate by Mustafa Kemal Ataturk had shaken the *umma* to the core and triggered efforts for its revival in various parts of the Muslim world, most of Kartosuwirjo's articles in *Fadjar Asia* focused on the Netherlands Indies and the *fitnah* caused by the Dutch colonisers and their collaborators. Here he asserted that the "people living in the colonized land called Indonesia" were living in a state of slavery with the ruled suffering greatly at the hands of the rulers.[43] Dutch laws had forced "tens, hundreds, even thousands of people ... to flee their homeland, their houses, their rice paddies and fields."[44] Farmers who had once "tilled their own land" were now "nomads without permanent income" who often went hungry.[45] Peasants were being exploited by foreign businesses or local capitalists.[46] He wrote that "the people of Lampung were treated like monkeys, who are chased from one tree to another," while people in Sulawesi and Borneo were subjected to forced labor.[47] Detainees and prisoners were treated arbitrarily, people's rights were violated, and "justice seem[ed] to elude the common people."[48] He accused the local nobility of sultans and *rajas* as well as *adat* chiefs of becoming "instruments" of the Dutch, driven by their "own egotistical needs," exploiting the people and punishing them arbitrarily.[49] He lamented that "those in power ignore the weak as long as they can serve their purpose in accumulating wealth."[50]

This *fitnah* posed a direct threat to Islam, as the Dutch also "pursued the politics of Christianization" through "the Christian missions which came here to eliminate Islam and Islamic values or at the very least to disgrace Islam in Indonesia."[51] Kartosuwirjo asserted that "Indonesian Muslims whose homeland is occupied by another nation are not allowed to worship in mosques," while "every Sunday afternoon, at the Lion Square in Weltevreden, the Christians hold sermons freely."[52] Moreover, politics based on Islam was maligned and Islamic nationalists were labelled "troublemakers, evildoers, people who incite conflict and create division among Muslims."[53]

In 1936, at the Twenty-Second PSII Congress, Kartosuwirjo was asked to put together a pamphlet explaining the party's position on *hijrah* as a response to the prevailing *fitnah*. In the first part of this two-part *Sikap Hidjrah P.S.I.I.* pamphlet, Kartosuwirjo discussed the meaning of the *hijrah* from Mecca to Medina, outlining its importance in Islamic history. He likened the *hijrah* to a door that opened into a *zaman baru* (new era) and a *dunia baru* (new world) and, ultimately, prepared the way into the *akhirat* (the hereafter).[54] It signified the *zaman baru* because of the changes in belief, behavior, and actions of the community, and because "falsehood is crushed by the truth" and the darkness of *jahiliyyah* (ignorance) is replaced with the light of Allah.[55] Medina itself became the *dunia baru*, the true *dunia* Islam, the first Islamic state.

In the second part, he defined *hijrah* for current times, the reasons for it, its meanings, its aims, its character, and how to undertake it.[56] *Hijrah* meant to leave behind, to distance from, to separate from, and to move.[57] It was an obligation "for every man and woman, young and old."[58] Kartosuwirjo also made it clear that "when talking about *hijrah* from Mecca to Medina we are not talking about Mecca in the Arab lands" but from "Mecca Indonesia" to "Medina Indonesia."[59] Once *hijrah* had been embarked upon it had to continue, as long as "idolatrous rules and regulations" were being implemented, and it should not be ended until the achievement of true *falah* (happiness) and *fatah* (victory).[60]

Kartosuwirjo distinguished between individual and communal *hijrah*, as well as internal and external *hijrah*.[61] However the aim of all forms of *hijrah* was the same, namely to hope for, to seek, and to receive the grace of Allah.[62] He wrote that *hijrah* was a part of *ibadah* (worship) and that once *hijrah* had been embarked upon, jihad would follow.[63] This jihad he defined as sincere efforts in the way of Allah towards the truth, carried out through *amal salih* (righteous deeds).[64] In this the lesser jihad, referred to in the history of the Prophet as *qital* or *ghazwa*, was for the defence of the Muslim community or the defense of Islam, whereas the greater jihad was fought against oneself.[65]

At the Twenty-Fourth PSII Congress in Surabaya in 1938, the decision was taken to issue a further pamphlet, *Daftar Oesaha Hidjrah P.S.I.I.*, which constituted the *hijrah* action program. In this *Daftar Oesaha Hidjrah* Kartosuwirjo explained that *hijrah* was figurative. It did not mean "moving from one place to another" but instead meant a shift in one's character, behavior, beliefs, and practices.[66] The aim of the *hijrah* was the establishment of an Islamic state, "where every Muslim and Muslimah can live by the laws of Allah, both individually and communally."[67] Interestingly, in light of the later debate in 1945 on Pancasila, an Islamic state, and the Jakarta Charter, Kartosuwirjo in *Daftar Oesaha Hidjrah* already stated his preference for "a perfect Darul Islam" over "a greater Indonesia (Indonesia-Raja)."[68]

The Japanese invasion of the Netherlands Indies in 1942 and the beginning of the Indonesian Revolution in 1945 saw a shift in Kartosuwirjo's conceptualization of the struggle for an Islamic Indonesia away from *hijrah* and toward jihad, although jihad remained a part of *hijrah* rather than becoming a standalone doctrine. This can be seen in Kartosuwirjo's *Haluan Politik Islam: Risalah Perjuangan Menuju Darul Islam*, published in 1946 as a set of guidelines for Masyumi.[69] In it he advocated for a dual revolution: a national revolution and a social revolution.[70] The aim of the national revolution was to rid the country of all occupiers, to achieve independence, and to have this independence internationally recognized.[71] Kartosuwirjo saw the Netherlands not only as having occupied Indonesian territory but as having enslaved the Indonesian nation, introducing *kekufuran* (unbelief) and infecting the people with "the disease of westernization that contains the idea of separation of church and state, the separation of this world from the hereafter."[72] Similarly, Kartosuwirjo charged the Japanese with introducing *kemusyrikan* (idolatry) into the Indonesian *umma*.[73] Both Dutch colonialism and Japanese fascism had to be "eradicated from the body of Indonesian society and from each individual."[74] Part of the cure was political engagement, what he refers to as *akida politik*, sacralizing it as a "political Islamic creed" and stating that "politics is a sacred obligation."[75] The national revolution was framed in religious terms as *fardhu ayn* (an individual obligation) for every Muslim to carry out *jihad fi-sabilillah bima'na qital* (struggling in the way of Allah through war) or *ghazwa* (a war guided by faith), to be fought "with property and soul, and whatever is required for sacrifice on this sacred path."[76]

The aim of the social revolution was to end the internal struggles and produce a stable government.[77] Kartosuwirjo left no doubt that this stable government was an Islamic one as it was a "requirement to establish a new world, a Muslim world, in other words: Darul Islam."[78] While the national revolution was *fardhu ayn*, the social revolution was *fardhu kifayah* (a communal obligation).[79] *Akida politik* ran as a connecting thread through both revolutions, as he stressed that the Islamic *umma* must be represented in all institutions from village level to the parliament, the Majles Permusyawartan Rakyat (MPR), and that it "must not forget about its obligation to be part of the executive and to make legislation."[80] He further explained that the social revolution would start with the individual and then "widen from yourself to your village."[81] Education was the key to turning the social revolution into an Islamic social revolution.[82]

The Darul Islam Rebellions: Phases and Dynamics

The first of the Darul Islam rebellions erupted in the context of the Indonesian Revolution, the nascent country's war of independence against the Dutch. They then evolved over three phases: 1947–1949, 1950–1959, and 1959–1965. The most often-cited starting point is the January 1948 Renville Agreement, which resulted in the withdrawal of Republican troops from West Java, leaving behind the Islamist fighters of Hizbullah and Sabilillah to fight the Dutch.[83] This chapter, however, takes the first Dutch *politionele actie* (police action) in July 1947, referred to in Indonesian historiography as the first *agresi militer Belanda* (Dutch military aggression), as the starting point, as it was in response to this Dutch invasion of West Java that Kartosuwirjo proclaimed a jihad not only to fight the infidel intruders but also to establish an Islamic state.

Phase 1

The first phase of the Darul Islam rebellions was characterized by three intertwining dynamics: first, Kartosuwirjo's defensive jihad against the Dutch; second, the emergence of a triangular war between Dutch, Islamist, and Republican troops; and third, the establishment of the Indonesian Islamic State—Negara Islam Indonesia (NII). The formal transfer of sovereignty from the Netherlands to the Republic of Indonesia in December 1949 concludes this phase, leaving two viable, yet competing visions of Indonesia—one based on Pancasila and an Islamist one.

The aim of the Dutch "police action" was to reduce the territory held by Indonesian Republican forces, to blockade the ports, and to access "essential ricelands."[84] It was also part of a broader strategy to undermine the Republic's ability to establish "its claim to be the sole government of Indonesia" and to force it to "participate in the United States of Indonesia."[85] In character, however, as explained by Amir Sjarifuddin, head of the Indonesian delegation to the United Nations (UN), it was more of "an actual war" than a police action.[86] "[Dutch] troops were landed after heavy naval bombardment. [Indonesian] troops and civilians were machinegunned from the air. Bombs were dropped and in the ground operation extensive use was made of heavy and light artillery. Paratroops were dropped in several instances."[87] This invasion cut West Java off from the rest of the Republican territory, which, as Chiara Formichi has shown, "laid the foundations for the region's divergent political path to independence."[88] It provided the space for Kartosuwirjo to transform Masyumi's West Java branch into what became the Darul Islam movement.[89] This transformation was prompted by the immediate need to defend the local Muslim population. Thus, on 14 August, Kartosuwirjo declared a *perang sabil* against the Dutch, calling upon all Muslims to rise against the enemies of Islam.[90] As a defensive jihad, this was *fardhu ayn*, and popular defense groups were subsequently set up, while Kartosuwirjo started to organize the resistance through Masyumi's paramilitary organizations Hizbullah and Sabilillah.[91] This was followed by the establishment of the Defense Council of the Islamic Community (Dewan Pertahanan Ummat Islam) in Garut and the Council of the Indonesian Islamic Community (Majelis Ummat Islam Indonesia) in Tasikmalaya to coordinate the struggle against the Dutch.[92] By the end of 1947 this had evolved into guerrilla warfare, and by August 1948 the entire population in the areas under Darul Islam's control had been mobilized.[93] Kartosuwirjo repeated his call for jihad after the second Dutch "police action." On 20 December 1948, he commanded the Indonesian *umma* to start a *"perang sutji muthlaq"* (absolute holy war), a *"perang totaliter"* (totalitarian war) against the Dutch colonisers until they "were destroyed" and until "the Indonesian Islamic State is established in its perfection throughout Indonesia."[94]

This first phase of the Darul Islam rebellion also saw the emergence of what in the literature is referred to as *perang segi tiga*, a triangular war, adding an intra-Indonesian dynamic. In 1947, competition over food supplies and weapons in West Java triggered clashes between Islamist fighters and the Siliwangi troops of the Indonesian military (Tentara Nasional Indonesia, TNI).[95] There was also more personally motivated violence, such as the cycle of revenge sparked by the TNI's execution of one of Sabilillah's leaders, Endang, for alleged treason.[96] Indeed, Endang's execution was one of the main factors driving support for Darul Islam in the regions of Garut and Sumedang.[97]

With the January 1948 Renville Agreement the battle lines became more clearly drawn. This agreement called for the withdrawal of Republican troops from most of West Java as well as parts of Central and East Java.[98] As some 35,000 Siliwangi troops redeployed to the Van Mook Line, the Islamist fighters stayed behind to continue the fight against the Dutch.[99] They were assisted by several hundred out-of-uniform TNI soldiers who had infiltrated into the Dutch-controlled territory.[100] The resistance was coordinated by Kartosuwirjo and his military commanders Kamran and Oni, with the Islamist fighters becoming the Indonesian Islamic Army (Tentara Islam Indonesia, TII).[101] They not only filled the vacuum left by the Republican troops in West Java but were also able to expand their territory into Central Java, establishing what Kees van Dijk refers to as "the offshoot."[102] This DI offshoot had its roots in the violent social revolution in the areas of Brebes, Tegal, and Pemalang. Hizbullah's Fifty-Second Battalion under Amir Fatah's command entered the area, adopted Pengarasan village as their central command base, and established a Majles Islam that had a "program for governance" from residency to village level, a police force, and the Heroes of Islam (Pahlawan Darul Islam, PADI) special forces.[103] Around March 1949 Fatah officially became the TII commander for Central Java and, in April, he proclaimed Central Java part of the NII.[104]

For most of 1948 it was the Islamist forces who fought the battle for Indonesia against the Dutch. Indeed, it was only after the second Dutch offensive that the Siliwangi troops began their "long march" to return to West Java.[105] As they tried to regain control, they were met with fierce resistance, which caught them off guard as they thought that Darul Islam backed the Republic.[106] The first armed contact took place on January 25, 1949.[107] On that day Kartosuwirjo had issued his first military decree, which described the Siliwangi as a *"tentara liar"* (illegal army) and designated them as the enemy of NII that had to be destroyed.[108] This armed conflict between nationalist and Islamist elements, as John R. W. Smail noted, became "the most striking feature" in rural areas of West Java in the late Revolution.[109]

During 1949 Darul Islam was active against the Dutch, the TNI, and the Dutch-backed State of Pasundan. DI's strategy was a territorial one, aimed at expansion and control. Territory was conceptualized in three categories: area 1 under DI control, area 2 partially under DI control, and area 3 fully under enemy control.[110] Expansion would be achieved by turning area 2 into area 1 and by making inroads into area 3 to turn it into area 2, which would eventually become area 1. Territorial control was, above all, achieved by controlling the people living there. This control was framed by the NII's Penal Code and its provisions for Islamic law in time of war. The latter divided the people into *ummat Muslimin* (community of the believers) and *ummat Kafirin* (community of unbelievers) and specifically designated the different types of enemy as *bughat* (those who do not recognize the laws of NII), *munafiq* (religious hypocrites), *fasiq* (sinners against Islamic law), and spies.[111] War was to be waged against the infidel colonial oppressors and those collaborating with them but also against the *bughat*, *munafiq*, *musyrik* (idolaters), and *muharrab* (those who have broken their loyalty oath).[112] This has led scholars such as Solahudin to assert that Darul Islam had a *takfiri* (practice of declaring Muslims apostates) stance.[113] It also explains the patterns of TII violence against civilians. These included kidnappings and the killings of Muslims and non-Muslims who did not agree with them.[114] Failure to follow DI regulations or failure to comply with "demands for food and services frequently met with sanguinary brutality."[115] DI paid nighttime visits to villagers to ascertain their loyalty, keeping those living in DI territory "in a constant state of submission" while keeping those living in adjacent territory "in constant terror."[116] People were robbed, mutilated, or killed, often after "being informed that they had been 'sentenced' by (secret) Muslim courts in accordance with the Islamic law of war."[117] "Cleansing" operations targeted "traitors against religion, state and people," resulting in "hundreds even thousands of traitors" having their throats slit, their "blood-covered corpses left in the streets and washed down the rivers."[118]

TII fighters also targeted Dutch and TNI posts, reportedly with *kiyai* (Muslim clerics) leading on the battlefield.[119] At times, the battle lines shifted with "reports that the Dutch were supplying weapons to Darul Islam in the Garut area," and of "casual co-operation" with leftist organizations.[120] Bandits also joined DI in order to benefit from "its military power and friendly peasant base of Darul Islam," exploiting "the local villagers in the DI's name."[121]

In this first phase, DI was able to carve out and control much of the mountainous regions of West Java. This became the base from which to establish the

Islamic state. Formichi divides this state building into four phases: First, from November 1947 to May 1948 when Kartosuwirjo established the TII. Second, from June 1948 to December 1948 when the NII cabinet was formed and the *kanun asasy*, NII's constitution, was drafted. Third, from December 1948 to May 1949, which she sees as leading to a clear "parting of ways" between Kartosoewirjo and the Republic. And fourth, from May 1949 to August 1949, which culminated in the formal proclamation of the Indonesian Islamic State.[122] The formal declaration of the NII, according to Kholid Santosa, also signaled the end of *jahiliyah* in Indonesia, which had been characterized by Dutch colonization and Japanese occupation.[123]

One area of contention in the literature on Darul Islam in the period of the 1945–1949 Indonesian Revolution, is to what degree Kartosuwirjo and the Indonesian Republic saw each other as enemies. B. J. Boland, who characterized this period as one of "relative unity-in-the-struggle," observed that it seemed that the government "did not wish to consider Kartosoewirjo's action a rising against the Republic, but only a regional counter-move against the Dutch-made 'State of Pasundan'."[124] George McTurnan Kahin noted that it was only in late December 1948 that DI became openly anti-Republican.[125] Here, Formichi argued that Kartosuwirjo and Darul Islam were not "arch-enemies of the Pancasila Republic," and Kevin Fogg, pointing to NII decree No. 6, highlighted that "even as late as December 21, 1948, Kartosuwirjo issued a proclamation emphasising his continuity and connection with the general Indonesian struggle for independence."[126] This chapter challenges these views. As discussed earlier, Kartosuwirjo believed his aim of establishing an Indonesian Islamic State to be incompatible with "secular" nationalism. This did not change when Sukarno laid out his vision of a state based on Pancasila, as illustrated by the rest of NII decree No. 6, which described the fall of Sukarno's government when the Republican cabinet was arrested by the Dutch as "a gift from God."[127] The fact that an open break with the Republic came so late in the revolution was thus purely tactical.

Phase 2

The second phase of the Darul Islam rebellions covers the period of January 1950 until February 1959 and is situated in newly independent Indonesia's era of liberal democracy. In this phase DI embarked upon a violent campaign against the Indonesian state, with the rebellion as a whole reaching its height in 1956–1957. NII's territory expanded beyond Java to South Sulawesi, Aceh, and South Kalimantan. There were also pockets of rebellion in the Lesser Sunda Islands and Halmahera.[128] This phase concludes with Sukarno's introduction of *demokrasi terpimpim* (Guided Democracy) in February 1959.

The departure of the Dutch after the transfer of sovereignty in December 1949 shifted DI's position from defensive to offensive as Sukarno defined and redefined the Indonesian state in the 1950s. His January 1953 speech in Amuntai, South Kalimantan, particularly spurred on the TII as he ruled out an Indonesian Islamic state and designated Darul Islam as an "enemy of the state."[129] Kartosuwirjo responded to this by declaring that the "war against the Pancasila state is a legal obligation."[130] This was followed in July 1953 by the TII launching "simultaneous actions," which became DI's new signature.[131] In August, Sukarno reiterated his designation of Kartosuwirjo and NII as enemies of the state in his speech to the special plenary session of parliament on August 16 and his independence day address to the nation on August 17, followed by a similar speech by Prime Minister Ali Sastroamidjojo on August 25. This prompted the release of a lengthy statement by Darul Islam in which Sukarno was called an "agitator" and a "Japanese agent" who "loves to lie."[132] Pancasila was labeled an ideology of *jahiliyah*, and the Indonesian Republic was referred to as the Communist Republic of Indonesia.[133] It was also pointed out that a declaration of war on NII amounted to recognition of the Indonesian Islamic State.[134] The statement concluded by calling upon every Muslim and every *mujahid* to reject the "*kafir* and *jahili* actions" of the Communist Republic of Indonesia, to protect the sacredness of the religion of Allah, and to defend the sovereignty of NII from aggression and attack.[135] The time had come for a struggle until death.[136]

Darul Islam's activities in the second phase of the rebellion in Java continued along similar lines as in the first phase, except that the targets were now only Indonesian. Its core territory was the mountainous regions "dominating stretches of two major roads: from Tegal to Purwokerto in Central Java and from Purwokerto to Bandung in West Java."[137] The key operational base was still Priangan Regency, and DI was particularly strong in Garut and Tasikmalaya.[138] DI's strength fluctuated between four thousand and fifteen thousand troops over the years, although the most often-cited number is ten thousand.[139] In 1956–1957, when the DI rebellions peaked, DI in West Java had two divisions, comprising seven regiments, twenty-four battalions, and 13,129 men.[140] These included former members of Raymond Westerling's Legion of the Just King (Angkatan Perang Ratu Adil, APRA) as well as Indonesian Army deserters.[141] The TII was thus "well armed," with Japanese, Dutch, and TNI weapons, including Sten submachine guns, Bren light machine guns, and some mortars.[142]

Foreign observers throughout the 1950s described West Java as "unsafe for Europeans" and as presenting the Indonesian government with a "chronic security problem."[143] The TII's targets fell into two broad categories: state and society. The first encompassed the Indonesian Republic's institutions, infrastructure, and those who represented it. This meant that government officials and offices, the security forces, public transport, and state infrastructure were attacked.[144] For instance, in January 1950, TII fighters launched an attack against Bantam during which they killed police chief Agus Jusuf Martadilaga, police bureau clerk Achmad, and first-class police constable Harjono, as well as military intelligence officer Raden Mochtar Surya Prawira and Bantam deputy resident Ahmad Fathony.[145] In June 1950, the fighting between the TNI and TII was concentrated in the areas of Tasikmalaya, Ciamis, Bandjar, and Garut. Three villages in the Ciawi District—Sukapada, Nanggewer, and Geranteng—were flagged as DI strongholds. The presence there of "not less than 6,000 troublemakers, among them 1,000 guest troublemakers who are armed and came from the area of Brebes, Indramayu, and who were led by Danu," was reported.[146] Indeed, these villages became one of the bases of DI's Tjakrabuana forces.

The tumultuous year of 1952 gives further insight into DI's operations. In April, the Indonesian military thwarted an operation to take over Bandung.[147] In May and June, DI increased its activities, ambushing security patrols and raiding small garrisons for weapons and ammunition.[148] A captured courier revealed orders for a "general attack" in West and Central Java to start on June 22, the beginning of the Islamic New Year, with targets "listed as small towns, army and police posts, and road traffic."[149] On the night of June 21 to 22, "600 fully armed and uniformed" Darul Islam fighters attacked President Sukarno's palace in Cianjur, partially penetrating the palace grounds. In the four-hour battle they killed ten TNI soldiers and wounded several more. Jakarta police also foiled a plot to assassinate government officials on June 22.[150] In late September, a TII regimental commander ordered a "determined attack" on all army and mobile brigade units in the Bogor Regency.[151] Observers at the time believed that Darul Islam had complete control of the civil administration at village level in the northeastern part of West Java, so much so that "the Indonesian army probably does not even enter the area."[152] In 1952, there were also repeated reports that DI was "gradually extending its influence into the eastern part of the island."[153]

In subsequent years, the TII sabotaged the Cibatu-Tasikmalaya train line, causing a train to derail, kidnapped four officers from the People's Committee of Jakarta and beheaded them in Mount Pantjar, and planned to disrupt the Asian-African Conference in Bandung.[154] At the height of the rebellion in 1956 and 1957, they managed to strike at the heart of the Indonesian government, targeting Sukarno's house in Puncak and Hatta's villa, as well as attempting to assassinate Sukarno on November 30, 1957, as he was attending a party at his children's school in Cikini.[155]

The second target was society. This included villages perceived as *kafir* because they were loyal to the Republic, refused to accept the NII, supported the communists, supplied Republican troops, or failed to follow Islamic law. Villages were also raided for funds and food supplies. And, according to Hiroko Horikoshi, "burning down villages and throwing corpses into the fire were seen as acts of *pembersihan* (purification), out of which a new and ideal state was to grow."[156] Much of this violence continued the patterns of terrorization seen in the first phase of the rebellion—looting, burning or destruction of property, killing or displacing residents, and sabotage. For example, in April 1950, it was reported that rubber and tea estates in Priangan were "almost deserted as a result of terrorization by Darul Islam."[157] In the last quarter of 1951, the TII was deemed to have been responsible for killing 414 people, burning 4,046 houses, carrying out 3,424 robberies, and leaving a total of 52,672 persons displaced.[158] In April 1954, the TII attacked Cisampang, leaving some three thousand people homeless in what the Indonesian military labelled "the method of the three Bs—*bunuh* (killing), *bakar* (burning), *bawa* (looting)."[159] On Indonesian independence day, August 17, 1954, Cikawung village was targeted, the houses and the mosque burned, "the people they encountered" shot.[160] In early 1955, the overall number of people displaced from "insecure areas" reached 209,355 persons.[161] In September 1956, the TII carried out continuous and simultaneous attacks for 17 days in the Tasikmalaya region, burning down 254 houses, two mosques, and a school.[162] In November 1956, they attacked Terayu village, burning down one hundred houses. Attacks in East Priangan also saw twenty civilians killed, three kidnapped, and 373 houses torched in the space of a week.[163] In total, in 1956 some 224 people were killed and 2,044 houses were burned down in East Priangan alone.[164]

While the attacks on villages were fairly indiscriminate, at times descending into massacres such as those at Cibugel, Ciinjuk, and Cikurahan, there were also attacks on specific individuals that were intensely personal, as they revolved around betrayal.[165] The most common targets here were DI members who tried to leave the movement. There were repeated reports of people "being hunted down and executed," as leaving was equated with apostasy.[166] The most high-profile personal attack was that against Kiyai Jusuf Tauziri, Kartosuwirjo's former teacher and confidant, who broke with Darul Islam when Kartosuwirjo declared the NII in 1949. This betrayal saw Cipari village, where Tauziri had his *pesantren*, attacked forty-six times between 1949 and 1958.[167]

During this second phase the rebellion and the Indonesian Islamic State expanded to South Sulawesi, Aceh, and South Kalimantan. There were three themes that underwrote this expansion. The first was Sukarno's centralization and with it the loss of regional autonomy. This was felt particularly acutely by the Acehnese, who had been promised special status in return for their contribution to the Indonesian Revolution. The second was the fear of Javanization. Not only was the national imaginary that Sukarno projected infused with Javanese culture and symbolism, but the existence of the Javanese as the largest ethnic group, and Java as the birthplace of Indonesian nationalism, ensured that the Javanese dominated the civil administration. Following independence, the Republican administration had been extended to the outer islands, often without incorporating or recognising those locals who had previously occupied administrative positions.[168] The TNI, too, saw its Javanese officers as key to asserting "firm Republican Army control over troops whom in their hearts they distrusted."[169] Thus it was reluctant to incorporate non-Javanese guerrillas. Demobilization certainly was among the grievances in South Sulawesi and South Kalimantan. The third theme was that of unfinished social revolution. This also applied more to South Sulawesi, where Kahar Muzakkar's rebels denounced the local aristocracy, and South Kalimantan, where Ibnu Hajar championed the oppressed and poor. Aceh had already undergone its social revolution in 1945.

These underlying dynamics have led to the DI rebellions in the non-Javanese areas being regarded as less Islamist in nature, as they were the result of dissatisfaction with Jakarta's policies.[170] This reading, however, misses the point made by Anhar Gonggong, who asserted that the rebellions in South Sulawesi and Aceh were as Islamic as that in West Java, as their leaders had all been immersed in Islam beforehand—Kartosuwirjo in Sarekat Islam, Kahar Muzakkar in Muhammadiyah, and Daud Beureueh in the All-Aceh Ulama Association (Persatuan Ulama-ulama Seluruh Aceh, PUSA).[171] Society in West Java, South Sulawesi, and Aceh was also staunchly Muslim. Building on Gonggong, it is argued here that all three rebellions in the outer islands, not disregarding the anticentrist and anti-Javanese dynamics, should be considered Islamist as their aim was an Islamic state, they all enforced Islamic law, and they each set out to implement their respective Islamist national imaginaries.

The first area where DI activity outside Java was noted was South Sulawesi. According to Boland, Kahar Muzakkar had reached out to Kartosuwirjo, was given, and had accepted "an appointment as Sulawesi commander of Kartosuwirjo's Islamic Army of Indonesia" on January 20, 1952.[172] On April 28, the Indonesian government announced that it "had conclusive evidence of a connection between the Darul Islam in West Java and the Mudzakkar rebels in the South Celebes."[173] Yet it was only on August 7, 1953, that Kahar Muzakkar formally proclaimed South Sulawesi as part of the NII.[174] By that point he had successfully established "closed areas," and by 1954 DI was deemed to have established control over most of South Sulawesi. The TII in South Sulawesi was believed to have had two divisions, the Hasanudin Division with twelve battalions and the "Division of 40,000" with sixteen battalions. There were also mobile combat units. Data from the TNI suggests that they had fewer arms than DI's divisions in Java but that this still included heavy weapons such as mortars.[175]

Darul Islam's targets in South Sulawesi resembled those in Java with attacks on army and police posts as well as attacks on villages, "murdering, plundering and burning."[176] Government offices and employees were attacked as they were seen as "*kafir* and *munafiq*."[177] In August 1955, Muzakkar also tried to interfere in the Indonesian elections, his forces occupying areas in order to prevent the vote from proceeding.[178] DI in South Sulawesi targeted pupils, youths, and soldiers for recruitment. Interestingly, women played a key role here: first, to lure urban male youths into joining DI; second, to lure TNI soldiers into joining DI; and third, to kill TNI personnel.[179] There were also reports of DI "atrocities against Christian Toraja," and forced conversions to Islam.[180]

The second territory to join the Darul Islam rebellions was Aceh. On September 21, 1953, Aceh's former military governor and founder of PUSA, Daud Beureueh, issued a statement proclaiming Aceh as part of the Indonesian Islamic State.[181] Here, the rebellion began with "coordinated attacks on police and army posts." Beureueh's followers, who numbered ten thousand according to the Indonesian defense minister, quickly moved to take over rural areas, which constituted their natural support base.[182] They also "launched major attacks on seven large centres," targeting Tapak Tuan in South Aceh, Meulaboh in West Aceh, Kutaradja (Banda Aceh) in Greater Aceh, Sigli and Langsa in East Aceh, and Takengon in Central Aceh.[183] These towns and cities were attacked in successive waves, each wave comprising more than one thousand men, spearheaded by Muslim youngsters armed with sharp weapons such as *rencong* (Acehnese daggers), machetes, and spears. Behind them were the adults with firearms, including Sten guns and Carbines.[184]

Beureueh's strategy aimed at gaining as much territorial control as quickly as possible. On September 24, reports emerged that DI had taken over "most of the territory" and it was considered that the Indonesian government faced the "prospect of indefinite guerrilla warfare."[185] On September 29, the American air attaché, who was monitoring the situation, asserted that "virtually all of the extreme northern end of Sumatra was held by rebel forces."[186] In November, Darul Islam shifted to guerrilla-style attacks in rural areas.[187] The targets over the next five years included the Indonesian security forces, who were regarded as *kafir* because, according to one of Darul Islam's leaders, Hasan Saleh, they hated "the prospect of Allah's law being carried out in Indonesian society."[188] The state infrastructure, in particular bridges and train lines, was also targeted, as were the non-Acehnese in Aceh, especially Bataks, who were seen as wanting "to gain control of Aceh."[189] And lastly, DI sought to infiltrate state institutions with the aim of taking them over from within. Here they were so successful that only a month after Beureueh's declaration, TNI Lieutenant Colonel Sutikno P. Sumarto lamented that about 70 percent of civil servants in Aceh had joined the rebellion.[190] When infiltration was resisted, civil servants, village heads, and also teachers became the targets of violence. For instance, in Central Aceh in 1955 village heads Abd. Madjid and Ramatsjah, as well as the teacher Ahmad, were killed. In the area of Takengon schools had to be shut and teachers relocated closer to the city for their protection.[191]

While Aceh was clearly part of the broader Darul Islam rebellions, Aceh maintained its distinctiveness, so much so that this allowed the Indonesian government to separate the rebellion in Aceh from the other Darul Islam rebellions and treat it differently. The first signs of this came in April 1957, when the TNI commander of the Aceh military area, Lieutenant Colonel Syamaun Gaharu, and the head of the Aceh police, M. Irsya, met with the TII Aceh commander Hasan Saleh and NII Aceh's prime minister, Hasan Ali, in the village of Lamteh.[192] This provided the basis for Hasan Saleh, Amir Hussein Al Mujahid, and Ayah Gani to move into negotiations with the Indonesian government, causing a split in the movement. Beureueh and his followers refused to engage in negotiations until Aceh had been granted the status of *daerah istimewa* (special region).[193] In fact, Beureueh held out even beyond that, until 1962, in solidarity with the continuing Darul Islam rebellions in West Java, South Sulawesi, and South Kalimantan, but also because he wanted to see the agreement actually being implemented.[194]

The agreement concluded on May 23, 1959, with Hasan Saleh stipulated that Aceh would become *Daerah Istimewa Aceh* on May 26, 1959. It further stated that DI/TII fighters would be integrated into the Teungku Cik Di Tiro troops of the TNI while those with civilian status would be given positions in the Indonesian civil service. The Indonesian government would also help Aceh develop. And in addition, the Aceh regional government would be permitted to draft regional legislation in accordance with *syariah* as long as it did not conflict with the "broad outlines of the state," the public interest, and national laws and regulations.[195] The DI rebellion in Aceh was the only one that was resolved through negotiations.

The last territory to join the rebellion in late 1954 was South Kalimantan, although contacts with DI in Java and South Sulawesi had been reported since 1952.[196] Under the leadership of Ibnu Hajar, what had started out as the Union of the Oppressed Indonesian People (Kesatuan Rakyat Indonesia Yang Tertindas, KRIYT) became the TII's Kalimantan division. This DI rebellion was smaller than the others in the sense that Ibnu Hajar and his men did not hold swaths of territory. Instead they were highly mobile, taking advantage of the dense jungle.[197] Armed with knives, machetes, spears, and some firearms, they targeted TNI and police posts, public transport, and plantations, as well as villages where they looted and burned down houses and kidnapped and killed people.[198] Van

Dijk noted that Ibnu Hajar's men became "more savage" after Sukarno's Amuntai speech.[199] They also became bolder, rendering not just the rural areas but now also the larger towns unsafe. As in Java, there were "visits" to villages where the residents were threatened or fined if they did not abide by Islamic law. *Hudud* punishments were also meted out.[200] Thus by 1955, the Indonesian government faced a multidimensional, multiterritorial rebellion by a rival Indonesian, albeit Islamic, state headed by Kartosuwirjo as imam and president, Beureueh as vice president, and Muzakkar as defense minister. Ibnu Hajar was only appointed Menteri Negara, the equivalent of minister without portfolio.

Phase 3

The third phase of the Darul Islam rebellions covers the period of Guided Democracy introduced in February 1959 until the death of Kahar Muzakkar in February 1965. This phase saw the Indonesian government tightening its control politically, the TNI being given more room for maneuver, the introduction of key tactical changes, and a waning of popular support for DI. The capture and execution of Kartosuwirjo in 1962 also dealt DI a massive blow, as the center of the Indonesian Islamic State collapsed.

The Indonesian Army's response to the Darul Islam rebellions from the 1950s onward had been a strategy of alternating combat and territorial operations with the aim of isolating the TII from its support base, cutting its logistics lines, and ultimately crushing it. Combat operations focused on gaining control over an area and clearing it of DI, expanding area by area, almost mirroring Darul Islam's strategy. Territorial operations were cushioned by *bhakti sosial* (social services), which had the soldiers rebuilding houses destroyed by TII fighters and restoring villages in a bid to win the hearts and minds of the people. This, however, was often undermined by the TNI's rough treatment of villagers when trying to ascertain their loyalty, punishing villages that supported DI, and drafting the local population into civilian defense organizations that then made them the targets of the TII.

While this strategy was broadly the same in West and Central Java as well as South Sulawesi, Aceh, and South Kalimantan, TNI commanders in their respective areas made their own mark on operations. For example, in Central Java the Indonesian military in early 1950 established the Gerakan Banteng Nasional (GBN) commando operation, which was drawn from the Siliwangi, Diponegoro, and Brawijaya divisions, followed by a new strike force, the Banteng Raiders, in 1952.[201] A young Lieutenant Colonel Suharto, who would later become Indonesia's second president, also introduced new training for his troops in order to raise their "fighting spirit."[202] Civilians, too, were drafted into support operations through people's defense organizations.²⁰³ In West Java in 1953, DI prisoners, especially those who had surrendered, underwent "a short period of indoctrination" after which they were released.²⁰⁴ In South Sulawesi, mobile commandos were used to pursue Muzakkar's forces in 1952, and in 1954 tactics shifted toward occupying areas controlled by DI and "herding the opponent towards the 'killing grounds'" where "the rebels" would be destroyed.²⁰⁵ In South Kalimantan the local population was given financial rewards for information on Ibnu Hajar's men, especially if this led to capture.²⁰⁶

Throughout these operations foreign observers regularly commented that "the army have found guerrilla tactics as difficult to counter as did the Dutch."²⁰⁷ They also noted that the Indonesian response to the rebellions had not been particularly effective, despite Darul Islam being proscribed, repeated orders to crush the rebels, and almost continuous military operations in the period of 1950–1957. Three main factors account for Indonesia's ineffectiveness. First, in the early 1950s Indonesia faced a multitude of insurgencies rather than just the Darul Islam rebellions. These included the APRA coup d'état led by Westerling, which succeeded in capturing the city of Bandung in January 1950, but failed at taking Jakarta; Andi Aziz's uprising in South Sulawesi against the incorporation of the federal states into the Republic of Indonesia; and the attempted secession of the Republic of South Maluku (RMS) under the leadership of Chris Soumokil, which lasted from April 1950 until December 1963. Troops, as a result, were often spread too thin or were withdrawn from areas of chronic insecurity to deal with acute challenges. Darul Islam was also seen as less of a priority compared to the RMS uprising, as DI did not threaten the territorial integrity of Indonesia. And last, but certainly not least, Sukarno himself was preoccupied with his campaign to incorporate Irian into Indonesia.

The second factor was the flow of information, weapons, and deserters from the TNI to Darul Islam. For instance, in September 1951, it was reported that "the irregulars have many friends" in the Indonesian Army and that these "connections keep the guerrillas informed of troop movements and of operations planned against them."²⁰⁸ In December 1951, the TNI was shaken by spectacular desertions when four TNI companies in Central Java left to join DI, followed by another two companies that took all of their equipment with them.²⁰⁹ By December 18, the total number of deserters had reached one thousand.²¹⁰ Foreign observers at the time were not all that surprised, as they saw the Indonesian Army as "a poorly trained, ill-paid, indifferently officered conglomeration of guerrilla bands" with "dubious" loyalties and frequent desertions, although usually "in smaller numbers than four companies."²¹¹ Documents captured in April 1952, when the security forces uncovered a Darul Islam plot to seize Bandung, indicated the degree of DI penetration of the "local army and leadership" in West Java as well as "the smuggling of large quantities of arms and ammunition from the armouries over a period of several months."[212] Reports in November 1952 also asserted that the army in East Java had been seriously infiltrated by Darul Islam.[213] In 1953, concerns were raised about DI infiltrations into the TNI in northern Sumatra as well as the reluctance by Muslim soldiers to take action against fellow Muslims.[214] In 1955, intelligence estimates cast doubt on the loyalty of as many as ten army battalions that may have had "sympathies" with one of the dissident groups, including Darul Islam.[215] In South Sulawesi, too, TNI soldiers often "ran to the jungle" between 1951 and 1960 to join the TII.[216] And TNI and police desertions to DI also occurred in South Kalimantan with the deserters taking their weapons with them, "thus augmenting the rebels' military potential."[217] The impact on the dynamics of the conflict was considerable. The TII's forces were boosted by ready-trained personnel, who brought with them modern military weapons. They refined the TII's tactics; the Indonesian military noted that its posts were being attacked "with better techniques."[218] Moreover, DI believed that it had been ideologically validated by these desertions while Republican troops had been weakened, not least because they now also had to focus on capturing the deserters and preventing further desertions.[219]

The third factor was the political uncertainty and increasing instability emanating from the Sukarno government. Two aspects, in particular, affected the Darul Islam rebellions: the reluctance of some TNI officers to go against the DI as they saw the DI as a potential ally in the battle against communism, and the factionalization of the army.[220] These internal TNI dynamics came in addition to the long-standing friction between the TNI and Masyumi. The TNI regarded Masyumi as a supporter of Darul Islam as it shared the goal of an Indonesian Islamic state. Masyumi's preference for a political solution to the rebellions, in turn, resulted in it blocking the TNI when it could.[221] Masyumi-driven attempts at negotiations with DI, however, were largely unsuccessful. In 1950–1951 the Natsir Cabinet sent emissaries to Kartosuwirjo, who then insisted that the NII be formally recognized first.[222] Negotiations with DI in South Kalimantan in 1956 looked more promising when they resulted in the surrender of some ten thousand fighters, including Ibnu Hajar. Yet, on February 2, 1957, Ibnu Hajar went on the run with seventy followers because the government had not kept its promise.[223] The greatest success was in Aceh, where "feelers from the Atjehnese rebels" prompted the Harahap government in 1955 to state that it would seek "to end the dissidence of fanatic Moslem groups through negotiations."[224] These feelers resulted in the 1957 Lamteh cease-fire agreement and 1959 special autonomy agreement discussed earlier.

In February 1959, Sukarno introduced "Guided Democracy" with the aim of creating national unity but that, in effect, shifted the center of power toward the president and toward the army.²²⁵ For the Indonesian military in its war on Darul Islam, this was a game changer. Guided Democracy created the political space for more extensive, intensive, and systematic operations against Darul Islam, especially after the 1957–1961 PRRI/Permesta rebellions had been put down and Masyumi had been banned in 1960. It had also become possible, for the first time, to turn all the state's resources against the DI, especially as Sukarno regarded Darul Islam as "a foreign controlled movement," believing that it was "manipulated and materially supported by the Dutch."²²⁶

Operational changes had already been introduced in 1957, outlined in Major General A. H. Nasution's Rencana Dasar 21 (Basic Plan 21). This plan stipulated that the enemy should be captured in a "specified area" and that the Indonesian troops needed to be consolidated and based in that area in order to carry out operations. Starting from Banten the troops would move eastward to close the escape route to Sumatra, "crushing" the enemy "one area after another." The local population was included in crushing the rebels; their role was to prevent the infiltration of the rebels into the villages.²²⁷ They became part of the "total isolation drive" that directed all of the local population to play an active role in the "annihilation" of the base of the rebels. This "total isolation drive" then developed further and, after being perfected, became known as *pagar betis* (fence of calves).²²⁸

Pagar betis operations aimed at weakening the DI by cutting logistical supply lines and decreasing its space for movement.²²⁹ They became an integral part of combat operations in 1961, the year that Kartosuwirjo issued an order for "total war," and were extensively used in the Brata Yudha operations from January 1962 until January 1963 in an effort to isolate DI.²³⁰ A *pagar betis* operation was usually set up at the foot of a rebel-held mountain. The men of the nearby villages would be mobilized or transported there while the TNI set up posts to mark the perimeter. Within this perimeter a chain of men, interspersed at intervals by three or four TNI soldiers, formed a ring around the area where the TII was suspected of operating. Together they would start marching up the mountain carrying torches, tightening the ring as they moved forward. Sometimes they were preceded by army patrols aiming to flush out the rebels and backed up by soldiers in case a siege was needed.²³¹ At other times it was the chain of civilians that was intended to draw out enemy fire, thereby revealing the location of the TII fighters. If fire was exchanged between the TII and TNI, it was usually the civilians who took the brunt of the casualties. Not only were the *pagar betis* operations an effective way to locate and trap the TII, but they were also extremely demoralizing for DI. Karl Jackson recounted that "rebel leaders spoke of the strain of waiting for the *pagar betis* while watching 'good Muslim peasants' praying in the hours before the morning march up the mountain."²³² Rather than fire on the civilians, many DI fighters surrendered, sweetened by the promises of clemency.²³³ Others were captured by the army's advance patrols.

By the beginning of 1962 Darul Islam in West Java had lost much of its strength. In April, Kartosuwirjo was wounded in a shooting. On June 4, severely weakened, suffering from diabetic complications and malnutrition in addition to his gunshot wound, he was discovered by the TNI on Mount Geber, between Bogor and Cianjur.²³⁴ According to Solahudin, the captured Kartosuwirjo then whispered to his son Muhammad Darda that "this is our Hudaibiyah" (quranic reference to the ten-year ceasefire agreed at Hudaibiyah between the Muslims in Medina and the idolators in Mecca) signaling that, despite his appeal for all DI fighters to lay down their arms, this was not a surrender but simply a temporary cease-fire.²³⁵

Meanwhile, in the outer islands Beureueh and his men came down from the mountains in May 1962, ending the last vestiges of the DI rebellion in Aceh. In the same month, Muzakkar seized the opportunity to shift the power center of the rebellion, declaring the establishment of the United Islamic Republic of Indonesia (Republik Persatuan Islam Indonesia, RPII).²³⁶ The following year, in July 1963, Ibnu Hajar and his followers "rejoined" the Indonesian Republic in a "brief ceremony in the village of Ambutun." According to van Dijk, he and his original fourteen thousand guerrillas even volunteered to assist the TNI in its konfrontasi with Malaysia, possibly in return for a pardon.²³⁷ This left Kahar Muzakkar as the remaining regional DI leader until he was shot dead on February 3, 1965.

Imagining an Islamic State in Indonesia

The Darul Islam rebellions were always more than simply uprisings. They tried to realize an alternative vision of Indonesia. Kartosuwirjo first started to conceptualize this Islamist national imaginary in the 1930s when he wrote *Sikap Hidjrah PSII*. This national imaginary was based on the first Islamic state established by the Prophet Muhammad in Medina. It was here that the first mosque was built by the Prophet and his companions, the community was unified, and *persatuan bathin* (inner unity), religious unity, and Islamic unity were achieved.²³⁸ It was also here that under the leadership of the Prophet the community's religious life was organized, social life was structured, and the first institutions such as the Baitul Mal (treasury) were set up.²³⁹ This became the core of Kartosuwirjo's national imaginary, which he further developed in *Daftar Oesaha Sikap Hidjrah PSII*, where he reiterated that the early Medina period at the time of the Prophet Muhammad was the ideal Muslim society and that this would form the basis of the Islamic state for which he was laying the foundations as "Medinah-Indonesia," the perfect Darul Islam.²⁴⁰ This, in turn, he defined as "the place were humankind receives *rahmat* (grace) and *ridho* (contentment) from Allah."[241] In this state, following the example of the Prophet, economic benefits would be distributed based on sincerity and patience, brotherly solidarity and collectivism. All wealth that exceeded the needs of individuals and households would be given to the Baitul Mal, from where it would be redistributed to those who had less.[242] "Medinah-Indonesia" would have the Quran as its *pedoman* (guidelines), and it would be based on the laws and commands of Allah as well as the *sunna* of the Prophet.[243]

However, it was not until the first Dutch "police action" in August 1947 that the institutional foundations for the Indonesian Islamic State were laid. In November 1947, Kartosuwirjo established the Dewan Pertahanan Ummat Islam in Garut and the Majelis Ummat Islam Indonesia in Tasikmalaya on behalf of Masyumi in order to coordinate local Muslim efforts in the struggle against the Dutch. In February 1948, in a series of meetings it was decided to set up a rudimentary regional government in West Java, by "duplicating the central government structure at all levels, extending down to the village levels."[244] According to Jackson both were based upon the *wadah* (receptacle) system whereby "administrative control was expanded by appointing an individual as village head before even part of the village had joined the rebellion. If the Darul Islam headman successfully filled his 'receptacle,' he would be promoted to subdistrict officer and again asked to fill the receptacle."[245] Existing Islamic organizations would be merged with the Majelis Islam headed by Kartosuwirjo, while existing guerrilla groups would become the TII. An Islamic police force was also established.[246] In May 1948, at a conference in Cijoho, the *kanun asasy*, comprising NII's constitution, were drafted. Their final version, in August 1948, conceptualized the Indonesian Islamic State as a *jumhuriyah* (republic), with a *majlis syuro* as parliament and *dewan imamah* as cabinet, and headed by the imam as president.[247] The imam was to be elected by the *majlis syuro* and had to be an Indonesian Muslim "obedient to God and his Prophet."[248] He was in charge of the armed forces, declared war, and concluded peace, and he was assisted in matters of Islamic law by the *dewan fatwa* (advisory council), headed by a grand mufti.[249] The state would be based on Islamic law with freedom of worship for non-Muslims.[250] As laid out in the Penal Code, religious backsliding by Muslims would be severely punished and Muslims could not change their religion.[251]

Kartosuwirjo himself became the imam of the Islamic State of Indonesia while Hizbullah and Sabilillah commanders Kamran and Oni became the minister and deputy minister of defense.[252] From this point onward the Indonesian Islamic State de facto existed, as exemplified by the decrees issued by Kartosuwirjo as the imam of the government of the NII. However, it was not until August 7, 1949, that Kartosuwirjo, in the village of Cisampang, formally proclaimed "the existence of

Negara Islam Indonesia," in the name of the Indonesian Islamic umma, with the document tellingly stating the location as "Medinah-Indonesia."[253]

The proclamation was accompanied by ten explanatory points that expounded that the Indonesian Islamic State was born in the midst of the national revolution, at a time of war, from the need "to fight against the cruelty of oppression and slavery practiced by the Dutch," that this fight had become an "Islamic revolution" or jihad, that the state thus would be governed by Islamic law in the time of war, and that the territory of the NII comprised the "whole of Indonesia."[254] Reflecting both the Islamic and Indonesian nationalist nature of the Indonesian Islamic State, its flag had as its base the red-and-white Indonesian banner with a white Muslim crescent moon and star on the red half of the flag.[255] The crescent moon and star clearly associated it with the last caliphate, the Ottoman Empire. The flag of the TII was green with a white crescent and star, and at times of war the flag of both the state and the military changed to a completely red one with a white crescent and star.[256]

When South Sulawesi, Aceh, and South Kalimantan joined the Darul Islam rebellions, their commanders joined the NII cabinet. Much in the way that the *wadah* system had been designed to "fill" villages and districts, thereby bringing them under DI control, NII was a *wadah* that was slowly being filled with regions, districts, and smaller areas across Indonesia.[257] However, while Aceh, South Sulawesi, and South Kalimantan were now united with West Java in the struggle for an Islamic Indonesia, each region had considerable leeway to implement its own policies and pursue its own national imaginary. Ibnu Hajar conceptualized South Kalimantan as an Islamic kingdom within the Islamic State of Indonesia, referring to himself as *ulul amri* (the authority).[258] He sought social and economic reforms, promoting Islamic law, Islamic values, and Islamic education.[259] He even commissioned an Islamic anthem that hailed God as "king" and "omniscient," to be obeyed and "served devotedly each day." It called on Muslims to unite and to "arise in spirit and body for the religion of the One and Only God."[260] This resulted in the Indonesian Islamic State effectively having two anthems.

Daud Beureueh established his own regional cabinet in NII's Aceh territory.[261] He also introduced his own currency. The banknotes referred to Aceh as a province of NII but also as Aceh Darussalam. He thus established continuity with the Sultanate of Aceh, which had been a major regional power in the sixteenth and seventeenth centuries as well as the "veranda of Mecca." This historic, fiercely Islamic Aceh was at the heart of Beureueh's national imaginary. Aceh's Islamic currency included half-rupiah, one-rupiah, and ten-rupiah notes, which following Islamic tradition refrained from depicting humans, with some showing distinctly Acehnese landmarks.[262] For example, the one-rupiah banknote shows a rough semblance of Baiturrahman Mosque in Kuta Raja/Banda Aceh on the left and the Islamic crescent moon in the center, with "propinsi Atjeh Darusalam" (Aceh Darusalam province) written in Indonesian on its left and "satu rupiah" (one rupiah) written in Arabic script on its right.

In South Sulawesi, Kahar Muzakkar envisaged the Islamic State of Indonesia as a revolutionary egalitarian Islamic republic, which he referred to as the Islamic Republic of Indonesia Eastern Section (Republik Islam Indonesia Bagian Timor). He proceeded to reorganize society and the economy. In an effort to remove all vestiges of feudalism he got rid of titles such as *"andi"* and *"daeng,"* and even "hajji," as well as *"bapak"* and *"ibu."*[263] He also introduced land reforms and restrictions on wealth in order to eradicate differences in personal prosperity.[264] The DI economy under Muzakkar drew financial support from merchants and traders, as key members of the South Sulawesi DI leadership came from a merchant trader background, and Muzakkar established the Special Secret Enterprise of the Revolutionary Organization (Usaha Rahasia Chusus Organisasi Revolusi, URCOR), which was granted a trade monopoly.[265] Moreover, a blockade was imposed to prevent trade between DI and non-DI areas.[266] Instead, products from within DI areas were sold directly abroad, often in return for bullets and weapons.[267]

DI's territory in South Sulawesi was divided into four regencies. In 1954 Kahar Muzakkar planned to establish a civilian government alongside a military one in each of the regencies, replicating Kartosuwirjo's system of governance in West Java. Each would be headed by a brigade commander who would become the resident.[268] In these areas DI's civil service collected taxes and ran schools.[269] His Islamic state was a puritan one where Islamic law reigned supreme and neither *adat* nor mysticism had a place.[270] A simple lifestyle devoid of jewelry, expensive clothes, makeup, and fancy foods was encouraged.[271] And he also endorsed polygamy as "an authentic Islamic solution" to "the social problem of widows."[272]

The highest institution was the *dewan fatwa*, which was headed by Haji Abdul Rahman Ambo Dalle, who was allegedly "kidnapped" by the TII in 1955.[273] This *dewan fatwa* fully subscribed to NII's *kanun asasy* but drew up additional regulations for its Eastern Section. The regulations on its justice system, for instance, stipulated that judges needed to be Muslim, adult, rational, independent, male, just, and knowledgeable in the law of the Quran and hadith. Moreover, a judge was not permitted to make decisions if he was angry, hungry, thirsty, or tired. Decisions would draw upon witnesses, oaths, confessions, and evidence. Witness requirements were two men or a man and two women, or if the case was female specific, four women.[274] In 1955, Muzakkar also outlined his ten-point program for revolutionary Islamic politics at the second conference of the Islamic Revolutionary Struggle in Eastern Indonesia. This included broad points such as rallying for Muslim unity (point 1) as well as realizing the dream of Islamic victory to create a peaceful world (point 9). The more specific struggle against Indonesia was addressed by his commitment to revive jihad (point 6) but also to prevent every Indonesian attempt at holding general elections (point 2). He reaffirmed his Islamic revolutionary credentials with his pledge to stand against ideas that undermined Islamic teachings, such as communism, imperialism, colonialism, feudalism, and *tarekat* (Sufism) (point 3), and to ensure social justice for the revolutionary society, particularly the families of victims of the revolution and the families of martyrs (point 8), as well as to fight corruption, loan sharks, and parasites in society (point 7). This was further underscored by the specific points pertaining to Islam: the guarantee to implement *syariat Islam* (point 10), the rejection of the *madhab* (schools of jurisprudence) in Islam (point 4), and the rejection of legal equality between men and women, which he denounced as Western emancipation.[275]

In his speech at the same conference his puritanical-egalitarian principles were even more pronounced, as he conceptualized the umma as *"ummat tauhid"* engaged in a "holy revolution" and whose obligation it was to carry out jihad that "would free man from all kinds of disasters and human habits on this earth."[276] He called upon the Islamic revolutionary fighters to self-limit their clothes and food, to defend the peasants and the poor, and to distance themselves from the arrogance of "the pharaohs."[277] Elaborating on some of the points in his political program he declared the Indonesian elections *"haram"* but, interestingly, endorsed Islamic democracy based on *"bermusyawarah"* (consultation).[278] He explained that the *madhab* must be rejected as they were the "result of human *ijtihad* [reasoning]" rather than the Quran, the book of Allah.[279] And he stated that the program would be implemented through the *"tri-tunggal"* (trinity) of *"berdjihad, beladjar, bekerdja"* (*jihad*, studying, working).[280]

In 1962, Kahar Muzakkar recast his Islamic state as the Republik Persatuan Islam Indonesia, headed by himself as "Caliph." In a speech to the mujahidin and the people in 1963, a year after Kartosuwirjo's execution, he denounced the Pancasila state as based on worldly ideas that would drag down the nation to the level of animals, which disregard moral and spiritual life. While he acknowledged that belief in one God was indeed one of Pancasila's core principles, he stated emphatically that all principles of Pancasila were only political principles, which were used as a "propaganda tool." He then called upon those DI/NII fighters who had surrendered to the government to return to the jihad if they were still "Islam-minded" and "Allah-minded." This jihad was necessary as the Indonesian nation stood at the "abyss of totalitarianism, oppression, rape, and enslavement by the totalitarian Pancasila state," trampled "under the feet of an unjust dictator . . . named Soekarno." It was the only way for the Indonesians to free themselves as "we are not Soekarno's slaves. We are not the slaves of the Pancasila state, and therefore we must fight and be willing to make sacrifices to obtain the freedom and independence that belong to us all."[281]

This speech also gives insight into how the Indonesian Islamic State's cabinet was reshuffled after the death of Kartosuwirjo, who was succeeded as NII imam by Abdul Fatah Wirananggati. Muzakkar retained his position as minister of defence and was the only remaining active military commander. Other ministers in the NII cabinet according to Muzakkar were Ahmad Marzuki Hasan as interim minister of the interior, Hasan Muhammad [di] Tiro as foreign minister, Achmad Sumarsono as communications minister, S. Barant as education minister, and KS Abdul Gani as economics minister.[282] Interesting in this lineup is Tiro, who was an Acehnese who had joined DI's struggle when Beureueh did. Tiro was based in the United States at the time as part of the Indonesian delegation to the UN. He thus not only was able to represent DI internationally but also remained part of DI after the rebellion in Aceh came to an end. He eventually led many of the "old" Acehnese Darul Islam fighters into a new movement for Acehnese independence in 1976.

Reflecting on Islam, Indonesian Nationalism, and the DI Rebellions

The Darul Islam rebellion that erupted in West Java was a response to the reoccupation of Muslim land by the non-Muslim Dutch colonisers in 1947 as well as the adoption of Pancasila as the foundation of the Indonesian state proclaimed in August 1945. Its roots, however, go back to the early Indonesian nationalist debates, in which Islamic nationalism was equally legitimate. It was this Islamic nationalist vision, advocated by Kartosuwirjo in the 1930s and 1940s, that led him to reject Pancasila as the foundational basis of the Indonesian Republic when it was proclaimed in August 1945. Here it is important to understand that Kartosuwirjo's objection to Pancasila had little to do with its actual principles and everything to do with the fact that it was a man-made philosophy, as can be seen from the way he conceptualized the struggle as *hijrah* and jihad in order to establish an Indonesian Islamic state that would allow Muslims to live their lives in accordance with *syariah* law. This aim was later shared by Kahar Muzakkar, Daud Beureueh, and Ibnu Hajar, who joined the rebellion in the early 1950s, although they all had different Islamic national imaginaries that they tried to implement in their respective territories. Thus the Darul Islam rebellions as a whole should be considered Islamist, even if the initial triggers were not necessarily so.

During the course of the rebellions the dynamics of the violence and the number of casualties differed considerably across DI's different territories. Aceh, which was the only rebellion resolved through negotiations, saw fewer casualties, as did South Kalimantan, where the rebellion itself was small. This contrasts with the higher number of casualties in West Java and South Sulawesi, where TII fighters held distinct territories. According to Jackson some forty thousand people were killed in the Darul Islam rebellions, with twenty-five thousand deaths in Java.[283] It is suggested here, in line with the argument of the book, that this high number of deaths overall can be explained by the extent of territory DI was able to carve out. However, the war in West Java was particularly bitter, as it was in West Java that the Indonesian Republic had been "saved" from being stillborn and the mere existence of the DI/TII challenged the "savior" narrative of the TNI/Siliwangi Division.

The Darul Islam rebellions came to an end in 1965. Kartosuwirjo and Ibnu Hajar were executed by the Indonesian government; Kahar Muzakkar was killed in a shootout. Only Beureueh survived. Since then scholars and Islamists have reflected on why the rebellions failed although Kartosuwirjo, Beureueh, Muzakkar, and Ibnu Hajar at times had considerable popular support.[284] An important factor certainly was the change in TNI tactics from 1961 onward, most notably the *pagar betis* operations.[285] As resource-intense operations they were particularly suitable for the population-dense areas of Java. The Darul Islam movement's lack of "significant financial resources" also played a role.[286] And finally, there is some consensus in the literature that the atrocities committed by the Darul Islam movement in the end alienated Indonesian Muslims.[287] This chapter takes this point beyond the nature of DI's violence, suggesting that the rebellions failed because the DI leaders did not succeed in establishing a stable state that met Islamic ideals. This did not, however, mean that the idea of an Islamic state in Indonesia ended with the rebellions. Indeed, as will be seen in chapter 2, the idea of an Indonesian Islamic state persisted, as did militant jihad in pursuit of it.

2

JEMAAH ISLAMIYAH'S JIHAD AND QUEST FOR AN ISLAMIC STATE, 1993–2019

At a secret meeting in late 1968 some DI/NII leaders, including Kartosuwirjo's son Dodo Mohammad Darda, decided the time was right to start reviving the movement.[1] Shortly thereafter DI's former finance minister, Djaja Sudjadi, met with former DI West Java fighters to socialize the concepts of *hudaybiyah* and *jihad fillah* (spiritual jihad), which would be in place until DI/NII had regained its military capacity.[2] He was joined by Kartosuwirjo's former aide Aceng Kurnia, as well as Kadar Solihat, in reaching out beyond Java to Gaos Taufik in North Sumatra and Daud Beureueh in Aceh.[3] Kurnia also introduced education programs for the children of Darul Islam members while his younger followers set up a DI/NII study group.[4] A new caderization process was initiated by, among others, Kartosuwirjo's son Tahmid Rahmat Basuki.[5] And Kartosuwirjo's one-time protégé Adah Djaelani oversaw the establishment of seven DI area commands of which West Java—the heartland of the 1947–1965 rebellions—was the most developed.[6] At the same time DI/NII embarked upon ideological renewal, embracing ideas from non-Indonesian Islamists including Abu Ala Maududi, Said Qutb, and the Egyptian Muslim Brotherhood. This reoriented the movement's ideology toward *tauhid* (oneness of God).[7] It was from this growing and increasingly heterogeneous DI/NII network that a new militant Islamist organization emerged in 1993: Jemaah Islamiyah (JI), this book's second case study of Islamist violence in Indonesia.

This chapter looks at how JI evolved out of the DI movement. It examines Suharto's policies, which closed the space for political expressions of Islam, criminalized Muslim activism, and led some Islamists to leave Indonesia for Malaysia and Afghanistan. It explores the establishment of JI and its return to Indonesia after the fall of Suharto. The chapter then proceeds to analyze JI's bombing campaign from 1999 to 2009 and its broader quest for an Islamic state from 1993 to 2019. Here it focuses on the ideological underpinnings of the violence and on the narratives and Islamist national imaginaries advanced by JI's founders, Abdullah Sungkar and Abu Bakar Ba'asyir, by JI's general guidelines, and by JI's *mantiqis* (regions). The chapter concludes with a discussion of the revived JI under the amirship of Para Wijayanto from 2008 to his arrest in 2019 and with a more general reflection on Muslim belonging and the persistence of Islamist violence in Indonesia.

This chapter shows that while the circumstances surrounding the Islamist violence in the 2000s differed greatly from those of the Darul Islam rebellions examined in chapter 1, the basis for contesting Indonesia as a state conceptualized through Pancasila rather than *syariat Islam* remained the same. Equally, the intertwining of Islam with Indonesian history as well as early Indonesian nationalism continued to provide legitimacy for reshaping Indonesia, thus explaining the persistence of periodic Islamist violence into the twenty-first century.

Suharto's New Order and Islam: Framing the Emergence of JI

The emergence of JI was framed by the New Order, which both allowed for the reemergence of DI/NII and created the political and social grievances that produced a new pool of recruits. The New Order saw the relationship between Islam and the state almost exclusively in ideological and security terms. This placed the Indonesian Armed Forces (Angkatan Bersenjata Republik Indonesia, ABRI) and the intelligence services at the forefront of fighting political expressions of Islam. Key roles were played by the State Intelligence Coordination Agency (Badan Koordinasi Intelijen Negara, BAKIN), the special operations unit (Operasi Khusus, Opsus), and the Operational Command for the Restoration of Security and Order (Komando Operasi Pemulihan Keamanan dan Ketertiban, KOPKAMTIB). Their activities were underwritten by articles from the Dutch colonial penal code criminalizing rebellion and sedition, incitement to hatred, and acts of hostility toward the government, as well as the 1963 Anti-Subversion Law, which defined any activity that "can distort, undermine or deviate from the ideology of Pancasila" as subversion.[8] Together these state agencies pursued a strategy that quickly moved from attempts at co-optation to manipulation and repression.

When Suharto rose to power on the back of the euphemistically labeled "events of 1965," Muslims and Islamists were cautiously optimistic as this signaled a pushback against the communism of the late Sukarno era. This ushered in a brief honeymoon period during which the Indonesian military, now having a common enemy with the Islamists, encouraged Muslim youths to actively participate, as partners, in the anticommunist purges of 1965–1966 in what François Raillon referred to as an alliance between "armed *priai* and unarmed *kiai*."[9] Eliminating the communists meant not only eradicating the agents of moral decline but also ending communist land reforms that had targeted the "pillars of the Muslim establishment," as well as removing the procommunist peasants' organization Barisan Tani Indonesia, "an irritating rival" to Nahdlatul Ulama (NU)'s "grassroots appeal in the Javanese countryside."[10]

In late October 1965, Indonesian special forces started training Muslim youths in rural Java. In Central Java, they "were incited to take up weapons (primarily knives and clubs) and run amok against the PKI."[11] In East Java, NU's youth wing, Ansor, played a "critical role in the massacres," needing "little encouragement to begin violent action," which was cast as revenge for the deaths of Masyumi and NU supporters during the 1948 Madiun uprising.[12] In the cities, the Muslim student organizations Himpunan Mahasiswa Islam (HMI) and Kesatuan Aksi Mahasiswa Muslim Indonesia (KAMMI) rallied support for the anticommunist campaign.[13] The previously defeated DI/NII also benefited, as incarcerated leaders were released after the deputy head of BAKIN, Ali Murtopo, and his Opsus team visited them in prison, and foot soldiers were recruited into the Siliwangi Division's anticommunist campaign. Murtopo also managed to recruit DI commander Danu Muhammad Hasan to work for BAKIN, giving him the task of "combing Jakarta to track down officials from the Soekarno regime that had gone into hiding."[14]

This cooperation placed Muslims in a position from which Islamists once again tried to sway the Indonesian government in favor of some of their aims. Thus in 1967, they attempted to reopen the Jakarta Charter debate, only to find this opposed by the military in the 1968 session of the People's Consultative Assembly (MPR).[15] They were somewhat more successful at achieving a partial rehabilitation of the previously banned Masyumi. In 1967, the Indonesian government permitted Mohammad Natsir to establish the Indonesian Islamic Propagation Council (Dewan Dakwah Islamiyah Indonesia, DDII). Moreover, in February 1968, Suharto approved a new Muslim political party, Partai Muslimin Indonesia (Parmusi). Parmusi, however, was no more than what Ruth McVey referred to as "Masyumi's pallid epigone."[16] Former Masyumi politicians were banned from Parmusi's leadership and its central executive was infiltrated by army intelligence, leading Natsir to comment that the New Order had treated them "like cats with ringworm."[17]

The New Order intelligence services kept an equally watchful eye on the DI/NII leaders who had now started to regroup. Key to continued cooperation between BAKIN and DI/NII was Danu's personal relationship with Murtopo. As Solahudin observed, "They had known each other since they were active together in the Hizbllah militia during the revolution. Danu greatly trusted Moertopo because he believed that he had once saved Darul Islam from extinction. . . . Darul Islam members like Danu even trusted Ali Moertopo's commitment to Islam. They were convinced that he shared their goal of establishing an Islamic state."[18] This provided an entry point through which BAKIN could monitor some activities and manipulate others. In 1969, BAKIN actively courted DI/NII's top echelons, offering them kerosene concessions for their areas.[19] Moreover, under the guise of seeking further anticommunist cooperation, Murtopo approached the remnants of the Central Java DI/NII under Haji Ismail Pranoto (Hispran), intending to use them as a vehicle for bringing in the Golkar vote.[20] BAKIN thus not only allowed but actively encouraged and contributed to the revival of DI/NII, which Sidney Jones has highlighted as "one of the worst mistakes made by the Soeharto government."[21]

However, not all of the reemerging DI/NII movement was willing to engage with BAKIN. Indeed, only about a third of the DI's twenty-six "core leaders" were cooperative.[22] And among those who were, many saw themselves as the manipulators rather than the manipulated, as explained by one of Aceng Kurnia's younger followers, Ridwan: "Actually, from the beginning we wanted to use BAKIN. We needed support for the movement. We didn't have funding, and support from the umma was less than total, so at the time we used BAKIN."[23] The New Order's intelligence approach toward DI/NII also set the context for the emergence of the militant Islamist Komando Jihad. Similar to the relationship between DI/NII and BAKIN, the relationship between Komando Jihad and BAKIN was a complicated one, in which Indonesian intelligence thought they had more control than they actually did. This is reflected in the comments by West Java commander Major General Himawan Soetanto, who in an interview with Ken Conboy stated that

> We were all concerned about his acquiescence to let Komando Jihad grow unchecked in our regions. Ali Moertopo told us not to worry. He said that he was letting them think they were a bulwark against communism, but was really using them for votes. Komando Jihad, meanwhile, was telling Ali Moertopo that they would guard against communism, but they were really using the opportunity to organize themselves. He was overly confident and assured us he could control them. It came down to a game of who was playing whom.[24]

In 1976, Komando Jihad embarked upon a campaign of violence as part of its strategy to bring about an Islamic state.[25] This saw the bombing of the Christian Immanuel Hospital in Bukittinggi as well as a Methodist Church, the Christian Budi Murni College, and the Riang Cinema and Apollo Bar in Medan, followed by the lobbing of a grenade into the Nurul Iman Mosque in Padang and an attack on a police station in West Java.[26] The selection of targets suggests that the aim was to provoke Christian-Muslim conflict as a way to undermine the government.

Komando Jihad's violence prompted a crackdown by Indonesian security forces on Islamists in 1977. Some seven hundred alleged members of Komando Jihad in Aceh, North Sumatra, Riau, South Sumatra, Lampung, Jakarta, West Java, Central Java, and East Java were arrested, most of them DI/NII members or supporters.[27] They included Hispran, Danu Muhammad Hasan, Dodo Muhammad Darda, Ateng Djaelani, and Gaos Taufik. Observers at the time believed that Komando Jihad was, in fact, a creature of Murtopo's, and that this violence had been encouraged, if not directed, in order to discredit Muslim parties in the runup to the 1977 elections, by linking "Muslim activism in the public mind with alleged terrorist activities."[28] However, according to Solahudin, it was only after these arrests that the government labeled the Sumatra and Java-based Darul Islam groups involved in the planned uprising as "Komando Jihad," suggesting that they had had considerable independence.[29] Similarly, Quinton Temby has asserted that simply seeing Komando Jihad as an Opsus "sting operation" is not an accurate presentation of the BAKIN-DI relationship.[30]

While Indonesian intelligence was busy trying to manipulate and control Islamist militants in the 1970s, the government adopted a less ambiguous position as laid out in Suharto's vision for the country. In this vision he sought to set "right the practice of and dedication to Pancasila and the 1945 Constitution in strict and consistent manner" and to "give top priority to economic development," through which "nation-building in a broad sense could be enhanced."[31] Suharto saw politicized or even too conservative Islam as a destabilizing force, as exemplified by his June 1971 Pasar Klewer speech in Solo, a month before the general elections.[32]

> I was critical of the vociferous voices which cried out that if the General Elections were not satisfactory, they would turn into a jihad, or holy war. That kind of thinking could only create chaos and conflict, while what we needed was security and unity. So I warned political leaders against provoking the people, and I also urged the people not to be influenced by such pronouncements. However, if there were trouble, then for the sake of development, Pancasila and the 1945 Constitution, there would be no other alternative for both the people and the Armed Forces than to meet jihad with jihad.[33]

In this speech he made it clear that Indonesia was not a theocracy, and that he would take "firm action against any attempt to exploit religious issues for improper political purposes."[34] The "wrong" kind of Islam was an obstacle to Indonesia's development and modernization. In order to encourage the "right" kind of Islam, the New Order urged Muslim scholars to study in the West rather than the Middle East.[35] Moreover, those who were close to the Javanese establishment were clearly favored.[36] With their support Suharto rolled out a series of policies aimed at promoting stability, Pancasila, and tolerance in which conservative Muslims quickly were directly targeted or became "collateral damage" of modernization and development policies. Examples of these policies included the 1970–1971 family planning program, which was welcomed by the United Nations, as well as the 1974 Marriage Law, which, according to Suharto, "marked a milestone in the history of the women's movement."[37] Its initial draft in 1973 would have allowed Muslim women to marry non-Muslim men, and *syariah* was to be replaced by "modern" laws "considered appropriate by the Westernized urban elite."[38] Open resistance by the ulama and Muslim organizations forced the government into redrafting the marriage bill, but the lesson was not lost on the government, which now saw itself confirmed in its assessment that Islam needed to be "tamed" and controlled.[39]

The first step towards domesticating Islam had already been taken after the 1971 elections when Suharto decided to "fuse" Indonesia's political parties into two, the Indonesian Democratic Party (Partai Demokrasi Indonesia, PDI), comprising nationalist and Christian parties, and the United Development Party (Partai Persatuan Pembangunan, PPP), which amalgamated all Muslim parties into what Michael Vatikiotis labeled a "decorative coalition of Muslim interests."[40] This move aimed at removing Muslim political identities and "defanging" the Islamists.[41] As Suharto himself noted, "I urged them not to overemphasize the religious aspects of Islam, voicing this warning from the outset. Therefore 'Islam' is not even mentioned in the party's name."[42] It also aimed at checking NU, which was not only perceived as antimodern and a "nuisance" as its ulama were "not so malleable," but also had demonstrated the capacity to mobilize Java's rural masses in 1965–1966.[43]

In 1973, the MPR session further removed religion as a foundation for development in the Broad Outlines of State Policy, and recognized *kepercayaan/kebatinan* (Javanese spiritual/mystical beliefs) as a separate religious orientation.[44] Not surprisingly this, too, resulted in fierce opposition by the ulama, who saw this as an attempt to dilute Islam by "encouraging" *abangan* (nominal) Muslims "away from the faith entirely."[45]

Having dissolved all Muslim political parties and closed off avenues for formal Muslim political expression, Suharto proceeded to co-opt as many of the ulama as possible. To this end, the Indonesian Ulama Council (Majelis Ulama Indonesia, MUI) was established in 1975.[46] Generous subsidies were also available to the "right" kind of mosques and *pesantren*.[47] Indeed, the New Order's cooptation strategy proved so successful that by 1985 the mainstream Muslim organizations had become almost completely compromised.[48]

The year 1978 saw the start of the New Order's "Pancasila-ization" drive with the introduction of two-week courses on the "Guidelines for Living and Practicing Pancasila" for all state employees. These courses were extended to all Indonesian citizens in 1983.[49] From 1980 onward, the "Pancasila-ization" of Indonesian public life began, inviting all political and social organizations to adopt Pancasila into their articles of association as *asas tunggal* (sole principle).[50] This *asas tunggal* requirement became Law No. 8/1985, after five years of resistance by political, social, and religious organizations that maintained that this requirement aimed at suppressing political opposition in general, and denying Islam as an alternative ideology in particular.[51]

The first open resistance came in the form of a petition brought to the Indonesian parliament by fifty Indonesian citizens on May 5, 1980, known as "Petisi 50" (the petition of fifty). This petition expressed concern about the interpretation of Pancasila and its use against political opponents, how ABRI had become a party rather than standing above politics, how some were seeing themselves as the personification of Pancasila, and how others were accused of subversion. The signatories of this petition included not only former Masyumi prime ministers Mohamad Natsir and Burhanuddin Harahap, former Indonesian emergency government president Sjafruddin Prawiranegara, and Muslim preachers such as A. M. Fatwa, but also former members of the Indonesian parliament (Dewan Perwakilan Rakyat, DPR) such as Ir. HM Sanusi and military officers such as retired General Jasin.[52] As a smaller working group they continued with meetings and statements of concern until the mid-1980s in their struggle "to restore the law, justice, and the sovereignty of the people . . . in the framework of enjoining good and forbidding evil."[53] Another challenge came from the National Movement for Veiling (Gerakan Berjilbab Nasional), which was formed in response to the Department of Education's decree 052/C/Kep/D/82 on uniforms in state schools in March 1982.[54] This decree forbade girls to wear the *jilbab*. Girls who insisted on wearing it anyway were sent home and asked to find a private school.

However, while resistance continued in pockets of civil society, *asas tunggal* made considerable inroads into formal political and social organizations. In 1984, the Muslim PPP was no longer permitted to campaign using the Ka'bah as its symbol.[55] In the same year NU withdrew from the PPP and from politics altogether. When the Muslim student organization HMI voiced resistance, its branches were infiltrated or disbanded and new ones created, until it was ready to conform.[56]

Resistance to *asas tunggal* tipped into full-blown violence in September 1984. The events that resulted in the Tanjung Priok massacre started on September 8 with a local sergeant taking down posters urging women to wear the *jilbab* from the walls of the Assa'dah mosque in Jakarta's dockland, Tanjung Priok.[57] In response to allegations that he had used gutter water to remove the posters and had entered the mosque wearing shoes, local Muslims mobilized over several days, culminating on September 12 in some 1,500 men marching on the local police station to free the four Muslims who had been arrested for trying to destroy the sergeant's motorbike. The protesters were fired on without warning by armed troops.[58] The following day Armed Forces Chief Benny Murdani stated that "armed" demonstrators had set out to attack a military command post that was protected "by only fifteen soldiers" and that nine of the attackers had been shot dead. Murdani's account was immediately challenged by the local community, some of whom asserted that "as many as six hundred" had been killed and that the army had trucks standing by onto which the bodies were loaded and later buried in a mass grave.[59] As one local resident later testified in court,

> The road was full of bodies, some people who had got down on the ground and were lying face down, and some who had been hit like me. While I was thinking this, I felt a kick and heard someone shout: "This one is still alive," followed by the order: "Finish him off!" A shot was fired from close range but it hit the ground close to my ear. . . . I don't know how long I lay on the road. Then I felt my hands and feet being grabbed and I was lifted up and thrown into a truck. Luckily, I fell on a pile of bodies. I felt around with my hands and realized there were two layers of corpses underneath me. They were stiff and cold, and were no longer moving. Twice I felt bodies piled up on top of me.[60]

The Tanjung Priok massacre provoked an outburst of protest beyond the affected local community. Murdani's account was challenged by twenty-two members of Petisi 50, who issued a white paper that stated that the source of the unrest was "the government's violation of the spirit and the contents of the 1945 Constitution" with its bills enforcing Pancasila as the sole principle for all parties and organizations. Thus the tragedy of September 12, 1984 was "not an isolated event but the consequence of the present system."[61] Petisi 50 signatory A. M. Fatwa even asserted that the regime wanted to use Pancasila as an ideology just as fascism and communism were used by totalitarian dictatorships.[62]

Human rights organizations accused the New Order regime of serious human rights violations, including summary killing, arbitrary arrest and detention, torture, intimidation, and terrorizing those detained, as well as involuntary disappearances.[63] Leaflets with accounts of Tanjung Priok were disseminated in mainstream and radical Muslim circles across Indonesia. Muslim magazines published further accounts. *Mubaligh* (lay preachers) railed against the *asas tunggal* regulations, Tanjung Priok, and the government's repression of Islam. A small number of militants even went as far as retaliating violently, bombing two branches of the Chinese-owned Bank Central Asia (BCA) in October 1984, a Catholic Church and Protestant seminary in Malang in December 1984, and Borobudur Temple in January 1985.

Striking back against this Muslim opposition, the government embarked upon large-scale arrests of Muslims, including those who had participated in the initial Tanjung Priok demonstration, members of Petisi 50, the lay preachers corps (Korps Mubaligh Indonesia, KMI), DI/NII, Komando Jihad, and *usroh* Islamic studies circles as well as Muslim activists involved in the bombings. They were all charged with political crimes, including violent resistance, incitement to rebellion, subversion, sedition, and the spreading of disaffection.[64] These arrests were followed by a series of trials "used to portray Muslim critics and opponents of Soeharto's regime as subversives and terrorists."[65]

The New Order's repressive Islam policy only changed in the late 1980s after Suharto realized that he could no longer rely on the army's backing and instead sought Muslim political support. In a highly symbolic move Suharto removed the Catholic Murdani from his post as armed forces commander. He also removed Christians from cabinet positions and reduced links with his former support group among Christians and Javanist Muslims.[66] He went on a well-publicized hajj, opened the finance sector to Islamic banking, allowed for the wearing of the *jilbab* in schools, and through his vice president, BJ Habibie, established the Indonesian Muslim Intellectuals Association (Ikatan Cendekiawan Muslim se-Indonesia, ICMI), which aimed at achieving "proportionality" for Muslims in the bureaucracy, whereby the proportion of Muslims in senior government positions would be roughly based on their proportion in the community as a whole.[67] Suharto's 1993 cabinet clearly reflected these shifts. It was also overwhelmingly staffed with ICMI members.[68]

For most of Indonesia's Islamists this shift in the New Order's Islam policy was too little, too late. By that point, many had decided that the fight for Muslim rights and an Islamic state could only take place outside the system.[69] Modernist Muslims from organizations such as DDII and Muslim youth organizations such as Pelajar Islam Indonesia (PII), Gerakan Pemuda Islam (GPI), and HMI became a new source for recruitment, made easier by the DI/NII's new emphasis on *tauhid*.[70] One such recruit was Abu Tholut, a university student, who later became a senior member of Jemaah Islamiyah. From a military rather than a

DI family, he explained how the New Order's Islam policies drew him into the struggle for an Islamic state:

> Tanjung Priok happened and then I met *ikhwan* (brothers) who presented a completely different history of DI than the one the government presented. They were not rebels like the government said. I became interested in this, so I started reading a couple of issues of this magazine. Then the editor was arrested, and the law was issued that all organizations had to be based on Pancasila. I was a HMI organizer and I said we cannot accept this. HMI split over this issue.... At the time, a lot of people were being arrested over Tanjung Priok. There was the big issue of the disappearance of the Islamist leadership—into exile, prison or they just kept quiet. I wanted to join the struggle and was told I should go to Malaysia.[71]

Abdullah Sungkar and Abu Bakar Ba'asyir: Trials, Sermons, and Tribulations

Two Solo-based ulama—Abdullah Sungkar and Abu Bakar Ba'asyir—who later became the founding fathers of JI, became caught up in the New Order's repressive Islam policy. Both Sungkar and Ba'asyir were from simple, but religious, families of Hadhrami Arab descent and both had been actively involved in *dakwah* since the mid-1960s. In 1967, they established Radio Dakwah Islamiyah Surakarta (RADIS) together, followed by another joint endeavor in 1971–1972: the Islamic boarding school Pondok Pesantren Al-Mukmin Ngruki.[72] Both were members of Darul Islam, and Sungkar was also a member of the DDII. In 1975 the New Order government banned RADIS, and in 1978 both Sungkar and Ba'asyir were arrested and detained for the next four years, undergoing repeated interrogation and intimidation, with confessions extracted under pressure after days of sleep deprivation.[73]

At their trials in 1982, the prosecutor accused the two men of not raising the Indonesian flag at Al-Mukmin Ngruki, of excluding the village head from *pesantren* events, of undermining Pancasila in the religious study sessions and sermons they held, and of being members of Darul Islam who had sworn a *bai'at* (loyalty oath) to Hispran, thus violating Law No. 11/PNPS/1963 on undermining the government and state foundation Pancasila.[74] Sungkar and Ba'asyir were both found guilty of subversion and sentenced to nine years in prison. These sentences, however, were almost immediately reduced on appeal to time served. By the end of 1982 both were free.[75]

Sungkar's and Ba'asyir's defense documents paint a vivid picture of the New Order regime and its policies. Sungkar, whose trial came first, charged the regime with "hijacking" all sections of society, starting with the political parties, followed by hijacking the mass social organizations, the labor unions, and youth and student organizations, as well as the parliament with guaranteed seats for ABRI in the DPR.[76] He further stated that the elections of 1971 and 1977 were marked by "detentions, arrests, persecution, the rape of human rights, prosecution of members of political parties in court," explaining that this was why he refused to vote as it was impossible to pursue Islamic aspirations through clean and free Islamic political parties.[77] Election regulations ensured that the regions were dominated by the political parties from the center and that candidates were vetted by KOPKAMTIB and, if unsuitable, then excluded.[78]

Indeed, KOPKAMTIB features large in Sungkar's defense, as he saw KOPKAMTIB as infringing Muslim rights through its surveillance and "reports on all forms of Muslim worship," as well as curtailing free speech. "Muslims are no longer allowed to talk about *syariat Islam*, Islamist ideology, and Islamic state ... if someone dares to talk about these issues, the regime is quick to accuse him of wanting to change the foundation of the state, extremism, and subversion."[79] He pointed out that "in the name of KOPKAMTIB" a wife could be kidnapped in order to obtain information; the house of a person could be searched and confiscated; a person could be "tortured until he is half dead"; a candidate for the DPR could be excluded from elections; newspapers and magazines could be banned; farmers could be pushed off the land they worked; an organization could be forbidden to hold meetings; universities could "be invaded and occupied by the military"; and a preacher could be arrested for giving a sermon which was critical of the government.[80]

In his defense Sungkar argued that legal provisions in Indonesia had actually given guarantees to Muslims to implement Islamic law for themselves, as stated in the presidential decree of July 5, 1959, which recognized the Jakarta Charter as the soul and an integral part of the 1945 Constitution.[81] This was also argued by Abu Bakar Ba'asyir at his trial, who highlighted further areas where he saw New Order policies infringing Muslim rights, including the 1973 draft marriage law and the wholesale assault on the Muslim education system, ranging from forbidding the building of a mosque "on campus in three locations" to withdrawing subsidies from and delaying assistance to private schools that give time off for Ramadan as well as reducing the value of religious studies in primary school.[82]

However, a close reading of Sungkar's and Ba'asyir's defense documents makes it clear that while the New Order's Islam policy framed their responses and curtailed their activities, it was Pancasila itself that was at heart of their resistance as Pancasila was an imperfect "product of human thought," which the New Order had sacralized as exemplified by the existence of "Hari Kesaktian Pancasila" (Pancasila Sanctity Day) on October 1, along with "objects" such as the emblem of Garuda Pancasila, the red-and-white flag, the grave of Sukarno, historical buildings, and the 1945 Constitution.[83] The way Pancasila was being implemented clearly stood in the way of "implementing *syariat Islam* in its totality," which "is an order from Allah" and as thus needed "to be followed without reservations and may not be rejected."[84]

Sungkar's objections to Pancasila were even more clearly stated in his sermons after his release from prison in 1982, in which he objected to Pancasila placing all religions on an equal level and lamented that Indonesian schools taught English, Dutch, French, and German, but not Arabic. Children were graduating from primary school without being able to read the Quran.[85] He accused the Indonesian government of using the education system to turn Muslim children into apostates by teaching them that "all religions are the same" and "all are equally good" because "all teach a noble character."[86] Sungkar then proceeded to pick apart this logic:

> So they say that all religions are the same because they are all equally true. In a Friday sermon I already explained—if a water buffalo has four legs, a cow has four legs, an elephant has four legs, a goat has four legs, and a mouse has four legs, is an elephant then the same as a mouse, the same as a goat, the same as a cow, the same as a water buffalo? Because the truth is they all have four legs. That is not correct, is it?[87]

Stating that all religions are the same to a Muslim was a *kalimat kufur* (sentence of unbelief). Pancasila itself and making Pancasila *asas tunggal* were "mental terror."[88] For Muslims there was only one *asas tunggal* and that was the Quran.[89]

After Sungkar's and Ba'asyir's release in late 1982, they proceeded to build their support base, expanding the *usroh* cadre recruitment program, which had been in its infancy when they were arrested but had "exploded exponentially after the Iranian revolution of 1979."[90] This *usroh* system had originated with the Egyptian Muslim Brotherhood and comprised small groups of seven to fifteen members that functioned as "compartmentalized" Islamic study cells, but also as the "building blocks" for a future Indonesian Islamic state.[91] Their purpose was to establish family-like ties—hence the name *usroh* from the Arabic for family—to provide mutual assistance such as collecting money to help pay for marriages or funerals.[92] These *usroh* dedicated themselves not only to studying Islam but to actually living it by avoiding alcohol, gambling, and smoking and by distancing "themselves from non-Islamic institutions" and rejecting "customs that are offensive to Islamic beliefs."[93]

These self-contained *usroh* groups differed considerably from DI/NII as they attracted university students and urban modernists. It is here where Sidney Jones sees one of the key contributions of the New Order to the emergence of JI: "By itself, DI could not have produced JI. It was a parochial, ideologically unsophisticated guerrilla movement with no significant international connections. Without the New Order restrictions on political expression that propelled a highly educated, modernist Muslim urban elite into its arms, DI would have remained an ongoing but very localized problem."[94] The *usroh* movement peaked between 1983 and 1985. However, its days were clearly numbered after the first of its members were arrested on subversion charges for "planning a three-stage revolt against the secular government, one of which involved the creation of a Jemaah Islamiyah."[95] In particular, Sungkar and Ba'asyir saw the writing on the wall, as state prosecutors had appealed their sentence and release. Indeed, the interrogation of *usroh* members had revealed that they "had circulated a book at Ngruki that reportedly urged Muslims to go to war against anybody opposing the implementation of Islamic law."[96]

In early 1985, first Sungkar and then Ba'asyir fled to Malaysia, where they set up another Islamic boarding school—Lukmanul Hakim—in Kuala Pilah, Negeri Sembilan. From there they began to send Indonesians from a DI/NII or *usroh* background, but also from Islamic student organizations such as GPI who were then inducted into DI/NII, to Pakistan for military training on the Afghan border in the context of the Afghan Mujahideen jihad against the Soviets.[97] There they not only acquired military capacity but were also introduced to the ideology of Abdullah Azzam and to the concept that "the correct understanding of *jihad* was *qital*."[98]

The Establishment of JI and Islamist Violence in the 2000s

In January 1993, Sungkar and Ba'asyir formally broke away from DI/NII and established Jemaah Islamiyah, an organization that was more salafi and more internationalist in outlook. In 1996, NII's *kanun asasy* and Pedoman Dharma Bhakti (NII guidelines) were replaced by a new set of General Guidelines for the Struggle (Pedoman Umum Perjuangan Al Jemaah Al Islamiyah, PUPJI), which stated that JI's aim was the establishment of *deen* (religion) and a *daulah Islamiyah* (Islamic state), and ultimately the reestablishment of the *khilafa* (caliphate) through "Islamic personal, familial and *jamaah* development" and by pursuing the path of "*iman, hijrah* and *jihad fi sabilillah*."[99] JI was regionally organized starting with two *mantiqis* (regions): Mantiqi 1 comprised Singapore and Malaysia and was tasked with fundraising while Mantiqi 2 covered Indonesia (excluding Sulawesi) and was designated the arena of jihad. In 1997, Mantiqi 3 was added, encompassing the Philippines as well as Sulawesi, which became the area for training. Completing the structure was Mantiqi Ukhro, sometimes referred to as Mantiqi 4 in the literature, which was active in Australia.[100] According to senior JI member Abu Rusdan, this *mantiqi* structure was the result of an inconclusive discussion on whether to make Indonesia or any other part in Southeast Asia a *qoidah aminah* (secure base).[101]

After the fall of Suharto in 1998, Sungkar and Ba'asyir, as well as other JI members, returned to Indonesia and started establishing structures and recruiting in the newly opened political space. In November 1999, Sungkar passed away and Ba'asyir became JI's second amir. This was also the year that the first JI members became involved in violence in Indonesia, as Christian-Muslim communal conflicts had erupted in Poso and Ambon. By that point JI had acquired considerable military capacity. Some 350 Indonesians had gone to Pakistan and Afghanistan, where they had received military training between 1985 and 1994, first in Abdul Rasul Sayyaf's Camp As-Saddah and then in their own military academy in Torkham (Pakistan) as well as in Khost (Afghanistan).[102] Between 1999 and 2001 another thirty JI members from Mantiqi 1 also trained at Al-Qaeda's Camp Al-Farouq in Afghanistan.[103] After the rise to power of the Taliban, JI's training base shifted to Mindanao in the Philippines. JI trainers were approached by the Moro Islamic Liberation Front in 1994 to provide training for the Bangsamoro at Camp Abu Bakar. JI was then permitted to set up a military academy in its own Camp Hudaybiyah, where JI trained its members until the Philippines Armed Forces overran Camp Abubakar in President Joseph Estrada's "all-out war." JI's training was shifted to a safer area, to JI's new Camp Jabal Quba.[104] Over the years somewhere between 150 and 160 JI members were trained in the Philippines.[105]

What became known as the Ambon jihad started in February 1999, a month after the communal conflict broke out, and ended after the attack on a police post in Loki on Seram in May 2005. It was spearheaded by the Afghan alumni with the approval of Sungkar and was conceptualized as a defensive jihad. Those JI members who volunteered did so because Muslims "were victimized by the Christians and by the security forces who helped the Christians," because they had "a responsibility to come to the defense of Muslims," and because they "felt about Ambon the way [they had] felt about Afghanistan."[106] The Ambon jihad was a war fought with an array of weapons ranging from automatic firearms to machetes, spears, bows and arrows, and fishing bombs, and "there was no grand strategy."[107] Attacks were driven by dynamics on the ground as well as revenge. Specific targets were often requested by the local Muslim population; others were clear because of the role they had played in previous violence.[108] Some were chosen for their religious symbolism, such as churches, or because they were seen as having discriminated against Muslims, such as the University of Pattimura.[109] Religious geography also played a role in determining attacks as Muslims "cleansed" Christians from their areas in order to create contiguous territory.[110]

A year after JI became involved in the Ambon conflict, it also became involved in the communal violence in Poso. The Poso jihad started after the May 2000 Walisongo massacre in which Muslim students and teachers from the Walisongo *pesantren*, as well as Muslim migrants from the adjacent village, were hacked to death by Christians. It ended with the mujahidin-police shootout in Tanah Runtuh in 2007. This jihad was led by Mantiqi 3 and the motivations for JI volunteers joining, as well as the dynamics of violence, were similar to those in Ambon. Where the Poso jihad differed from the Ambon jihad, however, was with respect to its place in JI's efforts to establish an Islamic countersociety in Indonesia and, ultimately, an Islamic state.[111] Indeed, Poso was deemed a suitable base as local Muslims showed interest in practicing a more salafi Islam and in the idea of an Islamic state, while Ambonese Muslims were ultimately deemed too heterogenous. Poso also had the advantage that it had attracted far less attention from the Indonesian security forces than Ambon.

In the same year as the start of JI's Ambon jihad, members of JI's Mantiqi 1 embarked upon a campaign of bombing foreign and economic targets in Indonesia. This campaign was more closely aligned with Osama bin Laden's global jihad. However, it was not wholly disconnected from domestic Indonesian dynamics. Intertwining the global with the local, Indonesian Christians were seen as allies of the West and bringing down the Indonesian government was necessary for establishing an Islamic state.

The first bombing targeted the Philippine ambassador, Leonides Caday, outside his residence in the Menteng neighborhood of Jakarta on August 1, 2000. A car bomb detonated as the ambassador's vehicle turned to pull into the driveway, wounding the ambassador, his chauffeur, and 20 others as well as killing a guard and a street vendor.[112] According to JI member Farihin, this attack was retribution for the destruction of Camp Abu Bakar and Camp Hudaybiyah by the Philippines Armed Forces earlier that year.[113] This attack was followed a month later, on September 13, 2000, with a car bomb that exploded in the parking garage below the Jakarta Stock Exchange, killing 15 and injuring 20. On December 24, 2000, a more ambitious operation was launched. Bombs were delivered to thirty-eight churches or priests in multiple cities across Indonesia, killing 19 and wounding another 120.[114] The Christmas Eve bombings were framed as revenge for the Christian violence against Muslims in Ambon that Muslims believed was planned on Christmas in 1998. The aim was to punish

Christians as, according to Abu Bakar Ba'asyir, who was JI's amir at that point, "Ambon was started by the Christians and Jews."[115] However, the idea to punish them "by attacking Christians in Java" did not originate with Ba'asyir but came from Hambali, the head of Mantiqi 1, who had extensive contacts with Al-Qaeda.[116] Hambali also saw the church bombings as a way "to provoke conflict and civil war," to "recreate" the Ambon conflict on a national level, and thereby to weaken the Indonesian government.[117] The August 2001 bombing of the Atrium Mall in Jakarta also had an Ambon link. Here the specific target was the Christian congregation that held "services on the second floor of the mall" and was believed to be sending funds to the Christians in Ambon.[118]

However, JI's most deadly bombings, carried out on October 12, 2002, targeted foreigners. Almost simultaneously bombs exploded in two bars and outside the US consulate in Bali, killing 202 and injuring another 300 people. Ba'asyir cast this operation as defensive jihad, claiming that Bali bomber "Amrozi is not a terrorist. He was defending himself." It is here that the global aspects of Mantiqi 1's bombing campaign but also of Ba'asyir's own framework become clear, as Ba'asyir saw the Bali bombs as a reaction to US imperialism, in particular the invasion of Afghanistan, asserting that "the US is the terrorist. We are only defending ourselves. Without US actions there would be peace."[119] Similar views were advanced by Bali bomber Imam Samudra in a statement posted on his *istimata* (prepare for martyrdom) website, where he stated that the bombings were in revenge for the killing of "600 thousand babies in Iraq and half a million children in Afghanistan" and that the Christian *kafir* "will bear the consequences of your actions wherever you are."[120] He further explained in his book *Aku Melawan Teroris* (I am against terrorists) that "the Bali bombing was part of the resistance aimed at the colonizer, America, and its allies."[121] Bali Bomber Mukhlas, in his unpublished manuscript *Jihad Bom Bali: Sebuah Pembelaan* (The Bali bomb *jihad*: A defense), listed three aims: "to terrorize, frighten and make tremble the enemies of Islam and Muslims"; "to reject the viciousness and brutality of the enemies of Islam (the Jews, America and its allies)"; and "to avenge their brutal attacks on Muslims."[122] He explained that Paddy's Pub and the Sari Club were not chosen because they were places of immorality, as "we need not have gone all the way to Bali" because "these days there are places of immorality everywhere."[123] Instead, Bali was chosen as "the area most visited by foreign tourists, particularly from Western countries . . . that ally themselves with America and participate directly in the coalition army led by it in the crusade to destroy the Islamic government of Afghanistan and slaughter Muslims there."[124] However, Bali bomber Ali Imron, who had selected the targets, pointed out in his book *Ali Imron Sang Pengebom* (Ali Imron the bomber) that it was not just about America but also about the lack of implementation of Islamic law, and the rampant destruction of morality, the economy, society, and culture across the world, including Indonesia, through the following of non-Muslim traditions such as free speech, prostitution, vigilantism, gambling, entertainment, and music as well as immodest clothing.[125] As with the Christmas bombings, the Bali bombings were conceived by Hambali. By targeting Paddy's Pub and the Sari Club they sought to kill Western, Christian unbelievers, and by targeting the US Consulate, they went after what they saw as the greatest oppressor of Muslims: the United States. But by targeting Bali, they also hoped to bring a financially struggling Indonesia to its knees, by destroying the only functioning part of the economy, which was propping up the Pancasila state.

The 2002 Bali bombings were followed by the 2003 Marriot hotel bombing in Jakarta, which killed 12 and wounded 150, and the 2004 bombing of the Australian Embassy that killed 9 and wounded 150. Similar to the Bali bombings, these targets represented foreign imperialism at a global and local level. These bombings were also carried out by suicide bombers. However, they were conceived by Noordin Mohammad Top rather than Hambali, who had been arrested on August 11, 2003, in Thailand. Unlike Hambali, who had relied on Mantiqi 1, Noordin drew on personal networks that included JI members but also outsiders, including from DI/NII. The repeat bombings in Bali in 2005 and of the Marriot hotel, as well as of the Ritz Carlton in 2009, were also carried out by Noordin's network.[126]

The Bali bombings and each bombing thereafter exacerbated the already existing tensions over leadership within JI, which had started after the death of Sungkar in 1999. His successor Ba'asyir was a divisive figure, so much so that senior JI member Abu Rusdan charged Ba'asyir with destroying JI, holding his weak leadership responsible for its factionalization.[127] Ba'asyir was seen as "too soft" by the younger hardliners in Mantiqi 1 such as Hambali, Mukhlas, and Imam Samudra.[128] They saw their views confirmed when Ba'asyir, together with Irfan Suryahardi Awwas, established the Majlis Mujahidin Indonesia (MMI) in August 2000 as a vehicle for JI to exploit the new political openness of *reformasi* Indonesia. To miss this opportunity, Ba'asyir had argued, "was not just wrong, it was sinful."[129] According to Abu Tholut, who was in charge of Mantiqi 3 at the time, Ba'asyir was simply implementing PUPJI, and MMI was established in order to pursue *dakwah jahriyah* (open *dakwah*).[130] Most JI members, however, disagreed because JI was a *tanzim sirri* (underground organization) and they believed it should stay so until the establishment of an Islamic state. Ba'asyir's "obsession with taking on America" was also criticized. Nasir Abas, for instance, saw this as coming at the expense of improving the *ummat Islam*, which Ba'asyir "was not interested in."[131]

The Bali bombings widened this internal debate with heated discussions about tactics, timing, targets, and Bin Laden's 1998 fatwa. It pitted those who wanted jihad now against those who believed that JI was not ready and should focus on *i'dad* (preparation); those who saw themselves as contributing to Bin Laden's global jihad against those who prioritized building the community and broadening JI's support base in Indonesia; those who "wanted to take the war to the civilians" against those who wanted to uphold the "values of NII," namely targeting the Indonesian government and state; and those who wanted to pursue the "far enemy" where he could be found against those who saw jihad only as an obligation where Muslims were under attack and the enemy was obvious, and this did not include places such as Jakarta and Bali.[132] In short, it pitted the group of bombers of Mantiqi 1 against most of the rest of JI.

The gap between JI and its "bombing wing" was never reconciled. Indeed, after the 2004 Australian Embassy bombing, JI leaders not only urged Noordin Mohamed Top and Azahari Husin to end their bombing campaign but, according to Julie Chernov Hwang, went as far as issuing a ruling that they would no longer be protected or assisted.[133] In 2005, Noordin and Azahari split from JI and named themselves Al-Qaeda in the Malay Archipelago, reflecting admiration rather than affiliation. They remained active until the death of Noordin in 2009.

The negative fallout from the Bali bombings in terms of large-scale arrests by the Indonesian, Singaporean, and Malaysian police forces, the collapse of JI's *mantiqi* structure, the splintering-off of the pro-bombing wing, and, above all, the loss of Indonesian Muslim support so essential for establishing an Islamic state, was followed by a further blow in 2007 when fourteen JI members were killed in a shootout with the Indonesian police in the Tanah Runtuh neighbourhood of Poso city.[134] This shifted the still-ongoing debate toward those who favored stepping back from violence and rebuilding the organization through *i'dad* as well as rebuilding its Indonesian support base through *dakwah* and *tarbiyah* (education).[135]

The Multiple National Imaginaries of JI: From the Founders to the *Mantiqis*

When JI was established in 1993, it sought to establish "a regional Islamic state together with the Moros and Pattani" that would eventually "become part of a global *khilafa* as envisaged by Abdullah Azzam."[136] As senior JI member Abu Rusdan recalled, "Our aim was not an Islamic state just in Indonesia. That would have been a nationalist aim and we were not nationalists."[137] This regional Islamist national imaginary, however, was not shared by all and disappeared in 1999 with the death of Sungkar, leaving a variety of old and new ideas on the question of *daulah Islamiyah*, *khilafa*, and the role of jihad as exemplified by the views of JI's founders, JI's general guidelines (PUPJI), and the different *mantiqis*.

The starting point for JI's founding fathers, Sungkar and Ba'asyir, was theological. As Sungkar explained in one of his sermons,

> We must follow the system put in place by Allah, "*ad-deen*" or the system of life, because the word *ad-deen* does not just mean religion. *Ad-deen* is best translated as the *system of life*. It concerns all aspects of our life. From the smallest to the largest. From relations between people to relations between states. Such is *ad-deen*. He who has the right to put in place the right system is only Allah SWT [subhanahu wa ta'ala, the most glorified]. We must submit to that system or we will be crushed by it. If we violate this system we will not reach our goal.[138]

At the core of this was implementing *syariat Islam*, as "all of the universe belongs to Allah and cannot be regulated by anything other than Allah's laws."[139] Ba'asyir took a similar line in a book he wrote decades later stating that "what is meant by *deen* is that it is also *daulah (negara)*."[140] He explains that "the community of believers must live under the leadership of the *ulil amri* [most authoritative] from the circle of believers. This means the system of living of the Islamic umma with respect to practising their religion has to be together under Islamic rule that is from *daulah* until *khilafa* not under a government based on nationalism or democracy led by *kafir* or people who claim they are Muslim but accept democracy."[141] It is an obligation for Muslims to have an Islamic government, a *daulah Islamiyah/khilafa*, in order to protect Islam, and only "a state based on *syariah* as the only form of governance model . . . can administer true justice."[142]

In addition to the theological obligation, the need for an Islamic state is also grounded in Indonesia's history and the denial of Islamic law by consecutive governments. Here Sungkar charged the Dutch colonial government with initiating a de-Islamization process, "separating the Islamic Community from the Qur'an."[143] He charged Sukarno with misleading the Indonesian nation with Pancasila, "a satanic understanding" derived from philosophy, and he charged Suharto with forcing the Muslim community to accept "a polytheistic ideology."[144] His conclusion that Indonesia's Muslims had "to pay the highest price for independence," and that the very existence of the *ummat Islam* was tied to Muslims becoming leaders and teachers, was shared by Ba'asyir, who contended that the Indonesian *ummat Islam*, despite being the majority, could not practice Islam in its totality (*secara kaffah*) because the *thoghut* (tyrants), who dominated the government, prevented it, and that the consequent *fitnah* would "not disappear as long as an Islamic state has not been established in Indonesia."[145] More globally, Ba'asyir saw an Islamic state as the only way to protect Muslims who were under attack, particularly by the United States, which had already attacked Muslims in Afghanistan and in Palestine where "Muslims are killed every day by Jews and the US supports that!"[146]

An Islamic state, according to Sungkar, would be established by "applying the strategies of *Eeman, Hijrah,* and *Jihad.*"[147] Jihad was seen as an obligation "within the framework of aiming to re-erect *Dawlah Islamiyyah,*" but also necessary because political parties seeking "to establish a *Dawlah Islamiyyah . . .* will be strictly forbidden." This jihad would draw upon three elements of strength: *quwwatul aqidah* (the strength of faith), *quwwatul ukhuwwah* (the strength of brotherhood), and *quwwatul musallaha* (military strength).[148] For Ba'asyir, too, *dakwah* and jihad were at the heart of the struggle to establish a *daulah Islamiyah/khilafa.*[149] He also stated that jihad was essential as "Muslims as well as *kafir . . .* block *da'wah,*" and as "without *jihad Islam,* the umma will weaken being trampled by the *kafir*" and the "*ummat Islam* will be slaughtered."[150] Moreover, struggling for an Islamic state through parliamentary democracy was forbidden "because the system is idolatrous."[151]

So how then did JI's founders imagine this Islamic state? Sungkar, in the first instance, conceptualized an Islamic state as "returning" to Kartosuwirjo's Negara Islam Indonesia, which is not all too surprising as Sungkar had been inducted into DI/NII.[152] Moreover, as seen in chapter 1, Kartosuwirjo's state had been based on the Prophet Muhammad's Islamic state in Medina—the original model. Ba'asyir, in contrast, found a range of models suitable, the most preferable being "the system of governance . . . by the Prophet and his companions, especially the righteous Caliphs as well as the way the *ummat Islam* lived until 1924."[153] He saw the *khilafa* as the place where "the *ummat Islam* lived in glory, peace, and happiness and the *kafir* who lived in the *khilafa* enjoyed justice, peace, and prosperity."[154] So the *daulah Islamiyah* that JI sought to establish, according to Ba'asyir, would be based on the Quran and Sunnah, regulated by *syariat Islam* in its totality, and united by *tauhid.*[155] This would include criminal law and *hudud* punishments (punishments specified in the Quran), which he saw as a system that is truly just, explaining that "under secular law if you get caught for theft you go to prison for ten years. Islamic law asks what will happen to the family if the breadwinner goes to prison for ten years? Under Islamic Law a thief will get his hand cut off. After a week he can return to work. That is real justice. It won't disrupt his life. He can still support his family. His wife and children don't get punished." When asked specifically about the place of non-Muslim minorities in this state, he stated that "*kafir* and *ahl al-kitab* [people of the book] would have to pay taxes" but that they also, as communities, would live according to their own religious laws. Islamic law would not require Christian women to wear the *jilbab,* "but according to their own laws Christian and Jewish women are also required to cover their hair."[156]

Jemaah Islamiyah's 1996 general guidelines, PUPJI, attempted to devise clear steps for establishing a *daulah Islamiyah* as the basis for an eventual *khilafa*.[157] This was to be achieved "by means of Islamic personal, familial, and *jama'ah* development," making state formation a bottom-up approach.[158] In addition to forming a *jamaah* the preparation for establishing this Islamic state required the formation of a *qiyadah ar-rasyidah* (rightly guided leadership), the formation of a *qoidah salabah* (solid base)—one of Azzam's key tenets—and a body to oversee the implementation of *syariat Islam*, the *hisbah*.[159] Territorial development, according to PUPJI, should be carried out continuously with the *jamaah* led by the *qoidah salabah* "as the core executive."[160] Once a suitable territorial base has been identified, a *qoidah aminah* (secure base) would be developed as a base against the enemy and as a place for migration—a *darul hijrah*.[161] This *qoidah aminah* would then become the nucleus of the *daulah Islamiyah*, which, in turn, was a stepping stone toward the *khilafa*. PUPJI defines the *khilafa* as a global entity with a world-wide *jamaah*, "which guarantees the implementation of Islamic law in its totality, the creation of security and peace in the purifying of service toward Allah, the collapse of polytheism, falsehood (that which is invalid) and injustice (tyranny) upon the earth as well as guidance of 'mankind' to the pinnacle of *akhlaq* (original pure behavior, 'morality') and civilization."[162] While PUPJI laid out the broad outlines, each of JI's *mantiqis* engaged with different parts of PUPJI. Mantiqi 1 was less Indonesia-centric. Instead, it focused on the global *khilafa*. As Mukhlas explained in his book, "an Islamic state is the embryo for establishing an Islamic Caliphate once more on earth, and the adoption of an Islamic Caliphate is a sign of the imminent fall of the power of the West and its allies."[163] They agreed with Al-Qaeda's analysis that the far enemy—the West—was the greatest obstacle to establishing this *khilafa* and that jihad against Western targets was the only way to rout and defeat this enemy. However, what exactly this *khilafa* would look like was less clear. For Mukhlas this *khilafa* would be established through jihad and territorial expansion and neither a "true Islamic state" nor a *khilafa* could be understood partially. "All of its parts are beautiful and great, including its laws of death by stoning, cutting off hands and jihad."[164]

While Mantiqi 1 pursued a vague distant global imaginary, Mantiqi 2 focused on Indonesia. It was the most cautious of the *mantiqis*, with little enthusiasm for Bin Laden's notion of global jihad as well as being reluctant to become involved in Indonesia's communal conflicts.[165] Indeed, Mantiqi 2's leadership believed that the timing was not yet right for jihad as they were still in the *i'dad* phase. They needed to focus on building their own organization, the *jemaah*, and the broader Muslim support base. Their approach was the bottom-up building of the *daulah Islamiyah*, one family at a time and one Islamic studies circle at a time. This approach was also firmly grounded in Indonesian history. As Abu Rusdan, who played a key role in Mantiqi 2, explained,

> Islam was put forward as one of the ways to establish Indonesia. It emerged at the time of Indonesian independence. The Islamists rejected Pancasila because it is a man-made philosophy. It was an ideological conflict from the beginning, which was further compounded by the problem that no one knows what Pancasila really means. Under Sukarno it was played as *gotong royong*. Under Suharto it became a tool of repression. So Pancasila is what? The only thing that is clear is that Pancasila is not Islamist and that it has been used by all politicians—Pancasila and NKRI—like a religion. But for us it is Islam as a way of life that unites the country.[166]

The starting point, not surprisingly, given that Mantiqi 2 encompassed Kartosuwirjo's old stomping grounds in the Javanese heartlands, is NII: "From 1949 to 1962 Karto had territory, a *qoidah aminah*. He established a state with effective laws. But after 1962 the state no longer existed. The sovereignty of NII was taken over by the Republic of Indonesia. So NII returned to being a *jamaah*. Since then it has struggled for *daulah* and then *khilafa*."[167] JI subscribed to many of the ideas of NII, but DI/NII "had not had an effective strategy for establishing an Islamic State since Kartosuwirjo" and that is why "we called ourselves Jemaah Islamiyah with focus on building an Islamic community rather than a *daulah Islamiyah*."[168] Thus the focus in terms of laying the foundations for any future state was on educating Muslims and on reviving *syariat Islam* as the basis for governance.

The *mantiqi* with the most concrete ideas was Mantiqi 3, which experimented with laying the foundations of an Islamic state in the district of Poso, Central Sulawesi. Its leadership believed that Poso met PUPJI's criteria for a *qoidah aminah*—a secure base. It was located in "an area favorable to defense," there were "available sources of logistics," "the majority of its inhabitants has received the call and is prepared to sacrifice," "the authorities cannot fully control the Islamic community," and the "leadership of the community both formal and informal [is] dominated by 'Abna'ul Ḥarakah'"—the children of the movement—meaning JI and JI affiliates.[169] The area could be developed into "a base for departure by concealing personnel, reforming as well as preparing *tanẓim*" through *jihad musallaḥ* (military jihad) in order to realize the *qoidah aminah*.[170]

The Amirship of Para Wijayanto: JI, Global Jihad, and Islamic Governance

JI's *mantiqi* structure collapsed as leaders and members were arrested following the 2002 Bali bombings, and the organization saw a succession of amirs and caretaker amirs who had little time to reconceptualize JI. The first steps in that direction were taken in 2005 during Zarkasih's amirship. Zarkasih tasked one of his men, Mindanao-trained Para Wijayanto, with devising a new structure and security system for JI to stop the organization from hemorrhaging further. This system was the Total Amniah Sistem dan Total Solution (Total Security System and Total Solution), better known by its acronym TASTOS, which was based on minimizing contact between the leaders and their subordinates as well as between cells. JI's new structure was disconnected and function based rather than area based.[171] In 2007, Zarkasih, too, was arrested. In 2008, Para Wijayanto was selected as JI amir, a position he held until his arrest in 2019, making him JI's longest-serving amir.

According to Para Wijayanto, JI's core aim was *iqomatuddin*—the restoration of Islam and *syariat Islam*—and the establishment of a *daulah Islamiyah*. Establishing an Islamic state was necessary because "the current condition was that the government is a democracy (religion and state are separated) so the plan for the future is to make religion and state one (*Khilafah ala Minhajin Nubuwah*) [a caliphate in accordance with the Prophet's method]."[172]

Abu Rusdan, the advisor to the *amir*, elaborated further on the unacceptability of the Indonesian government, focusing on Joko Widodo: "Jokowi's government is based on man-made secular law. You need to replace those institutions with *syar'i* [*syariah*-compliant] institutions. But in order to do that you need capacity and that means shifting capacity to Islam from the secular. This is not possible through Western democracy."[173] At the heart of this unacceptable system is Pancasila, which Abu Rusdan considered to be fundamentally incompatible with Islam. As he stated in one of his *pengajian* in 2018,

> Pancasila is not Islam and Islam is not Pancasila. . . . *Ketuhanan yang maha esa* [the first *sila*—belief in one God] will never become *tauhid* [the oneness of God] and *tauhid* will never become *ketuhanan yang maha esa*. . . . Pancasila is a philosophy, the product of man. *Tauhid* is based on revelation, the product of Allah. . . . So why then is Pancasila the basis of the state? So that Islam could not become the basis of the state![174]

While JI was clear in its need and aim for an Islamic state, establishing one was a long-term process. It had also, according to Para Wijayanto, not been very successful in Indonesia so far. Moreover, "JI was at its lowest point" when he became amir, "so the first priority was survival."[175] He asked for ten years to rebuild JI. This process included some reconceptualization of JI as an organization as well as its ideology. The first of these was rebuilding JI as a system, moving away from an organizational model that had been highly reliant on the personality and charisma of the amir. It is for this reason that Para Wijayanto chose to be an "unknown amir." The second was changing the recruitment criteria to reflect the needs of JI. The third was ideological, moving away from the *takfirism* that had crept in, which he believed was not *syar'i* and was also counterproductive.[176]

In 2015 JI started to move from the "survival period" to the "revival period."[177] The revival period was marked by an expansion of JI's structure and a reconceptualization of JI's strategy to establish an Islamic state, called *strategi tamkin* (consolidation strategy). This consolidation strategy aimed at forming an Islamic government in ten stages: first—*dakwah*, second—forming a *jamaah*, third—*tarbiyah*, fourth—finding a conducive territory, fifth—*hijrah*, sixth—*tamkin siyasi* (political consolidation), seventh—proclaiming a *daulah Islamiyah* in a suitable territory based on *syariat*, eighth—*tamkin siyasi* II (which entailed obtaining foreign recognition), ninth—*tamkin askari* (military consolidation) to defend the sovereignty of the *daulah Islamiyah* and to attack *kafir harbi* (enemy infidels), and tenth—global territorial expansion by attacking and liberating Muslim countries occupied by *kafir*.[178] When Para Wijayanto was arrested in 2019 he stated that JI was in the fourth stage, finding a conducive territory.

Interesting in this strategy are the two political consolidation phases as well as the question of where jihad fits in. Political engagement has not featured prominently in JI's previous strategies, as it was equated with legitimizing the system it opposed. JI has not shifted from this position. It has remained antisystemic and unwilling to participate in parliamentary politics, which a midlevel JI commander described as "a system which produces politicians who are like whores and thieves."[179]

Para Wijayanto conceptualized *tamkin siyasi* as JI joining in social and political activities that served Muslim interests, as JI fighting an information war through JI media raising issues about the global interests of America and democracy, and as reaching out to Islamic organizations such as Muhammadiyah and the Islamic Defenders Front (Front Pembela Islam, FPI). Together these would help create a broad basis for an Islamic state as well as shape the imaginary of that state. In his deposition Para Wijayanto gave the example of JI's involvement in 2016 in the Muslim demonstrations that cost Jakarta governor Basuki Tjahaya Purnama (Ahok), a Christian of Chinese descent, his reelection. JI participated in the "212 [December 2, 2016] activities, starting from presenting facts to joining coming out onto the streets and giving speeches."[180] Giving another example, Para Wijayanto stated that JI used the "Siyono case" to present facts and data about Siyono, who had been killed while in custody in 2016. JI also used the Siyono case to establish a pressure group against the Indonesian counter-terrorism unit Detachment 88 (Densus 88). This group coalesced around Muhammadiyah's Din Syamsudin and quite successfully launched a broader campaign against the brutality of Densus 88.[181]

As far as jihad was concerned, Para Wijayanto did not see a role for jihad in Indonesia at this point. In fact, he relegated jihad to the global level, stating that under his leadership "local jihad became global jihad."[182] This was linked directly to his decision not to focus on the territory of Indonesia, but instead to start with Syam (Syria) and Yemen. To Yemen, he sent JI members for religious studies and to build ties, as many Indonesians were of Hadhrami descent. Then, when the conflict erupted in Syria, he decided to send JI volunteers there for military training and some fighting, but more generally to show solidarity and provide humanitarian assistance.[183] Para Wijayanto's as well as Abu Rusdan's notion of global jihad thus was not that of Bin Laden, which Mantiqi 1 had embraced. Instead, it was the global jihad of Abdullah Azzam, which was based on global Muslim solidarity and aimed at the liberation of Muslim lands from occupation and the defense of Muslims under attack.[184] To this was added Abu Musab as-Suri's recasting of global jihad as *muqawama* (resistance).[185]

While Abu Rusdan agreed with Para Wijyanto on global jihad, he approached the question of *tamkin siyasi* slightly differently, situating it around restoring Islamic law. In his view "you restore *syariat Islam* until the people embrace it and then you have a *wilayah*." He contended further, "We as JI think that syariat Islam is something that needs to be implemented. Without syariat Islam you need to do jihad. But this jihad has to be with the umma. So that means it cannot be conducted without education or without politics. By politics I do not mean the dirty politics of democracy which have been forced on us by America. Democracy for us is like wearing other people's clothes."[186] Instead, he looked to Ibn Taymiyya's *siyasa syariah* (shariah politics) as the basis for what he labeled "jihadi politics" as opposed to parliamentary politics. These jihadi politics required five concrete steps: first, *tarbiyah*; second, *tanzim*; third, *i'dad*; fourth, *askariyah* (military training); and fifth, communication. The first and fifth steps were of particular importance as "this is all about how to make society understand what we are doing." He pointed out that "the Bali bombings made us hard to understand. The narrative that the public hears is about *amaliyah* (military operations). That is a big problem. Today they hear about rice cooker bombs, pot bombs, backpack bombs, and attacks on the police. So, they see us as terrorists that need to be countered."[187] At the same time, however, Abu Rusdan remained a sceptic in the discussion within JI's younger generation on whether JI should become more involved in social and political actions. As he explained,

> Muslims in Indonesia are getting stronger but the efforts to implement *syariah* are not yet serious. Just look at the demonstrations—411 [November 4, 2016] and 212 [December 2, 2016] have not changed anything. They have not moved the state closer to being an Islamic state. The leaders say now you have a Muslim governor and you can replicate this in other elections. You could elect a Muslim president. But the election of Anies [Baswedan] rather than Ahok did not change the system. The system is still the same system.

And here is where Abu Rusdan did not rule out jihad in principle, even if it was not something he personally advocated on Indonesian soil.

> The current Indonesian system is anti-Islam. It is trying to push this idea of Islam Nusantara but that is not pure Islam. It is Islam à la Indonesia. So you have to rely on jihad. That is how the Afghan mujahideen overthrew the communists. You can only change the system through jihad because this is not a problem of *akida* (creed) or rituals but a problem of *manhaj* (method) and basic understanding.[188]

In fact, in one of his *pengajian*, which he started by stating that "Islam was established by the sword," he contended that there are no examples in history where an idea, an ideology, a way of thinking was spread without being backed up by force.[189]

However, the midlevel JI commander quoted earlier asserted that "there is no plan for military action in Indonesia but the Quran says you need to prepare yourself so that is what we are doing." And that is where he saw Syria fitting in: "We sent people to Syria to get specialist training. More than sixty went—most have come back. If there is an opportunity in Southeast Asia or overseas, we need to send people for military training because we need security and the capacity to defend ourselves." Like Abu Rusdan, he too was not keen on JI getting too involved in politics, but he also stated that the younger generation of JI was split on this issue. "JI was divided over getting involved in the 212 movement. As agreement could not be reached, it was then left up to the individual. I was against it. JI needs to be involved in society but not in politics. It should have a presence in all social organizations. We need to particularly get involved with other Muslim organizations and support them."[190] This way a broad base for an Islamic state could be built. So how then should this *daulah Islamiyah* be imagined? The Islamic state Para Wijayanto had in mind was and is universally conceptualized, going back to the Prophet Muhammad's first Islamic state in Medina. It focuses on the fundamentals of Muslim unity, justice for Muslims and non-Muslims, and treaty relations over violence. It was also cast against the ISIS caliphate:

> What ISIS wanted to build is based on conflict. What JI wants to build is based on peace. Islam does not teach to force people. . . . It also has to be a genuine *daulah*. The Prophet never had any arguments with the Jews of Medina because they were Jews. He had an argument with some [Jewish] groups because they broke agreements.[191]

He further explained that

> The *daulah Islamiyah* that I mean is a *daulah Islamiyah* agreed on by the majority of Muslims through their representatives and is supported by the Muslim people, which then becomes *al-imaroh al-Islamiyah* (an Islamic government) that is implemented in accordance with the *manhaj nabawiyah* (the system the Prophet followed, peace be upon him). The *daulah Islamiyah* I mean is currently not formed and is still in the ideals of Jamaah Islamiyah and the role of Jamaah Islamiyah is to support the process of reestablishing the *daulah Islamiyah* globally.[192]

Abu Rusdan preferred to approach this question through Islamic governance rather than Islamic state, as the term "state" "is a Western idea, imposed by Europeans on the Muslim world."[193] He also maintained that Islamic governance, rather than an Islamic state, was Sungkar's aim, although he conceded that "to get there, you need Islamic governance starting at a local level—and that effectively means a state."[194] He explained that only governance based on *syariat Islam* enables Muslims to practice Islam fully and freely, but it also sets the boundaries to prevent transgressions. It thus regulates society and protects individual Muslims from sin.[195] "Islamic governance has two levels: First, the personal level—you live your life in accordance with *syariah*. Second, the public level—it is a public responsibility to provide and assure that Muslims can follow *syariah* in total. So it is not just personal."[196] *Syariat Islam*, Islamic governance, and Islamic punishment are an obligation, "but that does not mean it has to be a state with territory and borders as *syariat Islam* does not have borders" and "JI does not want to be limited to 'from Sabang to Merauke.'"[197]

Concretely conceptualizing what constitutes Islamic governance, however, has its own complications. For instance, "It is hard to imagine *hakimiyah* (the sovereignty of God) being implemented, especially if you approach this through European ideas about institutions of governance and the separation of powers into executive, legislative, and judicial. Islamic governance based on *syariah* does not have this separation. The role of the government will not be to make laws but to apply the laws of Allah." The institutions implementing them "will not be the same institutions as today as they are not suitable."[198]

A more concrete glimpse of how JI was conceptualizing the Islamic state it was seeking to build can be obtained from the 2013–2014 end-of-year report by JI's *tarbiyah* directorate. This report not only gives insight into the variety of educational activities JI was conducting for both men and women across nineteen *wilayah*, but specified that it was particularly targeting male and female students who were studying secular subjects with the aim of recruiting doctors, nurses, midwives, pharmacists, information technicians, chemists, mechanical engineers, electrical engineers, metallurgists, industrial technicians, nuclear engineers, publicists, communication specialists, journalists, lawyers, agricultural studies graduates, forestry studies graduates, fishery studies graduates, sociologists, accountants, economic management graduates, psychologists, Arabic teachers, English teachers, and Mandarin teachers.[199] This list of recruitment targets shows clearly that JI's Islamic state would not just be built upon religious institutions but that JI was aware that it needed a stable and functioning economy as well as social services.

Para Wijayanto's capture triggered the arrest of more than two hundred JI members in 2020 and 2021, including Abu Rusdan and many of those who had trained in Syria, who were of particular interest for the Indonesian police so that it could assess the extent of JI's new military capacity. However, the arrest of Abu Rusdan, who had not been involved in violence in Indonesia and who had even spoken out against Hambali's actions, shows that what Jakarta still feared the most was the progress that JI had made in terms of reorganizing, recruiting, and gathering support for its alternative national imaginary, an Islamic state.

Reflecting on the Islamist Challenge and JI

The crushing of the 1947–1965 Darul Islam rebellions did not spell the end of militant Islamists challenging the Indonesian state. It also did not spell the end of Darul Islam as a movement, which withdrew underground, reorganized, re-emerged, and factionalized. It was onto one of these factions that Jemaah Islamiyah was grafted in 1993 under the leadership of Abdullah Sungkar. JI was a more salafi and international organization that endorsed both local and global jihad. However, its opposition to the Indonesian state was exactly the same as Kartosuwirjo's, namely its conceptualization on the basis of Pancasila as a man-made philosophy rather than Islamic law as the product of divine revelation.

Indeed, for both DI and JI the starting point for establishing an Islamic state or Islamic governance was that it was an obligation, commanded by Allah.

The fall of the New Order in 1998 provided JI with the opportunity to return to Indonesia from Malaysia. Different JI commanders seized upon Indonesia's political chaos, security vacuum, and economic weakness to become militarily active. Some defended Muslims in the communal conflicts in Ambon and Poso while others participated in the bombings of Western targets. The communal conflicts also provided JI with the opportunity to experiment with establishing a *qoidah aminah* in Poso, which Mantiqi 3 leaders hoped could become the nucleus for establishing an Islamic countersociety and, ultimately, an Islamic state. These plans, however, were undermined by Mantiqi 1's bombing campaign, which not only made JI the target of extensive counterterrorism operations but also ended up fracturing JI.

The Indonesian state's response to JI differed considerably from Jakarta's response to the Darul Islam rebellions. Two key factors explain this difference: First, *reformasi* saw a pushback against the Indonesian security forces. The police were separated from the military, civilianized, and given the counterterrorism remit. This meant that there was an emphasis on forensic investigation after the 2002 Bali bombings, intelligence gathering, and arrests. They were also assisted by the international community, in particular the Australian Federal Police. Moreover, the police operations that did use force, notably those carried out by Densus 88, were, on the whole, carefully targeted. Second, JI did not hold territory. As seen in chapter 1, it was the military operations to oust Darul Islam from West Java and South Sulawesi, where DI held swathes of territory, that resulted in the largest number of casualties, comprising DI, its support base, and anyone caught up in the fighting.

While the state's response changed with respect to the use of force, from predominantly relying upon the military during the Sukarno era and the New Order to predominantly relying upon the police in the post-Suharto period, the fact that all Indonesian governments fully endorsed Pancasila made Muslim belonging in parts of the *santri* (pious) population in Indonesia somewhat equivocal. They faced the challenge of reconciling the obligation to live in accordance with *syariah* law with Pancasila. There was no singular response to this challenge. Masyumi members became involved in the PRRI/Permesta rebellions, Muhammadiyah focused on education, and NU withdrew from politics with *asas tunggal* but, later, decided to advocate for Islam Nusantara. DI/NII and JI were at the extreme ends of this *santri* population, a minority that felt dislocated in a Muslim-majority country in which successive Indonesian governments had an "Islam policy" that resembled that of Indonesia's former Christian colonial occupiers.

The repression and criminalization during the New Order, in particular, was formative for the first generation of JI. It contributed to the shift away from the "national" and away from DI/NII. Indeed, it is interesting to see how DI and JI positioned themselves with respect to belonging. DI under Kartosuwirjo clearly identified as Islamic nationalists. They belonged to Indonesia, but one with an alternative Indonesian national imaginary: the Indonesian Islamic State. JI rejected nationalism and projected itself more internationally through global Muslim solidarity and support for global jihad, and it even had non-Indonesian members as well as Mantiqi 1 members who identified with Al-Qaeda's political project. However, at the same time, the majority of JI members were and are Indonesian. When abroad, in Afghanistan, the Southern Philippines, or Syria, they established their own training camps rather than integrating into the Arab or Bangsamoro ones. Moreover, the arena of their jihad was Indonesia. And, most importantly, the starting point for their national imaginary whether it was a *daulah Islamiyah* or a *khilafah* was and still is in Indonesia. Indeed, at the same time as some eight hundred Indonesians left for Syria to live in the ISIS Caliphate and burned their passports on arrival as they did not believe an Islamic state in Indonesia would ever be possible, JI reembarked upon proto-state-building activities in Indonesia. Yet, belonging remained equivocal. As the midlevel JI commander explained, "I feel [Indonesian] and I don't. There is so much emphasis on the ceremonies with flag raising etc. If I look at those I don't feel Indonesian. And if you don't support Pancasila you are seen as not supportive of NKRI. If you are not active in society, you are not NKRI. If you pray too much you are seen as radical. If you wear ankle-length trousers or have a beard you are forced to participate [in Pancasila activities]."[200] This equivocal sense of belonging and the yearning for an Islamic state, combined with state repression and criminalization of Islamism, contributed to the periodic regeneration of Islamist violence in Indonesia and its persistence into the twenty-first century. At the heart of this persistence was the steadfastness of Islamist ideals, underwritten by the role of Islam in Indonesian history as well as early Indonesian nationalism. These continued to provide legitimacy for alternative Islamist narratives and an alternative national imaginary. Force was simply a means for achieving these ideals.

3

THE EAST TIMOR CONFLICT, 1975–1999

While the New Order in the early 1970s was depoliticizing its Muslim parties and projecting its developmentalist national imaginary, changes in Europe set in motion dynamics that would alter the boundaries of Indonesia's geo-body. On April 25, 1974, left-wing military officers overthrew the government of Portuguese prime minister Marcelo Caetano. The coup was the culmination of the "Carnation Revolution," which had started in March, driven by military and economic problems arising from the wars in Portuguese Africa. In mid-June, the new government in Lisbon announced that it intended to decolonize all Portuguese overseas territories, including the eastern half of the island of Timor in the Sunda Archipelago. Not long thereafter, in September 1974, BAKIN launched Operasi Komodo, a clandestine operation that aimed at preparing Portuguese Timor for integration into Indonesia. This was followed on December 7, 1975, by Indonesia's invasion of the territory, marking the beginning of twenty-four years of bitter conflict.

This chapter looks at the East Timor conflict from the Indonesian invasion in December 1975 to the postreferendum violence in September 1999. It starts by exploring the place of the island of Timor in the Indonesian national imaginary. The chapter then examines the conflict across several phases, analyzing Indonesia's strategies, tactics, and targets alongside those of the Revolutionary Front for an Independent East Timor (Frente Revolucionária do Timor Leste Independente, FRETILIN). This chapter also examines Indonesia's efforts to "Indonesianize" East Timor and the East Timorese, the competing narratives on the conflict, and the competing national imaginaries. It concludes with reflections on belonging and why the integration of East Timor ultimately failed.

This chapter shows that both the decision to integrate East Timor and the decision to allow it to have a referendum on independence were underwritten by Indonesia's national imaginary. The former was framed by the New Order's projection of Indonesia as a bastion of anticommunism as well as a geographic imaginary that covered the entire archipelago. The latter was enabled by a shift in the Indonesian national imaginary in the late New Order toward a more Islamic one, but above all by how Suharto's successor, Bacharuddin Jusuf Habibie, reimagined Indonesia as a democracy. Indonesia's national imaginary also framed the extreme violence during the invasion, the first phase of the conflict from 1976 to 1984, and after the 1999 referendum, influencing who was targeted and what was destroyed. FRETILIN's national imaginary also played a role in its violence, not only against the Indonesian military but also in the fratricide in the late 1970s.

Portuguese Timor in the Indonesian Imaginary

In order to understand where Portuguese Timor fit into the Indonesian national imaginary, it is useful to return to Sukarno's speech on the birth of Pancasila in June 1945. In this speech he advanced three geographic imaginaries that go beyond the Netherlands Indies. Two of these defined Indonesia in archipelagic terms as a unit encompassing *all* of the islands and waters between Asia and Australia.[1] The third defined Indonesia historically as "everything that had already been established in the era of Sriwijaya and Majapahit," which, in Indonesian eyes, included the whole of Timor Island as a tribute or vassal territory.[2]

Subsequent periodic references to these larger national imaginaries showed that expanding Indonesia's boundaries was not off the government's agenda. For instance, in 1950, Muhammad Yamin, while serving as minister of justice and education, argued that "Indonesia should incorporate the Dutch East Indies, North Borneo and the whole of Portuguese Timor."[3] In 1957, the Indonesian government issued a declaration that the territorial waters of the archipelago formed one unit with the islands. In 1959, a group of fourteen Indonesian exiles from the Permesta rebellion, who had sought asylum in Portuguese Timor the previous year, became involved in the Viqueque Revolt, attempting to overthrow the Portuguese colonial government together with a group of disgruntled Timorese civil servants and what Janet Gunter described as "minor royalty" from the Uatolari and Uatocarbau subdistricts.⁴ They were aided by the Indonesian consul in Dili, and by West Timorese supporters who "who had agreed to supply arms."⁵ Their objective, according to one of their leaders, José Manuel Duarte, was the integration of East and West Timor as "we have ancient links—we never had a border before Portugal colonized Timor."⁶ Not surprisingly, Indonesians have since regarded the Viqueque Revolt as "an early call for 'integration' with Indonesia," demonstrating the "aspiration for integration."⁷

Further initiatives in the early 1960s saw Ruslan Abdulgani, the deputy chairman of Sukarno's Supreme Advisory Council, at an Afro-Asian Solidarity Organization rally meeting in Jakarta in 1961, stating that Indonesia's "eyes and heart are directed towards Portuguese Timor" as it was still "under the power of colonialism."⁸ This was also highlighted by Foreign Minister Subandrio in his speech at the plenary session of the DPR in July 1961, where he emphasized Indonesia's geographic proximity and the Indonesian people's anger.⁹ That year also saw the establishment of a "Bureau of Liberation of the Timor Republic" in Jakarta, which "called on the people of Timor to drive out the Portuguese colonialists."¹⁰ This bureau belonged to a small movement for the liberation of East Timor, which was led by Mao Klao, a Timorese.¹¹

In October 1962, two months after Western New Guinea was transferred to Indonesia by the Dutch, foreign observers noted a "small build-up" of Indonesian troops in West Timor. Together with reports by the Indonesian news agency Antara, which accused the Portuguese of "unfriendly acts" including "firing on Indonesian coastal shipping," "inciting kidnapping," and the killing of three Indonesians, these foreign observers speculated that this "may signal the beginning of a campaign to justify eventual seizure of the territory."¹² In fact, Portuguese Timor officials positively "expected an Indonesian campaign against them."¹³

While a military campaign did not materialize, Indonesian "activities" continued. In spring 1963, the Timor Liberation Bureau announced that it had established a government inside Portuguese Timor. It comprised twelve ministers and was located in Batugade, just across the border from Indonesian Timor. These developments coincided with "reports of a military build-up in East Timor, with a thousand new troops being sent in by Portugal."¹⁴ Clearly the Portuguese continued to be concerned. In May 1963, Indonesian general Mokoginta in an interview with the *Washington Post* stated that "if the people of East Timor today or tomorrow started a revolution . . . we would support them" and "if they want to join Indonesia, we will talk it over."¹⁵ However, by July 1963, the government's eyes had shifted away from the east as Sukarno embarked upon his "crush Malaysia" campaign. Portuguese Timor could wait, not least because taking on the British would provide the ambitious Sukarno with greater anti-imperialist acclaim.

After the fall of Sukarno, the New Order recast the Indonesian national imaginary away from left-wing revolutionism, instead styling itself as a bastion against communism. In fact, its whole identity and legitimacy were tied to the narrative of having prevented a communist coup in 1965. Its power was asserted through the subsequent purges of alleged communists in 1965–1966; its stability and prosperity were tied to keeping Indonesia safe from communism. It was thus an ideological imperative to prevent the possible emergence of an independent socialist or communist East Timor just across the border.

However, there were also clear continuities with the national imaginary projected by the Sukarno government. Like Sukarno, Suharto saw Indonesia as the successor of the Srivijaja and Majapahit empires, including Timor Island as tribute territory. This was further underlined by the assertions of the Sultan of Ternate Moedaffar Sjah that Timor Island had been part of the vast territory of the sultanate, which stretched north all the way to the Sulu Archipelago and south all the way to East Nusa Tenggara.[16] Moreover, like Sukarno, Suharto conceptualized Indonesia as an anticolonial state and an archipelagic state spanning all of the islands between Asia and Australia.

Thus, once Suharto had secured his own position and the New Order had dealt with the PKI, Portuguese Timor popped back up on Jakarta's radar. In the late 1960s, BAKIN, while assessing Indonesia's security, came to the conclusion that Portuguese Timor, were it to become unstable or unviable, could pose a threat to Indonesia and should thus be incorporated into the country.[17] Unrelated, yet paving the way for a territorial claim, the Indonesian parliament in 1973 formally adopted the archipelagic principle, Wawasan Nusantara, in MPR Decree IV. Wawasan Nusantara designated Indonesia as an "inseparable entity of land and water."[18] The island of Timor as a whole and its territorial waters were an integral part of this. And not long after the 1974 coup in Portugal, DPR deputy speaker John Naro called upon the Indonesian government to "take preliminary steps and work out a special policy on Portuguese Timor so that the area will once again return to Indonesian control."[19]

The Road to Invasion

Less than a month after the April 1974 coup in Lisbon, politics in the sleepy backwater of Portuguese Timor sprung to life. The first political party to be established was the Timorese Democratic Union (União Democratica Timorense, UDT) on May 11, 1974. It advocated "progressive autonomy" under the Portuguese flag while calling for democratization, income redistribution, human rights, and self-determination.[20] Led by Mario Carrascalão, the UDT had a conservative social base comprising the colonial elite, Catholic smallholders, Eurasians, the *liurai* (traditional chiefs), some Chinese businessmen, and the Portuguese community.[21] With between eighty and one hundred thousand members the UDT was also the largest party.[22] However, it was soon eclipsed by the Timorese Social Democratic Association (Associação Social Democrática Timor, ASDT), which was established in the same month to "defend the right to immediate independence of the East Timorese people."[23] Led by Xavier do Amaral, the ASDT advocated socialism, democracy, anticolonialism, and East Timorese nationalism.[24] As a counter-elite movement the ASDT had a "progressive" social base of junior civil servants, sons of the *liurai*, teachers, urban workers, students, and peasants.

On September 11, 1974, the ASDT was transformed into FRETILIN, which strengthened the left-wing ideological elements as FRETILIN advocated revolution to bring about political and social change. A key role was played by the Timorese students who had studied in Lisbon, who formulated the early policies and carried out its immensely popular grassroots work in the rural areas.[25] They included Maoists such as Abilio de Araujo, who was especially "fond" of Mao's ideas from "the ultra-radical period of the Cultural Revolution of the 1960s," as well as Marxists such as Alarico Fernandes, who saw "Marxism as the only way of liberating our people from the exploitation of one man by another."[26] As Timorese resistance leader Xanana Gusmão recounted in his autobiography, Marxism was seen as "the 'immediate solution' to problems of an incredibly underdeveloped people" while Maoism was believed to be "a shining path to a revolutionary process."[27]

Foreign observers at the time described FRETILIN as "a militant left wing party organized by indigenous Timorese largely along the lines of FRELIMO in Mozambique."[28] FRETILIN was inspired by the struggles in other parts of the Lusophone world, such as those of Bissau-Guinean and Cape Verdean revolutionary Amilcar Cabral and Angolan Liberation Movement leader Agostinho Neto, as well as the ideas of Brazilian philosopher and educator Paulo Freire.[29] According to Jill Jolliffe, FRETILIN in the early days even "defined itself as a black nationalist movement."[30] This led FRETILIN to reject the label of "communist" as it "considered the communist parties of the Soviet Union and western Europe" to be "socialist-imperialist," which ran contrary to their own anticolonial and anti-imperialist orientation.[31]

The third party vying to shape the future of Portuguese Timor was the Timorese Popular Democratic Association (Associação Popular Democrática Timorense, APODETI), which was established on May 27. It called for "autonomous integration into the Republic of Indonesia" on the grounds of ethnic and historical links.[32] Many of its supporters had relatives across the Indonesian border.³³ Others were connected to the 1959 Viqueque uprising.³⁴ It was a significantly smaller party that, according to Don Greenlees and Robert Garran, never had more than a few hundred supporters.³⁵ APODETI became the vehicle through which Indonesia sought to influence the unfolding events.

Concerned by the left-wing nature of the coup in Portugal, by the Marxist influences on FRETILIN, and by the possibility of a hostile base just across the border, Indonesia did not believe that it had the option of simply watching. It feared that "an independent Timor state, cut off from current Portuguese subsidies, would need new foreign sponsors"—Soviet or Chinese—and "even if Timor avoided becoming a communist puppet . . . the regime would be instable and thus attract a great deal of attention."³⁶ The arrival of three openly leftist Portuguese officers to assist Timor's governor, Colonel Mario Lemos Pires, further stoked Jakarta's fears.³⁷

Indonesia's concerns were broadly shared by the United States. Cast in Cold War terms, the United States saw Suharto, who had crushed the Indonesian Communist Party in 1965–1966, as a reliable ally and Indonesia as the "most important non-communist Southeast Asian state." They feared that an unstable or indeed left-wing independent Timor would be an open invitation to communist influence. This became all the more urgent after the fall of Vietnam in April 1975. Thus, in US eyes, "a merger with Indonesia" was "probably the best solution for the colony if the inhabitants agree."³⁸

Australia, too, saw Indonesia's absorption of Timor as making "geopolitical sense."³⁹ So when Hari Tjan Silalahi, the director of the Center for Strategic and International Studies, and Lim Bian Kie (Jusuf Wanandi), personal secretary to Ali Murtopo, sought out Australian views on integrating Portuguese Timor, they were encouraged at highest level.⁴⁰ In early September, Australian prime minister Gough Whitlam at a meeting with Suharto in Yogyakarta effectively gave a "green light" to integration, when he stated that Timor was "too small to be independent" and would be "economically unviable."⁴¹

While the United States and Australia supported the integration of Portuguese Timor into Indonesia, propelled by Cold War concerns, Portugal, driven by the desire to unburden itself of this territory as quickly as possible, practically invited Indonesia in. Between the April coup and the October start of Operasi Komodo, Portuguese president Francisco da Costa Gomes and foreign minister Mario Soares repeatedly told Jakarta that "Portugal would not oppose annexation" as long as it was "orderly and peaceful."⁴² During Murtopo's visit to Lisbon right before the operation was launched, Da Costa Gomes and Prime Minister Vasco dos Santos Goncalves made it clear that Timorese independence was "unrealistic" and "nonsense."⁴³ And Portuguese minister for interterritorial coordination Antonio de Almeida Santos, during his visit to Jakarta after the operation had started, stated that he considered "a union a 'logical step.'"[44] Similar iterations continued throughout 1975. In March, Portuguese officials told the US Embassy that "they would not resist an Indonesian invasion of Timor."[45] In May, US officials reported that "Indonesia believes it has assurances from Lisbon that the Portuguese will give Jakarta *carte blanche* to influence the course of events in Timor."[46] And in June, US intelligence noted that Murtopo "believes the Portuguese will arrange matters so that Timor is eventually incorporated into Indonesia."[47]

Less than a month after the Suharto-Whitlam meeting in Yogyakarta and only days after Murtopo's visit to Lisbon, Indonesia launched Operasi Komodo to integrate Portuguese Timor through covert means. Operating from Atambua, West Timor, Komodo was based on a three-pronged strategy. First, it provided training by Indonesia's Kopassandha special forces (later renamed Kopassus) for several hundred APODETI "refugees."[48] Modeled on Murtopo's 1969 West Irian operation in which "volunteers" had been used to show that the local population was demanding integration with Indonesia, these Timorese "refugees" were prepared "to return to Portuguese Timor to play their part in persuading people to support integration."[49] The second element of Operasi Komodo was cross-border incursions. These were undertaken by some of the APODETI "refugees" as well as by some Kopassandha in order to gather tactical intelligence and gain an understanding of geography and society.[50] Third was an extensive propaganda campaign.[51] This included nightly broadcasts by Radio Kupang in Portuguese and Tetum, extolling the "wonders and advantages of Indonesia" while simultaneously issuing threats against communists in Portuguese Timor.[52]

It was against this backdrop that developments on the ground in Portuguese Timor began to unfold in 1975. On January 22, the UDT and FRETILIN joined forces in a "coalition for national independence."[53] Alarmed by these developments, Operasi Komodo stepped up its activities, now seeking to break up this coalition.[54] In April, the UDT started to fracture over what it saw as radicalization within FRETILIN, which was further underlined by the way FRETILIN dominated the coalition. Following a visit to Jakarta, where the two top UDT leaders, Francisco Xavier Lopez da Cruz and Augusto da Costa Mouzinho, were "feted" by Suharto, the UDT withdrew from the coalition on May 27.[55] This decision was also influenced by FRETILIN receiving 55 percent of the vote in the village head elections that month.[56]

In June, Indonesian newspapers began reporting that thousands of refugees were crossing into Indonesian Timor to escape FRETILIN atrocities while Portuguese diplomats tried to put together decolonization talks. In July, the British consul to Portuguese Timor reported from his tour that the Portuguese had "left themselves too much to do in too short a time" and that Timor's "diverse ethnic groups with their inexperienced politics and political parties provide fertile soil for passionate rivalries and disruptive tensions."[57] He noted that "trouble was almost certainly on the horizon" as "the Indonesians want ultimately to see Portuguese Timor an integrated part of Indonesia."[58]

Following several meetings with Indonesian officials, the UDT staged a coup on August 10 aimed at expelling all communists.[59] It quickly "moved against local Portuguese authorities," "occupied communication centers," "laid siege to the military headquarters," and "then delivered an ultimatum to the government in Lisbon demanding immediate independence and the arrest of the leftist Fretilin Party."[60] It also "captured the chief of police," "seized large quantities of arms," and "took over the airport."[61] As the UDT met with resistance from FRETILIN, Portuguese Timor descended into a civil war, which opened the door for violence "based on long-standing personal grievances," with rival families and tribes settling scores.[62]

The military balance swung in FRETILIN's favor when its call to all "patriots of the army" to crush the "UDT reactionaries" was heeded.[63] These soldiers brought with them "some 20,000 rifles and 80 percent of the heavy ammunition in the colony."[64] The defection of the troops, in turn, prompted Governor Lemos Pires with a skeleton staff of seventy to move to the offshore island of Atauro on August 17.[65] There he nursed "his hurt pride," reluctant to seek contacts with either the UDT or FRETILIN.[66] In the fourth week of August, in an attempt to shore up the UDT, Jakarta authorized a new operation, Operasi Flamboyan, which initiated covert cross-border paramilitary operations. The Timorese "volunteers" trained earlier were transformed into eight companies of full-fledged partisans who carried out hit-and-run attacks.[67] Amongst them were Kopassandha in civilian clothes.

FRETILIN's troops were better than either the Indonesians or the UDT had expected. On September 8 they declared victory in the short civil war, which had cost 1,500–3,000 lives and had displaced more Timorese to West Timor.[68] By October, the total number of refugees in and around Atambua had reached forty thousand. Of these 35 percent were women and 55 percent were children.[69] In response to FRETILIN's victory, UDT chairman Lopez da Cruz declared "that it was better to merge with Indonesia than live under communist rule," while Indonesia moved into the second phase of Operasi Flamboyan, namely to seize border enclaves in the name of the prointegration Timorese parties.[70] It was in this context that Indonesian soldiers and their APODETI auxiliaries assaulted the town of Balibo on October 16, killing, among others, five journalists—Australians Greg Shackleton and Tony Stewart, New Zealander Gary Cunningham, and Britons Brian Peters and Malcolm Rennie—all working for Australian television. They had been "eagerly waiting to get footage of Indonesian involvement in the escalating border conflict."⁷¹ The tepid British and Australian response, accepting Jakarta's explanation that "the newsmen were killed, almost certainly inadvertently, in the course of the attack," served to assure Indonesia that the path to integrating Portuguese Timor was clear.⁷²

Fearing that a full Indonesian invasion was imminent, FRETILIN unilaterally declared independence on November 28, announcing the establishment of the Democratic Republic of East Timor. FRETILIN believed that this would help mobilize international support and that the East Timorese people would be more prepared to fight for an independent state than a Portuguese colony. Two days later, on November 30, the UDT and APODETI, along with the small Kota and Trabalhista parties, which had united into the Anti-Communist Movement, declared Timor part of Indonesia in what has since become known as the Balibo Declaration.⁷³

As Jakarta publicly blamed Lisbon for FRETILIN's declaration, "implying collusion between the Portuguese and the Timorese radicals," Indonesia's generals revisited their invasion plans.⁷⁴ On December 5, the British noted "that Indonesia has now taken the decision to move on large scale into East Timor (possibly after the conclusion of President Ford's visit on 6 December)."⁷⁵ They were not wrong. During this visit, Suharto asked US president Gerald Ford and secretary of state Henry Kissinger for "understanding if we deem it necessary to take rapid or drastic action."⁷⁶ Ford responded that "we understand the problem you have and the intentions you have."⁷⁷

The East Timor Conflict—Phase 1: Large-Scale Military Operations and Mass Violence, 1975–1984

In the early morning hours on December 7, 1975, "more than 1,000 Army commandos," comprising paracommandos from Kopassandha and Kostrad airborne troops from battalions 501 and 502, "parachuted into the capital, Dili, in the first wave of the attack."⁷⁸ They were tasked with seizing the government buildings, securing the harbor and airport, and cutting off FRETILIN's escape route.⁷⁹ At dawn four Indonesian warships discharged more troops in landing crafts.⁸⁰

The quick victory the soldiers had been promised, however, did not materialize. Instead, the Indonesian military suffered heavy casualties. There was no clear chain of command between Kopassandha and Kostrad, and there was "inadequate coordination between air and land-borne forces with the result that they shot each other up."⁸¹ Some paratroopers were just dumped over the city center while others, instead of landing behind the FRETILIN forces, "were parachuted on top of them."[82] Several commandos landed in water and drowned, pulled down by their heavy gear. The Indonesian soldiers also came under fire by the two hundred FRETILIN "special troops" who had stayed behind in Dili.[83] Soon Indonesian casualties far outstripped the medical equipment brought, and more soldiers died because evacuation of the wounded was slow.[84]

It soon became clear that the invasion had been launched "without resort to known intelligence about FRETILIN's strong points."[85] Indeed, Indonesian soldiers had been told that the Timorese who had served in the Portuguese colonial army were "mere *hansip*"—civil defense forces.[86] According to Luhut Panjaitan, who was among of those first para-commandos, they believed "that the next day after the invasion FRETILIN will surrender. We parachuted in on a Sunday and the commander had already planned a parade for Monday."[87]

As they came under attack, the Indonesian paratroopers "experienced shock."[88] Foreign diplomatic reports described what happened next as officers losing "control over their troops," with units running "amok, looting, raping," and killing. According to James Dunn, it was the drowning of those whose plane had veered off course, that seemed "to have sent troops on the rampage, especially those of battalion 502."[89] Watching the invasion from the bishop's residence, Monsignor Martinho da Costa Lopes recounted that the Indonesian soldiers "started killing everyone they could find."[90] In one incident, in response to the killing of an Indonesian soldier, twenty-seven women were taken to the wharf and shot one by one, followed by a group of fifty-nine men who met the same fate as "a crowd which was being forced to watch, was ordered to count as the bodies fell back into the water."[91]

Among the women was Isobel Lobato, the wife of FRETILIN military commander Nicolau Lobato. Also executed on the wharf were Australian journalist Roger East, Timorese poet Francisco Borja da Costa, and the leader of the Timorese women's movement, Rosa Muki Bonaparte. One community particularly targeted was the Chinese, many of whom were taken to Licidere beach and shot.[92] Between five and seven hundred Chinese were among the estimated two thousand people killed in the first days of the invasion.[93]

The capture of Dili was followed by the capture of East Timor's other principal city, Baucau, with reports stating that Indonesian forces had established control by December 18.[94] A week later, on December 25, another fifteen thousand Indonesian troops arrived to reinforce the ten thousand already there.[95]

In 1976, the first year after the invasion, Indonesia had a total of forty thousand troops in East Timor. This number was further bolstered by recruiting local troops—battalions 744 and 745—in line with its territorial structure, and civilian auxiliaries in line with its total people's defense system (*sistem pertahanan keamanan rakyat semesta,* sishankamrata). Initially, Indonesia's strategy focused on extending its control over the remaining coastal areas, linking up with the troops that had landed in Baucau and those that had crossed the border from West Timor in order to establish a contiguous area under its control.[96] This involved bombing the towns, especially along the southern coast, and targeting the Timorese population in an effort to extract intelligence and to sever logistical links.[97] According to the Indonesian-appointed deputy governor of East Timor, Lopez da Cruz, some sixty thousand people had been killed by March 1976.[98]

This year also saw the highest number of Indonesian casualties in the whole conflict with 646 deaths, as crushing FRETILIN proved more difficult than expected.[99] FRETILIN, anticipating an invasion, had moved "large quantities of supplies and ammunition into the mountains."[100] Its military wing, FALINTIL (Forças Armadas de Libertação de Timor Leste, Armed Forces for the Liberation of East Timor), included a core of 2,500 Timorese colonial troops; their overall strength in December 1975 was estimated at 5,000–10,000.[101] As the Indonesian troops encountered the FALINTIL troops, they quickly realized that their enemy's "fighting capacity was strong" and their "motivation was high."[102] They also had NATO-standard weapons, "benefitted from the optimal use of the environment," and had the support of much of the population.[103] Thus, as predicted by foreign intelligence analysts, FRETILIN's "rural dissidence" would be "extremely difficult for Indonesia to eradicate."[104]

By 1977, the Indonesian military was in control of all the main coastal settlements.[105] FALINTIL, in turn, had consolidated its strongholds on Mount Matebian in the east and the Natabora plain near the south coast. In line with FALINTIL's revolutionary "people's war" strategy, it had established *zonas libertadas* (liberated zones) where FRETILIN leaders claimed 80 percent of the population was living, organized into *bases de apoio* (support bases).[106] These, according to Timorese resistance leader Xanana Gusmão, were introduced in May 1976 "to provide logistical and political support" and "as a mechanism to organize the people so they could continue to fight in the war."[107] According to Father do Rego, who had gone into the mountains with his parishioners from Soibada in mid-1976, it was in these bases that the people had succeeded in "preserving communal life, beyond the reach of the Indonesians." The extension of Indonesian control over coastal towns was thus, in his view, "only of geographic significance."[108]

In September 1977, the Indonesian military launched a major operation to separate the people from the insurgents, based on a strategy of "encirclement and annihilation." This typically started with intensive aerial bombardment of suspected FALINTIL bases, using low-flying counterinsurgency aircraft such as OV-10 Broncos, which were equipped with miniguns and rockets. "Forested areas were bombed in an attempt to defoliate ground cover," and then ground troops would move in and burn villages, kill livestock, and destroy crops and food.[109] The fleeing population was pushed "progressively eastward into steadily smaller and less productive areas."[110] Villages suspected of supporting FRETILIN were wiped out.[111] Others were relocated upon surrendering, initially into "guarded camps" and then into highly controlled "resettlement areas" locally referred to as *campos de concentração* (concentration camps).

Trying to evade the Indonesian forces, FALINTIL went on the run, taking the people with them. This compounded the devastating impact of the Indonesian attacks. Old people were left behind.[112] Parents abandoned "their children because they were afraid that they would slow them down, because their crying would put everyone else's life in danger, or because there was no more food to feed them."[113] Fields that had been planted in the *bases de apoio* could not be harvested. New crops could not be sown. Famine quickly set in.

As the Indonesian attacks intensified, some in the FRETILIN leadership started to question its strategy. One of the first to advocate allowing the people to surrender was Xavier do Amaral in 1977. For this he was branded a traitor and placed under arrest.[114] Thus it was only in late November 1978 that FRETILIN ordered the mass surrender of the civilians.[115]

In March 1979, Indonesia's encirclement and annihilation operations came to an end. FALINTIL had lost some 80 percent of its troops and more than 90 percent of its weapons.[116] Its lines of communication had been severed and the people with them had been ordered to surrender. Over the year more than half of the population of East Timor was relocated into 150 "resettlement areas," not least because Jakarta had limited humanitarian aid to these areas.[117] The offshore islands of Atauro, Alor, and Lirar were turned into prison islands for FRETILIN members and their families. In the resettlement areas, the people were restricted to growing limited amounts of food in small gardens, so they would not be able to supply the Timorese resistance, but also, as Gerry van Klinken has pointed out, because "hungry people do not revolt."[118] Geoffrey Robinson estimated that due to conditions of disease and malnutrition, some one hundred thousand of those displaced perished.[119]

The remaining FALINTIL reorganized into smaller, independent units scattered across the country, which shifted to more conventional rural guerrilla warfare and tactics.[120] These included the *ramahana* ("bow and arrow") maneuver in which small patrols were employed as bait to lure Indonesian soldiers into valley ambushes.[121] FALINTIL also used villagers as decoys.[122] They targeted Indonesian military posts not only to kill soldiers but also to capture weapons to replenish FALINTIL's depleted arsenal. By March 1981, FRETILIN had sufficiently recovered to bring many of its units together for a national conference.

This conference established the FRETILIN Marxist-Leninist Party (Partido Marxista-Leninista Fretilin) to increase the effectiveness of the struggle, as well as a new umbrella body for the resistance movement, the Revolutionary Council of National Resistance (Conselho Revolucionário da Resistência Nacional, CRRN), of which Xanana Gusmão had been elected president.[123] He also assumed the command of FALINTIL. Mobile FALINTIL units were introduced, a clandestine network was established, and *nucleos de resistencia popular* (nuclei of popular resistance) were set up to guide the people.[124]

It was in response to this resurgence that the Indonesian military launched a series of large-scale crackdown operations.[125] These included Operasi Kikis I and II. Operasi Kikis I aimed at laying siege to Mount Matebian, while Operasi Kikis II aimed at laying siege to Mount Aitana.[126] Both sought to flush out the remaining pockets of resistance. Similar to previous operations, these operations pursued an encirclement and annihilation strategy. This time, however, a new element had been added, the *pagar betis* that had been so successful in clearing out the remnants of Darul Islam in the early 1960s.

In May 1981, some eighty thousand East Timorese males, ranging in age from eight to sixty, were ordered "to form two human chains across the island from north to south at the eastern and western ends of East Timor."[127] They marched in front of and behind some eighteen thousand Indonesian troops.[128] In Operasi Kikis II, the East Timorese battalion 744 was the "main force on the front line in the pursuit operation," where according to Kiki Syahnakri, they provided "indisputable proof" of their reliability through "their toughness and dedication."[129] The main target of this operation was Xanana, who was believed to be in the center of the *pagar betis*.[130] At one point, Indonesian troops even believed that they had found his body when identifying corpses after a shootout.[131]

While Syahnakri gives insight into what the Indonesian military was trying to achieve, the account by Cristiano da Costa, one of the civilian participants in the *pagar betis*, paints a grim picture. He explained that "the front line was Timorese forced to take part. When the circle was small enough, the army bombarded the area, then soldiers went in to finish off any people left there."[132] He then described what he found when he accompanied a group of soldiers to "clean up" a week after the operation: "We smelt the bodies before we found them. The heads had been cut off the first bodies, one woman and four men. . . . We found three other men tied by the feet hanging upside down in trees . . . another two men were tied with their hands behind the trunks of trees. . . . On the ground beside them were six others, two women and two children and an old man and an old woman."[133] By March 1982, the Indonesian military had succeeded in capturing some 6,000 Mauser rifles, 5,000 G3 battle rifles, 3,500 hand grenades, 2,817 antitank weapons, 857 pistols, and 214 machine guns as well as explosives.[134]

They had also killed several FALINTIL guerrillas and forced others to surrender. However, they did not capture Xanana.

The *pagar betis* operations had enormous repercussions on East Timor's civilian population. Many of the men forced to participate died of exhaustion. The operations also disrupted the agricultural production.[135] There were no men to plant the fields. Consequently, there were no fields to harvest and the population was once again on the brink of starvation.

In early 1983, communications were opened between Indonesian East Timor commander Major Gatot Purwanto and José da Conceição, one of FRETILIN's local leaders in the eastern sector. Da Conceição then facilitated a meeting with Xanana, for both Purwanto and Indonesian commander in chief General Mohammad Yusuf.[136] This was followed by a cease-fire agreed on March 23, 1983.[137] However, when Murdani replaced Yusuf, this cease-fire was revoked, as not only was Murdani convinced that FALINTIL was using it to consolidate, but he also wanted to retain East Timor as a training ground for "the post-45 generation which didn't have a real battlefield."[138] Thus, when he announced a new offensive on August 17, he emphasized that "this time" they would "hit them without mercy."[139] Four days later, Indonesian troops killed between seven hundred and one thousand East Timorese in what has become known as the Kraras massacre.[140]

This first phase of the East Timor conflict was characterized by an enormous loss of life. The Commission for Reception, Truth and Reconciliation in East Timor (CAVR) estimated that some 102,800 civilians perished from deprivation while 18,600 civilians died in targeted killings.[141] Robinson argued that these deaths were the result of "conscious strategies rather than the by-product of conflict."[142] John Taylor explained the violence by the Indonesian troops in the early years, particularly 1976, as resulting from the "inability to make any headway militarily," which then led soldiers to take out their "frustration on the local population."[143] Robert Cribb explained the heavy loss of life resulting from "a sub-culture of violence" and "a military contempt for civilians dating back to the revolutionary period."[144]

The deaths from starvation and illness as well as the displacement were highest between 1976 and 1980, when the Indonesian military was pursuing a strategy that combined the American "Vietnam playbook" and its own "Darul Islam playbook." Looking at Indonesia's violence against the East Timorese through the New Order's national imaginary, and through its definition of what it meant to be Indonesian, provides a further dimension. In simple terms, as a bastion against communism New Order Indonesia had deployed its soldiers to East Timor "to prevent the establishment of a state affiliated with communism."[145] The soldiers had been told that FRETILIN members were communists and they had heard that China was supporting them. The soldiers also brought with them either direct experience of the anticommunist campaign in 1965–1966 or memories of what had occurred in their home villages. All of them had also been indoctrinated into the New Order's G30S/PKI (30th September Movement) founding narrative. Moreover, the fight against communism in Indonesia was not over. While Indonesian soldiers were hunting down "FRETILIN communists" in East Timor, Indonesian intelligence was still flushing out perceived communists in Java.

Against this backdrop, it is not all that surprising that in the first few days of the invasion the Chinese community of Dili was singled out, in Liquica "the entire Chinese population was killed," and in Maubara the Hakka men were separated from the women and then shot.[146] It is also not surprising that it was not just FRETILIN and FALINTIL who were targeted but also their members' families, relatives, friends, and supporters. As with the PKI in Indonesia, communism was seen as "infectious," passed on by association and passed down generationally. This explains why Indonesian soldiers executed entire families, and why in the town of Aileu "all those over three years old" were shot—because "they contained the seeds of FRETILIN."[147] As FRETILIN had received 55 percent of the votes in the village chief elections, the population as a whole was under surveillance for "signs of communism." Many of those deemed to be communists were simply killed, as the New Order did not see communism as being compatible with Indonesianness. They were thus seen as "unintegrateable." Indeed, the whole population needed to be cleansed in East Timor, just as it was still being cleansed in Indonesia well into the late 1980s.

Not all East Timorese deaths, however, were attributable to the Indonesian military. The Indonesian invasion radicalized FRETILIN, shifting it further to the left. At the second plenary session of its central committee, held in Soibada from May 15 to June 2, 1976, it adopted a Maoist strategy of a protracted people's war.[148] And, at its conference in Laline in 1977, Marxism became its official ideology.[149] This not only cast the fight against Indonesia as a war against imperialism, but also opened a new, internal, front.[150] This internal conflict between different FRETILIN factions included what Sara Niner referred to as "purging waves of massacres of nationalists."[151] One area of dispute was civilian supremacy, pitting FRETILIN's politicians against FALINTIL's military.[152] Another was allowing the people in the mountains with FRETILIN to surrender. And a third was establishing a classless society, which, as Xanana explained, required the upper classes, including the *liurai*, "to commit *suicide ideológico* (ideological suicide)" by abandoning their social status and wealth.[153] Those who objected to any of these principles were seen as reactionaries and as traitors who then became the targets of "revolutionary violence," including torture and killings. Those executed in this fratricide included FALINTIL deputy chief of staff José da Silva as well as commanders Agustinho Espirito Santo, Aquiles Freitas, and Martinho Soares.[154] Francisco Hornay and two companions were beaten to death, while Adao Amaral, Jose dos Santos, and Pedro Sanchez were tortured.[155] FRETILIN president Xavier do Amaral was arrested and his network was dismantled.[156] These internal conflicts only ended when the Indonesian military destroyed the *zonas libertadas*.[157]

The East Timor Conflict—Phase 2: Popular Resistance, 1984–1998

In the mid-1980s the East Timor conflict started to move away from being a purely military one. While periodic Indonesian operations continued along similar lines to those in the first phase and while FRETILIN continued its guerrilla war, three new elements characterized this second phase of the conflict: intermittent talks between Indonesia and Portugal under the auspices of the UN, public engagement by the East Timorese Catholic Church, and the emergence of an East Timorese civilian resistance. All three served to put and keep East Timor on the international agenda.

The first of the new elements to gain momentum was FRETILIN's diplomatic front, which was almost single-handedly run by José Ramos-Horta. Since Indonesia's invasion in 1975 he had annually sought a UN member state to sponsor a resolution on East Timor, which was designated as a "non self-governing territory" under Chapter XI of the UN Charter. In 1982, Ramos-Horta succeeded in bringing Portugal on board after years of the country's aloofness. This prompted the UN General Assembly to give the Secretary General's office the mandate to hold talks between Portugal and Indonesia on East Timor's political status. The first round of these tripartite talks was held in 1983.

The second element resulted from a shift in the position of East Timor's Catholic Church. When the Indonesians invaded, they assumed that the Timorese Catholic Church would become subsumed under the Indonesian Catholic Church. This had also been the assumption of Dili's bishop, Dom José Joaquim Ribeiro, who had been quite prepared to accept integration, as he believed it would be similar to when India took over Goa. He disliked FRETILIN, because he saw it as communist, and because it had "called for an end to the central position the Church had enjoyed under Portuguese colonialism."[158] The integration of Portuguese Timor into Indonesia, however, was nothing like that of Goa into India. In 1977, Ribeiro requested early retirement and returned to Portugal, spiritually broken from the violence he had witnessed. He was succeeded as apostolic administrator by Dom Martinho da Costa Lopes. Dom Martinho was the first to give the Church a public voice when he, on October 13, 1981, in front of twelve thousand people, condemned the atrocities perpetrated in the Lacluta massacre, in which more than five hundred Timorese were killed, including "pregnant women and children, whose heads were smashed against rocks."[159]

As Dom Martinho became increasingly outspoken and his words found their way into the international media, Indonesia pressed for his removal. In May 1983, he was replaced by the much younger Carlos Felipe Ximenes Belo, who had only recently returned from Portugal and whom the Indonesians believed they could mold. This did not, however, silence Dom Martinho, who continued to speak out from the safety of Lisbon and who travelled to the United Kingdom, Ireland, France, and the Netherlands in autumn 1983 to give accounts of the invasion, the suffering of the East Timorese people, Indonesian military operations, and how the lack of an international response showed that "the people in the west are losing their sense of sin."[160] In September 1984, he also visited the United States.

Bishop Belo followed in Dom Martinho's footsteps. By October 1983 he was condemning the "arrests and violence" after the collapse of the cease-fire.[161] This was followed in December by the Church adopting a position of "complete non-cooperation with the Indonesian military," with priests and nuns boycotting a meeting with Commander in Chief Murdani on Christmas Day in Dili.[162] Belo quickly became a powerful voice in East Timor, not least because the number of Catholics had increased fourfold since the invasion. The activism by the Church was also eased by the shift in the CRRN's ideology toward a more mainstream East Timorese nationalism, drawing upon shared history, shared languages (Tetum and Portuguese), and shared beliefs (traditional and Catholic). Reflecting Xanana's own disillusionment with what he later referred to as "political infantilism and thoughtless adventurism," he reconceptualized the ideology of the Timorese resistance as "*ukun rasik an*, self-determination," allowing the CRRN to adopt a policy of national unity in 1983 and to invite all East Timorese to join in 1984, including the Timorese Catholic Church.[163]

Bishop Belo also became a powerful voice internationally. His February 1984 letter to Dom Martinho in Lisbon, in which he recounted how the Indonesian military had "arrested people in all *postos*—600 people in Dili alone," how "others were made to disappear," how "the population is corralled," and how the Indonesians had "once more begun to mobilize the civilian population," was widely reported.[164] It even reached US secretary of state George Shultz, who then during his visit to Jakarta raised the issue of East Timor.[165] In 1985, Belo issued a statement that the "Church bears anxious witness to the facts that are slowly leading to the ethnic, cultural and religious extinction of the identity of the

People of East Timor."[166] And, in 1986, Belo led the boycott of the "Pancasila Programme for Church personnel in East Timor."[167]

By 1987, a credible civilian resistance was also in place. At the heart of this new resistance were the educated unemployed, students, and more generally East Timor's younger generation, which had grown up under Indonesian rule. They sought to draw attention to East Timor's plight through protests and demonstrations as well as by sending information to organizations such as Amnesty International and TAPOL.[168] It was this civilian resistance, often but not always directed by FRETILIN's clandestine front, that spearheaded the struggle against Indonesia during this second phase of the conflict.

The first protest took place in Dili on July 13, 1987 after Timorese pupils had received their school exam marks, which showed "that hardly any Timorese had passed while Indonesian pupils had all passed." Their anger increased further when they discovered that only "Indonesians had been accepted" to enter upper secondary school.[169] Education remained a key issue because, as activist Porfirio da Costa Oliveira explained, "We did not want the Indonesians to always look at us as poor and uneducated. We were fighting for education and we stood up against them."[170]

In 1989, Suharto opened up East Timor, as Indonesia wanted to show that the situation had normalized.[171] This provided the civilian resistance with an opportunity to hold demonstrations when international visitors were present. One of the first such visitors was Pope John Paul II in 1989. As he celebrated mass, youth activists "took off their Catholic scout uniforms, ran to the front of the altar, and began shouting, 'Long live the Pope' and 'Long live free East Timor.'"[172] Another opportunity presented itself when US ambassador John Cameron Monjo visited in January 1990. He was staying at the Hotel Turismo in Dili when some eighty to ninety students "occupied the entrance and forced Monjo to come out of the hotel." They then asked the United States to pressure Indonesia into withdrawing its troops "because we knew that if the US could give the green light for the invasion of East Timor, it could also give the red light to Indonesia's occupation."[173]

The power of global media exposure, however, was only fully realized with the Santa Cruz massacre on November 12, 1991. That fateful day had started with a memorial mass for Sebastião Gomes, a young Timorese killed by Indonesian soldiers.[174] The mass was followed by a procession to the cemetery. As Da Costa Oliviera recalled, "When we arrived at the cemetery, they massacred everybody. We were just demonstrating and they started to shoot. Everyone started to run. The first bullet that hit me was in my back and then in my leg. I fell to the ground. I saw others that had fallen but were still alive and then Indonesian soldiers killed them with knives."[175] Some 270 East Timorese were killed that day, although

Indonesia initially stated that the number of dead was a mere 19, a number later revised to 50.[176] Another 382 were wounded and a further 250 "disappeared."[177] The massacre, which echoed how Indonesia had "handled" the demonstration in Tanjung Priok in 1984, was caught on video by British filmmaker Max Stahl, whose footage severely damaged Indonesia's efforts to convince the world that most Timorese accepted integration. For the Timorese resistance it was the much-needed proof of the suffering inflicted upon the population. As Xanana explained in a radio interview in 1999, "before the massacre" they had tried "to say to the world that many, many people were killed but nobody" believed them.[178]

The Santa Cruz massacre boosted the efforts of the Diplomatic Front, as East Timor became increasingly viewed as synonymous with all that was wrong with the New Order: authoritarianism, corruption, and human rights abuses. The combination of the changes in the international environment with the end of the Cold War and the human rights abuses on the ground ensured that East Timor remained on the international agenda.

It was in this context that Ramos-Horta and Xanana in 1992 put forward a three-phased peace plan to the international community that called for "an immediate end to all armed activities in East Timor," the reduction and eventual withdrawal of Indonesian troops, the establishment of East Timorese political parties, elections for a "territorial assembly," and ultimately a UN-supervised referendum.[179] Interestingly, it was not just Jakarta that rejected this plan but also FRETILIN's external delegation, led by Mari Alkatiri in Africa and Estanislau da Silva in Australia, who believed that if East Timor was to become an autonomous region of Indonesia it would never gain independence. While this particular plan did not go anywhere, the Timorese resistance continued in its efforts to influence international opinion. Here the greatest success came in October 1996, when Belo and Ramos-Horta were jointly awarded the Nobel Peace Prize.

During this second phase of the East Timor conflict, the Indonesian security forces continued their pursuit of FALINTIL and FRETILIN, targeting high-profile commanders and leaders. In January 1992 they captured FRETILIN deputy chairman Mau Hudo, followed by the capture of resistance leader Ma' Huno in April 1993 and David Alex Dai-Tula, commander for the Baucau region, in June 1997. Their greatest success, however, was the November 1992 capture of Xanana, who had been hiding in a Dili suburb.[180]

As in the first phase, retribution played a key role in the dynamics of the violence. For instance, on August 3, 1986, "the entire population of Fo-Manu was wiped out" in response to a FALINTIL attack on an Indonesian military convoy, which had killed a whole company of soldiers, including its commander.[181] The capture and eventual killing of David Alex followed a FALINTIL grenade attack on a Brimob truck, which killed eighteen.[182] FALINTIL forces continued to target the Indonesian security forces as well as the resettlement areas, where they destroyed houses.[183] They also targeted the local government, the infrastructure, Indonesian doctors, teachers, and migrants.[184] Occasionally they staged larger operations, surrounding towns for several days, such as Soibada and Barique in December 1984, with the aim of isolating the Indonesian military there and forcing the trapped soldiers to surrender.[185]

The shift in the Timorese strategy toward civilian resistance added new, specific targets to the list of the Indonesian military. The first of these was the Timorese Catholic Church. Indeed, from the point that Dom Martinho and Bishop Belo started to speak out, the Catholic Church was seen as a problem. Consequently, the movement of priests and missionaries in East Timor was curtailed, they were harassed, and their pastoral work was "stopped."[186] Some priests such as Father Walter van Wouwe, the parish priest of Lospalos-Lautem, were beaten up by soldiers, as were teachers and students of mission schools.[187] Catholic schools were regularly searched and students interrogated.[188] Statues of saints were damaged or destroyed and churches desecrated with human excrement.[189] At the same time, Indonesia tried to get the Vatican to integrate East Timor's Catholic Church with that of Indonesia as a way to control it. In 1987, Indonesian Catholic and Protestant leaders lobbied Rome.[190] The pope's visit to East Timor was also an attempt to confer legitimacy on Indonesia's presence.

The second target was the civilian resistance, which was met with an Indonesian strategy of Timorization and militarization. More Timorese were recruited into the two territorial battalions, which according to East Timor commander Tono Suratman were about 80 percent East Timorese.[191] The security forces also embarked on further rounds of recruiting and training civilian auxiliaries. Robinson likened these new civilian auxiliaries, established in 1989 and 1990, to "death squads" as they were dressed in black, wore balaclavas, roamed the streets at night, and kidnapped as well as killed independence supporters.[192] They became the backbone of operations against the FRETILIN's Clandestine Front and the civilian resistance, tasked with infiltrating, disrupting, provoking riots, and even carrying out "mysterious executions" reminiscent of the Petrus killings in Java in the 1980s.

More civilian auxiliaries were recruited in 1993, with 3,844 East Timorese men joining the new Pasukan Adat (Customary Guardians), and in 1995 with the establishment of Garda Paksi (Youth Guard for Integration).[193] Garda Paksi was trained under Kopassus deputy head Brigadier General Prabowo Subianto and, unlike other civilian auxiliaries, offered employment opportunities through which it drew in the unemployed Timorese youth. Indeed, overtly it functioned as an employment agency. Peter Carey estimated that it had around three thousand members, with five hundred operating outside East Timor, mainly in Java and Bali, where they kept an eye on the political activities of East Timorese students.[194]

The final dynamic that characterized the second phase of the East Timor conflict was growing communal tensions between locals and migrants. On November 12, 1993, a riot in Dili was sparked by a Bugis trader stabbing a Timorese man. On January 1, 1995, a similar incident sparked a riot in Baucau, with shops in the market burned down. After these riots many Bugis left and Timorese anger shifted toward Javanese traders, resulting in further violence in July 1995.[195] The migrants also became a factor in the religious tensions that had started to emerge in the 1990s. Like Christians in Eastern Indonesia, the East Timorese worried about the openly pro-Muslim agenda of ICMI. Indeed, many Timorese, both East and West, believed that Muslim migrants were part of an Islamization strategy aimed at reducing the influence and number of Christians, particularly in Eastern Indonesia.[196] Incidents such as two Indonesian soldiers stomping on communion wafers during a mass in a village church on June 28, 1994, or the reports of Muslims insulting Catholicism that sparked riots in Dili in September 1995, confirmed Christian fears.[197] In February 1997, a year in which churches were burned in many parts of Indonesia, there were Muslim-Christian riots in Oecussi, sparked by an insult to a local priest following a Muslim *slametan* religious feast.[198] As Oecussi was an East Timorese enclave in West Timor, the riots spilled over into West Timor.[199]

Making East Timor Indonesian

The physical incorporation of the territory of Portuguese Timor by the Indonesian invasion was followed by three broad processes of "Indonesianization." The first constituted legal and political integration. The second aimed at developing East Timor economically. The third focused on "transforming" the local population into Indonesians. Legal and political integration started as soon as Dili was under Indonesian control with the installation of a provisional government headed by APODETI's Arnaldo dos Reis Araujo. At the same time Indonesia began to lobby the international community "for approval of the integration of East Timor into Indonesia," indicating that it planned "to organize a referendum a few months after order is restored" and that it hoped "to conduct the decolonization process under the auspices of the UN Security Council."[200]

The UN, however, proved reluctant, leaving Indonesia to devise its own, two-stage process for ascertaining the will of the people. The first stage saw the establishment of East Timor's people's assembly in April 1976, bringing East Timor in line with Indonesia's other provinces. This assembly, which had twenty-seven "elected" representatives from East Timor's thirteen districts as well as ten "prominent leaders" who were appointed by the provisional government, then convened for the "act of integration" on May 31.[201] Journalists had been flown in from Jakarta "to witness a short ceremony conducted in Portuguese," in which a petition "in the name of all of the people of East Timor" called on the Indonesian government to "affirm the integration of the population and territory of East Timor in the shortest time possible into the Negara Kesatuan Republik Indonesia, fully without referendum."[202] This petition was presented to Suharto by Dos Reis Araujo on June 7.

The provisional government of East Timor then invited observers to witness the second stage, the "act of self-determination," by the people's assembly.[203] A nine-member delegation of the DPR in Jakarta departed for East Timor on June 23, accompanied by some foreign dignitaries as well as foreign and Indonesian journalists.[204] The completion of this second stage paved the way for the Indonesian parliament to approve the integration of East Timor, which passed into law on July 17 as Law No. 7/1976. East Timor became Indonesia's twenty-seventh province.

Indonesia's electoral system and Indonesian national laws were then extended to East Timor, including Indonesia's family planning law, which had so angered *santri* Muslims in Java, and Law No. 5/1979 on village governance, which imposed the Javanese *desa* model across Indonesia. In addition, East Timor was opened to transmigration, a policy that sought to redistribute people from areas of high population density, particularly Java, to areas in the outer islands with smaller populations.[205] These three laws had a particularly detrimental impact as they diluted the East Timorese population and culture, thus directly playing into the conflict dynamics.

While the legal and political integration of East Timor replicated Indonesian political structures and processes, the economic integration was driven by the New Order's ideology of developmentalism. Development was seen as a sign of Indonesianness and as key to political stability in East Timor by creating loyalty to Jakarta. The "backward" territory that had been Portuguese Timor had to be developed in line with the New Order's national imaginary of Indonesia as a modern state.

Vast infrastructure projects were rolled out starting in 1980, when the Indonesian military believed East Timor to be sufficiently pacified. The extent of paved roads increased from 20 kilometers—all of them within Dili—to 2,957 kilometers by March 1984, extending across the province.[206] In 1981, Komoro Dili Airport was completed, which provided regular Garuda airlines flights to Jakarta via Kupang as well as to Surabaya.[207] The number of hospitals and clinics grew from two hospitals and 14 clinics in 1974 to ten hospitals and 197 village health centers by 1992.[208] The health infrastructure also included the building of 3,751 wells, 140 sewage systems, and 1,600 "family latrines."[209] These infrastructural achievements were accompanied by efforts to eradicate malaria and tuberculosis as well as immunization, family planning, and family nutrition programs.[210] The number of schools increased from 47 primary schools, two middle schools, and one high school in 1975, to 579 primary schools, 90 middle schools, 39 high schools, and three colleges by 1992.[211]

In urban areas low-cost housing complexes were built.[212] Modern resettlement villages were constructed in "newly opened locations" that were close to paved roads and boasted modern amenities: health centers, schools, fresh water, and a sewage system.[213] It is here where the Indonesian government hoped that the East Timorese "would gradually lose their old way of living," casting off their "primitive" culture and becoming Indonesian.[214] In rural areas agricultural intensification projects were introduced, irrigation systems were built, and skill training was organized to move East Timor away from shifting cultivation.[215]

By 1999 Jakarta had spent more than "100 times the average yearly expenditure for East Timor in the final period of Portuguese rule."[216] Indonesia's per capita expenditure on East Timor exceeded that for Irian Jaya.[217] More money was spent on East Timor than on West Timor, and, according to former BAKIN head Z. A. Maulani, East Timor received "29 times more money and subsidies than any other province in Indonesia."[218]

The third process of Indonesianization was social-cultural, aimed at turning the East Timorese into Indonesians. Central to this was education, which served not only to lower illiteracy levels, which had stood at 93 percent in 1974, but also to teach Indonesian values. These were delivered through teaching the Indonesian language, Indonesian history, Pancasila moral education, and citizenship. As in schools across Indonesia, flag-raising ceremonies were held regularly and patriotic songs were the order of the day. Textbooks taught Timorese history only up to 1976 and they taught that the East Timorese had requested the integration into Indonesia.[219]

The teaching of Indonesian values was reinforced by extracurricular activities, in particular the Indonesian scout movement Pramuka.[220] In 1984, there were 10,341 registered scouts in East Timor.[221] They participated in national scouting events and were actively involved in the celebration of national holidays such as Indonesian Independence Day and Integration Day.[222] Sports also served to bring the East Timorese into the Indonesian fold as East Timorese football teams played other Indonesian teams, in both home and away games.

At the tertiary level, East Timorese youths were sent to study at universities in places such as Jakarta, Bandung, Sukabumi, Malang, Yogyakarta, Manado, Ujungpandang, Palankaraya, Banjarmasin, and Samarinda.[223] Indeed, in 1989, some 1,500 East Timorese received university scholarships for such study.[224] The scholarships were embraced by the East Timorese who "found the educational opportunities offered by the Indonesians deeply desirable."[225]

At the extreme end of making the next generation Indonesian was the wholesale removal of East Timorese children to Java or Sulawesi. According to the United Nations High Commissioner for Refugees (UNHCR) 4,534 children were removed from East Timor between 1975 and 1999, with almost half of those taken by soldiers in the early years of the conflict to "to civilize and educate them in Indonesia."[226] The first official transfer of East Timorese children took place in October 1976 and was organized by one of the president's foundations. During the 1980s and 1990s, Indonesian Muslim organizations such as DDII, Hidayatullah, and Yakin also took some 1,000 East Timorese children, sent them to *pesantren* in Java and Sulawesi, and converted them to Islam, although this was discouraged by the government.[227]

While education aimed at turning Timorese children into Indonesians, transmigrants increased the overall Indonesianness of the population. Between 1980 and 1985, 13,092 transmigrants from Java, Bali, and Flores settled in East Timor. By 1990, this figure had almost doubled to 26,255.[228] The real number of outsiders, however, was far greater. Spontaneous migrants from Sulawesi followed in search of opportunities to set up small businesses in trade and transport. R. E. Elson estimated that by the early 1990s some 70,000 migrants had settled in East Timor and that by 1999 this number had swollen to 150,000.[229] On top of these were the families of soldiers, teachers, and civil servants. Together, these migrants diluted the "Timoreseness" of the population.

Jakarta's efforts to make East Timor Indonesian only had limited success, as Indonesia never managed to win the hearts and minds of the East Timorese, nor did it succeed in instilling a sense of loyalty or indeed of belonging. East Timor veteran Lieutenant General Kiki Syahnakri believed that "the East Timorese were disappointed with integration because of the corruption."[230] He asserted that "more than 50 percent of our money sent to East Timor did not get to the people."[231] Similarly, J. Kristiadi, MPR delegate for East Timor from 1987 to 1992, explained that "corruption was in the system on the civilian side and the military side. The money sent to East Timor went back to Jakarta."[232] As a result, "the central government" was only able to "get the land but not the people."[233]

For the East Timorese corruption was only one of many issues. The East Timorese never saw "development" as anything other than part of the occupation. Roads were built to make East Timor accessible to the army. Modern village settlements were designed for surveillance and control of the population. These settlements also cut the East Timorese off from their ancestral lands. The Indonesian health care programs, too, were seen as little more than an alternative way to control and reduce the population, as contraceptives were being promoted and rumors of women being sterilized without their knowledge were rife.[234] The vaccination programs were believed to be responsible for "children becoming deformed," and "fears of being poisoned" prevailed.[235]

Schools were seen as places of indoctrination that "wiped out Timorese identity," staffed with teachers from Java and Sulawesi who were "not the most qualified."[236] Often there was "no budget for the education programs they advertised," and to be eligible for scholarships students and families had to demonstrate their support for integration.[237] The Indonesian national curriculum had little impact or the "wrong" impact. As Da Costa Oliveira explained, "they taught us how wonderful Indonesia is and they tried to make us believe it. But after school all we ever talked about was fighting for our rights."[238] Others clearly saw the parallels between the Indonesian revolution and their own independence struggle.[239]

Integrating the youth through scouting and sport activities did not measure great successes either. Constancio Pinto, who was chosen from his school to go on a youth trip to Jakarta in 1985, recalled that it made him "feel more East Timorese." "It was as if the Indonesians were asking me, are you happy after I destroyed your home and stole your belongings? Now I'll take you to my house and show you all the marvellous things I have."[240] Children taken to Java or Sulawesi to be educated faced discrimination as they were stereotyped as "uncivilized and disruptive," especially when compared "with the submissive, obedient behavior expected of Javanese children."[241]

As more and more young adults graduated from school, a new problem arose, that of "educated unemployment," as East Timorese graduates lost out on jobs to the migrants.[242] Their presence quickly began to cause resentment among the locals as they started to dominate many sectors of the economy.[243] The Makassar and Bugis were particularly disliked as they were seen as aggressive.[244] The migrants were also seen as agents of de-Timorization "through the eradication of indigenous culture, language and religion," finishing the process started with Law No. 5/1979, which "broke the cultural structure."[245] East Timor's people's assembly was powerless to push back against national legislation. Nor was it able to stop the continued harassment of the population and human rights abuses by the security forces.[246] This is exemplified by the extraordinary report sent to President Suharto in June 1981, which raised the issue of behavior "that can only be described as being the behavior of conquerors towards a conquered people" in its lack of respect for local culture as well as "torture, maltreatment, murder and other unimaginable cases."[247] In light of this behavior no amount of development money could make the East Timorese feel that they belonged.

The Timorese Resistance: Narratives and National Imaginary

Indonesia's efforts to make East Timor Indonesian also ran up against the fact that the Timorese resistance never stopped advancing its own national imaginary. This national imaginary was both discursive and constructed. It reflected that the idea of an East Timorese nation and state, as opposed to identity, were relatively new. And it reflected the evolution of the ideological changes of the Timorese resistance. It was initially constructed against the Portuguese "other," whose colonialism FRETILIN's manifesto denounced as "oppressive and violating the most basic rights of the human being," stating that "it is urgent to awake the consciousness of the nation."[248] When FRETILIN was formed in September 1974, its president, Xavier do Amaral, described it as "the interpreter of the profound ideals of the people of all East Timor" and the "incarnation of the most profound aspirations of the people," making it "the only legitimate representative of the people."[249] It reiterated the aims stated earlier by the ASDT as the "total abolition of colonialism" and the "repudiation of neo-colonialism."[250] To this it added achieving Timorese independence from Portugal in the shortest possible time frame through a revolution that would also "erase the old social order" in order to replace it with "a new social structure without repression" and without the feudalism of the *liurai*.[251]

The state the ASDT envisaged in 1974 right after the Carnation Revolution was a social-democratic East Timor, as social democracy "stood for social justice, equitable distribution of the wealth of the country, a mixed economy and a democratic political system."[252] FRETILIN shifted this imaginary toward the left. Its political program spoke of the "creation of new political, economic, and social structures which will serve the interests of the people of East Timor."[253] These included the establishment of "cooperatives of production, distribution and consumption," agrarian reform with the expropriation of "all large farms," "the elimination of the colonialist education system," the introduction of an extensive rural literacy program, free health care, and the "abolition of the colonial administrative structure."[254] The booklet FRETILIN devised for its literacy program attacked "the greed of the colonists, economic exploitation under the Portuguese, the collaboration of feudal chiefs in exploiting the people and the methods of the colonial teaching system."[255] It thus not only served as a means to teach people how to read but also inculcated them with FRETILIN's ideology and nationalism.

To awaken the consciousness of the nation FRETILIN used the term "Maubere," a term previously used by the Portuguese for the "backward natives."[256]

As Ramos-Horta explained, "I began to concoct our own version of social democracy by coining the word Mauberism—from Maubere, a common name among the Mambai people that had become a derogatory expression meaning poor, ignorant.... Maubere became the symbol of a cultural identity, of pride, of belonging."[257] FRETILIN also tried to develop a national consciousness through the "cultural exchange" of local traditions such as songs and dances from one part of East Timor to another as well as using Tetum as a lingua franca.[258] Traditional East Timorese culture was affirmed, but some traditions, such as polygamy and the bride price, were also challenged, most notably by FRETILIN's women's organization, the Organizacão Popular da Mulher Timor (OMPT).[259]

The outlines of FRETILIN's national imaginary became clearer during its de facto governance in East Timor from September to December 1975. During this period, it established a protogovernance structure in the form of commissions for justice, agriculture, education, and health, among others. These commissions were "run collectively by army personnel, central committee members and professional advisers."[260] FRETILIN also emphasized the collective in its organization of society and the economy, setting up cooperatives and forming unions. It even had revolutionary brigades who lived "permanently in the villages in which they were implementing their literacy and health campaigns."[261]

When FRETILIN declared independence on November 28, 1975, the new Democratic Republic of East Timor was established as a democracy and as a republic that was, as expressed in its national anthem "Patria"—(Fatherland), anticolonialist, anti-imperialist, and revolutionary.[262] The republic was based on universal suffrage and equality of all citizens before the law.[263] The state was also a secular one as FRETILIN had "called for an end to the central position the Church had enjoyed under Portuguese colonialism."[264] Instead, "all citizens will have free choice of religion. Native religious houses, churches, mosques, and temples will be protected."[265] FRETILIN also envisaged the Democratic Republic of East Timor as nonaligned and on friendly terms with "the countries of the geographic area" but, above all, as part of the Lusophone world seeking "closer international co-operation with Portugal, Brazil, [and] Guinea-Bissau."[266]

These ideas were symbolized by the Timorese Republic's flag, which represented independence from Portugal and East Timorese self-determination as well as "ideas of a 'nation' and its history." As Catherine Arthur explained, "Red, which is the most dominant color, symbolizes the fight for national independence and freedom (*funu*); the yellow triangle symbolizes the remaining influences of colonialism; the black triangle represents the obscurantism left by colonialism that must be overcome; and the five-pointed white star represents the peace which has been desired for so long."[267] The East Timorese flag's resemblance to the FRETILIN flag, designed a year earlier in 1974, not only reflected their shared origin but also signaled that the national flag represented the culmination of FRETILIN's struggle for independence. Thus, when Indonesia invaded only days after the Democratic Republic of East Timor was declared, it was natural to revert to the FRETILIN flag and fight for renewed independence under its banner. The FRETILIN flag itself also bore similarities with those of other leftist revolutionary movements in former Portuguese colonies, most notably those in Angola and Mozambique, affirming its place in the anti- and postcolonial Lusophone world.[268]

When Indonesia invaded, East Timorese nationalism and the national imaginary also became constructed against the Indonesian "other." Here the narrative emphasized that the island of Timor, before the arrival of the Portuguese and Dutch, had been "a political entity in itself, largely untouched by the Hindu, Buddhist and Moslem empires that flourished in the region between the 7th and 13th centuries," thus rejecting Indonesian claims that it had been part of the Srivijaja and Majapahit empires.[269] Indeed, East Timor had "nothing, absolutely nothing, to do with the government of Indonesia, not in any political, economic, religious, cultural or ethnic aspect."[270] This narrative also rejected Indonesian claims that FRETILIN was communist and that Portuguese Timor had remained unstable after the civil war. Ramos-Horta branded both of these claims "an outright fabrication of Indonesia's propaganda machine."[271] He took particular issue with the invitation that the Indonesian government claimed to have received, stating that "the 'invitation' issued by the 'four political parties' was obtained under duress."[272] Moreover, of the four, only the UDT, which FRETILIN regarded as "white men with black faces," and whose leaders were virtual prisoners in West Timor, held any political influence.[273] APODETI was the object of particular contempt. Xanana in his autobiography referred to its members as "frustrated racist individuals," while Ramos-Horta described APODETI as a party that had "brought together a 'who's who' of corrupt incompetents and marginals," headed by "the only Timorese to be given a sentence for war crimes."[274]

The Timorese narrative advanced a range of views on Indonesia, the Indonesian military, the Indonesian government, and the Indonesian people. Here the voices outside and inside East Timor differed somewhat. Ramos-Horta, narrating the conflict from outside East Timor after December 1975, described Indonesia as a state based on "artificial 'unity in diversity,'" run by a regime that "is brutal, arrogant and militaristic."[275] He saw Indonesia as expansionist, with West New Guinea as "the first act of flagrant land-grabbing carried out by the Indonesian generals," and maintained that Indonesia was determined to annex East Timor "regardless of the wishes of the people, trampling upon their fundamental rights to self-determination and liberty."[276] Indonesian statements to the contrary in the run-up to the invasion only showed that "the word of an Indonesian official, civilian, or military, is meaningless."[277]

Narrating the conflict from inside East Timor, Xanana, FALINTIL guerrillas, and Timorese civilians referred to the Indonesian government as "the carnivorous Suharto and his corrupt generals," and the Indonesian military as "Javanese soldiers," "Jakarta's criminal soldiers," "barbarous occupiers," and "imperialist aggressors" who were at the same time arrogant, shameful, cowardly, and impotent.[278] Indonesia's special forces were singled out as "nanggala knife-killers," as many special forces units and operations were code-named Nanggala, and "red beret assassins."[279] The invasion and occupation were also often labeled "Javanese colonial expansionism."[280] This is not all that surprising. For one, most of the soldiers were indeed Javanese. More important, however, what both the Indonesian military and Indonesian government officials were projecting was a Java-centric Indonesian national imaginary and culture. Interestingly, both the "inside" and "outside" Timorese narratives made it clear that their fight was only with the Indonesian regime as "we know the Indonesian people are also suffering," showing awareness of political dynamics in Indonesia and reflecting also the experiences of East Timorese students at universities across Indonesia.[281]

The narrative of the Timorese resistance on the conflict and violence from the invasion in 1975 until the referendum in 1999 contrasted the rightful East Timorese claim to the land against Indonesia's illegal occupation, the abidance of FRETILIN by the Geneva Conventions against the brutality of the Indonesian military, and the heroic Maubere people against the cowardly Indonesians.[282] Xanana later also compared the Indonesian invasion of East Timor to the Iraqi invasion of Kuwait, the Russian invasion of Afghanistan, and the Vietnamese invasion of Cambodia.[283]

Indonesia's actions in East Timor and policies toward the East Timorese were likened to genocide.[284] Here Ramos-Horta pointed to the deaths of one to two hundred thousand Timorese, the "intent to decimate the indigenous population," the "forced removal of people from their ancestral lands," the "so-called 'resettlement camps' without medical care, sanitation or land for cultivation," the forced sterilization of women and men, arbitrary arrests, and the use of napalm.[285] Similarly, Xanana stated that "East Timor has been devastated by the horror of a genocidal war, sustained by the bloodthirsty clique of Suharto."[286] The act of integration in 1976 was labeled a "fantasy act," and Indonesian development was described as the "great Indonesian farce."[287]

The Timorese resistance narrative takes an interesting stance on the international community, which it needed but whose inaction it deplored. Ramos-Horta accused the Portuguese of having neglected Timor for centuries and having treated it as a "dumping ground for political dissidents, failed professionals and incompetent bureaucrats," only to abandon the territory "with neither honor nor dignity . . . to the mercy of a ruthless neighbor."[288] Particular contempt was reserved for Australia and the United States. Australian prime minister Gough Whitlam was seen as having "befriended the regional strongman," while the United States was charged with actively supporting "the mass murder of the Timorese women, men, and children," and the governments "of Australia, New Zealand and Japan and other capitalist countries" were seen "as accomplices in the extermination of the Maubere people."[289] In FRETILIN's radical years, the West was denounced as imperialist, Indonesia was considered the accomplice of the world imperialist powers, and the conflict in East Timor was seen as a war promoting imperialist interests.[290]

Over the twenty-four years of Indonesian occupation, the Timorese national imaginary shifted in line with the ideological evolution of the resistance. In the early years FRETILIN's national imaginary maintained its Marxist overtones, and during the first three years after the Indonesian invasion, FRETILIN was able to maintain some of the governance structures of the Democratic Republic of East Timor in its *bases de apoio*. There it had set up administrative divisions and "there were hospitals, schools, markets, and enough food was grown."[291] FRETILIN also "retained its essential participatory democratic features," holding regular meetings on topics ranging from the everyday issues of living in the bases to the struggle for independence.[292] In addition, it had a functioning justice system that included "corrective justice" for minor offenses such as theft and "popular justice" for major offenses such as treason. The former required a process of self-criticism, a light punishment, and forgiveness, while the latter required a public trial followed by punishments ranging from having to undergo "rehabilitation" to the death penalty.[293]

After the Timorese resistance shifted to a more mainstream nationalist ideology in the mid-1980s, the Timorese national imaginary reflected these changes in its commitment to political pluralism, a mixed economy, and nonalignment.[294] And, as an independent East Timor became a real possibility, Xanana articulated the quest to "construct a new nation, where we will secure respect for human rights, promote equality of rights and opportunities for all components of the Timorese society and defend the Timorese culture and identity."[295] The East Timor he envisaged was a state "that fights for peace, democracy and prosperity for all, regardless of political or religious convictions, race, color or social and cultural origins," a state that "will respect the universal principles relating to human rights, gender equality, freedom of speech and information and of assembly as they are defined in international conventions and treaties," and a state that would have a "market economy with selective intervention of the state to ensure equity, transparency and efficiency."²⁹⁶ Situated "between Asia and Oceania" it would seek membership of ASEAN (Association of Southeast Asian Nations), the South Pacific Forum, the UN, and APEC (Asia-Pacific Economic Cooperation) as well as solidarity with Portugal.²⁹⁷ It would also remain part of the Portuguese commonwealth and the Lusophone world.

B. J. Habibie, the 1999 Referendum, and Postreferendum Violence

The fall of Suharto on May 21, 1998, had an almost immediate impact on the conflict in East Timor. Less than a month later, on June 9, Suharto's successor, B. J. Habibie, announced to the foreign press that he was willing to consider giving East Timor wide-ranging autonomy.²⁹⁸ This was followed on June 18 by Foreign Minister Ali Alatas presenting new autonomy proposals to Portugal. And on June 24, Habibie met with Bishop Belo in his office in the pursuit of open dialogue, asking him what he could do "to fulfill the expectations of the East Timorese."²⁹⁹ In his memoirs, Habibie later stated that this discussion reinforced his "decision to resolve the East Timor problem as quickly as possible, so that it would no longer burden the reform process."³⁰⁰

On January 27, 1999, he took everyone by surprise when he announced that a popular consultation would be held in East Timor later that year in which the East Timorese would be asked to choose between autonomy and independence. Faced with the prospects of lengthy economic recovery after the Asian monetary crisis, the Indonesian government had little enthusiasm for spending money on a province that had undermined the country's international standing. As Habibie confidant Z. A. Maulani explained, "If we could get rid of East Timor those billions of rupiah could go into development. And we would also be free from international humiliation."³⁰¹ Habibie, in his memoirs, also emphasized the urgency he felt to resolve the "East Timor problem" before the next elections so that "the next president and vice president would be free of this problem and could put all their energy into the reform process and concentrate on its political and economic challenges."³⁰²

Habibie's decision to let East Timor go was framed by his conception of what constituted Indonesia and, above all, his vision of a reformed Indonesia. The former saw Habibie reverting to Indonesia's smallest geo-body, that of the Netherlands Indies, seeing the shared colonial experience as the defining criterion for Indonesia's boundaries.³⁰³ The latter saw him advance an Indonesian national imaginary that had at its heart "an independent, free, cultured, democratic system of government," in accordance with "the spirit of the 1945 constitution" while embracing modern technology.[304] It was a decentralized Indonesia, home to "a new Indonesian society" that was based on "openness and respect for human rights," led by a government "that is clean and works responsibly."[305] It would have "centers of excellence" for the oil and gas industry.[306] A restive East Timor was an obstacle to this vision.

Support for "letting East Timor go" also came from the Muslim intellectuals of ICMI, who had been actively advocating a more Islamic Indonesian imaginary since 1991. Here the overwhelmingly Catholic province was seen as an impediment to the promotion of Muslims into leading positions across Indonesian society, especially in Eastern Indonesia. Already in 1996, ICMI's think tank produced an internal paper arguing for East Timor to be set free, as there was "little point in Indonesia's reputation continuing to be harmed by clinging to a Catholic province."[307] Indeed, many ICMI members saw East Timor as "full of ungrateful Catholics who wanted to live off Jakarta," and they resented the fact that Indonesia, which was the largest Muslim country in the world, had become the target of international criticism because of its East Timor policies.[308] To them this constituted an indirect attack on Islam.[309]

Habibie's decision was also influenced by Australian prime minister John Howard's letter of December 19, 1998, which praised Habibie's decision to offer East Timor autonomy as a "bold and clear-sighted step" and then proceeded to suggest a deferred referendum along the lines of the Matignon Accords in New Caledonia, stating that "the successful implementation of an autonomy package with a built-in review mechanism would allow time to convince the East Timorese of the benefits of autonomy within the Indonesian Republic."[310]

This letter, according to Habibie's aide Dewi Fortuna Anwar, "made Habibie mad. He saw it as presumptuous of Australia to tell Indonesia what to do. And he did not like to be compared to France which had been a colonial power. Indonesia was not a colonizer."[311] Habibie later jotted some notes in the margins of the Howard letter and gave copies of it to his ministers and the military. In these notes he asked "whether it would not be fair and democratic after 24 years of the East Timorese not feeling Indonesian to allow them to part peacefully."[312] He then consulted a small circle, including Defense Minister Wiranto and retired general Sintong Panjaitan.[313] This was followed by a political and security affairs meeting on January 25 and a full cabinet meeting on January 27, 1999, at which Coordinating Minister for Security and Political Affairs Feisal Tanjung introduced the topic. As Anwar recalled, "Feisal reported the results of the ministerial meeting a couple of days before, saying that they had agreed that if East Timor did not want to be part of Indonesia it should be allowed to depart peacefully. Then [Foreign Minister] Ali Alatas made a presentation and supported the president's suggestion. Then Wiranto also agreed with the president to support the idea but with the caveat that the integration of East Timor in 1975 should not be regarded as a mistake because of the tremendous sacrifices by the soldiers."[314] Habibie concluded the meeting saying that "if everyone agreed they should give East Timor two options—autonomy and if autonomy was rejected independence."[315]

Wiranto's lack of opposition retrospectively confounded many in the international community who witnessed the violence surrounding the popular consultation, a violence that clearly reflected the New Order's national imaginary and went against Habibie's. The head of the United Nations Mission in East Timor (UNAMET), Ian Martin, in his memoirs attributed Wiranto's as well as Feisal Tanjung's silence to them "not [being] among the generals who had the greatest stake in ET."[316] However, according to East Timor veteran Luhut Panjaitan, Wiranto had not objected because he genuinely believed that 70 percent of the vote would be cast in favor of autonomy.[317] Indeed, Wiranto's update on the situation in East Timor, which he sent to Feisal Tanjung in June 1999, certainly asserted that the "'silent majority'... supports the pro-integration group."[318] Similarly, Indonesian intelligence estimated that between 55 and 60 percent of East Timorese would vote for integration.[319] And, lastly, it is worth noting that Feisal Tanjung had prior referendum experience, having been involved in the 1969 "Act of Free Choice" in Irian Jaya, and he believed that the East Timor popular consultation could be similarly finessed under UN auspices.

While the new Indonesian government under Habibie grappled with the East Timor issue in Jakarta, the situation on the ground was deteriorating rapidly. According to East Timor military commander Colonel Tono Suratman, after the fall of Suharto proindependence organizations mushroomed overnight "to launch a systematic assault on pro-integration politics."[320] FALINTIL commander Taur Matan Ruak announced that some six hundred new recruits had joined, and FALINTIL was thus able to renew its armed resistance.[321] One of the first incidents was an ambush on three soldiers and a civilian engineer who were surveying a farming plot for transmigration on 28/29 October in the area of Weberek in Alas Subdistrict.[322] According to Lela Madjiah, they were suspected of being spies, and were apprehended, tied up, and taken away by FALINTIL. The bodies of three of them were later found near Weberek River. The fourth, Private Siswanto, "managed to escape and reach a military post in Alas, however he later died from his severe wounds."[323] Attacks continued throughout November and into December when two FALINTIL gunmen charged into a primary school classroom in Viqueque District and shot the fifty-six-year-old teacher Francisco Amaral in front of his class.[324] The renewed military campaign targeted the Indonesian security forces, their local allies, the Indonesian infrastructure, and migrants. After Habibie's announcement that there would be a

TABLE 2. Civilian auxiliaries in East Timor, 1999

NAME	LEADER	AREA OF OPERATIONS
Tim Saka	Juanico da Costa	Baucau
Tim Sera	Augustinho Boavide Ximenes "Sera Malik"	Baucau Manatuto
Tim Alfa	Joni Marques	Lautem Los Palos
Tim Makikit	Afonso Enriques Pinto	Viqueque
Halilintar	Joao da Silva Tavares	Bobonaro Maliana
Garda Paksi	Abilio Jose Osores Soares Marcal d'Almeida	Liquica
Tim Sakunar	Simao Lopes	Ambeno
Aitarak	Eurico Guterres	Dili
Pejuang 59–75	Martinho Fernandes	Viqueque
Jati Merah Putih	João Belo Edmundo da Conceicão Silva	Lautem Los Palos
Ahi	Horacio	Aileu
MAHIDI	Cancio Lopes de Carvalho	Ainaro Suai
PPPI (Peace Force and Defender of Integration)	Tomas Gonçalves	Dili
Ablai	Nazario Vital Cortereal	Same Manufahi
Laksaur Merah Putih	Olivio Mendoza Moruk	Suai
Dadurus Merah Putih	Natalino Monteiro	Bobonaro
Darah Integrasi	Lafaek Saburai	Gleno Ermera
Naga Merah	Paulo da Costa Suarez	Ermera
Besi Merah Putih	Manuel de Sousa	Liquica
Kaer Matin Merah Putih	João Franca da Silva	Bobonaro
Mahadomi	Vital Doutel Sarmento Aquino Caldas	Manatuto

referendum on independence, these attacks, according to Robinson, became part of a concerted strategy of displacement.[325] By early August some seventy thousand bureaucrats had left, as had non-East Timorese staff in schools, medical facilities, and small businesses.[326]

In December 1998, the Indonesian Army embarked upon yet another round of recruiting civilian auxiliaries. In February 1999, both new and old auxiliaries (see table 2) were placed under the umbrella of the Pro-Integration Forces (Pasukan Pro-Integrasi, PPI) led by Joao da Silva Tavares. In August, the month of the popular consultation, Indonesian military documents showed that there were around 1,100 armed prointegration forces with 546 weapons and a total of 11,950 supporters.[327]

Their initial aim was to fortify the lines of defense against the resurgent Timorese resistance.[328] With Habibie's announcement of the referendum, however, the civilian auxiliaries became the Indonesian military's primary instrument in a strategy aimed at ensuring a pro-autonomy anti-independence vote. Their role was to prevent the effectiveness of the proindependence campaign, "to bottle up" foreign media and UN staff "to stop them from collecting evidence on the operation to subvert the referendum," and to provide plausible deniability for the military.[329] They also waged a campaign of intimidation against the Timorese population. Bishop Belo recounted that villagers were told that "to vote for independence is a sin" while Father Albrecht explained that militias in the western part of East Timor had terrorized whole villages into fleeing.[330] "The militias then burned down their houses and the refugees were persecuted."[331]

As the campaign progressed toward the referendum date, auxiliaries openly operated side by side with the Indonesian military. Indeed, in Maliana, Halilintar openly operated out of the local TNI headquarters.[332] Between February and September the various auxiliaries issued death threats to Australian journalists, burned down houses, and attacked the CNRT, proindependence activists, and students.[333] This included the shooting and hacking to death of fifty-seven people in Liquica Church in April, as well as the attack in the same month on Manuel Carrascalão's house where twelve were killed, including Carrascalão's teenage son.[334] The latter was the direct result of Aitarak commander Eurico Guterres's order to "all prointegration militias to conduct a cleansing of all those who betrayed integration."[335] At another prointegration rally on August 26, Guterres prophetically declared that Dili would be turned into a "sea of fire" should the referendum results favor independence.

When UN secretary-general Kofi Annan on September 3 announced that 21.5 percent had voted in favor and 78.5 percent against the proposed special autonomy status, Aitarak members in their black T-shirts and brandishing automatic firearms started cruising the streets of Dili targeting foreigners. Journalists were attacked and beaten up, *Financial Times* correspondent Dutch journalist Sander Thoenes was killed, and most of the media was driven out of East Timor.

UNAMET staff, too, were targeted, their offices and houses burned. In Maliana, "two UNAMET local staff were killed."[336] The UNAMET compound in Liquica was assaulted and the convoy of fleeing staff came "under heavy fire from automatic and homemade weapons, fired by militia, police, and at least one TNI soldier."[337] UNAMET was also forced to withdraw from Suai and Manatuto on September 5, from Ermera and Viqueque on September 6, and from Baucau, Lospalos, and Oecussi on September 7. In Baucau, staff lay on the floor for two hours as Indonesian police fired automatic weapons into the UNAMET office at chest height, before the TNI commander came to escort them to the airport.[338] After that UNAMET was effectively restricted to its compound in Dili.

The third target was the Timorese Catholic Church: priests, nuns, buildings. On September 5 the office of the Catholic diocese in Dili was attacked and set on fire. The next day, on September 6, Indonesian soldiers and auxiliaries surrounded Bishop Belo's compound, evacuated the bishop, and then Indonesian officers gave the order for and directed the attack.[339] The residence was burned down and 18 of the 5,000 Timorese who had sought refuge there were killed.[340] The rest were forcibly evacuated to the police station and from there to West Timor.[341] On the same day the compound of Our Lady of Fatima Church in Suai was attacked by Laksaur Merah Putih (LMP). More than one hundred people were killed, including Father Dewanto Tarcisius, who tried to negotiate with the LMP but was cut down by machete blows. Father Fransisco Soares met a similar fate.[342] The prointegrationists then entered the church, which was packed with women and children, "firing indiscriminately with automatic weapons."[343] There they killed Father Hilario as well as two nuns. Then, according to Sister Mary Barudero, who witnessed the massacre from the window of a house nearby, they threw three grenades and when they left, "blood was spattered everywhere."[344] Another witness explained that "the militia used machetes" and that people running out of the church were hacked to death.[345] While the LMP was on the front line, the attack on the church had been led by Suai military commander Lieutenant Sugito.[346] A Christian policeman in West Timor later testified that he and some colleagues had caught Sugito burying twenty-six bodies near Belu village in West Timor.[347] When the bodies were later exhumed they included "3 priests, 12 males, 8 females, and 3 bodies of undetermined sex. One was a child, two in their teens, six in their teens to mid-20s, twelve middle-aged and two elderly."[348]

Two days after the Suai massacre, on September 8, news was received by Sister Gabriela, head of the Canossian convent in Jakarta, that four nuns had been killed in Baucau. On September 9 it was reported that the head of Caritas in Dili, Father Francisco Barreto, was killed.[349] On September 11, German Jesuit Priest Father Albrecht was shot. And on September 25, nine nuns and priests were killed in Lospalos.[350]

The Indonesian military's narrative on the postreferendum violence portrayed it as spontaneous and as carried out by the pro-integration supporters with possibly some rogue TNI elements, most of whom were of East Timorese origin. Armed Forces Commander Wiranto asserted that "the violence was an emotional outburst neither premeditated nor controllable."[351] He blamed the inability of the security forces to stop the violence on "psychological obstacles" that made it difficult for Indonesian soldiers and police to confront the "very people who had supported them in East Timor."³⁵² He denied having given any orders to destroy the infrastructure and even claimed that when the prointegration forces indicated that that would be their response if the vote favored independence, he ordered them not to.³⁵³ He further maintained that he went to East Timor on September 5 exactly because his orders were being ignored. He tried to stop the violence but was not able to, which is why he asked for the imposition of martial law.³⁵⁴

Yet the violence was clearly not random. The targeting of the foreign journalists, UNAMET, and the Church reflected how they were perceived by the Indonesian military, the first two as "lacking objectivity" and neutrality, and the third as a long-term supporter of independence.³⁵⁵ They were also in line with the targets listed in a TNI document dated August 1999 discussing contingency plans should the referendum fail.³⁵⁶ Moreover, they were seen as obstacles to the Indonesian military's displacement strategy. They thus needed to be removed and witnesses and their buildings needed to be destroyed, as they provided refuge to the civilian population. British UN ambassador Sir Jeremy Greenstock noted, the "massive forced relocation" of the population had been designed to give the impression of widespread dissatisfaction with the referendum as well as bringing large numbers of people under Indonesian control.³⁵⁷

According to Robinson, around 400,000 people, half of East Timor's population, was forced to flee their homes.³⁵⁸ Some 280,000 of these were moved to West Timor while thousands of others fled to the mountains.³⁵⁹ This displacement strategy also raised the prospects of partitioning East Timor, with the westernmost districts opting out of independence and remaining within Indonesia. Indeed, already in August Aitarak commander Guterres explained how "autonomy was the compromise between integration and independence" and if the vote was cast for independence "but was not 100 percent in favor then the territory had to be partitioned in accordance with the results."³⁶⁰

Also strategically framed was the widespread destruction of property in East Timor. On the night of September 7, as Madjiah recounted in her book, Dili "became a *lautan api* (sea of fire) as almost all of the provincial capital was burned."³⁶¹ This, too, had been discussed as one of the possible scenarios in that August 1999 TNI document, referring to *bumi hangus* (scorched earth actions) against vital installations and public facilities.³⁶² *Bumi hangus* and *lautan api* were also deeply ingrained in TNI culture and doctrine, invoking the Indonesian nationalists' setting fire to Bandung in March 1946 in order to deny the Dutch the city.³⁶³ This was later formalized as military doctrine by General Sudirman in Decree No. 1 of June 12, 1948, advocating the destruction of property and removing all items of value and evacuating the population.³⁶⁴

Moreover, the destruction of parts of East Timor after the referendum constituted a form of "de-Indonesianization." It was the development and the new infrastructure that had been central to making the territory Indonesian. The destruction of the infrastructure, government buildings, and houses was a way to reverse the integration process, to return East Timor to the "primitive" state in which the Indonesians had found it, and to punish the people for rejecting Indonesia.

Reflecting on the East Timor Conflict, Violence, and the National Imaginary

The Indonesian national imaginary played a key role in the East Timor conflict. Its larger geo-body, as projected through its archipelagic conception, paved the way for Portuguese Timor's geographic incorporation; the New Order's G30S/PKI foundational narrative and its core identity as a bastion against communism made the invasion of East Timor in December 1975 ideologically and strategically imperative. The decision after the fall of Suharto to allow for a referendum on independence, too, was underwritten by how Indonesia was conceptualized. As Habibie reimagined Indonesia as a democracy, East Timor came to be seen as a stumbling block.

The New Order's national imaginary framed the violence by the Indonesian military, determining who was targeted while drawing upon both national and international strategies as exemplified by the "Darul Islam playbook" of encirclement, *pagar betis*, and killing fields, and the "Vietnam playbook" of OV Broncos, exfoliating agents, and strategic hamletting. The New Order's national imaginary also framed Indonesia's efforts to "make" the Timorese Indonesian, transforming them from "primitive" to "developed," from illiterate to educated.

Despite being framed by the same national imaginary, Indonesia's military and civilian strategies were fundamentally contradictory, which is why the integration of East Timor ultimately failed. While the military operations succeeded in incorporating East Timor territorially into the Indonesian geo-body, the violence made it impossible for the East Timorese to feel any sense of belonging to Indonesia. This was further exacerbated by the displacement from ancestral lands as the East Timorese were corralled into strategic resettlement areas. Development was also not unproblematic. It destroyed local culture, created new inequalities, and was riddled with corruption. Thus, over the twenty-four years of Indonesian control the Timorese resistance grew, disparate East Timorese identities fused, and East Timorese nationalism matured.

Yet, most Indonesians, in and out of government, did not expect a proindependence vote. Many blamed the West for their loss of East Timor, pointing to "Australian oil interests" and asserting that "the referendum was rigged."[365] They saw Indonesia as the victim of international interests, a country that had been "the darling of the US because we were anti-Communist" only to become "the pariah and object of humiliation" after the fall of the Berlin Wall.[366]

Nevertheless, on October 19, 1999, the Indonesian parliament ratified the referendum results, reversing the integration of East Timor. The way the conflict ended, however, had tremendous repercussions for conflicts in other parts of Indonesia. As the Indonesian Commission of Inquiry into Human Rights Violations in East Timor released a detailed report naming thirty-two officials and leaders of auxiliaries as responsible for grave human rights violations amounting to crimes against humanity, soldiers and police on duty in other restive areas worried that their actions could land them in court.[367] Thus, especially in the communal conflicts of Poso and Ambon, they stood by watching Muslims and Christians kill each other out of fear that armed intervention would be deemed a violation of human rights. East Timor's successful bid for independence also inspired other separatist movements. As will be seen in chapter 4, parts of the Acehnese population demanded a referendum while the Free Aceh Movement (GAM) tried to emulate FALINTIL.

4
THE ACEH CONFLICT, 1976–2005

Almost two years after the Indonesian invasion of Portuguese Timor and while Indonesian counterinsurgency operations there were in full swing, signs of trouble appeared at the other end of the Indonesian Archipelago. On October 20, 1977, leaflets from a hitherto unknown organization, Aceh Merdeka (Free Aceh), materialized in and around the newly established Lhokseumawe industrial complex in North Aceh. These leaflets called upon all foreign employees of Mobil Oil Indonesia and the construction company Bechtel to leave Aceh as they were deemed "collaborators" with the "Javanese colonialist thieves" who were "robbing" Aceh's resources. Just over a month later, in early December 1977, three foreign contractors came under fire, one of whom was killed. These were the first signs of the insurgency that would wrack Aceh for the next three decades, destroy the province's social fabric and its infrastructure, and cost some twelve to twenty thousand lives.

This chapter looks at the second case study of separatist violence in this book, the 1976–2005 Aceh conflict. It examines the causes of the conflict, Acehnese grievances since independence, and how this conflict related to Aceh's participation in the Darul Islam rebellions. The chapter then proceeds to analyze the Free Aceh Movement (GAM), focusing on its narrative, national imaginary, and military and political strategies. It concludes with a discussion of "belonging" in Aceh.

This chapter shows that the roots of the Aceh conflict lie in the Indonesian state's unitary and "secular" pluralist character. This left little room for Aceh's more Islamic identity, which the Acehnese believed would be accommodated when they supported the Indonesian nationalist project and the war of liberation against the Dutch. "Belonging" in Aceh was thus conditional from the beginning and remained contentious thereafter. As seen in chapter 1, Aceh participated in the Darul Islam rebellions, driven by its rejection of centralization and its support for a more Islamic national imaginary. During the New Order, the Acehnese experience of Suharto's Islam policies resembled that of the *santri* and Islamists in Java discussed in chapter 2. There were also parallels with East Timor with respect to the impact of developmentalism. However, GAM's response was above all framed by Acehnese history. Consequently, GAM did not seek to change the nature of the Indonesian state, but to separate from it.

This chapter further shows that the existence of GAM's alternative Acehnese national imaginary and narrative was seen as a greater threat by Indonesia than GAM's military activity and capacity. The Indonesian security forces sought to counter this national imaginary while also seeking to validate the Indonesian government narrative, as exemplified by their emphasis on loyalty ceremonies, *pembinaan* (guidance programs), and attempts to bring GAM members back into the fold. The Aceh conflict was thus, above all, an ideological war of competing narratives and national imaginaries pursued by military means.

The Roots of the Aceh Conflict

The roots of the Aceh conflict lie in the way the Indonesian state was conceptualized. Its centralized nature and its foundational ideology of Pancasila sat uncomfortably with Aceh's strong commitment to Islam in all aspects of life. However, Aceh's relationship with Jakarta was not antagonistic from the start. While Aceh was the last territory to be incorporated into the Netherlands Indies following its invasion by the Dutch in 1873, and while the Acehnese continued to resist the Dutch until 1942 in what Paul van't Veer has referred to as the four Aceh wars, the encounter with colonial modernity, as Edward Aspinall has argued, pulled Aceh in line with the political developments in other parts of the archipelago. Its premodern identity, which developed in the sixteenth century with Sultan Iskandar Muda's territorial conquests as Antony Reid has shown, was transformed into a modern Acehnese national identity.[1] Thus there were considerable parallels with the development of Indonesian nationalism. Crucially, these two modern nationalisms were not initially constructed against each other, as Islam was important to both.[2] It was only after the formal transfer of sovereignty to Indonesia in 1949 that an increasingly antagonistic dynamic of center-periphery relations and shifts in Acehnese nationalism were set in motion, leading to a divergence of national imaginaries and the role of Islam in them. At the heart of this new dynamic were two core issues. The first was the subordination of Islam to Pancasila and the second was Aceh's loss of autonomy within the Indonesian Republic.

The importance of Islam to Acehnese identity cannot be overstated. According to some accounts Islam arrived in Aceh as early as the seventh century, significantly earlier than the rest of the archipelago.[3] As a result Islam has been embedded deeply in Acehnese traditions and culture. Politically, Aceh became a sultanate in which the ruler cooperated closely with the ulama. Socially, Aceh was organized around religion and its education system was under the control of the ulama.[4] Acehnese *adat* (customs) was based and continues to be based on *syariah*. Being one of the historical entry points of Islam into the archipelago as well as the departure point for Muslim pilgrims going on hajj or *umroh* pilgrimages to Mecca, Aceh became known as *serambi Mekkah* (the verandah of Mecca), a moniker the Acehnese closely identified with.[5] When the Dutch attacked Aceh in 1873, Aceh's response was, not surprisingly, articulated as a jihad, a *prang kaphé* (infidel war), and those who were killed were revered as *syahid* (martyrs).[6] As the Dutch consolidated their occupation of Aceh over the next decades, the ulama in their *dayah* (Acehnese Islamic boarding schools) continued to frame this occupation in Islamic terms, referring to the Dutch as *kafir* who must be resisted by true Muslims.[7] This gave rise to sporadic martyrdom attacks by some Acehnese against Dutch officials, which the latter referred to as *Atjeh-moorden* (Aceh murders).[8]

The ulama were also at the heart of the continued Acehnese resistance to the Dutch, with a key role played by the All-Aceh Ulama Association (Persatuan Ulama-ulama Seluruh Aceh, PUSA), which was established in 1939 to oust the Dutch from Aceh's territory as well as ousting the *uleëbalang* (notables), Aceh's local elite through whom the Dutch ruled, from governance positions.[9] Its aim, as articulated in its first public statement, was "to proclaim, uphold, and maintain the greatness of the holy Islamic religion, especially in the land of Aceh."[10] PUSA was "an exclusively Acehnese affair," which focused on reviving the golden age of the Acehnese sultanates.[11] Its position was strengthened with the Japanese occupation of the Netherlands Indies from 1942 to 1945. As the Dutch were interned, many of the *uleëbalang* who had cooperated with the Dutch lost their administrative positions.[12] After the Japanese surrender, the conflict between the ulama and the *uleëbalang* turned into an outright civil war in which the ulama and their supporters attacked the *uleëbalang*, forced them out of their positions, confiscated their property, displaced their families, and killed hundreds of them.[13] In Indonesian historiography this became known as the "Cumbok Incident" or the "Cumbok War" while Western scholars have generally referred to it as Aceh's social revolution, as it was social and political rather than religious in nature.¹⁴ Aceh's regional government cast it as a struggle against traitors (the *ulèëbalang*) who were preparing for the return of the Dutch.¹⁵

Crucial for understanding the changing dynamics between Aceh and Jakarta is that the social revolution enabled the positions previously held by the *ulèëbalang* to be filled with members of PUSA, including Daud Beureueh, who in 1953 would lead Aceh into joining the Darul Islam (DI) rebellions.¹⁶ Equally crucial is that this happened at a time when the Indonesian nationalist leaders Sukarno and Hatta decided to endorse the pluralism of Pancasila rather than Islam as the basis of the Republic of Indonesia that they had declared on August 17, 1945. In the debate over the role of Islam in the new state, the Acehnese found themselves on the losing side along with Masyumi. This created a rift between Aceh and Jakarta, although this was initially dampened by the fact that the Acehnese still believed they would have autonomy within Indonesia once the Indonesian Revolution was over, and that this would allow them to continue to place Islam at the heart of how Aceh was governed. Aceh was the only territory of the Netherlands Indies that did not see a return of Dutch forces and thus it became a base from which the Dutch could be fought. Acehnese merchants also raised $US130,000 for the Republic's first planes, two Dakotas, after Sukarno visited on June 16, 1948, as well as money to fund Indonesia's diplomatic efforts to gain international recognition.¹⁷ In return, Aceh, like Yogyakarta, was to be granted special status, which the Acehnese believed would mean autonomy to safeguard their identity, customs, and, above all, Islam.

Yet achieving this autonomy was fraught with difficulties as Jakarta's approach to the territory was inconsistent, moving back and forth between seeing Aceh as separate from and as part of North Sumatra. After the Japanese surrender, Aceh was autonomous in all but name. However, formally it was one of the residencies making up the province of Sumatra. In mid-1947, in response to the first Dutch "police action," Aceh was designated a *daerah militer istimewa* (special military area) and placed under the command of military governor Daud Beureueh.¹⁸ When Sukarno visited Aceh that year, Beureueh was able to extract a promise from him that Aceh would be permitted to keep implementing *syariah* after independence. According to M. Nur El Ibrahimy, Beureueh asked Sukarno to put his promise in writing, to which Sukarno "tearfully" responded that this was not necessary.¹⁹ In April 1948, Aceh's designation as *daerah militer istimewa* was revoked and Aceh reverted to being part of the new province of North Sumatra, headed by Governor Sutan Mohamed Amin Nasution.²⁰ By the end of the year, however, as the Dutch launched their second "police action," Aceh was redesignated a special military area, again under Beureueh as military governor.²¹

In December 1949, Indonesian deputy prime minister Sjafruddin Prawiranegara, following an earlier visit to Aceh, where he had come under considerable pressure from PUSA, issued a regulation that divided North Sumatra into two provinces: the province of Aceh and the province of Tapanuli/East Sumatra.[22] Beureueh was installed as the governor of the former while Ferdinand Lumbantobing became the governor of the latter. Aceh's status changed again in August 1950 with the abrogation of the United States of Indonesia and the proclamation of the Unitary Republic of Indonesia. This new republic comprised ten provinces and Aceh, after the revoking of Prawiranegara's regulation, once again became part of the province of North Sumatra.[23] The Acehnese rejected this decision, arguing that Aceh needed to be treated differently because of its distinctive situation with respect to education, religion, law, and economics.[24] Not surprisingly, by the end of 1950 Acehnese guerrilla leaders, who had fought during the Indonesian revolution for Indonesia, had reactivated their troops, this time for an autonomous Aceh.[25] In official Indonesian historiography, Aceh's rejection is attributed to Beureueh's personal aspirations rather than to a position held by the Acehnese as a whole. As the second volume of the history of the TNI narrates, "Daud Beureueh was not satisfied . . . as he assumed that his power would be downgraded. Because of that he resigned and for [the next] three years he and his friends prepared themselves."[26] They gained the sympathy of the people by advocating "regional sentiments and Islamic sentiments," they provided military training, and they "forced the residents [of Aceh] to follow their wishes" by threatening them with "death and the burning of their homes."[27] This account ignores that in an attempt to prevent unrest, Indonesian prime minister Mohamed Natsir concluded an agreement with Beureueh in January 1951 according to which the Acehnese would drop their resistance to being part of the province of Sumatra in return for the Indonesian government's acceptance that Acehnese autonomy would not be ruled out.[28] It also ignores that the Aceh residency was placed under the supervision of a non-Acehnese resident-coordinator, that a number of Acehnese *bupatis* (regents) were removed, that PUSA members in Aceh government positions were now subordinated to officials from Java and Medan, that Acehnese troops were replaced with non-Acehnese troops, that the funding of Islamic schools was cut, that the authority of the *syariah* courts was reduced, and that Acehnese businesses were required to send their export goods from the port of Belawan in North Sumatra rather than being allowed to trade directly with Malaysia as they had done in the past.[29] These grievances were further exacerbated by Acehnese suspicions that the Batak of North Sumatra were trying to gain control over Aceh, aided by "fellow-Bataks in Jakarta, namely the generals Nasution and Simatupang," and that, to make matters worse, many of these Bataks were Christian, which meant infidels ruling over believers.[30] Thus when Sukarno visited Aceh in July 1951, it is not surprising that he was greeted by demonstrators holding signs stating that "Aceh must not be treated as a stepchild" and "We love the President, but we love religion more."[31] A month later, in August, some fifteen thousand people were arrested across Indonesia and charged with undermining the government. Among them were members of the Masyumi Party, Aceh's closest ideological ally, and PUSA's top leaders, including Daud Beureueh.[32] Two years later, in September 1953, Beureueh announced that Aceh had joined the Darul Islam rebellions, which had already been pitting Islamist fighters under Kartosuwirjo against Republican forces since 1948.

The New Order and Acehnese Grievances

When Suharto succeeded Sukarno, it quickly became clear that the agreement that had brought to an end the Darul Islam rebellion in Aceh in 1959 was meaningless. The Aceh regional government's permission to draft regional legislation in accordance with *syariah* as long as it did not conflict with the "broad outlines of the state" was effectively revoked, reversing Aceh's special status in all but name.[33] Old grievances were reopened and new grievances were added. The latter resulted from the New Order's centralization policies and ideology of developmentalism, exemplifying what Herbert Feith referred to as the repressive-developmentalist state.[34] In this developmentalist paradigm Jakarta saw Aceh not only as economically underdeveloped and "backward" but also as "narrow-minded" and "fanatic."[35] Jakarta's solution to Aceh's problems was to develop its infrastructure, especially roads, in order to better integrate it with the rest of the country. The discovery of natural gas in North Aceh in 1971 raised hopes in Jakarta that Aceh could be fully modernized. It also raised hopes among the Acehnese of sharing in this wealth. Economic centralization policies, however, ensured that the Acehnese benefited little. From 1980 onward Aceh contributed between $US2 and $US3 billion annually to Indonesian exports, but the revenue flowed to Jakarta and from there to the rest of Indonesia.[36] Only a small amount of Aceh's export surplus was "recycled" in the form of central government expenditure in the province.

Centralization, both economic and political, was seen as the means to protect the unity and integrity of the state and as an integral part of the nation-building effort. The impact of Suharto's centralization policy on Aceh cannot be overstated. Political centralization policies included the imposition of the "Javanese village model" on Aceh through Law No. 5/1979 on village governance. This not only relegated the Acehnese village model to history, but also undermined Acehnese *adat*. As Vice Governor Azwar Abubakar explained in 2001, "Socioculturally in Aceh you have the *mukim* (Acehnese village). That was based on the traditional wisdom of how to care for the forest, how to farm, how to fish. That system was changed to the *desa* (Javanese village). The process of change introduced new leaders not by *musyawarah* (traditional consultation). *Mukim* leaders no longer had roles, so culture and society has been destroyed."[37] Abubakar also pointed to the interlinked nature of Acehnese *adat* and Islam: "*Adat* is not just customs. Traditional rule here is based on *syariat Islam*," but *syariah* was replaced by a secular system in which "they send people to prison."[38] However, that was not the only impact centralization had on Islam in Aceh. Hassan Basri has argued that Aceh's ulama became "little more than a political commodity used for the legitimization of power and authority" as they were used by Suharto "to mobilize the masses in order to win the general election for Golkar."[39] In return, Basri asserted, "the ulama were given money, cars and even their own *dayahs*, where they teach students loyal to them."[40] Similarly, Malik Musa, head of the Muhammadiyah Youth, elucidated that the Suharto regime "co-opted the ulama into the government through Golkar" and "if there was criticism from the ulama they would be sent to prison."[41] The result was that there were few ulama left that the people would follow because "the people don't believe in the ulama anymore."[42]

Aceh's social and religious structures were further affected by modernization and socio-economic dislocation, both of which were directly linked to the discovery of natural gas, which started to transform the hitherto agricultural economy. In 1971, the province's per capita GDP was 89 percent of the national average; by 1983 it had increased to 282 percent.[43] Between 1971 and 1979 Aceh underwent rapid development, peaking in 1978–1979. Aceh's manufacturing sector grew at an average annual rate of 13.7 percent and the percentage of the province's GDP derived from oil and gas rose from 17 percent in 1976 to 69.9 percent in 1989.[44] This rapid pace of development was welcomed by then Aceh governor Muzzakir Walad, but the Acehnese population was "woefully unprepared for the arrival of the modern industrial complex." In the mid-1970s there was not even a technical high school in North Aceh.[45] Not surprisingly, at grassroots level the efforts at industrialization were viewed with suspicion, which soon turned into resentment. Foreigners and Javanese took many of the higher-paying jobs as the Acehnese often lacked the required technical and educational qualifications.[46] This situation was further exacerbated by the unrealistic expectations of the villagers. As a local military commander in the 1980s, Sofian Effendi, recalled:

> I had a lot of contact with Arun and Mobil. They tried with community development but there was a problem with skills. The Acehnese did

not have the skills for the good jobs. There was resentment in the villages next to Arun and Mobil, so I asked them to employ more Acehnese but their education was just too low. It was a real mismatch—a real problem. When I talked to villagers they said they wanted to be managers. And they complained that they didn't get those jobs. What made things worse was that those same villagers had no electricity and would sit in the dark next to the brightly lit Arun and Mobil complex.[47]

Some fifty thousand migrants from other parts of Indonesia came to the Lhokseumawe area in search for work.[48] Added to these were Javanese transmigrants, who were settled in Aceh by the Suharto regime between 1974 and 1987. As North Aceh's population rose from 490,000 to 755,000, greater Lhokseumawe was unable to absorb these numbers and its infrastructure and social services quickly became overstretched.[49] Local farmers were dispossessed and local fishermen forced from their traditional occupations, often by the effects of industrial pollution.[50] The price of staple foods rose, coinciding with the decline of per capita income in the outlying rural areas of Aceh.[51]

Dislocation, unmet expectations, unemployment, social jealousy, and urban poverty placed considerable strains on Aceh's social fabric. This was further compounded by the emergence of "prostitution, gambling, alcohol, drugs, and strong-arm thugs," which the Acehnese associated with the military but also, rightly or wrongly, with the Javanese migrants.[52] In Acehnese eyes, the province was being bled dry for the benefit of Jakarta, and resentment quickly took on ethnic overtones, translating into the belief that the government was "stealing" from the Acehnese to "give" to the Javanese.[53] The Acehnese grass roots felt exploited and trapped. Mutually reinforcing political and economic centralization ultimately created broad popular discontent upon which GAM was able to draw.

The Free Aceh Movement

It was in this context of political and economic grievances that the Aceh Sumatra National Liberation Front (ASNLF), which became locally known first as Aceh Merdeka (AM) and later as Gerakan Aceh Merdeka (GAM), was established. Its founding father was Hasan di Tiro, grandson of Teungku Cik di Tiro, hero of the anticolonial struggle against the Dutch. Di Tiro was born in Aceh on September 4, 1930. At the age of twenty, he left Aceh to study in the United States, where he also worked at the Indonesian Mission to the United Nations. In 1953 he resigned his post to support Daud Beureueh's Darul Islam rebellion. Thereafter he continued as a businessman in the United States until his return to Aceh in 1976. Di Tiro attributed his decision to return to two events in particular: first, the death of his brother in hospital in 1974, "murdered by Javanese military intelligence 'doctors,'" and second, in 1975, an almost-fatal plane accident that reminded him of his yet-unfulfilled obligation as a member of the di Tiro family—to fight for Acehnese independence.[54] As di Tiro recalled, "I had to go back to Aceh. It's part of my history."[55] Arguably, a third reason should be added. In 1974, di Tiro lost out to the American construction company Bechtel on a bid to build one of the Aceh pipelines for Mobil Oil Indonesia.[56]

On October 30, 1976, di Tiro arrived in the fishing village of Pasè Lhok on Aceh's east coast.[57] He then gathered a small number of Darul Islam veterans, most of whom were from his home district of Pidie. Together they embarked upon a guerrilla campaign against Indonesian state and security forces targets. AM saw itself as a national liberation movement whose stated aim was to ensure "the survival of the people of Aceh Sumatra as a nation; the survival of their political, social, cultural and religious heritage which are being destroyed by the Javanese colonialists," reopening "the question of decolonization of the Dutch East Indies alias 'Indonesia,'" and reestablishing an independent Acehnese state.[58] AM's Acehnese nationalism was ethnically defined through blood ties, religion, and *suku* (ethnic group) affiliation. It was asserted through the Acehnese language, culture, and history. As Aceh was 98 percent Muslim, Islam was an integral part of AM's ideology, but mainly as a reflection of Acehnese identity and culture rather than Islamist political aspirations. However, it must be pointed out that AM and later GAM allowed for different emphases on Islam within its ranks. The leadership in Sweden made few if any references to Islam through the whole period of the conflict, while at village level AM and GAM often relied on the mosque network and presented its struggle in Islamist terms, "involving the condemnation of the impious behaviour of the rulers, promises of restitution of *syariah* law and an Islamic base to an independent Aceh."[59]

Throughout most of the conflict, AM's and GAM's top leadership was in exile. As AM evolved into GAM in the late 1990s, the organization became more structured. GAM's *wali nanggroë* (guardian/head of state) Hasan di Tiro, prime minister and defense minister (operational) Malik Mahmud, foreign minister and health minister Zaini Abdullah, and information minister Bakhtiar Abdullah resided in the Stockholm suburb of Norsborg. The organization's education minister, Musanna Abdul Wahab, was based in the United States and its defense minister (procurement and intelligence), Zakaria Zaman, operated out of Thailand. In July 2002, at a meeting in Stavanger, Norway, GAM's leadership in Sweden became the State of Aceh government in exile.

GAM's midlevel leadership, troops and members were based in Aceh, which GAM had divided into seventeen *wilayah* (regions). Each *wilayah* was "governed" by a governor who oversaw GAM's civilian functions such as tax collecting as well as the issuing of birth and marriage certificates. However, as most decisions on the ground were dictated by military imperatives, it was the *panglima wilayah* (regional military commanders) who held the real power.

GAM's civilian structure was shadowed by the parallel structure of the Armed Forces of the Free Aceh Movement (Angkatan Gerakan Aceh Merdeka, AGAM), renamed Army of the State of Aceh (Tentara Negara Aceh, TNA) with the Stavanger Declaration. The TNA was under the TNA *panglima*. Under his command were the seventeen *panglima wilayah* at regional level, who in turn were responsible for four *panglima daerah* at district level. Below the *panglima daerah* were the *panglima sagoë* at subdistrict level. The troops under the command of the *panglima sagoë* were organized in a cell structure. It was at this level that the TNA's command structure was the most highly factionalized and the troops were the most undisciplined. In fact, it was not uncommon for actions carried out for hardline ideological reasons or personal economic gain to be at odds with directives of the top leadership.

Contact between the exiled leadership and the GAM guerrillas in Aceh was maintained by telephone.[60] According to field commander Amri bin Abdul Wahab, orders were given by Malik Mahmud to the AGAM/TNA *panglima*. They were then discussed with the *panglima wilayah*, who in turn discussed them with the *komandan lapangan* (field commanders) and *komandan operasi* (operation commanders). The actual decisions on strategy and tactics were made at field commander level.[61]

When AM was established in 1976 it comprised only 70 guerrilla fighters. It grew significantly in the mid-1980s and again after 1998. The first increase was accompanied by Libyan training that significantly raised AM's military capacity. According to di Tiro, as many as 5,000 GAM guerrillas were trained in Libya between 1986 and 1989; the Indonesian military intelligence set the number at 583.[62] The second increase of what had now become GAM was accompanied by territorial expansion. Before 1998 its territorial base was the east coast: Pidie, Bireuen, North Aceh, and East Aceh. After the fall of Suharto GAM expanded westwards. However, while it was genuinely backed in its "traditional" areas, especially among the less educated, poorer, and rural sections of society, support for GAM from the better-educated urban population, Acehnese political and commercial elites, and the wider, ethnically different, population in West, South, Southeast and Central Aceh, was equivocal. The former benefited politically and financially from ties to Jakarta while the latter sought to project their own ethnic identity.

The key factor motivating young Acehnese to join GAM after 1998 was the full revelation of the scale of human rights abuses by the Indonesian military. This new generation of GAM was fueled by vengeance and the quest for justice.

They were joined by local thugs and petty criminals who saw the GAM label as a useful tool for obtaining easy money.[63] There is anecdotal evidence that GAM in some areas ordered villages to provide it one or two volunteers.[64] In February 2002, GAM prime minister Malik Mahmud claimed that GAM had an active guerrilla army of 30,000 and a reserve of almost the whole population of Aceh.[65] Indonesian military intelligence estimates set the number of GAM fighters in April 2003 at 5,500.[66] And foreign observers, such as the International Crisis Group, believed that GAM comprised 3,000 active fighters.[67] However, GAM's fighting capacity was a lot smaller than its membership suggested. In 2001, most observers believed that AGAM had between "1,000 and 1,500 modern firearms, a few grenade launchers, even fewer rocket-propelled grenade launchers, and perhaps one or two 60mm mortars."[68] In May 2003, the TNI estimated the number of GAM's weapons at 2,137, comprising a mixture of *rakitan* (homemade) and standard firearms.

In November 2003, Malik Mahmud claimed that GAM had spent more than $US10 million on weapons for the struggle.[69] This money came from three main sources of revenue: "taxation," foreign donations, and criminal activity. GAM levied an Aceh state tax, *pajak nanggroë*, on all elements of society. According to senior GAM negotiator Sofyan Ibrahim Tiba *pajak nanggroë* had been collected ever since the organization was established and it was based on religion. "In Islam if there is a struggle there is *infaq* (financial donation)."[70] Similarly Pasè (North Aceh) commander Sofyan Dawod explained that "the Acehnese do not object to our taxes . . . because that money [is used] to defend them."[71] The level of taxation depended on the project or the salary. There were two bases for taxation: first, taxation of profits, which Dawod claimed was around 2.5 percent, and second, the value of the project. Farmers and teachers did not pay taxes, "but we do ask for a voluntary contribution of one day's earning per month. We also ask for donations from Aceh's wealthy to help society, to cover state functions and expenses, and also to buy weapons."[72] GAM particularly targeted merchants in Greater Aceh (many of whom were ethnic Chinese), contractors in the Lhokseumawe industrial area, Javanese migrants in the coffee plantations of Central Aceh, and civil servants.

The second important source of funding for GAM was foreign donations, which came primarily from Acehnese expatriates. The largest amount of this money probably originated from Malaysia. It was estimated that in Kuala Lumpur alone at least five thousand Acehnese provided GAM with regular donations.[73] The third source of funding was generated from criminal activity, mainly drug trafficking and kidnapping for ransom. GAM was actively involved in the cultivation of marijuana, and GAM's involvement in drug trafficking was directly linked to the arms-drugs nexus, both regionally and domestically. Marijuana was sold to obtain weapons from Cambodia and Thailand but also from individuals in the Indonesian security forces, Indonesia's arms manufacturer Pindad, Jakarta's black market, and even as far away as West and East Timor, where arms from former pro-Jakarta militias were widely available.[74]

Kidnapping for ransom was another means for raising funds, although this was denied by the GAM leadership. Here the targets included local legislators, businessmen, and oil workers.[75] For instance, in early 2001, GAM kidnapped a senior executive of PT Arun and demanded $US500,000 to release him. In late August 2001, six Indonesian crewmembers from the *Ocean Silver* were abducted and $US33,000 demanded for their release.[76] In April 2002, three oil workers contracted to Pertamina were kidnapped. One was released the following day; for the other two GAM demanded a ransom of Rp200 million ($US20,193).[77] On July 2, 2002, it was reported that nine crewmen servicing the offshore oil industry were kidnapped from their ship, the *Pelangi Frontier*.[78]

The Aceh Conflict: Phases and Dynamics

The conflict in Aceh underwent three distinct phases: 1976–1982, 1989–1999, and 1999–2005. The first phase started with di Tiro's launch of a limited guerrilla struggle on the ground in Aceh in 1976. The struggle was geographically limited to the east coast and focused on the area of North Aceh. It was also limited by the fact that Aceh Merdeka only had seventy fighters. According to di Tiro this was the educational phase of the struggle, and the aim was to awaken the national consciousness of the population.[79] That did not, however, mean that military action was absent. In May 1977, di Tiro described AM's strategy in classical guerrilla terms. AM kept "to the hills" in order to "nullify Javanese superiority in armored vehicles, naval and air power" and hovered "in the enemy's neighborhood, preventing him from gaining any permanent base." He emphasized that "engagement must be done at the place and time of our choosing" and explained that AM's aims were "to cripple [the] enemy's communications and economy and to destroy his foreign backers' confidence."[80]

Indonesian counterinsurgency operations began in October 1977, after AM had threatened foreign workers employed in connection with the recent discovery of liquid natural gas (LNG). These took the form of intelligence operations carried out by Indonesia's army special forces, Kopassandha (now Kopassus). The first *sandhi yudha* (combat intelligence) detachment in the field was code-named Nanggala 16.[81] The main objective was "to neutralize the situation, restore security, to enhance the construction of the LNG project, and to destroy Aceh Merdeka."[82] The Nanggala detachments pursued a strategy of isolating AM by severing its logistical and communications lines and destroying AM's military command structure.[83] As AM guerrillas virtually disappeared into the local population, one of the key elements of the operations became the gathering of intelligence on AM fighters and supporters. For this purpose Nanggala 21 raised civil defense groups (*perlawanan rakyat, wanra*) in line with Indonesia's Total People's Defense System (sishankamrata).[84] By the end of 1979, the Nanggala operations had effectively deactivated AM's first cabinet. Its members had either been killed, captured, or forced into exile. Di Tiro sought asylum in Sweden, from where he supported the struggle by sending "recorded speeches and writings."[85] In 1982, AM decided upon a tactical withdrawal.

The second phase of the Aceh conflict began in May 1989 with the reemergence of a larger AM with greater military capacity, which was the result of military training in Libya. As one of AM's exiled leaders, Malik Mahmud, who was residing in Kuala Lumpur at that time, recalled, "the Libyans had the policy and we fit in. We were invited to Tripoli and we established relations and then went there for training."[86] According to the testimony of a Libyan-trained AM guerrilla in detention in 1991, the first group of recruits numbered only 45 and was sent to Mattabah Tajur Training Camp in Libya in 1986. The following year, 1987–1988, some 400 were sent and in 1989, another 150.[87] Mahmud maintained that there were around 500 trainees every year.[88] The Acehnese recruits were trained in guerrilla warfare by the Libyans during the day while di Tiro, who had moved to Tripoli "to be close to our people," taught them in the evening "about the political future of Aceh ... history, politics and our ideals."[89] Each year-long course ended with a graduation ceremony at which "Libyan officials like Gadhafi were present."[90] After that the graduates returned to Aceh where they reorganized the movement, establishing "para-commandos."[91]

The return of the Libyan-trained AM to Aceh changed the situation on the ground significantly. Not only did AM now have skilled fighters, it also had acquired better military equipment purchased from donations given by the Acehnese *diaspora* in Malaysia. Moreover, it had far wider support from the local population, whose economic, political, and social grievances had been further exacerbated as a result of the New Order's development and transmigration programs.[92]

The reemergence of AM took the Indonesian security forces by surprise.[93] As in the 1970s, the Suharto regime opted for a military response. In mid-1990, the military operations implementation command, Kolakops Jaring Merah (Red Net), was established in Aceh, which became more conventionally referred to as DOM, the acronym for *daerah operasi militer* (military operations area). Some six thousand nonorganic (centrally recruited and trained) troops were sent into Aceh, including the Kopassus special forces, to join the six thousand organic (locally recruited territorial) troops already there. Together they set out to crush

AM. Their strategy was to separate the insurgents from the local population, to isolate them, and then to destroy them. This included a "campaign of terror designed to strike fear in the population and make them withdraw their support from AM," referred to as "shock therapy," which saw the "houses of villagers suspected of providing shelter or support to the rebels... burned to the ground," and kidnappings and rapes as well as "targeted killings and public executions."[94] As in the first phase, the Indonesian security forces also raised local defense organizations to help hunt down AM.[95] In this phase of the conflict AM took a severe beating. It had not, however, been defeated. Subsequent investigations revealed that in the period from 1989 to 1998 between 1,258 and 2,000 people were killed and 1,958 disappeared.[96] After the end of DOM seven thousand cases of human rights violations were documented and at least twelve mass graves were investigated.[97]

The third phase of the Aceh conflict began in 1998 after the fall of Suharto. Reformasi initially ushered in a period of respite. Armed Forces commander in chief General Wiranto announced an end to DOM, withdrew nonorganic forces, and even apologized to the people of Aceh for the abuses perpetrated by his soldiers. AM guerillas and Acehnese civilians who had fled to Malaysia returned. However, as the efforts by Indonesian civil society organizations to push the military out of politics continued and President B. J. Habibie, who had succeeded Suharto, took the unprecedented step of granting East Timor a referendum on independence, AM—which now called itself GAM—saw an opportunity. The returned guerrillas, joined by scores of volunteers whose families or friends had been victims of DOM, filled the vacuum left by the withdrawing Indonesian troops. GAM expanded territorially across the whole of Aceh and renewed its attacks, driven by the belief that Indonesia was on the brink of territorial disintegration and that Acehnese independence was just a matter of a final push. East Timor's referendum outcome in September 1999 only strengthened this belief, and East Timor thus became a blueprint for GAM's exiled leaders, making internationalization their new strategic cornerstone. The East Timor parallel became central to wooing an international community that hitherto had not paid much attention to Aceh. For instance, a GAM press release in June 2001 stated that the "Indonesian government has been committing gross human rights violations in Aceh, in a degree much worse than they did in East Timor."[98] Further efforts at drawing the parallel with East Timor were evident in the emphasis on the existence of the *wanra*, depicting them as similar to the militias operating in East Timor.[99] This strategy, however, did not result in an outpouring of Western sympathy as anticipated. Western support for the East Timorese had been predicated upon the testimonies of Indonesia's brutal invasion, the accounts of human rights abuses coming from the Timorese Catholic Church, and the fact that the East Timorese were Christians. GAM and the Acehnese as Muslims were approached with caution by the West, which was fighting a "war" against Al-Qaeda and which, by and large, saw Aceh as an integral part of Indonesia.

The end of the New Order changed Jakarta's handling of the Aceh conflict from a purely military approach to one that combined decentralization and negotiations with security measures. Laws No. 22/1999 and No. 25/1999 on decentralization devolved extensive governmental powers to the regions and permitted local governments to retain some of the net income from the exploitation of natural resources. In addition, Aceh under Law No. 44/1999 was given autonomy with respect to culture, religious affairs, and education. Law No. 18/2001 granted special autonomy to Aceh, formally changing the province's name to Nanggroe Aceh Darussalam (NAD). Special autonomy allowed for the introduction of *syariah*, and it provided Aceh with control over 70 percent of its oil and gas revenues for the next eight years.[100] Indonesia hoped that special autonomy would undermine popular support for GAM, and that GAM would lay down its arms and give up its struggle for independence.

In January 2000, under President Abdurrahman Wahid, a parallel process of negotiations was added that aimed at finding an end to the conflict between GAM and the Indonesian government. This process was facilitated by the Swiss-based Henry Dunant Center (HDC). The first "result" of these talks was the May 12, 2000, Humanitarian Pause, which was accompanied by the establishment of two joint committees, one on humanitarian action and one on security modalities, as well as a monitoring team. However, the implementation of the Pause lacked commitment from both sides and violence actually escalated. In April 2001, Jakarta decided to launch a security recovery operation, Operasi Pemulihan Keamanan, after ExxonMobil had halted its production due to GAM threats. Three months later, in July 2001, negotiations broke down, only to resume again in February 2002, now under President Megawati Sukarnoputri. In December 2002, the Cessation of Hostilities Agreement (COHA) was concluded, which called for the cantonment of GAM weapons, the relocation of the Indonesian security forces and reformulation of their role, and the establishment of peace zones. However, the COHA started to disintegrate after GAM failed to meet the February deadline for the cantonment of its arms, and it collapsed completely on May 18, 2003, when Indonesia demanded that GAM relinquish its armed struggle and recognize NKRI (Negara Kesatuan Republik Indonesia, Unitary State of the Republic of Indonesia). The following day Aceh was placed under martial law and a "comprehensive" counterinsurgency operation, Operasi Terpadu, was launched with the aim of crushing GAM. Operasi Terpadu decimated the lower and middle ranks of GAM's command structure, which had a severe impact upon the movement's military capacity. GAM reverted to smaller groups and a more basic type of guerrilla warfare.[101] Even greater damage was inflicted upon GAM's civilian structure, which collapsed as its "tax collectors" were turned in by members of the public and its "governors" were captured, arrested, and put on trial. TNI commander in chief Endriatono Sutarto claimed that during the martial law period 1,963 GAM fighters were killed, 2,100 were captured, and 1,276 surrendered, totaling 5,339 from the organization, which he estimated to have a strength of 8,000.[102] When the tsunami hit Aceh in December 2004, GAM received another blow. Its "logistic support bases, mainly villages and hamlets along the coastlines, [were] decimated."[103] Many captured GAM field commanders in prisons along the coast also perished. GAM had no military option left. Only a return to the negotiating table would place GAM back in the center of action, and the price for such a return was agreeing to something less than independence. Importantly, by this point, internal discussions within GAM's leadership had already produced conceptual shifts toward embracing Malik Mahmud's view of pursuing a more step-by-step "decolonization strategy" that would entail accepting autonomy in the interim.[104] It was this shift, rather than the tsunami, that provided an entry point for Indonesia's new government under President Susilo Bambang Yudhoyono and Vice President Jusuf Kalla, who were trying to come up with a way to bring the Aceh conflict to an end.[105] In fact, a secret channel had already been opened months before the tsunami between Kalla's team and GAM leaders on the ground and in exile. This enabled negotiations to be restarted in January 2005 in Helsinki, facilitated by the Finnish NGO Crisis Management Initiative (CMI), which resulted in the August 2005 Memorandum of Understanding, bringing the Aceh conflict to an end.

The GAM Narrative and National Imaginary

The Free Aceh Movement's national imaginary was both discursive and constructed. It also evolved over time, adapting to the changing political dynamics in Indonesia with the fall of Suharto and democratization as well as changing international dynamics from the Cold War to the post–Cold War new international order. These changing ideas originated largely from the leadership exiled in Sweden, thus also reflecting the influences of their immediate environment.

AM's narrative and national imaginary were first outlined in Hasan di Tiro's diary, written during the first phase of the struggle for independence in 1976–1979 and published from exile a few years later. The Acehnese national imaginary constructed by di Tiro was imbedded in a historical narrative that emphasized that the Kingdom of Aceh had existed as a sovereign and internationally recognized independent state before the Dutch invasion in 1873, as exemplified by its political relations with the Ottoman Empire, Great Britain, the United States,

Germany, and Italy.[106] The narrative stressed that the Dutch were unable to fully subdue the Acehnese during their subsequent occupation and that their control thus remained contested. Moreover, after the Second World War, the Dutch failed to reoccupy Aceh. Consequently, di Tiro argued, the Dutch should have returned sovereignty to the Acehnese rather than transferring it to Indonesia: "Sovereignty over a colonial territory resides with the people of that colony and not with the colonialist power. This has been stipulated in UN Resolution 1514-XV. Holland's transfer of 'sovereignty' over Acheh Sumatra to Indonesia was therefore illegal. The most outrageous of all was the fact that when Holland did that, it was not even in control of Acheh Sumatra where Holland had no presence since she was chased out of Acheh Sumatra by the Achenese resistance movement in March 1942!"[107] Di Tiro then proceeded to assert that Indonesia, unlike Aceh, did not exist prior to the arrival of the Dutch. Only ever referring to Indonesia in his diary as "Indonesia" within quotation marks, he labeled it a "fraud," "artificial" and "fabricated," without history and without "root in the hearts and minds of the people in this region."[108] Indeed, he wrote that "the only common denominator among these diverse peoples was the fact that they were unfortunate enough to be colonized once by the Dutch."[109] He then cast the transfer of sovereignty to "Indonesia" as an act of Javanese colonialism and Western neocolonialism: "'Indonesia' is nothing but a new label to replace the old, used one, the Dutch East Indies, and to justify the Javanese perpetuation of Dutch colonial administration for Western colonialist economic interests. 'Indonesia' is an artificial creation, fabricated to serve imperialist economic interests under their Javanese puppets."[110] The Javanese he described as a "colonial horde worse than the Dutch."[111] The Dutch, di Tiro lamented, "were at least civilized people with some sense of justice" while the Javanese were "barbarians without any concept of justice and without any understanding of human dignity and compassion."[112]

To illustrate this di Tiro not only explained that the Javanese used torture, denied prisoners medical treatment, and dishonored the dead, but he also pointed to their treachery, highlighting three events in Acehnese history.[113] The first is an account of the role the Javanese played in the 1873 Dutch invasion of Aceh. Not only were the Dutch "aided by Javanese mercenaries" but "the man who brought the infamous Dutch colonialist ultimatum to the independent State of Acheh Sumatra was none other than Mas Sumo, a Javanese servant of the Dutch whose descendants and kinsmen have the impudence now to claim the right to colonize us Achehnese Sumatrans."[114] The second event is Aceh's contribution to Indonesia's war of independence. Here di Tiro explained that

> the Achehnese helped the Javanese Indonesian struggle against the Dutch mainly because the Achehnese considered the Dutch as their

enemies. It was Teungku Daud Beureueh who gave financial help to enable the Javanese maintained [sic] their mission to the US in New York and other places in the world. It was the Achehnese who gave the money to the Javanese to buy the first two planes for the Indonesian Garuda airways for use to smuggle arms to Java from the Indonesian Emergency Government [when it] fled to Acheh in 1949 after Yogyakarta fell to the Dutch without a fight. They came to Acheh under protection of Teungku Daud Beureueh.[115]

The Acehnese helped the Javanese and were then once again betrayed by them by being colonized. This then directly leads to third event, the Darul Islam rebellions, which di Tiro saw as starting in 1950 and which he recast as a "revolt against Javanese Indonesia" and a "revolt against Javanese Indonesian colonialism."[116]

Aceh, according to the GAM narrative, experienced three decades of Javanese colonialism before di Tiro redeclared Aceh's independence in December 1976. This included the stealing of Acehnese resources and putting the Acehnese "people in chains of tyranny, poverty and neglect."[117] It also included "large scale Javanese migration" to Aceh "to create Javanese settlements to help Javanese occupationary forces."[118] And it further included the use of "schools and the mass media to destroy every aspect of our nationality, culture, polity and national consciousness."[119]

The duplicity and treachery of the Javanese stood in stark contrast to the Acehnese, whom di Tiro endowed with honesty, bravery, steadfastness, and the willingness to die as martyrs for their beliefs. He defined Acehneseness in ethnic, almost primordial, terms in which the land is inherited by a nation whose generations are tied by blood. Genealogy occupied a central place. Every Acehnese, he wrote, must know "who you are, who your fathers and mothers are, what is your patrimony."[120] The other core element in Acehnese identity was Islam. "Islam is an inseparable part of Achenese identity. As far as my people are concerned Acheh and Islam have the same meaning. If Acheh is a coin, Islam is the other side of that coinage. Acheh is a nation founded on Islam and lives by the laws of Islam."[121] This Acehnese nation and Acehnese history were the foundation upon which GAM's national imaginary was built.

In di Tiro's diary, the model of the Acehnese state was a historical one. After the redeclaration of independence in December 1976, di Tiro and his followers set out to reestablish "the historic territorial divisions of the country as they were before the arrival of the Dutch, and the Javanese."[122]

> On the village level we re-established the traditional and centuries old democratic system of administration. Each village is headed by a village chief, called Geutjhik, who wields great prestige and social influence. . . .

> The administrative division above the village is the Mukim. Several villages make a Mukim. The head of the Mukim is called Imum (from Imam, community leader). Several Mukims would make a Sagoë (District), and a Sagoë is headed by an Uléë Sagoë. He is assisted by a Panglima Sagoë (District Military Commander). Several Sagoë make a Nanggroë (Province).... All of them are appointed by the Head of State.[123]

This head of the Acehnese state had several historical models, including King/Queen, Sultan/Sultana, and Wali Neugara/Wali Nanggroë (Guardian of the State). It is the latter title that di Tiro chose for himself, suggesting that ultimately it would be the Acehnese people who would determine the final shape of the Acehnese state.[124]

Acehnese history was also referenced in demarcating Aceh's territorial boundaries. These were not just the boundaries of the Kingdom of Aceh right before the Dutch invaded in 1873, when Aceh "covered half of Sumatra until Djambi and the Riau archipelago," but the boundaries of the Sultanate of Aceh Darussalam under the twelfth sultan, Iskandar Muda (1593–1636), which was seen as Aceh's golden age, when "Malaya, West Borneo, and the Banten region of Java were also under Achehnese-Sumatran sovereignty." Here di Tiro's diary is clear that the return "to the *status quo ante bellum*, to March 26, 1873," only "constitutes the minimum legal claim."[125]

The model of GAM's Acehnese state was not just an ethnic one but also an Islamic one. According to di Tiro only a devout Muslim could lead this state. Indeed, "if a man is not fit to lead in prayer, he is not fit to lead the country and the state."[126] He pointed to Islam as "a complete system requiring total submission from the believers to Allah and his laws without any concessions to the Caesars," "because the law of Islam concerned equally to spiritual life, material life, moral life, political life, economic life, to relations between men and God, between men and other men, between men and women, between communities, and among nations."[127] Here, too, there was a historical precedent from the golden age, namely the Islamic Code of Iskandar Muda, which di Tiro saw as "the base of our [AM's] *stare decisis*."[128] Aceh's Islamic identity was also illustrated by di Tiro's choice of flag as well as holidays recognized by his Acehnese calendar. The flag comprised the white crescent and star on a red background of the Sultanate of Aceh Darussalam, but replacing the sword below the crescent and star with a black-and-white stripe above and below it. In these stripes the black represents the Acehnese martyrs in the resistance against the Dutch, the Japanese, and Indonesia, while the white symbolizes the sanctity of the struggle as well as the purity of the Acehnese nation.[129]

Aceh's calendar, as outlined in di Tiro's diary in March 1977, had holidays that commemorated "Muslim events such as the Birth of the Prophet, the Revelation of the Quran, Id al Fitr and Id al Adha but also Ashura" alongside "the deaths of key Acehnese such as Al-Malik Tengku Tjhik di Tiro, Sultan Mahmud Shah, Sultan Iskander Muda, Tjut Njak Dien and Teuku Umar as well as the battles of Alimon, Alue Simi, Alue Bhot, and of course the re-declaration of independence."[130]

GAM's narrative in the decades after di Tiro wrote his diary changed little. It remained discursive, drawing upon Acehnese history, and Acehneseness continued to be constructed against the Javanese "other." For instance, GAM negotiator Amni Ahmad bin Marzuki in 2001 explained that the Dutch in 1949 "did not own Aceh as the Acehnese had never surrendered" and that therefore the transfer of sovereignty was "totally against international law." He referred to the Indonesian government that took control of Aceh as a "Javanese government" that was "trying to re-establish the Majapahit kingdom" by reclaiming "all the territories ever claimed by Javanese kings. So no wonder they treat the islands outside Java as occupied territories."[131] Similarly, GAM minister of state Malik Mahmud in 2002 stated that "the creation of Indonesia was a ploy by the Dutch and some Western countries betraying our right to an independent state" and that "Javanese colonialism is the biggest problem." Like di Tiro, Mahmud also charged Indonesia with corruption, oppression, depleting Aceh's resources, and damaging Aceh's ecosystem.[132]

Some new elements, however, started to appear in AM/GAM's narrative in the 1990s. As the international community became more critical of Indonesia's human rights record with the end of the Cold War and, particularly, in reaction to the 1991 Santa Cruz massacre in East Timor, GAM incorporated both human rights and comparison with East Timor into its discourse. Shifts were also visible in how GAM's national imaginary was articulated. Here, the Islamic references started to be toned down while the democratic references were emphasized. In February 2002 Malik Mahmud responded to the question of what the Acehnese state would look like after independence by saying, "That is up to the Acehnese—ultimately it is up to the future generation."[133] Five months later, in July 2002, the Stavanger Declaration was issued, which stated that GAM sought the establishment of a democratic system in Aceh.[134]

National Imaginaries at War

The competing national imaginaries had a direct influence on how the war between GAM and the Indonesian security forces was fought. They determined aims, strategies, tactics, and, above all, the targets.[135] As to be expected, AM and

GAM targeted the Indonesian security forces as they were the "colonial occupiers." More illuminating in terms of the national imaginary are GAM's civilian targets: Indonesian government structures in Aceh, the Indonesian education system, Javanese transmigrants, and the oil industry in Lhokseumawe.

GAM targeted Indonesia's "alien" local government structures in Aceh in order to loosen Jakarta's control. Accordingly, GAM attacked public buildings and targeted civil servants at all levels.[136] This was particularly evident in the third phase of the conflict. Civil servants, judges, members of the regional parliaments, and village heads were intimidated, kidnapped, or shot. In 2000–2001, such actions caused the collapse of Aceh's legal system. In several districts courthouses were destroyed and many judges, prosecutors, and lawyers were subject to repeated intimidation.[137] Most judges fled.[138] Local legislators, especially those who criticized GAM, as well as the governor and deputy governor, were also targeted because they were all seen as the "lackeys of Jakarta."[139] Aceh governor Abdullah Puteh was blamed for the death of GAM commander Abdullah Syafi'i in January 2002, for the reestablishment of the regional military command in 2002, and for lobbying for a military solution in 2003.[140] GAM went as far as stating that with these acts Puteh had "lost his civilian rights in the war."[141] Other examples include the June 2003 shooting of Lhokseumawe's city secretary, Bachtiar, as he was traveling to Banda Aceh.[142] Later that month GAM kidnapped twenty-three village heads in Bireuen.[143] Langsa city councilor Budiman Samaun was also taken hostage. When martial law was declared in May 2003, TNI commander in chief General Endriatono Sutarto stated that 99 out of 228 districts and 4,750 out of 5,947 villages did not have a functioning local government.[144]

GAM's second civilian target was the Indonesian education system, as the national curriculum taught that Aceh was an integral part of Indonesia. It emphasized Pancasila over Islam and prioritized national history and identity. GAM saw the Indonesian education system as actively destroying Acehnese history and culture while promoting "the glorification of Javanese history."[145] One way of countering this was the tailoring of school curricula in GAM strongholds to a local view of history.[146] Another way was to burn schools so "that they were not used to turn Acehnese children into Indonesians."[147] The burning of schools and teachers' houses, as well as the intimidation and killing of teachers, began in the second phase of the Aceh conflict. Between January 1989 and June 2002, 527 schools, 89 houses of teachers, and 33 houses of principals were burned down.[148] Teachers were intimidated into not teaching the state curriculum. Many teachers quit their jobs and recruitment of new teachers became difficult as 60 teachers were killed, 200 others physically assaulted, and another 170 seriously injured or tortured during this period.[149] In the first two weeks of martial law in May 2003 over 600 schools went up in flames.

GAM's third civilian target was Javanese migrants. This also started in the second phase of the conflict as Javanese workers flocked to Aceh to take up jobs in the Lhokseumawe industrial complex. Others were being settled on new palm oil plantations when Aceh became part of the government's transmigration program in 1975. As in East Timor, transmigration to Aceh was also intended to bring "development" to the "backward" Acehnese. And as in East Timor, loyal Javanese were settled there to shore up Jakarta's claims. Thus Aceh needed to "absorb as many transmigrants as possible."[150] AM and GAM viewed this as a Javanization policy that aimed not only at taking Aceh's land but also at eradicating Acehnese culture, declaring that "Javanese transmigrants are marrying our own Sumatran daughters and dragging and forcing them to live under Javanese culture."[151] Seeing them as colonizers, thieves, and potential collaborators with the security forces, AM went on an offensive against them in mid-1990.[152] According to Amnesty International thousands of Javanese transmigrants and their families were intimidated into leaving their homes.[153] As GAM expanded into other parts of Aceh in the third phase of the conflict, more Javanese transmigrants were targeted. In September 1999, the *Jakarta Post* reported that thousands of Javanese transmigrants were fleeing North Aceh after being terrorized by GAM.[154] The Central Java transmigration office said that since July that year, 1,006 had left Aceh with their families.[155] GAM also started routine inspections of vehicles traveling through their areas looking for Javanese passengers.[156] In early 2001, GAM harassment of ethnic Javanese began to escalate. In May-June, GAM guerrillas and local sympathizers attacked the ethnically mixed Aceh-Gayo-Javanese areas of Central Aceh.[157] In Kresek village ten houses were burned and five people killed on the night of June 5, 2001.[158] Over a two-week period, the death toll reached sixty-four people, of whom fifty were Javanese. Some one thousand houses were burned. According to Staffan Bodemar, who worked in Aceh for the UNDP (United Nations Development Programme) in 2001, between 120,000 and 176,000 people, mostly Javanese, had fled to North Sumatra since 1999.[159]

GAM's final target was the oil industry in the greater Lhokseumawe area. Employees of both domestic and foreign companies lived under the threat of intimidation, kidnapping, or death since AM's early days. AM actions, according to di Tiro's diary, aimed at closing "down foreign oil companies . . . to prevent them from further stealing our oil and gas."[160] His diary entry for October 16, 1977, recounts how in an AM cabinet meeting the decision was made to safeguard Aceh's natural resources "that are being increasingly plundered by the Javanese and their foreign cohorts, especially our oil and gas."[161] Four days later, on October 20, AM leafleted the Lhokseumawe industrial complex, calling upon all American, Australian, and Japanese employees of Mobil Oil Indonesia (MOI) and Bechtel "to pack and leave this country immediately ... for we cannot guarantee the safety of your life and limbs. Your employers, Mobil and Bechtel, have made themselves co-conspirators with Javanese colonialist thieves in robbing our unrenewable gas resources for their mutual advantage."[162] In early December 1977, three foreign contractors for Bechtel, an American and two Koreans involved in the construction of the Arun Field Cluster III, came under attack. The American was killed by what di Tiro in his diary described as "stray bullets."[163] However, Bechtel's doctor at the time recorded events differently. According to him there was no evidence of a gun battle, only an armed attack on the unarmed foreign contractors. The American was shot dead while the two Koreans were able to flee the scene and hide in the rice paddies. Sofian Effendi, commander of special forces unit Nanggala 16, which was operating in the area at the time, claimed that the killing had been carried out by AM troops under Fauzi Hasbi's command.[164]

In the third phase of the conflict GAM stepped up attacks on the vulnerable oil and gas production facilities and pipelines now operated by ExxonMobil Oil Indonesia (EMOI). In March 2001, EMOI was forced to close production from its four onshore gas fields and to evacuate workers. GAM was also believed to have been responsible for firing at aircraft transporting ExxonMobil workers and hijacking the company's vehicles, as well as stopping and burning buses and planting landmines along roads to blow them up.[165] As EMOI public affairs manager Bill Cummings described the security situation:

> Between May 1999 and the onshore shutdown in March 2001, acts of vandalism increased and over 50 vehicles were hijacked from public roads. In 2000, two chartered airplanes carrying ExxonMobil workers were hit by ground fire. In one case in March 2000, a gunman on the back of a motorcycle fired at the plane as it was taxiing to the terminal in Point A, the Arun Field control center, wounding two passengers. Through a news story in a local newspaper a few days later, GAM claimed responsibility for the attack.[166]

GAM's issue with the oil and gas industry was twofold: it was seen, first, as exploiting Aceh's resources, and second, as collaborating with the Indonesian military, which was securing the industry's premises and receiving funds for this service from state oil company Pertamina. So GAM regarded these corporations as legitimate targets. As its spokesman Isnander al-Pasè explained in April 2003, "ExxonMobil is a legitimate target in war. Why? Because it helps the opponent's military and now Exxon is housing a military base within its complex. And the people living next to Exxon tell us that they do not get anything from Exxon while Exxon takes our oil."[167] Just as GAM's narrative and national imaginary played a determining role in target selection, so did the narrative and national imaginary advanced by the Indonesian government. As defenders of NKRI, the Indonesian security forces targeted GAM as a separatist organization, but they also targeted the Acehnese more broadly to discourage them from supporting GAM. At the top of their list in all three phases of the conflict were GAM's political and military leaders, who were targeted in the belief that without its leaders GAM would disintegrate and its directionless supporters could be brought under control more easily. Targeting the leaders was also a way to target GAM's military and civilian structures, in short, GAM's shadow state.

In the first phase, Kopassandha teams pursued di Tiro and his men into the jungle and succeeded in killing, capturing, or forcing into exile most of AM's first cabinet. In the second phase too, the focus was on taking out AM's leaders. By the end of 1991, many AM field commanders had been captured or killed.[168] The killing of AM *panglima wilayah* Samudra-Pasè Yusuf Ali and the subsequent capture of his wife Mariani Ali, who had led the guerrillas after her husband's death, brought to an end organized AM resistance in the stronghold of North Aceh. AM had been virtually crushed, its remnants driven underground or into exile to Malaysia.[169] During the third phase, the Indonesian military killed GAM's commander in chief Abdullah Syafi'i in January 2002 as well as a number of low-level GAM commanders. The introduction of martial law in in May 2003 also saw the arrest of GAM negotiators Amni bin Marzuki, Teungku Kamaruzzaman, Sofian Ibrahim Tiba, Nashiruddin Ahmad, and Teungku Muhamed bin Usman Lampoh Awe. They were charged with treason and terrorism and sentenced to between twelve and sixteen years in prison.

Pressure was also exerted upon high-ranking GAM personnel to give themselves up. Those who surrendered included West Aceh district commander Teuku Ali Said, Tamiang governor Zulfauzi, Bireuen district commander Dedi, and Tiro field operations commander Amri bin Abdul Wahab. Others were captured, such as GAM spokesman Irwandi Yusuf and the district commanders of East Aceh, South Aceh, and Aceh Besar. Those killed included Samudra Pasè governor Said Adnan as well as Pasè deputy commander Teungku Ibrahim. Peureulak operational commander Ishak Daud, who baited the TNI throughout martial law with high-profile operations and kidnappings, was shot dead on September 8, 2004.[170] In all three phases the targeting of the leaders weakened AM's and GAM's military and civilian structures, sometimes eliminating them until they were revived years later.

In addition to the AM and GAM leaders, the movement's members of all ranks were targeted. Here the aim was to reduce the overall strength of AM and GAM as an organization and its territorial control. In the 1970s, when AM was still a small organization of some seventy men, targeting the leadership virtually overlapped with targeting members. This changed with the second phase of the conflict when AM expanded considerably. The houses of suspected AM members were systematically burned down and AM members themselves were hunted.[171] Similarly, in the third phase, operations commander Major General Djali Yusuf stated that GAM concentrations and training camps were specifically targeted.[172] When martial law was imposed, TNI commander in chief General Sutarto ordered his troops to "destroy GAM forces down to their roots" by "finishing off, killing, those who still engage in armed resistance."[173] The Indonesian security forces conducted house-to-house searches for GAM members.[174] By May 2004, 1,963 GAM members had been killed, 2,100 captured, and 2,075 had surrendered.[175]

During all three phases the families of known AM and GAM members were also targeted. Parents, wives, siblings, and children were routinely interrogated and sometimes tortured in order to obtain information.[176] Starting with the Nanggala operations in the first phase, female family members were held as hostages in order to get their male relatives to surrender.[177] Many of the women suffered humiliation, sexual abuse, and rape at the hands of the security forces.[178] In the third phase of the conflict, the houses of the families of GAM members were marked with a red "X" by the military and kept under surveillance.[179]

In August 2003, known GAM wives were registered with the security forces and many were obliged to report to the security forces twice a day.[180] Some GAM wives such as Jamilah, the wife of GAM Aceh Rayeuk governor Teungku Achyar, were even forced to divorce their husbands.[181] On April 7, 2004, TNI troops arrested GAM commander in chief Muzakkir Manaf's wife Aisyah and her young children, detaining them first at a TNI post and then moving them to a "controlled village."[182] On April 23, all GAM families in the Keude Bieng area were called to the Kopassus post in Lhokgna, and told that if their GAM relatives did not surrender within the next twenty days, their identification cards would be revoked and their houses marked.[183] On April 30, members of the extensive family of GAM Aceh Rayeuk commander Tengku Muharram Idris were arrested and detained in order to force him to surrender.

Another specific target that directly relates to competing national narratives was human rights activists and NGOs. This was particularly evident in the third phase of the conflict when, in the context of Indonesia's transition to democracy, alternative narratives on the Aceh conflict and Acehnese history could be openly voiced, and the security narrative advanced by Jakarta during the first two phases of the conflict could be challenged. In the eyes of the security forces, human rights activists and NGOs were endorsing the GAM narrative on Acehnese independence. As a result, from 2000 onwards security forces' pressure on local and foreign NGOs in Aceh increased significantly. Some NGOs, such as the Aceh Referendum

Information Center (SIRA) and Student Solidarity for the People (SMUR), were seen as particularly close to GAM.[184] Indeed, according to Major Edi Sulistiadi, "GAM and SIRA are the same. SIRA is the political wing of GAM."[185]

On September 19, 2000, two leading SIRA activists, Mohammed A. Saleh and Muzzakir, were abducted by out-of-uniform officers of Brimob (police mobile brigade). They were interrogated, beaten, and then released.[186] In November, SIRA's office was raided by the police, and its chairman, Muhammad Nazar, was later arrested. As Nazar explained, "I was accused of separatism. Also, SIRA members in Jakarta were arrested. I was not arrested because I was part of GAM but because I organized people power. SIRA has no institutional relations with GAM, but we do not reject GAM's struggle."[187] Other NGOs, both foreign and local, were also subjected to repeated harassment and intimidation. One of the most brutal incidents occurred on December 6, 2000, when four volunteers from RATA, a local organization for the rehabilitation of torture victims, were abducted and three of them killed.[188]

In June 2001, Colonel Endang Suwarya asserted that the NGOs did not just give support to the people, "they give money to GAM."[189] They were also seen as tools for foreign intervention, as foreign spies, and as agents of conflict.[190] In April 2003, a month before the imposition of martial law, General Ryamizard Ryacudu stated that the problem with NGOs was that "they get money only when there is conflict so they don't want the conflict to end."[191] Not surprisingly, during the first week of Operasi Terpadu, military authorities systematically started to arrest activists and NGO personnel. Between May 19 and 27, forty-five students and activists were apprehended on suspicion of links with GAM.[192] According to Amnesty International, twenty-one activists were brought to trial during the martial law period. These included SIRA chairman Muhammad Nazar, who was sentenced to two years in prison for campaigning for a referendum; Cut Nur Asikin of the Aceh women's rights organization Srikandi, who was accused of being the commander of GAM's Inong Bale women's battalion; Husni Abdullah and Mahyeddin, members of the People's Crisis Centre, a humanitarian organization that helped Acehnese internally displaced persons (IDPs); Daun, a university student and volunteer for the local Monitoring Committee for Peace and Democracy in Aceh; Nuraini, a member of the Commission for the Disappeared and Victims of Violence (Kontras); and two volunteers with the Indonesian Red Cross.[193]

The final target of the Indonesian security forces was much less narrowly defined but is equally illustrative of how Jakarta perceived Aceh's challenge to the Indonesian national imaginary. This target was the Acehnese population, which was seen as potential supporters of GAM both politically and logistically. Or in the words of Colonel A. Y. Nasution, "GAM and the community are like fish and water. So long as there is water, the fish will live. But if the water is completely drained away, then the fish will die."[194] The aim thus became cutting any links between the Acehnese and GAM, isolating GAM, deterring the Acehnese from supporting GAM, and "inoculating" the population against GAM's ideas and ideology.

Deterring the people from supporting AM characterized much of the second period of the Aceh conflict. This took the form of heavy-handed military reprisals against villages believed to be providing logistical help or sanctuary to the insurgents. Common tactics included the burning of the homes of suspected independence supporters or sometimes their entire villages. This "shock therapy" was described as a "campaign of terror designed to strike fear in the population and make them withdraw their support from GAM."[195] Anyone suspected of contact with AM was vulnerable to arbitrary arrest and detention, torture, "disappearance," or summary execution.[196] "For a period of about two years after the start of combat operations, the corpses of Acehnese victims, generally young men, were found strewn in public places—beside main roads, near village security posts, in public markets, in fields and plantations, next to a stream or river—apparently as a warning to others not to join or support the rebels."[197] In the third phase of the conflict, deterrence took the form of collective punishment, such as that meted out against the East Aceh town of Idi Rayeuk in March 2001, or the burning down of the house of the head of Simpang Mamplan village in May 2001.[198] These punishments ran in parallel with forced relocation of people—as in East Timor—akin to "strategic hamleting" and systematic "loyalization" efforts.[199] In 2001 over six thousand villages were compelled to declare their loyalty.[200] During the martial law period "loyalization" began with the military mobilizing people to attend loyalty ceremonies to swear allegiance to the Republic of Indonesia. Mass participation in the recitation of oaths of loyalty to the Indonesian state was even broadcast on television.[201] The population was encouraged to fly Indonesia's red-and-white flag, as "flying the flag is an indication of whether they are really Indonesian or not," as army spokesman Colonel Ditya Soedarsono put it.[202] This was followed by the mobilization of nationalist youth groups such as Pemuda Merah Putih that demonstrated in favor of martial law, and whose key function was to display loyalty to Indonesia and hatred of GAM. "Loyalization" further included the introduction of "loyalty tests" for some sixty-seven thousand civil servants.[203] Those who failed the test were replaced, as was the case of thirteen district heads and two Acehnese councillors.[204] Another administrative measure was the issuing of new "red-and-white" identity cards in efforts to distinguish civilians from GAM members.[205] These new ID cards needed to be produced at checkpoints and people unable to produce them fell under the suspicion of being GAM.[206] Suspected GAM supporters as well as suspected members were also put on *pembinaan* (guidance courses). Major Prasetyo, who was running the *pembinaan* in Lhokseumawe, explained that a course lasted for around five months and was designed to teach them "what is NKRI, Pancasila, and the Indonesian constitution."[207] The first three months focused purely on Indonesian nationalism. After that, skill training was added. The course he was running at the time had 672 participants.[208]

"Belonging" in Aceh: Conditional and Contentious

GAM defined "Acehneseness" in juxtaposition to both "Javaneseness" and "Indonesianness." Being Acehnese and being Indonesian were therefore mutually exclusive and as di Tiro explained in his diary, "any Acehnese who has come to believe that he is not Acehnese but 'Indonesians' [sic] he is suffering an identity crisis."[209] Di Tiro further stated that "when a people lost [sic] their national consciousness and forget their history, they can no longer exercise their right of self-determination. That is what happened to the Acehnese generation of 1945," thus accounting for why Aceh did not resist becoming part of Indonesia when the latter became an independent state.[210]

While di Tiro adopted an unequivocal position, for most of the Acehnese population the question of belonging was far more complicated. It was tied to how they read the causes of the Aceh conflict and experienced it. This sometimes shifted over time and divided not only society but also families, as this account from Teuku Kamal shows:

> I myself come from a family which has both GAM and NKRI. The conflict has been passed on from generation to generation. This conflict started within the house and went from house to house, village to village, region to region. It is really a civil war in that sense although it does not look like that from the outside. . . . The society feels frustrated and some parts of society are so frustrated that they have become separatist. There are some who choose NKRI and some who choose GAM.[211]

The popular discourse on how the Acehnese see their place in Indonesia has revolved around six core issues: broken promises, the place of Islam, the place of local *adat* customs, inequality, injustice, and human rights abuses. One of the most commonly iterated factors undermining Acehnese support for Jakarta is the history of promises broken by the central government. For instance, Malik Musa, the head of Muhammdiyah youth in 2001, saw this as key to understanding why many Acehnese were disillusioned with Indonesia: "For the Acehnese there have been so many promises from the government. The Acehnese don't believe them anymore and for the Acehnese it is difficult to forget. This will be passed on to the next generation."[212] According to Yusny Saby, a lecturer at the state institute for Islamic Studies IAIN Ar-Raniry Darussalam, "the Acehnese felt part of it [Indonesia] when independence was declared on 17 August 1945, but then Aceh was included into North Sumatra" despite having been promised a province of its own.[213] It was this broken promise that gave rise to the 1953 Darul Islam rebellion, which was about returning "special status to Aceh" because "Aceh was meant to be different."[214] Saby also attributed the 1976 insurgency to the failure of the central government "to accommodate the needs of Aceh in unity in diversity."[215] Broken promises were also flagged up by Abdullah Puteh, the governor of Aceh in 2004. He too stated that "Aceh was first to support Indonesia." In fact, he called it the "model of the region." But then "Aceh was placed under the leadership of the Karo and the Batak, Aceh's provincial status was removed, Aceh was ignored by the central government, and Acehnese dignity was stepped on."[216]

The removal of Aceh's provincial status and special status had a direct bearing on the place for Islam and local *adat* customs in the governance of Aceh. The subordination of both to Indonesian state law and national culture caused considerable discontent. As Imam Suja, the chairman of Aceh's branch of Muhammadiyah, asserted in 2001, Aceh's ulama "felt particularly hurt" because Aceh had been promised *syariah* as part of its special status and also because the ulama "were used" by both the Indonesian government and GAM "as a political tool . . . to get legitimacy from the people."[217] The head of Aceh's *syariah* services, Alyasa Abubakar, concurred. In 2002, he saw the reintroduction of *syariah* as necessary because "Aceh will become better with *syariah*." While *syariah* would not solve the conflict in the short term, he asserted that "if *syariah* is not implemented the killing will never stop. We need to break the cycle of revenge. This can only be achieved through religion."[218]

According to Malik Musa *syariah* and Acehnese *adat* were closely intertwined "like essence and substance—it is difficult to differentiate them." He gave the example of *musyawarah*. "*Syariah* asks us to solve problems through *musyawarah* and *adat* also uses *musyawarah*. . . . So violence cannot be a solution for the Acehnese. If you want to solve this conflict it must be through respect, nonviolence and without the military. For the Acehnese the most important thing is sitting in the *musyawarah* to solve all problems by *musyawarah*."[219] This view on the importance of local *adat* was also held by Teuku Kamal, who advocated "*adat* law not politics" as a way "to deal with the mentality of the separatists," alongside honesty from the government because "if *adat* is not revived morality will totally disappear."[220]

Closely related to the narrative on broken promises is the narrative on the inequality that Aceh experienced. Azwar Abubakar, deputy governor of Aceh in 2001, saw Aceh's political and economic marginalization by Jakarta as the key factor that undermined the Acehnese sense of belonging to Indonesia. "All the resources from Aceh go to Jakarta. If there was equality there would be no conflict. But they cannot share. This is the problem. The government is centralized like the VOC during the Dutch era. It is getting many resources. This is exacerbated by corruption. It is like that in almost all provinces of Indonesia but the Acehnese feel that their resources are bigger and they get less than other provinces."[221] This view was shared by Saby, who asserted that "the Acehnese feel discriminated against in every aspect of life—economics, politics, and education."

> The roads here are like they were 100 years ago. We should have a much better infrastructure. We used to have a train and then the central government stopped subsidizing it. We were active and you could go everywhere. It was a regular line until the 1960s but after that nothing has been developed. Some houses are bigger but far more have degenerated.... Education is decreasing simply because of corruption. There is no mobility and there are no values. Education is meant for enriching society but here it is only enriching the education managers. And in the military who is Acehnese? Always the driver and that's the feeling.[222]

Puteh believed these feelings were exploited by AM in 1976 as "Hasan di Tiro's concept was to eradicate poverty." He explained that "during the 1970s the situation was poor" and "that's when Hasan di Tiro appeared and promised change."[223]

Inequality and perceptions of inequality in Aceh were further exacerbated by the sense of injustice. Nasrullah Dahlawy, who was part of the team monitoring the Humanitarian Pause in 2001, believed that "most Acehnese consider Indonesia as alien because the suffering is so much. Many of the Acehnese want to separate from Indonesia because they can't trust the Indonesian government any longer." He placed particular emphasis on the Javanese "pushing themselves onto all other peoples of the archipelago without warning" and their "impunity," adding that "no one here can have a fair trial."[224]

Not surprisingly, human rights abuses by the Indonesian security forces during the three decades of the conflict also occupy a central place in the discourse on injustice. For instance, Muhammad Nazar, the head of SIRA, recounted that "Suharto described Aceh as special territory," and then declared, "What did he mean?—human rights abuses and massacres!" These also included the destruction of "identity and culture." He further believed that "there is no philosophy that the Acehnese can subscribe to in the Indonesian state," which is why SIRA organized a referendum on independence in November 1999, taking its cue from the referendum on East Timorese independence two months earlier. According to Nazar, 92 percent of the 2.7 million Acehnese polled voted for independence and only 1 percent for remaining part of Indonesia. For Nazar there was only one solution, namely to let the Acehnese people decide for themselves as "Indonesia has had 55 years' time for every political experiment" to make this work. In the end, "Acehnese political culture and Javanese political culture are too different."[225]

Saby, too, highlighted the human rights abuses in Aceh and the correlation between human rights abuses and the support for independence. "In 1976 very few people supported independence, but the treatment of GAM by the central government—the kidnapping, torture, and killings—created resistance. By the end of DOM, people supported the idea of independence but not necessarily GAM. The treatment we had received was as if Aceh was not part of Indonesia."[226] This snapshot of views clearly demonstrates the degree to which the Acehnese felt alienated from Jakarta. Their belonging was both conditional and contentious. It was conditional on the original bargain which saw Aceh's efforts during Indonesia's war of independence rewarded with special status. It was contentious, as Acehnese values were defined by Islam. This conditionality and contentiousness were strengthened with every promise broken by the Indonesian government, by Aceh's marginalization, and by the military force used to subdue Acehnese discontent. Thus, for many Acehnese being Indonesian held little meaning.

Reflecting on Three Decades of Conflict in Aceh

The 1976–2005 Aceh conflict, just like the 1953–1959 Darul Islam rebellion in Aceh, was rooted in the way Indonesia was conceptualized as a state based on Pancasila. This sat awkwardly with Aceh's strong Islamic identity and undermined Aceh's sense of belonging. Jakarta's "mechanism" for reconciling the differences as well as recognizing Aceh's contribution to Indonesia's war of independence was to give Aceh autonomous status, including the right to implement *syariat Islam*. The breakdown of this mechanism paved the way for both Aceh insurgencies, as autonomy became subsumed by Indonesia's centralization drive, first under Sukarno and again under Suharto. However, while the root causes of the violence were similar, the Acehnese response to Jakarta differed considerably. Aceh's Darul Islam rebellion sought to change the nature of the Indonesian state to make it a better fit for Aceh; GAM's 1976–2005 insurgency sought to secede from it.

This resulted in different narratives and national imaginaries. GAM's narrative was shaped considerably by its leader, Hasan di Tiro, who wrote most of the foundational tracts, interweaving his personal history with that of Aceh. He reframed the latter to argue that Aceh had been incorporated into the Indonesian Republic illegally, as sovereignty should have been transferred from the Dutch to the Acehnese. GAM's ability to build upon existing popular narratives such as the golden era of Sultan Iskandar Muda, Aceh's place in the Muslim world, and Aceh's heroic resistance to the Dutch, as well as its ability to draw upon Acehnese grievances resulting from Sukarno's and Suharto's policies, gave GAM credibility in the eyes of large parts of the local population. This was reinforced by how GAM's quest for independence and its national imaginary of a more Islamic Acehnese state were constructed against an Indonesian national imaginary that had repeatedly failed to accommodate Aceh's more Islamic identity. Not surprisingly, GAM's alternative narrative and national imaginary were seen as a greater threat to Indonesia than GAM's military capacity. The Aceh conflict was thus, above all, an ideological war pursued largely by military means.

The Aceh conflict was brought to an end in August 2005 with a Memorandum of Understanding (MoU) between the Indonesian government and GAM. In simple terms, the MoU was a return to the "mechanism" that bridged the gap between Pancasila and Acehnese identity. Aceh was granted wide-ranging autonomy within Indonesia. It received the right to use regional symbols including a flag, a crest, and a hymn as well as the right to establish Aceh-based political parties, which provided a way for GAM to enter politics. Aceh also had jurisdiction over living natural resources in its territorial sea as well as being entitled to retain 70 percent of the revenue from all current and future hydrocarbon deposits and other natural resources. The MoU stipulated that the legal code for Aceh would be redrafted on the basis of the universal principles of human rights, and that Aceh would receive its own independent court system, a human rights court, and a truth and reconciliation commission.[227] After the MoU was signed, GAM members were granted amnesty and those imprisoned were released. GAM demobilized 3,000 troops and decommissioned 840 weapons between September 15 and December 31, 2005, while Indonesia withdrew all nonorganic security forces, leaving 14,700 TNI and 9,100 police.[228] In 2006, the Law on the Governance of Aceh introduced provisions for the implementation of *syariat Islam*, with respect to not just civil and family law but also criminal law. The Acehnese thus for the first time achieved what they believed they had been promised since Indonesia's struggle for independence. The peace has held for the last two decades, despite sporadic violence, mostly in the run-up to elections. This peace, however, remains fragile and Acehnese "belonging" remains conditional and contentious.

5
THE POSO CONFLICT, 1998–2007

The fall of Suharto invigorated the push for independence in East Timor and Aceh. The resulting power vacuum, with the Indonesian security forces politically on the defensive in Jakarta or battling separatism in the regions, allowed for simmering Christian-Muslim tensions in Poso Regency, Central Sulawesi, to break out into the open. On December 24, 1998, a brawl broke out between a Christian and a Muslim youth in Poso city. Within hours both religious communities had mobilized, clashing repeatedly over the next five days. When the violence subsided on December 29, some two hundred people had been injured and more than four hundred houses had been looted and then burned, most of them Christian. The conflict continued for almost a decade, during which churches, mosques, shops, and houses were destroyed, and massacres were perpetrated. Over this whole period, politicians in Jakarta were largely uninterested while the security forces focused on the greater threat posed by separatism in other parts of the archipelago. The Poso conflict was thus allowed to evolve from urban riots, to communal clashes, organized offensives, jihad, and terrorism.

This chapter examines the first of two case studies of communal violence: the 1998–2007 Poso conflict. It starts with an analysis of the roots of the conflict, focusing on Christian-Muslim relations, in-migration, Islamization, and the opportunity structure for change provided by *reformasi*. The chapter then looks at how the violence evolved from urban riots to wide-spread communal confrontation and from a local conflict that was joined by non-local volunteers. It examines the combatants involved, their aims, strategies, and national imaginaries, and concludes with a discussion on belonging and feelings of alienation of Poso's Christians and Muslims.

This chapter shows that it was the shift of the Indonesian national imaginary in a more Islamic direction in the late New Order that triggered the Poso conflict. It further demonstrates that the organized violence from 2000 to 2007 was underwritten by misaligned national imaginaries between Jakarta and Poso. For the Christians in Poso this misalignment began in the late New Order when Suharto started courting the Muslims. The in-migration of Muslims and the more Islamic national imaginary together were perceived as an existential threat by local Christians, which explains the nature and extent of their offensive in May 2000. For the Muslims in Poso this misalignment started during the conflict when the election of Abdurrahman Wahid as Indonesia's fourth president shifted the national imaginary back to a pluralist one, but above all when Jakarta failed to respond to the Walisongo massacre. This disconnected them from the center and made them receptive to the alternative national imaginary—an Islamic state and *khilafa*—advocated by the mujahidin from Java, who had come to Poso to defend their Muslim brethren. It is important to note, in light of the previous conflict case studies in this book, that neither Christians nor Muslims in Poso developed their own alternative national imaginaries. The Christians stayed tied to the dominant national imaginary projected by Jakarta, namely the pluralist Pancasila Indonesia, while Muslims supported the more Islamic Indonesian national imaginary projected by the late New Order and ICMI or the alternative national imaginary advocated by JI.

The Roots of Conflict in Poso

The majority of Muslims and Christians in the coastal city of Poso and the highland town of Tentena were surprised by the outbreak of the conflict as well as its intensity and protractedness. Virtually every person interviewed for this book maintained that Christians and Muslims had lived peacefully together in the past and that there was a long tradition of intercommunal cooperation exemplified by the concept of *sintuwu maroso* (brotherhood ties) and the tradition of *padungku*, in which the Christians would invite the Muslims for *silaturrahmi* (friendly get-togethers) after the harvest. However, a closer examination of Christian-Muslim relations, in-migration, and Islamization during the New Order, as well as the impact of the fall of Suharto, explains both the eruption of intercommunal violence and the fault lines of the conflict.

When Dutch Protestant missionaries came to Central Sulawesi in 1892, they encountered a population comprising local Muslim fishermen in the coastal areas and animists, who practiced shifting cultivation, in the interior.[1] The relationship between Muslims and animists was complex, as they were geographically separated yet economically interdependent, largely peaceful, albeit with a "routine existence of small-scale warfare."[2] The animist Pamona and Mori were the first to embrace Christianity, deciding "*en masse* to adopt the religion of the new rulers" after a brutal Dutch pacification campaign in 1905.[3] The highland town of Tentena then became the local center of Christianity as the Netherlands Missionary Society set up its headquarters there. After Indonesian independence, Tentena continued to be the region's Protestant stronghold, home to the synod of the Central Sulawesi Protestant Church (Gereja Kristen Sulawesi Tengah, GKST).

The introduction of Christianity and the incorporation of Central Sulawesi into the Netherlands Indies affected the relations between the communities of the highland and the coast in three important ways. First, Christianization united the animist communities. Second, the missionary schools gave the Christians an educational advantage that ensured that Protestants were given preference over Muslims in local bureaucratic positions right up until the 1980s. And third, Dutch regulations and imports disrupted precolonial highland-lowland alliances.[4] Thus by the time the Japanese invaded in 1942, Poso's Protestants were both economically and politically linked to the colonial regime, which then resulted in both Japanese and Muslim repercussions. According to Reverend Tarau, "During the Japanese occupation a lot of Christian teachers and clergy were killed or imprisoned by the Japanese army. Some were executed. And this was carried out by local Muslims. They told the Japanese that the Christians were friendly with the Dutch."[5] Indonesian independence stopped the maltreatment of the Christians, but it did not bring the two communities closer. During the early Sukarno years, Central Sulawesi found itself geographically wedged between Muslim-majority South Sulawesi, which had become one of Darul Islam's territories, and Christian-majority North Sulawesi, which had joined the 1957–1961 Universal Struggle Charter (Piagam Perjuangan Semesta Alam, Permesta) rebellion.[6] Not surprisingly, local history refers to this period as the time of the *gerombolan* (gangs) as both DI and Permesta forces often carried out attacks in Central Sulawesi.[7] As local Christians assisted the Indonesian security forces in fighting both rebel groups, the army favored Christians right into the 1970s.[8] Yet, as the communists gained more influence in the late Sukarno era, Poso too experienced changes. Reverend Tarau recalled that "the communists came and became the majority in politics also in Poso. There was no more community organization to give a voice to the aspiration of local people."[9]

The position of Poso's Christians started to decline politically.[10] This was exacerbated with the rise of the New Order and its transmigration program. Between 1975 and 1990 181,696 transmigrants were settled in transmigration sites in Central Sulawesi.¹¹ Further spontaneous migration followed with the start of the construction of the Trans-Sulawesi Highway from Makassar to Manado as part of the New Order's developmentalist ideology. This large influx of migrants affected the demographic balance in no uncertain terms, with respect to both the indigenous-migrant and Christian-Muslim ratios. As most migrants were Muslim, it was in the latter that the greatest changes were seen. As explained by Jusuf Kalla, coordinating minister for people's welfare at the time of the Poso conflict, "Poso had been 60 percent Christian and 40 percent Muslim. That was in the 1960s and 70s until the Trans-Sulawesi Highway was built. Then the Bugis came from the South and Javanese transmigrants came from the north. The demography changed to 60 percent Muslims and 40 percent Christians."¹² This large influx of migrants had an enormous economic impact. The new migrants flocked to the extractive industries such as ebony and cash crops, soon dominating the clove, cacao, coffee, and copra trade as well. They also owned the majority of small shops.¹³ Even the market in Tentena became dominated by migrants of Bugis, Gorontalo, and Arab descent, with the effect that pork was no longer sold because the traders were Muslim.¹⁴ By the 1990s the key sectors of the economy were dominated by migrants, partially because the local Christians were more interested in civil service positions and partially because the migrants were able to tap into existing ethnic trade networks. Not surprisingly, those who posed the largest economic threat were subsequently targeted in the conflict. Reverend Irianto Kongkoli elaborated that "The Christians went against the Bugis, Gorontalo, and Javanese because they were an economic threat. They did not go against Balinese migrants because they interacted differently. The Bugis and Gorontalo were aggressive. Also the Bugis, Gorontalo, and Javanese tended to be Muslims and disturbed the religious balance. The Balinese and Florinese migrants did not."¹⁵ While most spontaneous migrants settled in the coastal areas in and around Poso city, transmigrant sites tended to be located more in the interior. Coupled with Sukarno-era and New Order land policies, this settlement pattern led to encroachment upon Pamona and Mori *adat* land. This process began with the 1960 Basic Agrarian Law, which transferred legal control of *adat* land to the state for potential development purposes. In 1967 two further laws were passed, one on forestry and one on investment, which allowed foreign companies to finance and control industries in Indonesia's forested interiors. In 1973, Presidential Instruction No. 2 designated Central Sulawesi and nine other outer island provinces as new transmigration sites. This legal framework was completed with the 1974 Regional Government Law and the 1979 Village Government Law, which removed power from local *adat* councils of elders and placed it in the hands of the national civil service bureaucracy. Deemed as vacant state land, Pamona *adat* land was used for transmigration sites and hundreds of hectares of Mori *adat* land were taken for palm oil plantations.[16] *Hutan lindung* (protected forest) was sold over repeated protests by the indigenous population, and during the last decade of the New Order there were intermittent outbreaks of violence between the indigenous people and transmigrants that were put down by the military.[17]

From the 1990s onwards, spontaneous migrants also started to push into the interior of Poso district searching for land, especially for cacao plantations.[18] Indeed, after the 1997 Asian financial crisis migrants flocked to the area to grow cacao, "which had become a 'hot' export crop because it was pegged to the US dollar."[19] Some migrants did not even bother to purchase land but simply entered Pamona ancestral forests with chainsaws and cut down the trees to clear fields for cacao and other cash crops.[20]

The loss of *adat* land had a traumatic impact on the indigenous highlanders, as the land was intrinsically connected to indigenous beliefs, and that had not changed when the Pamona, Lore, and Mori had become Protestants. The land was still considered sacral as it tied the present generation to their ancestors. The commodification and alienation of Christian ancestral lands thus translated into not only impoverization but also cultural dislocation.

The loss of land, however, was not the only issue to have an impact on indigenous culture. The behavior of migrants, who came with their own culture, also created tensions. Expectations by the indigenous population that local *adat* should be respected were not met, giving way to a wave of complaints. Albert Tumimor, the district attorney in Tentena, recalled his grandfather, the *raja* of Poso, saying, "I did not call you or invite you. But if you want to stay here, respect our traditions." He further elaborated that "many Muslims came to Poso. But they did not behave like guests or what you would expect from newcomers. When they were there for a while and had become rich, they started to suppress the indigenous."[21] Indeed, Muslim transmigrants were seen as more aggressive and more violent than local Muslims, and also as arrogant, looking down on indigenous customs.[22] These tensions increased further when the government in Jakarta started to apply the label "primitive" to groups with recent animistic traditions.

And last, but certainly not least, there was the impact of migration and transmigration upon the education sector, the civil service, and local political constellations. The impact of the Muslim migrants pushing into higher education and the civil service was felt particularly acutely, as these were the areas that Poso's Christians saw as theirs. They were central to the Christians' self-identity but also to their economic survival. As coreligionists they had occupied a privileged position in the colonial civil service. Their educational advantage had also ensured that they remained dominant in these positions throughout much of the Sukarno era and the New Order. However, in the 1990s Muslims started to push into these positions, as they had caught up educationally. Rinaldy Damanik gave the example of the University of Tadulako, where locals on the eve of the Poso conflict only comprised 20 percent of the lecturers and administrative staff.[23] The other 80 percent were largely Muslim migrants. Thus, in the late New Order, Christian resentment was already visible as Protestants started to feel that they were losing key positions such as *bupati* (district head) and *sekwilda* (district secretary) and with them, of course, access to government funds and contracts.[24]

The in-migration had clearly marginalized indigenous Christians and to a lesser extent indigenous Muslims—economically, socially, culturally, and politically. It had ensured that "the elite and the middle class became Muslim and the Christians found themselves at the bottom."[25] And while these developments were recognized by some of the local Muslims, concerns were overridden by Muslim solidarity, on the one hand, and dismissed as consequences of the laziness of indigenous Christians, on the other. As explained by Muslim businessman Mohamed Daeng Raja, who himself played a not insignificant role in the early stages of the conflict:

> The migrants worked day and night. This created an economic gap. It is the fault of the Christian leaders. They received aid and they kept Christian society dumb. You have to work if you want to be rich. The Christians were still a majority when the transmigrants came. Cacao is the main harvest here and it raised expectations in society. Fifty years ago, the local government was full of Christians. 90 percent of the positions were Christian including the *bupati*. In 1984 the first Muslim *bupati* was appointed for Poso. Until that point all *bupatis* had been Christian. Also the *sekwildas*. Since then Muslims have started taking civil service positions and there has been social jealousy.[26]

In-migration had the effect of Islamizing society and politics in Poso, initially as a by-product. However, many Christians believed that Islamization actually was one of the aims of transmigration to areas with large Christian populations.[27] This Islamization was strengthened by two factors: first, the Islamic revival since the late 1970s and second, the redirection of government policy toward state-driven Islamization in the 1990s. Lorraine Aragon noted that "as early as 1978, Muslim demands led Protestant proselytizing and mission funding to be more closely controlled by the Suharto government."[28] By the 1990s many clinics and schools that had previously been funded and operated by Protestant churches had been seized by the government while Muslims, especially modernists such as Muhammadiyah, started increasing their educational networks. Indeed, it is this period that Poso and Tentena Christians see as start of the "radicalization" of *pesantren* Walisongo, the site of one of the largest atrocities in the third phase of the conflict in 2000. GKST synod head Reverend Tobundo asserted that "already before 1998 they were becoming quite fanatic. It was under Muhammadiyah when a Javanese named Marban came there in 1987. For fifteen years already Christians had to move from that place."[29]

State-driven Islamization is usually dated to the establishment in 1990 of ICMI. High on ICMI's agenda was increasing the number of Muslims in leading positions in government and society in Indonesia's eastern provinces with large non-Muslim populations. These changes, driven by grassroots Muslims from below and government policy from above, created fear among Poso's Christians as well as communal entrenchment. They reinforced psychological and physical segregation, as exemplified by separate education from elementary school to university. The University of Sintuwu Maroso even had two campuses, one in Poso for Muslim students and one in Tentena for Christian students.[30]

As ICMI gained in influence in Poso, it disturbed the unwritten power-sharing agreement that had existed between Muslims and Christians. This tradition stipulated that if a Muslim was appointed, his deputy would be Christian and vice versa. If the executive branch was dominated by Christians, then the legislative was dominated by Muslims. Between 1989 and 1999 the top fifty positions in the office of the *bupati*, the heads of offices, agencies, divisions, and subdistricts saw the percentage of Christian officeholders drop from 54 percent to 39 percent.[31] According to Damanik, these developments started with the appointment of Arief Patanga as *bupati* and were further entrenched by his successor, Abdul Muin Pusadan. Not only were all leaders of the executive and legislative branches Muslim, but they were also members of ICMI.[32] Not surprisingly, many Christians believed that ICMI was at least partially responsible for the conflict in 1998 as exemplified by Albert Bisalemba, Lucas and Rasip Ley: "The Muslims want a Muslim Poso. That is a national program. ICMI started this policy. It was Habibie's program. He kicked all Christians out of leading positions. ICMI wants to occupy all positions in the army, the police, and the bureaucracy."[33] When Suharto fell in May 1998 and the tight control that the New Order had exercised over ethnicity, religion, race, and intergroup relations referred to by the acronym SARA (Suku, Agama, Ras, Antar-Golongan) came to an end, the opportunity presented itself for policy reversals at local level.[34] Four issues, in particular, had an impact on Christian-Muslim relations in Poso. The first was the spate of attacks on Christians across Indonesia in the late New Order. Churches were burned and in some cases Christians killed in what John Sidel described as places "known for the Islamic piety of their inhabitants": Purwokerto, Tasikmalaya, Situbondu,

Pekalongan, Makassar, and Banjarmasin.[35] Poso, too, saw tensions during this period:

> It started with the anti-Chinese violence in 1997. After that the prices of goods increased enormously and the Muslims were angry about that. Then when Christians from the highlands wanted to enter Poso, they were only permitted to park at the airport. The students at Muslim universities set up checkpoints. They forced the Christians to get out of the car and read out passages from the Quran. Then in late 1998 the police issued warnings to everyone in the tourism business not to drive past the *pesantren* [Walisongo] at the edge of Poso. The police could no longer guarantee safety. We then withdrew to Pendolo [on the far end of Lake Poso].[36]

The second factor was B. J. Habibie's assumption of the presidency, which emboldened ICMI in Poso to push for the complete Islamization of the top positions in politics, society, and business. This resulted in a Christian-Muslim struggle over the control of the civil service, culminating in the competition for the post of *bupati*.[37] This also resulted in ethnic tensions, as a large number of the ICMI members who already held positions in local government were Muslims from the Bungku area of Morowali.[38] The third factor was the first post-Suharto local elections. The political scramble was started with the announcement on December 13, 1998, by the incumbent Poso *bupati* Arief Patanga, whose term was due to expire in 1999, that he would not seek reelection. A struggle then ensued between Muslims, Christians, and the military. Yahya Patiro, a Pamona Protestant who was *sekwilda* and thus second in command to Patanga, quickly emerged as the Christian favorite. He was championed by Herman Parimo, a Pamona member of the Regional People's Representative Assembly, who had widespread Protestant support. His main competitor became Damsyik Ladjalani, whose family originated from the Togian Islands. The political competition between Patiro and Ladjalani quickly turned "dirty" with fliers, banners, and graffiti that Christians described as "a successful intimidation campaign" aimed at preventing Patiro's selection.[39] The fourth issue was, more generally, the impending reform of the electoral mechanisms and expected decentralization of government functions. This created "local-level uncertainties over how different groups could seek and secure access to state employment and contracts in post-New Order Indonesia."[40] This process continued to feed the conflict once it had erupted. The regional autonomy laws that were passed in 1999 stipulated that the rights, origins, and customary traditions of villages and regions were to be respected, but "without saying exactly how that is to be done in multi-ethnic areas."[41] *Reformasi* thus exacerbated Christian-Muslim intercommunal tensions in Poso. It was these that came to the fore when conflict erupted in December 1998, although the root causes of the conflict were political and social rather than religious.[42]

Political Competition and Urban Riots: The Poso Conflict December 1998 to April 2000

The Poso conflict saw five distinct phases. The first two phases were short-lived urban riots that disintegrated into communal clashes connected to local political interests. The first phase started on December 24, 1998. It was triggered by a clash between a Christian and a Muslim youth. In the Christian version of this incident, Roy Bisalemba and Ahmad Ridwan had an argument over a borrowed screwdriver. Bisalemba stabbed Ridwan, who then fled into a local mosque and broadcasted via the loudspeaker that a Muslim had been persecuted by a Christian inside the mosque.[43] In the Muslim version a drunk Roy Bisalemba entered the Darussalam Mosque looking for the Muslim youth he had had an argument with earlier. He was carrying a machete and he cut the son of the imam who was sleeping there. "Then the clash started. Other youths got involved, their parents got involved, and as it had happened in a mosque it took on religious characteristics."[44]

Rumors that the Muslim youth had been killed led to Muslim attacks on Christian houses in the Sayo neighborhood, including that of Roy's family. The next morning, on December 25, the situation escalated as religious leaders banned alcohol for the duration of Ramadan. The police had started confiscating bottles when some overzealous Muslim youths decided to conduct raids of their own. In the afternoon crowds of Muslims entered Sayo to ransack the houses of Roy's extended family and "then went on to raid shops and hotels selling alcohol across the city."[45] Protestant youths rallied to the defense and street battles ensued between the Bugis Muslim residents of Kayamanya and the Pamona-, Mori- and Minahasa-descent Christian residents of Sayo and Lombogia.[46] On December 26, Muslims outside Poso city started to mobilize. They had heard that Ahmad had been killed in the mosque; others had heard that an imam had been slaughtered while praying.[47] At the same time rumors that churches had been torched led to the mobilization of Christian Pamona farmers. Reverend Nelly of Silancar village recalled hearing the rumor about the burned churches. "After that the Christians went down. They went to the bridge and stopped by every house along the way mobilizing others."[48] On the night of December 27, local Protestant figure Herman Parimo organized trucks to bring the Pamona, who had gathered in Tagolu, to Poso city to defend their coreligionists. They were armed with machetes and headed toward the harbor and the market areas. As many as two thousand Christians and Muslims clashed in the early hours of December 28 and a battle erupted at the bridge that separates the two halves of Poso city. This full-scale riot went on all day with both sides throwing rocks at each other, or using traditional weapons such as knives, spears, catapults, swords, machetes, blowpipes, and arrows.[49] According to Dolfi Monding, the rector of an English-language school in Kasintuwu, many of the Muslims who took part in this violence were outsiders. "The residents of the Muslim villages on both sides of Poso city participated in the attacks, including members of the local police and Brimob. The bus terminal was burned down and then my school which was right across from it."[50]

By the end of the day more than one hundred houses had been looted and burned, mostly in the Christian areas of Lombogia, Kasintuwu, and Sayo. Some eighty people were injured, including one Christian who was doused with gasoline and set alight.[51] The *bupati*'s residence came under attack and Patanga and Patiro were evacuated in what Dave McRae called the beginning of the "campaign of insurrection of local Christian officials."[52] However, places of worship were not targeted despite the religious connotations that the conflict had assumed and despite earlier rumors about burned churches. On December 29, community leaders from Palu met with the governor. They then accompanied the governor and provincial security leaders to Poso where, according to Reverend Irianto Kongkoli, they were "greeted by people brandishing spears." It was this intervention that brought the violence to an end "before it spread to the churches and mosques."[53]

The first phase of the Poso conflict saw some two hundred people injured, some of whom had been "tortured by being stabbed, burned, or dragged by ropes from vehicles."[54] Four hundred houses were looted and burned.[55] Most of those injured were Protestant, and the vast majority of houses destroyed were also those of Protestants. In an attempt to head off a religious interpretation, government authorities declared the violence *kriminal murni* (purely criminal), and Wirabuana regional military commander General Suaidi Marassabessy announced on December 30 that the riot had been caused by eight troublemakers—all Protestant—who had all been arrested, including Roy Bisalemba and Herman Parimo.[56] On January 9, 1999, the National Human Rights Commission, Komisi Nasional Hak Asasi Manusia (Komnas HAM), announced that the conflict in Poso was the result of miscommunication and there was no indication of any involvement of local elites. This interpretation was fully endorsed and maintained by Jakarta for a long time, despite the fact that there was considerable evidence that Muslim and Christian leaders had "whipped up the people."[57]

The second phase of the Poso conflict erupted on April 15, 2000, and lasted for five days. It, too, took the form of an urban riot that was linked to local political competition, in this case the appointment of the *sekwilda*. And as in the first phase, Christian and Muslim narratives differed. Muslims believed that the Christians had started the violence and had, in fact, been preparing and training for it throughout 1999.[58] As Samsu Mohamed, the former *lurah* (ward head) of Kayamanya, explained, "The Christians were consolidating up in the mountains. When the second phase of the conflict erupted they had *rakitan* [home-made firearms]. So it was true that for the last year they had been consolidating and training."[59]

In contrast, Christian accounts highlight the ominous warning by PPP DPRD member Haelani Umar that if Damsyik Ladjalani was not selected for *sekwilda*, then there would be another riot in Poso.[60] Damanik saw this warning as "proof" that the second phase was engineered to serve specific Muslim political interests. He pointed to the timing of renewed violence during the selection of the *sekwilda* as well as the trial of Arief Patanga's younger brother Agfar Patanga, the corruption case against Daeng Raja and Aliansyah (Maro) Tompo, the rising demands for an investigation into the possible corruption of Japanese aid money intended for the rehabilitation of victims of the first conflict, and the money politics of the *bupati* elections.[61] The timing also coincided with the Easter celebrations, which like the coincidence of Christmas and Ramadan during the first phase of the Poso conflict, provided for heightened communal sensitivities. In light of this, Damanik maintained that the youths and alcohol associated with the initial brawl were never more than scapegoats.[62]

According to Forum Cheq and Recheq, the planning began on January 14, 2000, after Friday prayer in Poso's Baiturrahman Mosque when a meeting was convened by the Forum for the Defense of the Islamic Umma. The meeting was led by Haji Adnan Arsal and attended by Maro Tompo, Muktar Lapangasa, Yusuf Dumo, Ahmar Laparigi, Karman Lamuka, Daeng Raja, and Mandor Pahe.[63] They decided "to burn a mosque and a church to incite new violence," "to direct the Muslims to burn and destroy the court in Poso if the court's decision was not acceptable and then to direct them toward the houses of the Christians in Lombogia and Kasintuwu to destroy the basis of the Christians in Poso," and "to urge the government to appoint Damsyik Ladjalani as *sekwilda*."[64]

A similar account was provided by Syarifuddin Lukman, deputy head of PAN in Poso, who described the second phase as a "game" by "economic whores" and "political whores." He, too, highlighted the meeting at Baiturrahman Mosque and asserted that the most important decision taken at this meeting was "to lure the masses" at the time of Agfar's trial by "burning a mosque in Lawanga and then burning a church."[65]

The initial brawl, which McRae called "contrived even from its first moments," took place near Poso's bus terminal between a Muslim youth, Firman Said alias

Dedi, from Kayamanya and two Christian youths from Lombogia.[66] Dedi punched one of the Christian youths and left, only to return an hour later on a motorbike with two friends and a sword. The Christian youths chased Dedi and his friends away with knives. Dedi then "bandaged his healthy arm and began telling people that he had been knifed."[67] This compelled Muslims from Kayamanya and Lawanga neighborhoods to go to Lombogia in search of the attacker. The police managed to keep the gathering crowds apart until the following day. On Sunday, April 16, Muslim youths from Lawanga, carrying machetes, went in search of Angky Tungkanan, one of the Christian youths. The *lurah* of Lombogia went to meet them, accompanied by Angki's father, Paulus Tungkanan. However, while the police were facilitating negotiations, Muslim youths started to set fire to Christian houses and one attacked Paulus with a machete.[68] Attacks were also directed at the Pniel Church by a group from the Bonesompe Mosque Youth.[69] Samsu Mohamed later explained that they believed that the church had been "full of weapons."[70] In the clashes that ensued seven civilians and three policemen were injured, large parts of Lombogia were burned, and thousands of Christians were displaced.[71]

The local parliament was paralyzed. Herry Sarumpaet, deputy head of the DPRD, recalled that "we were scared. We talked about getting in the TNI and the police but with their record of human rights abuses we were reluctant to call on them. So the Muslims protected their community and the Christians protected theirs."[72] Poso's police chief called for Brimob reinforcements from Palu, which arrived on April 17. They set up a roadblock at the Tentena intersection to keep Muslims and Christians separated. The initial impact of the roadblock was the displacement of violence to the majority-Christian Kasintuwu neighborhood. Then the Muslims, whose numbers had been reinforced by "help from the villages" upon rumors of Dedi's death, broke through the police blockade.[73] At this point Brimob officers started firing shots into the crowd, killing three and injuring eight others, one of whom later died. After the funerals that same afternoon angry Muslims launched another attack on Lombogia and burned houses, schools, and churches.[74] They also turned against the police, attacking several residences of police officers as well as other police-owned buildings in the neighborhood of Bonesompe.[75]

On April 18, Governor Paliudju, the provincial police chief, and the regional military commander came to Poso in an attempt to calm the situation down. Paliudju was met by a Muslim delegation led by Maro Tompo who presented him with a list of demands: first, to dismiss Poso police chief Dedy Woerjantono; second, to withdraw Brimob; third, to halt the lawsuit against Patanga; and fourth, to install Ladjalani as *sekwilda*. Brimob was redeployed that night, but the rioting continued, spurred on by the next morning's discovery of the body of a

Muslim youth near a Christian house in Lombogia.[76] More Christian houses, the local headquarters of the Indonesian Democratic Party of Struggle (Partai Demokrasi Indonesia Perjuangan, PDI-P), and two more churches were set on fire.[77] Muslims then set up roadblocks and started "sweeping for Christians," demanding to see identity cards, and pulled two Protestants "from vehicles and publicly slashed [them] to death."[78] Another was "burned to death in his car."[79]

Provincial police reinforcements and some six hundred soldiers from Kodam Wirabuana were sent to Poso. On the night of April 20 order was restored and a series of reconciliation meetings were held.[80] The conflict was officially declared over on May 3. In this second phase six were killed and thirty-eight injured.[81] However, the destruction was vast and almost exclusively Protestant. Virtually all of Lombogia had been destroyed. Some seven hundred houses were burned. Three Protestant schools, seven churches, one police dormitory, and Poso's courthouse had been attacked. The documents pertaining to the trials of Agfar Patanga and Maro Tompo were burned, leading to the suspension of the trials.[82] There were also thousands of Christian refugees, most of whom had fled to Tentena.[83]

Kelompok Merah and the Christian Offensive May–June 2000

In the third phase of the Poso conflict in May–June 2000 the Christians went on the offensive in response to the destruction of Christian property in the first two phases. It was also a response to the role Muslim migrants had played in that violence and in the cultural dislocation of indigenous Christians, as well as the perceived radicalization of Muslims in Poso.[84] And finally it was a response to the failure of the security forces to respond effectively, Muslim impunity, and the local and national government blaming the Christians for the conflict.[85] One Christian lawyer asserted that "the whole justice system, the police, the courts and the judges are pro-Muslim."[86] Christian politicians saw the political system in a similar vein.[87] Christians also believed that another Muslim attack was imminent, and their offensive was thus preemptive as "we were convinced the Muslims would attack Tentena next. They wanted to kill us and they wanted to take our land."[88] The destruction of churches also played a key role in the decision to hit back as "burning churches is an insult. After that we had no other option than to strike back."[89] Albert Tumimor summarized the reasons for the Christian counterattack as follows:

> First, the arson attacks were carried out by people who were guests—Bugis, Javanese, Gorontalo—they were all guests here. They were

welcomed to Poso but then stopped behaving like guests. Second, the residence of the *raja* was burned down by these guests. Third, the people from Ujung Pandang, Java, and Gorontalo, who became rich, displaced the locals. Until today Christians do not dare to live in Poso. Fourth, the burning of churches was the greatest insult. Fifth, they murdered.[90]

The Christian offensive was spearheaded by the newly formed Fighters for the Restoration of Security in Poso (Pejuang Pemulihan Keamanan Poso), more commonly referred to as Red Group (Kelompok Merah). Kelompok Merah's aim was to defend the Christian community, Christian property, and Christian land from Muslim attack. The fighters also shared an ethnoreligious discourse challenging the depiction of conflict in Poso as purely religious. Instead, they saw the conflict as one of indigenous communities defending themselves against migrant encroachment. In this discourse indigeneity was virtually interchangeable with Christianity and, arguably, Pamona Protestantism. Poso was thus defined as Christian territory in both historical and *adat* terms.

Kelompok Merah did not have a formal leadership. Instead, a number of different geographic locations were brought together under the group's umbrella, led by what McRae calls the "organized core."[91] Among these was A. L. Lateka, a Protestant civil servant from Kelei village who was employed at the Central Sulawesi Regional Investment Coordination Board in Palu. He was looked up to because he was an engineer and a civil servant. He had also suffered a direct loss in the conflict; he was the brother-in-law of Herman Parimo, who had died in prison.[92] Another leadership personality was Fabianus Tibo, a Florinese transmigrant living in Beteleme where he worked on a rubber plantation.[93] He was a known *preman* (thug/gangster) who had a previous conviction for killing a man during a dispute between Balinese and Florinese transmigrants. In the context of the Poso conflict, this provided him with useful "credentials of violence." As a Catholic, he also represented the small Catholic community, many of whom were worried about their children who attended Santa Theresia boarding school in Poso city. He became one of the most important field commanders of Kelompok Merah. The third key leader was retired police officer Paulus Tungkanan. He represented Poso city's Christians, who had taken the brunt of the early violence. His background as a police officer, as well as the fact that he himself had been wounded in Lombogia while negotiating with the Muslims, qualified him for leadership. Important roles were also played by Tungkanan's sons Angky and Berny, Lateka's brothers Bakte and Kade, and Tibo's associates Marinus Riwu and Dominggus da Silva. Within the three constituencies they represented, there were also smaller groups of core combatants, whom Human Rights Watch referred to as "red bats," "black bats," and "ninjas."[94] They led the search-and-destroy missions aimed at eliminating Muslim provocateurs.

Kelompok Merah's central base was in the village of Kelei. On its outskirts the training of combatants started in early May 2000. According to McRae there were two training sessions every day, the first from 4 A.M. until 12 P.M. and the second from 3 P.M. until 6 P.M.[95] The training was conducted by Marinus Riwu as well as others, and lasted until May 21, the day before the Christian offensive was launched.[96] Witnesses at Tibo's trial claimed that a seven hundred-man militia had been prepared, that the training was funded by retired army officers, and that a helicopter had supplied a large number of M16s from Manado, North Sulawesi, that had originated in the Philippines.[97] Muslims further alleged that sixteen members from the local army command, Kodim Poso, were involved in supplying training and ammunition as well as information to the Christians.[98] These claims, however, were never substantiated. The number of those trained was much smaller, comprising young men directly connected to one of the three key leaders as well as some youths from the surrounding villages who had gained fighting experience during the first two phases of the conflict.[99] The training given to them included instruction in the use of arrows as well as making improvised, home-made *rakitan*, which would hardly have been necessary if they had had a large supply of M16s. Moreover, when the offensive began, there was little evidence of modern standard firearms. While it is possible that some firearms were used by the few military and police who had joined the ranks of the fighters, on the whole Kelompok Merah fighters were armed with catapults and blowpipes, as well as "spears and machetes and some *rakitan*."[100] Indeed, when the police disbanded the Tagolu *posko* (command post) the weapons they seized included no M16s and only one *rakitan*. The rest were traditional weapons, including twenty-seven dum-dum, fifteen slingshots, and 550 arrows.[101] (Dum-dums were improvised weapons that used a pipe and the explosive material from fireworks to shoot metal fragments or glass shards. They had a range of between 10 and 20 meters.) The notion of weapons having come in from Manado was also rejected by the local military commander, who asserted that in 2000 and 2001 "any help from Manado or Toraja" had come in the form of "money rather than guns" and that any guns that were used were "*rakitan* not standard."[102] He also rejected the claims that active army personnel had been involved in either training or supplying Kelompok Merah.

The Christian offensive, which was effectively the third phase of the Poso conflict, started on May 23 with Kelompok Merah setting up several *posko* in strategically vital areas. It then launched the first of two targeted operations, which Aragon described as a nighttime strike against Kayamanya and Moengko by about a dozen black-clad "ninjas" armed with machetes.[103] Led by Lateka—although it is Tibo who stands out in Muslim accounts—this group went in search of the Muslim provocateurs.[104] They had drawn up a list that included Adnan Arsal, Daeng Raja, Maro Tompo, Agfar Patanga, Nani Lamusu, and Mandor Pahe.[105]

Samsu Mohamed recalled the Christians entering from Lombogia and heading for Adnan Arsal's house. However, before reaching their intended target the masked men ran into a police officer who tried to stop them. In the ensuing scuffle Sergeant Major Kamaruddin Ali was killed along with a Muslim resident of Kayamanya.[106] Similarly BR recounted that "Tibo came with his forces, on foot, via Gebrangrejo, through the city to the market. They had some targets that they were searching for and they burned some houses. One policeman was killed and some others wounded. When they entered, we followed them all the way to the Catholic church in Moengko. I was later told that Tibo had gone there because the children were threatened. He wanted to save them."[107] According to Arsal the ninjas killed the retired *lurah* Abdul Surkur before they then proceeded to Santa Theresia Catholic School.[108] As Tibo was negotiating with the police, the crowd of Muslims, led by Adnan Arsal, Nani Lamusu, and Mandor Pahe, arrived, brandishing traditional weapons.[109] Upon seeing them, the Christian fighters fled through a back door of the dormitory and "disappeared into the jungle."[110] The Muslim crowd then proceeded to burn down the school, church, and orphanage.

Kelompok Merah's strategy comprised several elements: It sought to eliminate known Muslim provocateurs and to evacuate indefensible vulnerable areas, as exemplified by the first targeted operation. It also sought to take out areas of Muslim radicalism. And lastly it aimed to open the roads to other Christian areas, to eliminate Muslim-minority pockets, and to push the Christian-Muslim boundary into Muslim territory in order to create a larger, contiguous, and more defensible Christian territory.

After their escape from Moengko, the Christian fighters gathered in Kelei village. It was here that Lateka gave the order that Poso be razed.[111] A *posko* was then established at Tagolu village, which is located at the point where the road from Tentena splits into two, one road leading to Poso and the other to Ampana. From the *posko* in the house of Lateka's brother Bakte, they were thus able to block Muslims trying to get to Tentena while also being able to attack along both roads.

On May 25, Christian assaults were launched along the Tagolu-Ampana road, "against villages on both sides of Poso" where Muslims fleeing Poso had sought refuge.[112] At the same time, seven truckloads of Muslims from Ampana joined with local Muslims to attack Bategencu, triggering the flight of Christians to Sepe and Silancar villages.[113] There they were joined by "those from Tagolu *posko* including Tibo, Dominggus and Berny Tungkanan."[114] On May 26, Muslim fighters attempted to push up toward Tentena but were stopped by Christian fighters at Toyado village. The Christians proceeded to burn much of Toyado, and subsequently Tongko and Labuan villages.[115] It was at this point that the decision was made to attack the Walisongo *pesantren* and the adjacent Javanese transmigration site Sintuwulemba in the second targeted operation. This resulted in the single most violent incident during the third phase and possibly the conflict as a whole.

The Walisongo *pesantren* was located nine kilometers south of Poso city between Tagolu and Tentena, placing it in Christian territory. At the time of the attack, it was attended by some 150 students.[116] Since the 1990s Christians had seen this *pesantren* as a source of radicalism, and after the Poso conflict erupted many Christians were also convinced that the Walisongo *pesantren* was the "place where they [the Muslims] set up the headquarters for their forces to attack Tentena. There were guns in the mosque and Christians who tried to pass that area were shot at by snipers from the mosque."[117] And then there was the two-way antenna that Christians believed "was being used to plan an attack on Tagolu."[118]

Tibo had already requested that the *pesantren* take down the antenna, and the school had agreed to do so in return for assurance that the Christians would not attack it. On May 26, fearing the worst, the police tried to evacuate the *pesantren*, but their convoy was blocked in Tagolu. Reinforcements were then requested but none were available. As a result, the police turned back and no further efforts at evacuation were made.[119] On May 28, Christians carrying traditional weapons attacked the *pesantren*.[120] They then moved on to Sintuwulemba, which was seen as a source of Christian dislocation, where migrant cacao farmers prospered and had "continued to purchase more land."[121]

Led by Tibo, they set about killing Muslim men, many of whom were hacked and chopped to death.[122] Some thirty-eight people were killed in the *pesantren*'s mosque alone.[123] Over the next couple of days the Christian fighters rounded up those who had fled into the nearby forest. The women and children were held in Tambaro village hall, where some women were "subjected to strip searches and inspections of their vaginas by Dominggus, who claimed to search for hidden Javanese amulets."[124] The men were tied up and led by foot to the village hall in Ranononcu.[125] There they were questioned about the Lombogia attacks in April and tortured. Then they were loaded onto trucks and taken to Poso River, where around twenty-eight of them were executed and thrown into the water. Others were dumped in a gorge near Pandiri village or buried in mass graves near Sintuwulemba.[126] One Tentena youth who had participated in the attack "returned to Tentena with fifty identity cards which he had taken off the people he had killed."[127] Tibo, too, initially confessed that he personally executed about forty of the hundreds who were thrown into the Poso River or other mass graves.[128] The overall death toll was estimated at between one and three hundred.[129]

Muslim migrants were also targeted in other areas, and Muslims in overwhelmingly Christian villages were often expelled, as was the case in the 90 percent Christian village Tangkura.[130] As the attacks on Muslim villages continued, Al-Khairaat in Palu called for jihad against the *kafir*, started recruiting fighters, and ordered weapons.[131] Two trucks of volunteers left for Poso on the evening of May 27.[132] However, after the first mujahid was killed on May 29, their enthusiasm quickly waned.[133] Blaming Lateka for the violence, Governor Paliudju requested assistance and 1,500 soldiers were sent from Kodam Wirabuana.[134]

On June 2, during a Christian attack on Kayamanya, Lateka was killed. According to Damanik he was stabbed to death.[135] Christians later claimed that Lateka had been chopped into small pieces.[136] In the days following Lateka's death the predominantly Muslim villages on the roads to Palu and Ampana were attacked, with the result of closing Poso city's major transportation and communication system. On June 6, in a battle with the police just east of Poso city, more than sixty Christian fighters were killed.[137] On the same day Christian leaders met in Tentena, after which Tibo and Dominggus presented the police with what has become known as "Lateka's mandate."[138] This mandate sought to "restore the human rights of the Poso community" and to "free the Poso community of the oppression by the rioters" by calling upon the government to allow "the indigenous inhabitants . . . [to] live in freedom in their own birthplace," to stop protecting the provocateurs, to stop the security forces taking sides, and to "give us the opportunity and freedom to help the government to pursue the provocateurs/rioters and to take action against them as a guarantee of restoration of security as a component of national security."[139]

After this the violence declined drastically, and most analysts agree that by July the third phase of conflict was over. The *Mercusuar* newspaper estimated that the death toll during this period was as high as 1,000, with around 165 bodies alone found in Poso River.[140] The police recorded 577 deaths.[141] Some 3,500 houses and two schools were destroyed in twenty villages. More than seventy thousand persons fled their homes.[142] Indonesian government data, which were collected up until the formal conclusion of the third phase of violence on August 22 with a "traditional" *adat* ceremony attended by President Wahid, show that seventy-three mosques, eighty-seven churches, and one Hindu temple were burned.[143]

Enter the Mujahidin, 2000–2001

The Christian offensive shook Poso's Muslims to the core. Samsu Mohamed and Adnan Arsal both maintained that they had expressed concerns about a possible attack to the local government and security forces and that they had been assured there was not going to be one.[144] Iwan Ambo, too, knew they would attack as "the Christians wanted the Muslims out of Poso. They wanted to establish a *wilayah* Kristen Pamona Raya [a Greater Christian Pamona Region]" and "they wanted to kill us all."[145] The Christian attacks also left no doubt in Muslims' minds that this was a religious conflict, as "they sang 'Halleluya' and 'Darah Yesus' [the blood of Jesus]. That means they were attacking Islam. So the Muslims responded with 'Allahu Akbar.' That's how it became a religious war."[146]

The single most traumatic incident was the Walisongo massacre. Arsal, who subsequently became one of the local mujahidin leaders, maintained that "at Walisongo three hundred were slaughtered. Women were raped. Bodies were cut open."[147] Ambo, who later joined the Mujahidin Tanah Runtuh, recounted how he saw "the bodies in the river after Walisongo. Bodies of women, children, babies—all mutilated."[148] The importance of the Walisongo massacre cannot be overstated. It shaped the rest of the conflict, as the news of the attack drew in mujahidin from other parts of Sulawesi and Java, locally referred to as the "outside mujahidin." Walisongo was also the reason most cited by local Muslims for joining the jihadi affiliates that the "outside mujahidin" established. And further, it motivated specific acts of retribution for years to come.

The "outside mujahidin" arrived in Poso in two waves. The first wave mobilized after Walisongo and comprised members of Jemaah Islamiyah, the Java-based Mujahidin KOMPAK and Darul Islam, as well as the South Sulawesi–based Laskar Jundullah and Wahdah Islamiyah. The second wave followed the 2001 Buyung Katedo massacre and comprised mainly members of the Java-based Laskar Jihad.

The first to arrive in early June 2000 was Mujahidin KOMPAK, which had evolved out of the Action Committee for Tackling the Consequences of the Crisis (Komite Aksi Penanggulangan Akibat Krisis—KOMPAK) established in 1997 by DDII in the context of the Asian financial crisis to help ordinary Muslims. It had also provided humanitarian aid to Ambonese Muslims after the conflict there had erupted in January 1999.[149] After Walisongo, the head of KOMPAK's Ambon office, Abdullah Sonata, led a six-man team to Poso in order to defend the Muslims just as they had been doing in Ambon. While they were few in number, they came "carrying Rp17 million ($US1,960) in cash and 14 guns," which they had captured after the raid on the Brimob arsenal in Tantui, Ambon.[150] In Ambon they also had gained experience recruiting, training, and organizing local mujahidin. Their initial involvement was assisting with the evacuation of bodies and documenting their work with video cameras.[151] KOMPAK also made a number of VCDs (video compact discs) on the atrocities, which were then used for recruitment. This first KOMPAK team was followed by a second team of

KOMPAK Maluku veterans in August 2000, whose mission was to distribute aid but also to recruit local mujahidin. They were accompanied by JI members Farihin and Ali Fauzi.[152]

JI's head of Mantiqi 3, Abu Tholut, also took a keen interest, as Sulawesi was part of his territory. He had been to Palu and Manado several times since the Poso conflict had first erupted, as both of those areas were "part of the JI strategic plan". He recounted that "when Walisongo happened the Palu JI explained what had happened. We sent a team to Poso to investigate. They met Haji Adnan Arsal. After that we went to Poso to protect the Muslims from genocide and to see if Muslims in Poso would be open to JI."[153] Both Mujahidin KOMPAK and JI sought out informal local Muslim leaders. One of these was Srie Handono Mashudi alias Abu Hakam, who worked as a civil servant in Palu in the Ministry of Settlements. Abu Hakam saw the conflict in Poso as "religious from the beginning." He also believed that it was part of "a grand design" that sought "to wipe out the Muslims" and that "all of the conflicts across Indonesia had been engineered and in all of them the victims were Muslims."[154] Abu Hakam became a key local figure for Mujahidin KOMPAK.[155] The other key local figure was Adnan Arsal, who was often referred to as the commander of the Poso mujahidin.[156] Arsal had both the necessary conflict and religious credentials. Not only had he been active during the first three phases of the conflict, but he was also an employee in the Poso district office of the Ministry of Religion; had his own *pesantren*, Amanah; held a senior position in MUI; and headed a religious endowment foundation, Yayasan Badan Wakaf Ulil Albab, which raised funds across Indonesia for Muslims in Poso.[157] Arsal had relations with several of the outside mujahidin groups, but it was JI that he was closest to.

The last to arrive was Laskar Jihad, almost a year after Mujahidin KOMPAK and JI. Laskar Jihad shared the desire to defend Poso's Muslims and to introduce *syariah* with the other Javanese mujahidin, but it differed greatly in its attitude toward the Indonesian state, whose unity and integrity it sought to defend against what it saw as Christian-separatist threats.[158] The violence in Poso, according to Laskar Jihad leader Jafar Umar Thalib, was driven by a Christian separatist movement, which aimed to link up with Christians in other parts of Sulawesi in order to establish a Tanah Toraja Raya (Greater Toraja state).[159] Laskar Jihad thus styled itself as an auxiliary to the Indonesian security forces and, as an aboveground organization, was able to court the local political establishment and formally open offices in Palu and Poso. It obtained permits from the governor for providing medical aid to Poso's Muslims, and claimed that its members were free to carry arms and train openly "because their presence in Central Sulawesi was sanctioned by the local government and security forces."[160]

The outside mujahidin as a whole were able to significantly increase the fighting capacity of local Muslims by providing them with training and weapons. Their presence also boosted morale. Each of the outside groups set up base in a different area. In Poso city, Mujahidin KOMPAK settled in Kayamanya while JI embedded itself in Tanah Runtuh. Laskar Jundullah, led by Agus Dwikarna, set up its local headquarters in Pendolo on the other side of Lake Poso, thus encircling the Christian areas. Laskar Jihad spread across the villages not just because it was the "late-comer" but also because it wanted to replicate the village-defense strategy it had so successfully pursued in Ambon.[161]

KOMPAK started training the first local Muslims in October 2000 after establishing its affiliate Mujahidin Kayamanya. It had the largest program, as it also trained mujahidin from other organizations and its local training sessions were short.[162] The graduates were then sent into immediate action, following a "learning by doing approach."[163] KOMPAK did not have formal training camps in Poso but sent the more promising recruits to its camps on Buru and Seram in Maluku. JI began to conduct training in December 2000, having set up its affiliate Mujahidin Tanah Runtuh. The first batch had forty-five local recruits, who were trained by Afghan veterans.[164] JI's training lasted for at least three months and comprised both *tadrib* (military training) and *taklim* (Islamic studies).[165] According to Cecep, the training started with "*taklim umum* [general Islamic studies]." The next stage was *taklim khusus* [special Islamic studies], "where we learned about military science." And then *tadrib*, "where we learned how to assemble weapons and put things into practice in the field."[166] However, the first batch, as BR explained, did not quite follow this order: "For the first batch the *tadrib* came before the *taklim khusus* because of the security situation. Fighters were needed immediately as attacks were still going on. We were suffering hit-and-run attacks on Sayo and Lawanga so we needed to focus on this." The *tadrib* included the "study of strategy, tactics, warfare, force formation," and how to shoot as well as camouflage, "making bombs, and protecting yourself from the enemy but also *tafsir* [Quranic exegesis] and *fikh jihad* [Islamic laws on jihad]."[167] It was followed by two months of *taklim khusus*, where the *ustadz* (honorary title for a religious teacher) determined whether you could move on to the next stage. Then came further Islamic studies sessions called *dauroh*, which covered "*jamaah*" (community), "*bai'at*" (loyalty oath), and "*khilafa* (caliphate)."[168] When the training was completed, the newly minted mujahidin took the loyalty oath. Cecep and BR swore theirs to JI's Abu Rusdan. Later batches often swore their *bai'at* to Adan Arsal.

Laskar Jihad also conducted training, but its sessions were often only a day long and specifically geared toward setting up a string of village defenses. Together with local Muslims, they targeted Christian enclaves and outlying Christian villages through frontal attacks, in an effort to establish a contiguous and defensible Muslim area.[169] Being rurally based, Laskar Jihad was involved in the day-to-day harassment of Christian farmers, but its volunteers were also active in health care and *dakwah* (Islamic outreach), as well as rebuilding destroyed Muslim villages.[170] And, last but certainly not least, Laskar Jihad pursued aggressive information warfare through its website, magazine, bulletins, press releases, flyers, and pamphlets. In the period of May to August 2002 this escalated into a full-blown media war with "a press statement from Laskar Jihad and from the [Christian] Crisis Centre every day."[171]

Together the outside mujahidin paved the way for the Muslims to gain the upper hand in the Poso conflict in its fourth phase from June to December 2001. This fourth phase followed the same religious, economic, and ethnic battle lines as the previous phases, pitting Christians against Muslims, and the indigenous population against migrants. It saw a continuation of Christian attacks, including more massacres. The fourth phase, like the first two phases, was also linked to local politics. Renewed violence coincided with the revived debate about power sharing and the selection of a new district secretary as well as the *bupati*'s decision to appoint Muslim civil servant Awad al-Amri to this position.[172] At the same time, however, the fourth phase was clearly a Muslim offensive that sought retribution.

It began with clashes on June 30, 2001. Rumors that the Christians were planning a protest against the *bupati*'s decision resulted in the mobilization of Muslims from Ampana who clashed with the TNI, police, and Christians in Malei-Lage.[173] Then, on July 2, a delegation of thirty Christians went to Poso city to protest at the DPRD but were stopped by the police and a crowd of Muslims from Sayo.[174] According to Lasahido, it was the blocking of the protests that prompted the attack on Buyung Katedo on July 3.[175] Kelompok Merah, armed with sharp weapons, launched a predawn attack on the Muslim hamlet. Almost all of the houses were burned or razed to the ground. The Nurul Amin Mosque had its walls "desecrated with provocative slogans" and was then set on fire with Musa, the imam, inside.[176] In total fourteen were killed. All but two of the victims were women and children and most of them suffered several deep machete wounds to different parts of their bodies.[177] As Daeng Raja recounted, "They chopped them to bits. There were rapes. Babies had their heads cut off. Crosses were cut into the bodies. Women's breasts were cut off. And that is when the Muslims decided upon full-scale revenge."[178]

The following day, on July 4, local Muslims together with their mujahidin allies embarked upon an offensive aimed at "sterilizing" twenty-two Christian hamlets and villages.[179] Their strategy comprised two elements, both firmly situated in the religious geography. The first was to "cleanse" all Muslim areas of

Christian pockets. The second was to target those villages that were seen as the Christian strongholds during the third phase. They, too, had a list of "provocateurs," comprising eighty Christian names, including A. L. Lateka, who was already dead, and Tibo, Dominggus, and Marinus, who were in prison.[180]

Betania village was attacked and houses burned. Christian houses and a church were also burned in Poso city. On the same day Christian fighters attacked Sayo, where they torched a *musholla* (prayer house) and IDP barracks. On July 5, more Muslim IDP barracks were set on fire in Toyado and six Christians were killed nearby as well. On July 6, the conflict shifted to Poso Pesisir with Muslim attacks on Saatu and Pinedapa. One Christian was killed and more than a hundred houses burned. On July 7, officials declared the region quiet.[181] This quiet, however, was deceptive. On July 14, Laskar Jihad's reconnaissance team very openly arrived in Palu and after their meeting with Governor Ponulele, Poso *bupati* Muin Pusadan, and MUI, they publicly declared war on the Crisis Centre run by Reverend Damanik.[182] *Mercusuar* newspaper reported Laskar Jihad as having stated that "Christians whether in Ambon, East Timor, or Poso have a Crisis Centre. Its purpose is internationalization in order to corner the Muslim umma. For the Christians there are two big enemies, those are the Muslims and the TNI. . . . Don't talk reconciliation, reconciliation for them means consolidation."[183] Within a week Laskar Jihad's presence had increased to thirty-one and its website started recruiting for jihad in Poso. Laskar Jihad's very public arrival and its provocative language reinvigorated the conflict. Reverend Kongkoli recounted that "they called Christians pigs. They said Jesus is a pig. They said this in the mosques. They said the Christians started the conflict and that it was because the Christians wanted to be by themselves, wanted independence. They said the Christians and their leaders have helped themselves to aid money, that they were stealing money that should help Muslims. And then they taught the Muslims how to make bombs."[184] Local Christians as well as outside observers soon attributed the change in Muslim fighting capacity to Laskar Jihad, as epitomized by the subsequent Human Rights Watch report, which credited Laskar Jihad with turning sporadic attacks into organized assaults, the introduction of automatic weapons, and the leveling of entire villages.[185] Similarly, Graham Brown and Yukhi Tajima asserted that Laskar Jihad's arrival shifted the dynamics of the violence and that as a result of that organization's possession of automatic rifles the "fighting quickly became more organized and deadly."[186] However, both local Christians and observers were mistaken. They had missed the entry of Mujahidin KOMPAK and JI, who months earlier had quietly started to train, arm, and organize Muslims in Poso. It was their presence, their rigorous training, their bomb-making skills, and their firearms that shifted the dynamics in the conflict rather than the arrival of Laskar Jihad.

On July 25, the police headquarters in Palu were bombed. Periodic attacks were conducted against farmers working in cacao or clove orchards. In early August, there were clashes in Pendolo and October saw a spate of attacks on buses, churches, and villages. In early November, fighting erupted in Sayo and Kayamanya. This was followed by clashes at Bridge II in Poso city on November 11, which turned into open conflict between Kawua village and Ranononcu village early in the morning of November 12. There were also clashes in Tanah Runtuh and Lembomawu on that day.[187] On November 18, Laskar Jihad ominously announced that it "would not be satisfied until we have seen Lake Poso" and that "the umma will struggle until the last drop of blood is spilt."[188]

On November 27, Muslim fighters launched another offensive. Their targets were eight villages in Poso Pesisir and Lage subdistricts: Betalemba, Tangkura, Sanginora, Dewua, Patiwunga, Padalembara, Silancar, and Sepe. In less than a week, all of them were razed to the ground. Like the July attacks, the November-December attacks followed a strategy of cleansing Muslim areas of pockets of Christians and targeting the main centers of hostility. The first target was Tibo's hometown of Betalemba. According to the accounts by both Laskar Jihad and Mujahidin KOMPAK it was Betalemba that had fired the first shot.[189] They also attacked the Christian stronghold of Tangkura, which had played such a central role in the violence of the third phase. According to Tangkura resident Deki Molilo, "Laskar Jihad came on November 28 and all the houses were burned, both Christian and Muslim. But there were no victims as a school had already been attacked in a neighboring village and everyone [in Tangkura] fled. So we were not here when they came."[190] In both Betalemba and Tangkura Christians tried to defend themselves by barricading the roads with oil drums and trees. They were not, however, able to repel the mujahidin. On November 29, Muslim fighters overran Sanginora and Dewua villages, killing four Christians and sending another eleven thousand scrambling for safety to the hills. On December 1, Laskar Jihad reported destroying Bategencu hamlet adjoining Sepe village, in "a sea of fire."[191] Then, according to Reverend Nelly, "Sepe was attacked by men who were dressed in white and had turbans.... They used automatic rifles. We only had *rakitan*. We were evacuated again. They entered the village on December 1, 2001. In November they had already attacked Tangkura. They went by car. The attackers always took everything before they burned the houses. We heard the shooting and we fled. Then the TNI came with ten soldiers and three TNI were shot. Also some mujahidin died."[192] *BUNYAN* magazine, a publication that at the time was linked to KOMPAK but later was closer to JI, stated that Bategencu and Sepe had been targeted because they had harassed Toyado and that the attack had been launched during Ramahan in order to ensure success and secure "greater rewards."[193] Local Muslims saw the attack on these seven villages mainly in terms of revenge. "Everyone wanted revenge for the killing of the fourteen [Buyung Katedo], for the massacre at kilometer 9 [Walisongo], for the slaughter of the children. It was revenge on Kelompok Merah not on the Christian community. Betalemba, Tangkura, Pattiwunga, Padalembara, and Sanginora were attacked because those villages had helped Kelompok Merah."[194] The extent of the Muslim offensive, the use of modern standard firearms, and the degree of coordination prompted Christian leaders in Tentena to appeal to the United Nations for help.[195] It also caught the attention of decision-makers in Jakarta.

Post-Malino Terror, 2002–2007

The fifth phase of the Poso conflict started after the communal violence had been brought to an end with the Malino Agreement on December 20, 2001. It was characterized by what Brown and Tajima labeled "targeted terror."[196] For the first six months of 2002 this terror was sporadic and came mainly in the form of homemade explosives. These bombings caused predominantly material damage. As there was no popular mobilization in response to these bombings, the security conditions gradually normalized.[197] Nevertheless, these bombings served as a periodic reminder that the mujahidin were still present, that they still had considerable military capacity, and that there were still outstanding Muslim grievances as Christians who had participated in the Walisongo and Buyung Katedo massacres were still at large. They were also an indication of what was to come once Operation Sintuwu Maroso had ended on July 31, and many of the TNI troops were redeployed.

The targeted terror was perpetrated by a small number of local and outside mujahidin almost exclusively against Christians. McRae called it a new kind of "collective enterprise," in which the core combatants of multiple groups merged into a smaller, more deadly group, comprising locals from Mujahidin Kayamanya and Mujahidin Tanah Runtuh alongside outsiders from Darul Islam offshoot Bulan Sabit Merah, Mujahidin KOMPAK, and JI.[198] Adnan Arsal, too, remained deeply involved as was the JI *markaziyah* (central leadership), which supplied weapons and explosives to JI members through the logistics unit of the military command controlled by Abu Dujana. Indeed, the International Crisis Group has argued that the violence against Poso's Christians was not only condoned but sanctioned by the JI leadership, as "the legitimacy of the jihad against the *kafir* enemy there, even after the Malino peace accords, was something that all factions of JI could agree on, regardless of their stance on bombing western targets."[199] Thus the post-Malino violence served the additional function of achieving a semblance of cohesion in JI by papering over the cracks of a quickly factionalizing organization.

The targeted terror originated from three areas, Kayamanya and Tanah Runtuh in Poso city and Pendolo/Pandajaya on the other side of Lake Poso. It took a number of forms, including arson attacks on Christian villages and churches, assassinations of high-profile Christian leaders and public officials, shootings of farmers, the killing of foreigners, and the bombing of buses with Christian destinations, markets, and police stations.

It was a series of arson attacks that signaled the turning point from a comparatively low level of violence during the first six months following the Malino Agreement to a new campaign of violence from August 2002 until January 2007. On August 4, the Christian village of Matako in Tojo Subdistrict was attacked. Two churches and dozens of houses were burned, and seven villagers were injured. Matako was targeted not only because it was a Christian village but also because "it was a symbol of peaceful coexistence."[200] Two days later on August 6, Malitu and Betania in Poso Pesisir were attacked. Some twenty-one houses and a church were torched and the IDPs, who had been staying there, were displaced again.[201] On August 12, Silanca, Sepe, and Bategencu were attacked. Unlike Sepe and Bategencu, which already had been set on fire during the conflict, Silanca was targeted for the first time. This was particularly symbolic as it was one of the few untouched Christian strongholds.[202] Reverend Nelly from Silanca, who at the time of the attacks on Sepe and Silanca was in Palu for a meeting evaluating the implementation of the Malino Agreement, explained the local perception of events at the time: "On August 9 we received information that one Brimob had disappeared. People here were angry because it was not true. I was in Palu at that time. Then Laskar Jihad showed up with Brimob. My house was burned. People were evacuated by Damanik with trucks. Five people were killed. Five churches were burned. Two people were wounded. People here believe that Brimob and Laskar Jihad were working together. In Silanca 563 and in Sepe 295 houses were burned."[203] Not surprisingly, by that point some Christian leaders considered the Malino Declaration to be a failure. Like the residents of Silanca, many Christians not just blamed the security forces for failing to prevent these attacks but accused them of actual involvement. Damanik recalled raising this question at an official level: "We asked if there was a possibility that Brimob was involved but they said Brimob could not have been involved as they do not use M16s."[204] McRae, however, maintains that the locals were correct about Brimob's involvement. Presuming their missing colleague had been murdered by locals, they allowed Muslims to attack the villages.[205] Where the locals were wrong was in believing that these Muslims were Laskar Jihad, as they tended to conflate various mujahidin, usually blaming Laskar Jihad as the most visible organization.

Another spate of attacks and executions were carried out on October 9–10, 2003, when a group of gunmen attacked Beteleme, killing two and wounding three. Two nights later gunmen appeared in Saatu village, Poso Pesisir, surrounded the houses, ordered the inhabitants out, and then shot them, killing four and wounding one. They then moved on to Pinedapa village, where they entered the houses and shot a man and two women, followed by Pantangolemba village, where they shot the night watchman, injured another five people, and then shot two girls aged nine and eleven. Five other villagers, three men and two women, were executed. These attacks were attributed to KOMPAK special forces members and were deemed to be in response to rumors that "a few of the sixteen men named by Fabianus Tibo as the masterminds of the Walisongo massacre were now occupying land seized from Muslims." Thus "it was no coincidence that the first village attacked in October was Tibo's hometown."[206]

In addition to attacks against villages, there were what locals referred to as "mysterious killings." Many of the victims of these mysterious killings were farmers. For instance, on June 9, 2002, a man was killed in an ambush in his coconut plantation in Kayamanya.[207] On May 30, 2003, another farmer was hacked to death in Kayamanya. On June 2, two people were killed in Madale. On July 9 a farmer was killed in Pinedapa. On July 11, another farmer was killed in Lembomawo. On October 1, a farmer was killed in Pandimi. On October 27, another farmer from Pinedapa was shot dead.[208] The killing of farmers not only spread fear among the rural population, but also had a detrimental follow-on effect on Poso's economy as many farmers left fields unharvested for fear of being killed. Others started to harvest in groups rather than individually, and work teams hurried to finish before sunset.[209] The insecure farming situation was also a setback for the return of the IDPs.

In addition to lone farmers who were easy targets, the mujahidin also sought out high-profile targets: tourists, church leaders, and government officials. These more high-profile killings included the August 8, 2002, killing of Italian tourist Lorenzo Tadi when the bus he was traveling on was fired on as it passed through Mayoa village near Pendolo. Four other passengers were wounded. It was initially assumed that Tadi had been accidentally killed in a random shooting. However, it later emerged that Tadi had been targeted because he was suspected of being a foreign spy.[210] He had been under mujahidin surveillance and was assassinated by members of JI/Tanah Runtuh, although this was initially attributed to Bulan Sabit Merah.

Examples of the targeting of church leaders include the November 16, 2003, beating to death of Orange Tadjoda, the treasurer of the GKST synod; the July 18, 2004, shooting dead of Reverend Susianti Tinulele in front of her congregation while giving a sermon in Effata Church in Palu; and the October 16, 2006, assassination in a drive-by shooting of the head of the Central Sulawesi Protestant Church, Reverend Irianto Kongkoli, as he was buying construction materials. Police, at the time, believed Kongkoli's killing was linked to him leading numerous protests against the execution of Fabianus Tibo, Marinus Riwu, and Dominggus da Silva on September 22, 2006.[211] According to *Kontras*, Kongkoli was the fifty-seventh incidence of violence in 2006, most of which were targeted shootings.[212] Reverend Susianti Tinulele, as later investigations revealed, had not actually been the target. As Iwan Ambo explained, the target had been Reverend Kongkoli and they "only realized when we started shooting that it was not Kongkoli but Susianti."[213]

The next attempt on Reverend Kongkoli's life was more successful. Abdul Muis, who was part of the assassination team, stated in his interrogation in January 2007 that Kongkoli had been killed "because he was the person who was made leader of the Christians by Damanik and he was the person who most frequently led demonstrations by Christians and in particular, demonstrations against the execution of Tibo."

Other high-profile Christians who were assassinated included the dean of Sintuwu Maroso University's law faculty, Rosye Pilongo, who was shot on March 30, 2004, on campus, and Carminelis Ndele, head of Pinedapa village, who was found murdered on November 4, 2004.[214] He had been mutilated and beheaded. On November 19, 2005, Tadulako University lecturer Puji Laksono and his wife, Novlin, were shot in Palu. The targeting of officials was not just restricted to Christians but also included symbols of the *thoghut* (tyrant) state, such as the 2004 shooting of attorney general Ferry Silalahi and the 2006 shooting of Poso police chief Rudy Sufahriadi.[215]

The mujahidin also conducted a bombing campaign, particularly targeting bus routes servicing Christian destinations. For example, on June 5, 2002, a bomb inside a bus from Palu to Tentena killed four people and injured sixteen.[216] This was designed to instill fear, constrict the mobility of the Christians, and result in high numbers of *kafir* casualties. Markets also became the targets of bombings and many of these bombings were symbolic in terms of target or timing. For example, on November 13, 2004, on Idul Fitri a bomb exploded in Poso's Central Market, killing six. On December 31, 2005, a bomb detonated in Pasar Maesa's pork market in Palu, killing nine and wounding fifty-five. This bomb had initially been scheduled for December 24 but failed to explode.[217] The most spectacular bombing, however, was the Tentena market bombing on May 28, 2005, in which two bombs detonated in the Christian heartland. The first bomb went off in the crowded market; the second bomb followed fifteen minutes later next to a branch of Bank Rakyat Indonesia, killing many who had rushed to aid the victims of the first bomb. The bombings resulted in twenty-two dead and fifty-three wounded and were the deadliest bombings since Bali 2002.[218] They were carried out in the hitherto unpenetrated Christian heartland, but it was the timing that was most telling: the fifth anniversary of the Walisongo massacre. As Ambo, who had been part of the operation, explained, "Tentena was bombed because it was responsible for Walisongo. There was no way they did not know. They were the base. That is why we bombed Tentena market. Tentena let them come down. Women were raped. Children were cut up. It was sadistic. They were not just killed but tortured beforehand. They cut off their heads and took the heads back with them. It was all about revenge."[219] And last but certainly not least, there were "spectaculars" intended to provoke and to instill the ultimate terror. On October 29, 2005, during Ramadan, a group of seven black-clad, masked mujahidin carrying machetes ambushed four Christian schoolgirls—seventeen-year-old Alvita Polino, sixteen-year-old Theresia Morangki, fifteen-year-old Yarni Sambua, and sixteen-year-old Noviana Malewa—who were on their way to school from Bukitbambu village. Noviana managed to escape the attackers with her cheek slashed; the other three were beheaded.[220] Their heads were taken and later dumped with accompanying notes, all in a different handwriting, stating that "we are still looking for 100 Christian (Kongkoli) heads" as "Lebaran [Idul Fitri] gifts," that "blood must be avenged through blood, a life for a life, a head for a head," and that "this reprisal is nothing compared to your sadism, your barbarism. You will not be safe or calm until our [desire for] vengeance has been healed."[221]

The attack on the schoolgirls had been carefully planned. It was carried out by local mujahidin Lilik Purnomo alias Haris, Irwanto Irano alias Iwan, Mohamad Basri, Agus Nur Muhammad alias Agus Jenggot, and Rahman Kalahe alias Wiwin. Personal motivations of revenge played a key role. Basri later stated at his trial that twenty-six of his relatives had been killed in the Walisongo and Buyung Katedo massacres. "All that was found of one of my relatives was the head. Another had his hands cut off. My auntie's stomach was torn open, and she was pregnant. I rescued their remains. I wanted to avenge their deaths. I wanted revenge against those Christians. They killed my family."[222] The religious justification was provided by JI's Hasanudin, who asserted that the attack was sanctioned by the Quran, which deems it permissible to carry out retribution in the same form as the original violence.[223] As Christians had beheaded Muslim women at Buyung Katedo, the beheading of the schoolgirls was treated as like for like. Moreover, as four girls had been designated, the one that had escaped needed to be "compensated for" and thus Wiwin, who had failed to achieve his objective, was compelled to seek a "replacement target." He selected seventeen-year-old Ivon, a student at the Poso Protestant High School. Ivon and her friend Siti Nuraini were shot and wounded in a drive-by shooting on November 8.[224]

It was also no coincidence that the schoolgirl beheadings were carried out during Ramadan, not only commemorating the outbreak of the first phase of conflict in Poso but also reflecting the belief that the rewards for jihad during Ramadan were greater than at any other time.[225] Indeed, the targeted terror between 2002 and 2007 spiked each year at Ramadan, including the killings of Irianto Kongkoli and Carminelis Ndele. The specific idea of "Lebaran gifts" was adopted by Hasanudin with the blessing of Ustadz Sanusi, who, while training with the Moro Islamic Liberation Front in the Philippines, had heard of such a practice.[226]

The killing of the schoolgirls prompted a national and international outcry as well as condemnation from within JI. Senior JI leader Abu Dujana disowned the beheadings of the schoolgirls as a "loss of command" and senior JI member Abu Rusdan later exclaimed that "Hasanudin will be held responsible by Allah for the mutilations."[227] This set the ball rolling for removing the remaining jihadis from Poso. A special criminal investigative unit was established and sent to Poso, comprising personnel from the police bomb-disposal unit and Densus 88. A series of subsequent arrests and interrogations provided the police with enough information to piece the Poso puzzle together, but left them facing the challenge of separating the perpetrators of the violence from the society that supported them and in whose eyes the police had little legitimacy.[228] As the mujahidin denounced the police as *thoghut*, *kafir*, and *pengkhianat* (traitors), and Poso Muslim leaders, including Arsal, traveled to Jakarta and called for a new jihad in Poso,[229] the police launched counterterror operations in January 2007. The first came on January 11 in Gebangrejo near Tanah Runtuh. Four suspects were arrested, and two others—Dedi Parsan and JI leader Ustadz Rian—were shot dead, Rian allegedly as he came out of Arsal's *pesantren* carrying a bomb.[230] This was followed by a further counterterrorism operation on January 22, targeting twenty-four "wanted" suspects. One member of the police and thirteen mujahidin were killed in the battle that ensued in Tanah Runtuh; dozens were arrested.

National Imaginaries and the Poso Conflict

The shift in the Indonesian national imaginary in the late New Order toward a more Muslim one, and the role ICMI played in this, were key factors in the eruption of the Poso conflict. Islamization was one of the core grievances of the Christians, who saw their community best preserved through the national imaginaries of the early Sukarno and early Suharto periods, a national imaginary that emphasized Pancasila, pluralism, religious equality, and monotheistic ecumenicism.

Conversely, many Muslims saw themselves as victims in those very same national imaginaries the Christians perceived as safe. They thus wholeheartedly embraced the new direction ICMI was pursuing. However, as the conflict transitioned from urban brawls to communal offensives, a further shift in the Muslim national imaginary took place. This was partially the result of the uncertainties that *reformasi* had introduced with respect to how the state was defined. But above all it was a response to Jakarta's lack of interest in the Poso conflict and how Muslims were killed in the Walisongo massacre, as well as the inability of the local government to handle the increasing violence. As Adnan Arsal elucidated, it was the result of its false assurances that "the local government lost society's trust."[231] This provided an opening for the outside mujahidin to introduce Poso's Muslims to their notions of *daulah Islamiyah* and *khilafa*.

Here JI stood out, as it had clear aims of establishing an Islamic state, its *dakwah* was accompanied by the introduction of *syariah* in areas where it was based, and, most importantly, it had territory. Indeed, JI established three new *wakalahs* (divisions) in the area in 2002: Wakalah Uhud in Palu, Wakalah Khaibar in Poso, and Wakalah Tabuk in Pendolo/Pandajaya.[232] Poso's Muslims were also seen as receptive to JI's *taklim* and local community leaders shared JI's commitment to Islamic law. Thus, JI believed that through intensive *dakwah* it could expand the community prepared to live by salafi principles.

It was these elements of receptive society and territory as well as the geographic remoteness of Poso that prompted the first head of Mantiqi 3, Abu Tholut alias Mustopha, and his successor, Nasir Abas alias Suleiman, to experiment with "the idea of establishing a *qoidah aminah* there as outlined in PUPJI."[233] Abu Tholut took his idea to the JI *markaziyah*: "I said let's try it. Come here and see for yourself and if it doesn't work it doesn't work. Don't judge before you have even gone to Poso. Abu Rusdan came because I invited him to see. Abu Bakar Ba'asyir came as the head of MMI." Abu Tholut believed that throughout the course of Indonesian history the Muslims had been "cheated." "The Jakarta Charter was put forward as a compromise but Sukarno and his friends did not want it. So the nationalists destroyed it and the Islamic group got nothing." Since then Muslims have been in conflict with the state: "Muslims felt that they have to struggle for their rights" and that "if you don't support Pancasila you are the enemy of the state." He also believed that the way to establish an Islamic state was through jihad as the establishment of "every state has included the use of the military." The Islamic state that Abu Tholut wanted to establish the foundations for in Poso "would be a state that guarantees that its people can practice Islam to its fullest. It has two characteristics: First, the ruler must be a Muslim. Second, the law must be *syariah*. Other than that, you can have any system you like. It can be a kingdom or a democracy."[234] In the end the *markaziyah* did not approve Abu Tholut's plan, seeing the Poso conflict as a temporary situation. They then sent only a few junior *da'i* (preachers) and *mubaligh* (lay preachers) in order to nip any attempts at setting up a *qoidah aminah* in the bud.[235] That did not, however, prevent Mantiqi 3 leaders from venturing out on their own.

In April 2001, after Abu Tholut's arrest, Nasir Abas became the new head of Mantiqi 3. He also had ideas about the possibilities the Poso conflict offered. "Local jihad in Indonesia is all about establishing an Islamic state in Indonesia. It's in PUPJI. There are two aims: first, to revive Islam through *dakwah* and, second, *iqomatuddin*—to establish an Islamic state. The strategy is twofold: first, through education—*tarbiyah rasmiyah*—to strengthen the umma and to restore *daulah Islamiyah* and second, through *pembinaan teritori* (preparation of the territory) to set up a *qoidah aminah* before, during, and after establishing *daulah Islamiyah*."[236] So after the Malino Agreement in December 2001, Nasir Abas set about establishing a *qoidah aminah* in Poso, starting with its economic base.

> After Malino, I did not want to continue jihad in Poso because it would backfire against the local Muslims. I was questioned by others in JI—why do you want to end jihad? I said I am not ending jihad, I have a different plan. I wanted to turn Poso into our new economic *wilayah*. Because of the conflict the price of land was cheap. Farmers were scared to farm and were selling. I wanted to buy up this cheap land with coffee and cacao trees. We had lost Mantiqi 1 Singapore and Malaysia, which was our economic *mantiqi*. We could turn Poso into our new economic area and help Muslims there as well. I surveyed the territory around Poso. It was perfect for a *qoidah aminah*. It would be similar to Basilan for Abu Sayyaf. We could bring in weapons and set up weapons factories and supply other areas in Indonesia.[237]

Abas thought that he would need approximately four years "to set this up and get our agro-business running." Then JI "could start establishing an Islamic state with Poso's Muslims at its core."[238] His vision of an Islamic state drew upon Muslim rather than Indonesian history, which is not all too surprising as Nasir Abas is Malaysian. It was also cognizant of Poso's multireligious and multicultural composition.

> An Islamic state is a fairer system. In Indonesia Muslims pay *zakat* and tax. Non-Muslims only pay tax. So Muslims are taxed twice. In an Islamic state a Muslim pays *zakat* and a non-Muslim *jizya*. So they pay the same.
>
> Non-Muslims can live among Muslims and exercise their rights. Non-Muslims have the right to build houses of worship. Relations be-

tween Muslims and non-Muslims would be the way they were under Caliph Umar or maybe like they were under the Ottomans.²³⁹

This was also reflected in JI's implementation of *syariah*.

> In Poso we implemented *syariat Islam*, not by force like the Taliban in Afghanistan but by persuasion. JI in Poso encouraged people to follow it. There were patrols and if they saw women without *jilbab* they'd ask them why. They also carried a bag of *jilbabs* and if women were not wearing because they could not afford one, they could choose one from the bag. The *jilbabs* had been donated from Java for the women in Poso.... We had the same approach to people drinking alcohol. The patrol team would stop them and ask if they had been drinking and why they were drinking.²⁴⁰

In April 2003, Nasir Abas was arrested and his plans for a *qoidah aminah* were shelved, but the ideational seeds had been sown. As one member of the first batch of Mujahidin Tanah Runtuh explained, they were taught that a *khilafa* "needs to be established because the *jamaah* in Indonesia is weak. This *khilafa* would encompass all Muslims in the world. The focus was on the global *khilafa* but also on restoring *syariat Islam* in Indonesia. You had to do this in order to move toward the global *khilafa*."²⁴¹ When a new jihadi group, Mujahidin Indonesia Timur (MIT), emerged in Poso in 2012, it became clear that the seeds had germinated. Not only did MIT draw upon Muslim grievances going back to the Poso conflict, but it also linked itself to the global Islamic struggle, reaching out first to Al-Qaeda's Global Islamic Media Front and then pledging allegiance to Abu Bakar al-Baghdadi and ISIS (Islamic State of Iraq and Syria) in 2014.²⁴²

Reflecting on Communal Violence in Poso

The 1998–2007 Poso conflict was rooted in the changing Christian-Muslim and indigenous-migrant demographics, particularly during the New Order. These impacted upon the division of political offices, social positions, employment patterns, and ancestral lands. As argued in this chapter, the shifts in the Indonesian national imaginary as projected by the central government in Jakarta also played a key role. The shift from the religiously pluralist imaginary of the early and mid–New Order toward the more Islamic one of the late New Order was, together with the demographic changes on the ground, perceived as an existential threat by Poso's Christians. This explains the Christian offensive in the third phase of the conflict. Conversely, the more Muslim national imaginary initially emboldened Muslims in Poso, but when there was little reaction to the Walisongo massacre, and as the Indonesian national imaginary had reverted to a more pluralist one under Abdurrahman Wahid, this provided an opening for a shift toward support for an Islamic state in Indonesia and a global *khilafa*. While this latter shift was only embraced by a minority of Poso's Muslims, this was all that was needed to keep the violence going after the December 2001 Malino Agreement and to reignite it under a different name in 2012.

What the Poso conflict clearly shows is how complicated belonging was for both Christians and Muslims, not least because they had separate colonial experiences. Neither Poso's Christians nor Poso's Muslims had been key players in the Indonesian Revolution. They thus related to the national imaginaries projected by Jakarta without having been part of constructing them. The fact that Indonesia's national imaginary shifted several times complicated belonging further. Indeed, the uncertainty at the center during the early years of *reformasi* meant that, in the end, communal belonging superseded national belonging. Christians stressed the need for indigeneity and cast their local imaginary in ethnoreligious Pamona-Christian terms. Muslims in contrast cast their local imaginary in purely religious terms, with Islam serving to bridge the gap between locals and migrants. Continuing, escalating violence in the face of inaction by Jakarta pushed belonging beyond Indonesian state boundaries. Muslims sought refuge in the ideas of a global *khilafa* while Christians appealed to international Christian organizations, the Western media, Western states, and the UN. Both had become alienated from the state. However, they never stopped identifying as Indonesian.[243]

The persistence of Muslim grievances after Malino and the persistence of the alternate national imaginary of an Islamic state or *khilafa* provided a basis for reviving the Poso jihad in 2012. This second jihad specifically targeted the Indonesian police as *thoghut*, but also, to a lesser extent, local Christians. The linkage between the "old" Poso conflict and "new" Poso jihad is best exemplified by Basri, who had lost most of his extended family in the Walisongo and Buyung Katedo massacres. He was among the first to join the Mujahidin Tanah Runtuh, where he also met Santoso, and in fact trained him. In 2012, Santoso established MIT and asked Basri to join. Basri later explained during a meeting in Cipinang Prison that "the locals joined MIT because there was still no justice after the Poso conflict. Many Muslims suffered but the Christians responsible have not been punished."[244] He added that he personally had joined because he wanted to continue the war, because he wanted revenge, and because Santoso had asked him. At the end of the meeting he had a message for his Muslim brethren in Poso—to be vigilant as the Christians could come down from the highlands again.[245]

6

THE AMBON CONFLICT, 1999–2005

Three weeks after the violence broke out in Poso on Christmas Eve 1998, the Ambon conflict erupted on Idul Fitri 1999. On January 19, two Bugis Muslim migrant youths, Usman and Salim, asked a Christian Ambonese transport driver, Jacob Leuhery (Yopi), for Rp500 at the Batu Merah Transport Terminal in Ambon city. They claimed the van that Yopi was driving belonged to a Bugis on whose behalf they were collecting rent. Yopi saw this as an attempt at extortion and refused to give them any money. Usman and Salim then asserted that Yopi had threatened the Muslim bus conductor. The youths drew a traditional *pisau badik* knife, at which point Yopi drove off to the Christian Mardika neighborhood, ostensibly to pick up some fares. When he returned to the terminal, he saw Salim and Usman waiting for him. So he went home, got his own knife, and returned. Along with other Christians who joined him, he chased the Bugis youths into the Muslim Batu Merah neighborhood, where the Bugis youths disappeared. Shortly after Yopi returned home hundreds of Muslim youths from Batu Merah attacked Christian Batu Merah Dalam, where Yopi lived.[1] Violence quickly spread to other neighborhoods in Ambon city, to other villages on Ambon Island, and from Ambon Island to other islands in Maluku. By the time the communal conflict was formally brought to an end with the Malino II Agreement in February 2002, some 4,000 to 10,000 people had been killed and between 123,000 and 860,000 displaced.[2]

This chapter looks at the 1999–2005 Ambon conflict, examining the causes of the conflict and the place of Ambon and the Ambonese in the Indonesian national imaginary. It then analyzes the phases and dynamics of the violence, with a focus on local Christian and Muslim combatants as well as the mujahidin from other parts of Indonesia who remained militarily active until the 2005 Loki attack. This is followed by a discussion of the alternative national imaginary that was advanced by some Christians before concluding with a reflection on Ambonese belonging and alienation within the Indonesian state.

This chapter shows that the Ambon conflict, like that in Poso, was rooted in the changing ethnoreligious demography and its impact on political, economic, and social dynamics. As in Poso, the shift in the Indonesian national imaginary toward a more Islamic one in the late New Order period raised fears among Ambon's Christians. However, unlike in Poso, the Ambon conflict was read through "filters of history" with collective historical memories playing active roles. This history was defined by the distinctly different colonial experience of Ambon's Christians as well as the attempt to establish an independent Republic of South Maluku (Republik Maluku Selatan, RMS) in 1950. Together these ensured that "belonging" to Indonesia for many Ambonese Christians remained contentious. This history also ensured that the Indonesian military, many Ambonese Muslims, and Laskar Jihad never regarded the conflict that erupted in Ambon in January 1999 as purely communal but instead suspected separatism. The RMS also provided a historic Ambonese alternative national imaginary that was dusted off and revived in 2000 by the Maluku Sovereignty Front (Front Kedaulatan Maluku, FKM) when Ambonese Christians felt that they were being left to die by the Indonesian government.

The History of Christian-Muslim Relations in Maluku

The 1999 Ambon conflict can only be fully understood by considering the *longue durée* of Christian-Muslim relations in Maluku. Local history credits a Javanese trader named Hussein with the introduction of Islam to Ternate, North Maluku, around 1460. Four decades later Islam arrived in Ambon, Central Maluku. Hitu, a confederation of some thirty villages, became Ambon's first Muslim community.[3] In 1511, the first Portuguese ships arrived in search of spices, carrying with them Catholic missionaries.[4] One of these, Fransiskus Xaverius, is commonly seen as having established the Catholic Church in Maluku.[5]

Both Islam and Christianity became intertwined with commercial interests and colonial control. This led to tensions between Christians and Muslims, not least because the Catholicism practiced by the Portuguese was fiercely anti-Islamic, colored by centuries of *Reconquista*, the liberation of the Iberian peninsula from Muslim control. The first Christian-Muslim conflict erupted when the Portuguese confiscated the clove harvests in North Maluku and Sultan Hairun declared jihad against the Portuguese settlers in Ternate as well as Malukan Christians who he saw as vital to Portuguese expansion. Military expeditions sent by him and later by his son Baabullah resulted in the persecution and massacre of some eighty thousand Christians on Moro and Bacan.[6] On Ambon, the Muslims of Hitu spearheaded the anti-Christian campaign, killing around seventy thousand.[7] By 1573, the Jesuits acknowledged that almost their entire mission in North Maluku had been destroyed, and in December 1575 the Portuguese withdrew to Ambon, where the church had managed to survive.[8]

It is at this time that Ambon town was established, as Christians settled around the new Portuguese fort where they could seek refuge.[9] For the next twenty-five years it was an almost exclusively Catholic town, from which Captain Sancho de Vasconcellos waged a brutal war with his Christian Ambonese supporters against Ambonese Muslims.[10] In 1597, Ambon was besieged by a Javanese Muslim fleet that had come to aid their Muslim brethren, leading many Christians to fortify themselves in the hills. This marked the beginning of the end of Portuguese rule, a period that went down in the Muslim collective memory as brutal foreign colonization and in the Christian collective memory as a brutal jihad. Two years later the first Dutch forays were made into Ambon.

The Dutch period from 1599 to 1942 saw the Protestantization of Ambon and eventually the rise of Ambon's Christians politically, socially, and economically. This period is crucial to understanding the Malukan Christian psyche as Protestantism came to be understood as providing both protection and power. G. J. Knaap estimated that there were about sixteen thousand Catholic Ambonese when the Dutch arrived.[11] Most of them became Protestants, bringing their religious and communal identity in line with that of their new colonial overlords. As Ambon became the political center of the Dutch United East India Company (Vereenigde Oost Indische Companie, VOC), Ambon town became a Protestant bastion and the Christian *raja* (village heads) on Leitimor dominated the highest legal and administrative body in which Ambonese participated: the Landraad.[12]

The VOC quickly moved toward establishing its monopoly over the nutmeg and clove trade, forcing the Ambonese Christians from their mountain settlements down to the coast in the mid-seventeenth century in order to control the clove cultivation.[13] The Christians established separate *negeri* (villages), sometimes right next to or in between Muslim villages. This perpetuated religious segregation while, at the same time, moving Christians and Muslims territorially closer together. Christian-Muslim relations were strengthened by a system of intervillage alliances known as *pela* that often tied Christian and Muslim villages together on the same island or across islands.[14] These *pela* assured mutual aid in times of need, but this did not prevent different *pela* alliances from fighting against each other.[15]

The VOC's assertion of monopoly also triggered another cycle of violence in Maluku, driven by commercial interests, colonial rivalries, and local alliances.[16] It included the 1636 and 1646 popular revolts—which were both Christian and Muslim; the 1635–1638, the 1650–1656, and the 1679–1681 Maluku wars between the Dutch and Ternate, Tidore, and Spain; and intervillage battles such as the 1632–1651 Iha War. Most of these conflicts divided local populations along religious lines, whereby Ambonese Christians fought for the VOC against their Muslim neighbors.[17] This dynamic of the Christians allying with the Dutch colonizers ingrained itself deeply into the collective Muslim memory, as did particular incidents of violence. Muslim community leader Thamrin Ely recalled the appearance of flyers just after the 1999 Ambon conflict had erupted, which recounted how in 1699 Passo's Christians "walked on hundreds of Muslim bodies" as they expelled Hitu's Muslims and confiscated their land.[18]

In January 1800 the Dutch government took over the assets of the bankrupt VOC.[19] Shortly thereafter, the Napoleonic Wars inaugurated another period of instability that in the Netherlands Indies started with the repressive rule under Governor General Herman Willem Daendels, followed by the British occupation of Ambon from 1810 to 1814, and culminating in the 1817 Pattimura Rebellion after Ambon had been returned to the Dutch. Ambon then became the seat of the Dutch proconsul until the Japanese invasion in 1942. It is during this latter half of the Dutch colonial period that the Dutch openly started to favor Ambon's Christians. By the 1830s, Ambonese Protestants, as loyal coreligionists, became the preferred recruits of the Dutch colonial army (Koninklijk Nederlands-Indisch Leger, KNIL), where they were used as "as shock troops, to conquer the enemy's position."[20] Ambonese Christians also became an important source of administrative manpower for the expanding colonial bureaucracy, having benefited from education through missionary schools.[21]

This created a clear-cut social stratification along religious lines in Ambon, with the emergence of an exclusively Protestant middle class whose communal interests were tied to the Dutch. Not surprisingly, this period of rapid Christian advancement ingrained itself as one of injustice in the collective memory of Ambon's Muslims and was seen as one of the long-term causes of the 1999 Ambon conflict. As Muslim community leader Ali Fawzi explained, "The Muslims were put down and the Christians were preferred. They gave the Christians facilities to go to school but not the Muslims. They gave the Christians positions in the administration but not the Muslims. They gave them positions in the police and in the army; there were fewer positions for the Muslims. That is the long-term cause of the conflict."²² The Second World War reversed the fortunes of Ambon's Christians. Japan's attack on January 24, 1942, destroyed more than four-fifths of Ambon town. By February 3, some three thousand Australian and Dutch forces, who were fighting the Japanese alongside the KNIL, had surrendered.²³ Ambon's Muslims welcomed the Japanese as liberators from Dutch oppression; the Christians saw their arrival as "a great misfortune for their souls and security."²⁴ Christian Ambonese soldiers were interned in camps alongside the Dutch.²⁵ Christian Ambonese civilians lost their privileges and social position. As the Japanese saw Christianity as part of the Western influences that they sought to eliminate, the Malukan Protestant Church (Gereja Protestant Maluku, GPM) suffered greatly.²⁶ Church buildings were destroyed and clergy were punished.²⁷ Some ninety clerics and church employees were executed.²⁸ Christians were removed from administrative positions and Muslims were installed in their place. Most of the senior positions went to members of the pro-Indonesian nationalist organization Sarekat Ambon, thus facilitating the rise of a new pro-Indonesian nationalist elite.²⁹ This marked the beginning of a struggle for hegemony and competing political imaginaries that characterized much of the postindependence period. It also resulted in renewed intercommunal tensions. According to Richard Chauvel, after the arrival of the Japanese, Muslims looted Dutch and Christian property and carried out assaults in "revenge against the Dutch and the Christians for the discrimination they felt they had suffered."³⁰ The collective Christian memory of the Japanese occupation and, in particular, the collaboration of Ambon's Muslims with the Japanese also became one of the long-term causes of the 1999 Ambon conflict.³¹

The RMS Rebellion and Ambon in the Indonesian National Imaginary

When Sukarno and Mohammad Hatta declared Indonesian independence on August 17, 1945, Ambon and the neighboring islands of Seram, Buru, Saparua, Haruku, and Nusa Laut were clearly situated within the Indonesian geo-body. However, the historical experience of Ambonese Christians equally clearly stood at odds with Sukarno's national narrative of 350 years of oppression by the Dutch. The close relationship of Ambonese Christians with the Dutch provided them with a significantly different colonial experience to that of much of the rest of the Indonesian population. It also provided them with a distinct identity. In 1926, Dutch missionary Hendrik Kraemer stated that the Christian Ambonese "feel themselves to be Europeans" and considered "themselves the pacifiers and conquerors of the Indies."³² Ben van Kaam pointed out that "there were many

Ambonese who themselves believed that loyalty to the Netherlands and the House of Orange was a major characteristic of their history."[33] And, according to Chauvel, Ambonese soldiers, in particular, developed "an acute ethno-religious identity."[34] It was this identity that ensured that Ambon's Christians, and with them Ambon, would occupy an awkward, equivocal place in the Indonesian national imaginary. Indeed, as Muslim politicians in Jakarta voiced their support for a more Islamic Indonesia, most Ambonese Christians continued to side with the Dutch during the Indonesian Revolution. They allowed the Netherlands Indies Civil Authorities (NICA) to land on Ambon and take control.[35] They then joined the KNIL and fought the Indonesian Republican army across the archipelago. The Ambonese soldiers were even credited with securing the Dutch reoccupation of Jakarta.[36]

The reaffirmation of allegiance to the Dutch by many Ambonese Christians, as well as the behavior of the "trigger-happy Dutch and Ambonese soldiers," resulted in the declaration of the Ambonese, who had already been "regarded with deep suspicion by the *pemuda* [youths] and much of the public," as the enemy.[37] Equating Ambonese with Ambonese Christians, nationalist vigilante youth groups called upon the population to kill the Ambonese, and the Indonesian People's Army declared "a guerrilla and economic war against the Ambonese."[38] The Ambonese, alongside the Dutch and other Eurasians, became the targets of "atrocities and terrorism."[39] In October 1945, Pastor J. C. Hoekendyk, the Dutch mission's "Consul" in the Netherlands Indies, reported that in Batavia "more than 10,000 Ambonese (all Christians) are persecuted and some are killed."[40] In November, a committee of Dutch civilians in Java headed by the Vicar Apostolic of Batavia called upon the Netherlands and the Netherlands Indies governments to evacuate Ambonese women and children on Java as "the deeds of terror" were "increasing from day to day."[41]

There is no doubt that many Indonesian nationalists considered the Ambonese KNIL soldiers, their families, and Ambonese Christians more broadly as collaborators. They were also seen as an obstacle to the implementation of Sukarno's vision of Indonesia as a unitary republic as they supported Dutch plans for a federal Indonesia, the United States of Indonesia (Republik Indonesia Serikat, RIS). As such they were denounced as "Dutch puppets."[42] Later, Sukarno would describe the supporters of federalism not only as "Dutchified groups" but as "chameleon and 'cockroach' groups."[43] Not surprisingly, as soon as the transfer of sovereignty was completed on December 27, 1949, Sukarno set about implementing his own vision of a unitary Indonesia by dismantling the federal structure. For him federal Indonesia had only ever been an "interim period," a "tactic" to obtain independence, and the treaties signed with the Dutch, in the words of Muhammad Yamin, were nothing more than "snapshots of the revolutionary torrent."[44]

It was this dismantling of the RIS that caused Christiaan Soumokil, an Ambonese Christian who had been appointed justice minister in the federal component state of East Indonesia, to flee from Makassar to Ambon in April 1950. Several days and meetings later, on April 25, Johannes Hermanus Manuhutu and Albert Wairisal declared an independent Republic of South Maluku. This declaration put further strain on Christian-Muslim relations, both in Ambon and between Ambonese Christians and the Muslim-majority Indonesian state. Jakarta deemed this declaration a direct attack on the Indonesian geo-body and on its "true" unitary national imaginary in accordance with the August 17, 1945, proclamation of independence.

Sukarno's initial response was to send a peace mission led by Indonesian health minister Dr. Johannes Leimena, who was of Ambonese origin. Leimena's mission, however, failed as the RMS government refused to even meet with him. Yet his account of the mission is instructive, as it exemplifies the Indonesian government narrative: Soumokil was "the *auctor intellectualis*," supported by "Dutch circles."[45] The proclamation of the Republic of South Maluku was "not based on the popular will in the South Moluccas" but was "forced upon the South Moluccas Council by the KNIL green- and red-caps."[46] Indeed, the KNIL was the core of the problem, terrorizing "all sections of the population which do not line up with them." The result was that the population "in Ambon and the adjoining islands" lived "in fear and alarm."[47] He concluded his report by calling upon Ambonese Christians "to become good Indonesians, besides being good Christians," stating that as a Christian, he regretted "the activities of Soumokil and his armed followers," and that "viewed historically and from the angle of the Church, the Ambon islands are passing through a crisis."[48]

After the Leimena mission the Indonesian government quickly shifted to "the second and third stages, that is 'blockade and military operation,' to crush them [the RMS]."[49] The blockade was imposed in May and all air, shipping, and telegraphic services were suspended. Military operations against the RMS commenced on July 13, when the first 850 Indonesian troops landed on Buru, but it was not until September 28 that the TNI set foot on Ambon.[50]

The battle for Ambon was a bitter one in which ground troops were supported by warships and bombers. While the official TNI history asserts that Ambon was occupied "in the matter of a few days," it also records that this did not include "the southern part where the RMS had based all of its forces" and that the RMS defense of Waitatiri caused so many deaths that the TNI had to request help from Jakarta.[51] Casualties for the period of July–December 1950 were considerable. The chief of operations in Maluku, Captain J. Muskita, estimated that the TNI lost four to five hundred men.[52] According to British sources there were "no less than 6,000 [TNI] casualties" inflicted by a "determined Ambonese resistance."[53] Civilian, mainly Christian, casualties were estimated at five to eight thousand.[54]

While Ambon city was taken by the Indonesian military by the end of 1950, the RMS rebellion continued for another thirteen years in the jungles of Seram Island. During this time Jakarta pursued two parallel policies. The first was a propaganda war against RMS representatives in the Netherlands and the United States. In this struggle the Indonesian government stressed that the South Maluku rebellion was an internal affair, and it emphasized that "every effort had been made to settle this issue peacefully but Soumokil and his followers had not wanted a peaceful settlement so the Government had been reluctantly compelled to apply the law of force."[55] Sukarno stressed that the military operations were not directed against the people of Ambon. Similarly, Indonesian foreign minister Mohammad Roem contended that the people of Ambon were the victims of "the terror and intimidation perpetrated by the armed ex-KNIL forces."[56] The RMS was labeled a "non-existent entity," "nothing but a farce," the product of "adventure politics," "foreign-inspired and foreign-supported."[57] Those who supported it were "misguided rebels," led astray by "unscrupulous and irresponsible adventurers, who keep themselves under cover."[58] They were seen as separatists, counterrevolutionaries, and "blandistis" (pro-Dutch), and their views were branded as "heresy," while their military operations were dismissed as "insignificant."[59]

The second policy aimed at bringing the Ambonese back into the Indonesian fold. Sukarno placed the small number of Ambonese Christians who had been active in supporting the Republic in important positions in the government, even appointing some to his cabinet. In Ambon, too, Christians were able to reclaim their social hegemony, largely as a result of their educational advantage that allowed them to dominate the civil service, the education system, and the media for another generation. Sukarno also located several national development projects in Maluku such as the Wayame shipyard, the Oceanography Research Institute, and the Makariki sugar mill. He even named Indonesia's first research nuclear reactor Siwabessy—after an Ambonese engineer.

However, while the Indonesian government and military publicly considered "the Indonesian people in the South Moluccas victims" of the RMS, to many the rebellion privately confirmed the disloyalty of Ambonese Christians.[60] This ensured that while the territory of Ambon was clearly part of the Indonesian geobody, its population continued to be viewed with suspicion by Jakarta. For instance, Indonesian nationalist of Ambonese origin Johannes Latuharhary, who became the first Indonesian governor of Maluku, was never fully trusted by Jakarta, because he, according to British politician Edward Heath, who was touring Maluku in February 1954, was seen as "leaning too far over the Ambonese side of the fence." Heath reported that Latuharhary "is distrusted at the Centre (though a personal friend of the President) and starved of authority in his province. So great are these limitations, and martial law is still in force in Territory

VII, that Mr. Latuharari makes no secret of the fact that he regards his hands as tied."[61] And, as the Republic continued down the road of total centralization, government policies started to favor the more populous areas of Indonesia: Java and Sumatra. When rice production became a high priority, funds were channeled to rice-producing regions in Western Indonesia, and Maluku started to stagnate.[62] The capture of RMS leader Soumokil in December 1963 further directed Jakarta's attention away from Ambon.[63] On April 12, 1966, Soumokil, like Darul Islam leader Kartosoewirjo, was executed by firing squad on the small island of Ubi off the coast of Jakarta and buried in an unmarked grave.

The RMS insurgency had a profound impact on Ambon's Christians and Muslims. The former continued to often feel alienated from the state, acutely aware of their minority status in the Indonesian Republic, fearful of any shift toward Islam locally or nationally. The latter remained suspicious of Christian behavior and motivations, knowing that in an independent Malukan state they would be the minority, cut off from Muslim Indonesia. The RMS rebellion also ensured that when the communal violence erupted in January 1999, the central government, the military, and many Muslim Ambonese were convinced that the conflict had been started by the RMS in a renewed bid for Malukan independence.

The New Order Causes of the Ambon Conflict

While the pre–New Order history of Christian-Muslim relations in Maluku challenges the notion of historically continuous religious harmony—an image perpetuated by the New Order—and while it shows how Christian-Muslim social stratification and historical memories fed into the 1999 Ambon conflict, it was the New Order period that directly prepared the ground for intercommunal violence. The first challenge to Christian-Muslim relations and Ambon's social fabric during the New Order came from Suharto's transmigration program. Between 1969 and 1999, 97,422 transmigrants were resettled in Maluku.[64] While this number only comprised about 5 percent of Maluku's population, there was a significant number of spontaneous migrants—Bugis, Butonese, and Makassar, locally referred to as BBM—from Sulawesi who arrived on the back of the transmigration program and found their niche in the informal sector. As highly entrepreneurial small merchants they were drawn to Ambon not only by economic opportunities but also by historical connections. This was particularly true for the Butonese, who as small farmers, mainly from the island of Binongko, had already started settling on Ambon in the last decades of the nineteenth century. Yunanto estimated that unofficial transmigration right before the eruption of conflict in Ambon in 1999 was as high as two hundred thousand, and in Ambon city the BBM were estimated to make up between a quarter and a third of the population.[65]

The impact of the in-migration into Maluku and especially Ambon affected the religious balance considerably, as the majority of both transmigrants and migrants were Muslim. Between 1971 and 1990 the proportion of Muslims in Maluku Province grew from 49.9 percent to 56.8 percent.[66] In 1997, according to the Bureau of Statistics, the population of Maluku Province was 59.02 percent Muslim, 35.29 percent Protestant, and 5.18 percent Catholic in a population of 2.1 million.[67] In Ambon city the religious balance shifted from a 57.5 percent Christian majority to just under fifty-fifty with at least fifty thousand migrants from South Sulawesi.[68] Religious difference and identity were further emphasized by the segregation of Ambon city into Muslim and Christian areas with only a few mixed neighborhoods. Most of the Christian areas were considered as well off, contrasting particularly with overcrowded, poor Muslim areas with large numbers of migrants such as Batu Merah.[69]

The loss of the demographic majority in Ambon was acutely felt by the Christians, many of whom saw this as a deliberate New Order policy linked to Ambon's rebellious past. It was no coincidence that most of the Javanese migrants were settled on Seram, the island where the RMS fighters had been active until 1963. Seram also had a significant amount of natural resources; thus, it is not surprising that it was designated an area for development.[70] As Suharto began to court Muslim support in the 1990s in order to broaden his power base, Christians in Ambon started to believe that official permission for transmigrants was for Muslims only, linking transmigration to Jakarta's new Islamization policy. As Jesuit priest Ignatius Ismartono recalled, Ambonese "ministers and priests started talking about a threat."[71]

The socioeconomic balance in Maluku also started to change during the New Order. At the heart of this was the expansion of Muslim education. In April 1950, a foreign military observer team touring South Maluku noted that "there is practically no illiteracy among the Christian population" while "the percentage of illiteracy among the Mahometans is as high as anywhere also in Indonesia (approx. 85%)."[72] Thus, the Christians, despite the RMS rebellion, occupied most of the higher echelons in the civil service, the bureaucracy, and the education system in the 1950s. While educational opportunities for Muslims during the colonial period were virtually limited to the children of Muslim *rajas*, this changed with Indonesian independence.[73] Muslims had access to better schools, and their children were encouraged to study as part of Indonesia's drive to improve its human resources.[74] By the 1990s the educational gap between Christians and Muslims had narrowed considerably and Ambonese Muslims started to set their sights on those civil service, education, and media jobs that the Christians had hitherto seen as their prerogative.

While Ambonese Muslims were moving up educationally, the BBM filled the emerging gaps in the informal economy and the labor market. Butonese migrants in the 1960s took on employment as laborers in the harbor.[75] By the 1980s, they had also pushed into fishing.[76] Bugis migrants quickly took over as *becak* (pedicab) drivers, and they soon started to dominate local transport.[77] The BBM spread into small trade and similar urban occupations, not just filling genuine gaps but forcing out Ambonese Muslims. This was aided by the fact that the police in Ambon city "was dominated by BBM officers. So it was easy for the BBM to get licenses. Local Muslims were very frustrated by this."[78] The BBM "took over" whole neighborhoods, usually adjacent to the markets where they plied their trade. Batu Merah was one of the most crowded; it was also about 40 percent BBM.[79] By 1996, locals found that they were losing in the competition with the outsiders.[80] So they started to blame Butonese fishermen for the pollution of Ambon's harbor, and the BBM as a whole for the rise in prices, the rise in Ambonese Muslim unemployment, and the declining economic opportunities for the Christians.[81]

Part of the problem was that Maluku under the New Order had continued to stagnate. It had also lost its "prestige projects," which were relocated to Java. At the same time Suharto-linked conglomerates "began to feast on Maluku's abundant natural resources."[82] Licenses for fishing, timber, and cloves were handed out by Suharto in the 1990s to big Jakarta-based Chinese-run companies. The situation became particularly acute in the clove sector, 75 percent of which was dominated by Christian villagers who relied on the production of spices as their main livelihood. When Suharto's son Tommy acquired a monopoly "poverty started to appear in Maluku with the Christian community hit disproportionately."[83]

Social friction between migrants and locals increased. There was a rise in intervillage feuds over boundaries as well as neighborhood disputes in Ambon city. The Bugis and Makassar were seen as particularly aggressive and adverse to integration.[84] Different customs and traditions clashed. Ambonese *adat*, however, was not only diluted by the migrants. It had already been undermined by the New Order through Law No. 5/1979 on village governance, which saw the traditional village head—the *raja* or *upu lattu*—replaced by an elected *kepala desa*, exchanging a hereditary "ascribed status" for one that all adults living in a village could assume.[85] Over time the *kepala desa* became increasingly discredited, with the result that when the conflict erupted in January 1999 and local leaders tried to calm the violence, they had no real authority to do so and were often simply ignored.[86]

Adat had also been weakened by reforms in both Ambonese Islam and Protestantism. The former was influenced by the modernism of Muhammadiyah and

Masyumi, making it more Indonesian and increasingly more universal. The latter's "delocalization" was initially a political decision when the GPM endorsed the Indonesian state during the RMS rebellion. In 1960, this was underwritten by theological reforms embodied in the "message of repentance" issued by the GPM synod, which highlighted the need for purification by breaking the link between religion and *adat* as "you cannot be a Christian if you worship your ancestors."[87] The religious reforms in both Malukan Islam and Christianity weakened the *adat* bond to such an extent that "the communities lost their buffer" and when the conflict erupted, "it blew up and spread on massive scale."[88]

The final blow to Ambon's political, demographic, and social balance came with the appointment of its first Muslim governor, Akib Latuconsina, in 1992. He was the first civilian to hold this position during the New Order. He was also the provincial head of ICMI.[89] In line with ICMI's national policy, Latuconsina quickly embarked upon "reforming" Maluku's civil service by removing "top bureaucrats with Christian names" and replacing them with Muslims.[90] Many of these were from the Muslim clans of Hatuhaha, including the Latuconsinas, Marassabessys, Salampessys, Tuasikals, and Sangajis, in what Sumanto Al Qurtuby referred to as Governor Latuconsina's "nepotism, 'regionalism' and 'clanism.'"[91] By 1996, all the *bupatis* in Maluku Province were Muslim.[92] Most new teachers hired by the government were Muslim. Many originated from outside Maluku with only 10 percent hired from the education department of the University of Pattimura (Unpatti) as opposed to the previous 90 percent.[93] In 1997, Akib Latuconsina was succeeded by Saleh Latuconsina, who favored "graduates who came from the Haruku island villages Ori, his own village Pelauw, and Kailolo."[94] Nine out of twelve regional government offices were headed by Muslims.[95] Adding insult to injury he filled the remaining Christian positions in the bureaucracy with Catholics, choosing Paula Renyaan as deputy governor. He even tried to appoint a Muslim rector of Unpatti, which led to an eight-month deadlock during which 230 professors threatened to resign.[96]

When Suharto fell in May 1998, Ambon's elite was overwhelmingly Muslim, as was its middle class.[97] The Christians felt marginalized politically, socially, and economically as the loss of positions in the bureaucracy meant the loss of patronage. They believed the stigma of the RMS was affecting their career advancement, they saw themselves as "the 'stepchildren of progress' and guests in their own house," and they were terrified by ICMI's references to *syariah* and its "targeting of the population in Eastern Indonesia because it had been instrumental in stopping the inclusion of the Jakarta Charter."[98] This loss of power and these fears of becoming a minority, according to the emeritus Catholic bishop of Amboina, Monsignor Sol, were at the heart of the conflict.[99]

Phases and Dynamics of the 1999 Ambon Conflict

The Ambon conflict can be broadly divided into three phases. The first lasted from January 1999 until May 2000, while the second covered the period from May 2000 to February 2002. The third constituted the postagreement violence until 2005.

Phase 1

The eruption of large-scale communal violence on January 19 was preceded by days if not weeks of Christian-Muslim tensions. These were linked to the announcement in December 1998 of the date for the next general elections in June 1999. This set in motion party political competition, which, as Gerry van Klinken explained, ensured that when the conflict erupted, prominent political figures such as Dicky Wattimena, Agus Wattimena, Ali Fawzi, Yusuf Ely, and Thamrin Ely were among the militants.[100] Preparations in the run-up to both Christmas and Idul Fitri also saw both communities, as Patricia Spyer noted, setting up *posko* in their areas.[101] On the morning of January 19, 1999, tensions were running particularly high. As one Muslim humanitarian aid worker recalled, "There was an incident at Al-Fatah. People were coming out of the mosque after the morning prayer and Christians coming from Silo [Church] started throwing rocks at them. People were angry. Then in the afternoon there was the clash between Batu Merah and Mardika and it all exploded."[102] Following the argument at Batu Merah bus terminal, rumors circulated that the Muslims wanted to torch Silo Church and "the burnings started."[103] The first burnings, according to Jacky Manuputty, who was on the front line, "were in a Muslim area. Then Christian houses in Mardika and then Waihoang and Silale were burned." The latter were mixed areas and this marked the beginning of the "religious cleansing." In just five hours all Christians were pushed out.[104]

A church was set alight in Silale.[105] Another church, in Batu Merah, where an emergency meeting was taking place, found itself under siege with some two hundred Christians trapped.[106] The news of attacks on churches turned what many Christians had initially seen as simply another of the regularly occurring clashes between Batu Merah and Mardika into something much greater. Indeed, Emang Nikijuluw contended that "it only exploded after the church in Silale was burned. That is when the conflict spread to the masses."[107]

Christians in Kudamati gathered and descended from their hilltop neighborhood to assist their coreligionists below. They were led by members of the Handsome Boys (Cowok Keren, Coker), a gang established by Berthy Loupatti in 1985.[108]

Other residents, including church elder Agus Wattimena, quickly joined in.[109] They came marching down the hill carrying traditional weapons and singing "Laskar Kristen Maju" ("Onward Christian Soldiers"), which later led Muslims to assert that the Christians had already established a Christian militia—Laskar Kristen—and this was proof that the Christians started the conflict.[110]

Christians attacked pockets of Muslims in predominantly Christian neighborhoods such as Batu Gajah and Karang Panjang.[111] By 7 P.M. the Bandanese area near Kudamati had been burned to the ground. According to Bandanese leader Des Alwi, who was on the first investigative commission into the Ambon conflict, "The church bells began to ring. This was the sign to start the attack. When the Muslim houses caught fire, the inhabitants ran out shouting 'Allahu Akbar' so that if they died, they would die praising God."[112]

At around 8 P.M. some thirty Muslims tried to attack Silo Church but were held off.[113] In response, Christians torched a number of kiosks and *becak* owned by the Bugis and Butonese. By 11 P.M. the violence had spread to Kampung Paradeys, where a Christian mob claiming that Bethlehem Church had been burned went on a rampage, destroying houses with iron pipes and rocks. Two more waves of attack followed in which the houses of Bugis, Butonese, Minang, and Javanese migrants were targeted.[114]

On the following day, January 20, Christians set the major markets in Ambon city on fire, where most stalls were Bugis owned.[115] They also burned a Butonese settlement around Gambus market. When the news of the burning of the markets, embellished by rumors that Al-Fatah Mosque had also been torched, spread to the Muslim villages of Hitu and Mamala, their residents decided to march to Ambon city. On their way they passed the Christian village of Benteng Karang and took revenge, hacking to death sixteen residents with machetes and burning down the entire village.[116] They then proceeded to the Christian village of Passo, where they encountered fierce resistance at the bridge near Air Besar. The Indonesian army intervened and tried to take the Hitunese back to Hitu by truck. However, some of them turned back on foot, torching Christian homes from Benteng Karang to Nania along the way.[117] Passo's men in revenge burned the Muslim houses and destroyed the mosque in Nania and Negeri Lama. They were seen raising the RMS flag, while further RMS flags were spotted floating attached to balloons over Benteng Atas and Kudamati.[118] Violence also erupted in Hative Besar, Kamiri, and Wailete, where Christians attacked property belonging to Bugis, Butonese, and Makassar.

These first two days of communal violence set the patterns and dynamics for the rest of the first phase of the conflict. Christians attacked Muslim migrants with the aim of pushing them out. The destruction of churches and mosques, or simply rumors that they had been burned, brought in people from other areas.

Christians were expelled from Muslim-dominant areas while Muslims were kicked out of Christian-dominant areas. Revenge became the key driving force. And the raising of the RMS flag ensured that Ambonese Muslims and Jakarta believed that the RMS was involved.

In February, the first attempts at organization were made. Muslims initially grouped under the umbrella of the Indonesian Ulama Council (Majelis Ulama Indonesia, MUI), which set up a task force headed by Yusuf Ely. He attempted to bring together various neighborhood youths "to protect the refugees in Al-Fatah" Mosque and "to protect Al-Fatah."[119] These neighborhood youths were then joined by Muslim volunteers from the villages of Morela, Tulehu, Hitu Lama, Mamala, Wakal, Hila, Negeri Lima, Asilulu, Larike, and Laha. Some of these "sent up to one hundred people in accordance with tradition. They came with swords, spears, bows and arrows."[120] They all came to Al-Fatah, where the MUI task force attempted to coordinate them but was only successful with respect to some of the smaller groups.[121]

Christians, too, started to mobilize, doing so on the basis of church *klasis* (districts).[122] As in the Poso conflict, there were Protestant ministers who led Christian combatants in prayer and blessed their weapons.[123] From late February onward there was rudimentary coordination, and clear leaders had emerged "because people followed them."[124] Foremost among these were Berthy Loupatti, Agus Wattimena, and Emang Nikijuluw. Loupatti's leadership remained limited to Coker as he was keen to maintain his independence.[125] Wattimena became the grassroots leader on Ambon Island while Nikijuluw became the grassroots leader in Ambon city.

While there were obvious Christian and Muslim leaders, what can be loosely regarded as combatants was a very fluid concept. The number of fighters varied from battle to battle, depending upon the particulars of each incident. Much was determined by geography in the sense that it was usually people from adjacent neighborhoods or villages who joined clashes spontaneously.[126] Both Christian and Muslim fighters included children, who often spearheaded the attacks.[127] According to George Aditjondro, two to four thousand children took part in the violence over the course of the Ambon conflict.[128] Malukan children aged ten to seventeen were present at most battles, either as combatants or as scavengers. The latter were Butonese known as *pasukan linggis* (crowbar troops), who were not, as asserted by Aditjondro, Van Klinken, or Spyer, child fighters. Well known among Muslim child fighters was "Sam's group," whose members gained notoriety for their invulnerability in battle.[129] In contrast to the Muslim child fighters, who operated independently, the Christian child fighters were associated with the adults. The *agas* (sandflies) were linked to Coker while the *cicak* (geckos) were linked to the grassroots leaders.[130]

February also saw the arrival of mujahidin from Java.[131] The first of these were members of Jemaah Islamiyah's special forces, Laskar Khos, which had already been set up before the Ambon conflict by JI's top military commander Zulkarnaen to train those JI members who had not yet received training.[132] It comprised mainly, but not exclusively, "Afghan alumni." Laskar Khos member Ali Imron recalled that "when the conflict broke out, we had to help."[133] Zulkarnaen, who was in Malaysia at the time, went to Ambon to see the situation for himself. "I went to a [Muslim] refugee camp. Their houses had been burned. This was at the beginning of the conflict. They had machetes and rocks. I heard the Christians had guns. So, I wanted to find weapons and bomb-making material—to balance it out. We needed to find weapons for the Muslim side."[134] Some weeks later Ali Imron, together with Nurudin and Saifudin, started instructing small groups of Muslims in houses in different neighborhoods and villages "on how to use a gun and how to make bombs but the most important was *fiqh jihad*."[135] JI was soon joined by other organizations—NII, DI, Laskar Jundullah, and Wahdah Islamiyah. Collectively they were referred to as Laskar Mujahidin.[136] Over the next months and indeed the whole of the conflict, there was a steady stream of these clandestine mujahidin into Buru, Ambon, and Seram. Many initially entered under the umbrella of KOMPAK, which provided them with a legitimate cover as KOMPAK's Solo branch, headed by JI member Aris Munandar, had been invited to Ambon by the head of DDII's Ambon branch, Ali Fawzi.[137]

In mid-February the communal violence started to spread to other islands. Christians armed with sharp weapons attacked Muslims in Kairatu, Seram.[138] On Saparua, Christians burned down a Muslim dormitory.[139] On February 17, violence erupted in Haruku.[140] On March 31, clashes broke out in the Kei Islands, and in April they spread to the Banda Islands, where the Indonesian navy evacuated the entire Christian population, with the exception of fifteen households on Ai who refused to leave.[141] Only in May was the situation brought under some degree of control with a series of peace ceremonies initiated by the military.

Ambon police characterized this first wave of violence as "pure communal conflict" since there was no evidence of organized fighters or any weapons other than traditional ones.[142] Ambon's Christians and Muslims, however, understood the conflict differently. Most Christians perceived it as a conflict between Ambonese and migrants.[143] As Nikijuluw explained, "it was not a clash between Ambonese Muslims and Christians but between Ambonese Christians and the BBM."[144] That is why Muslim migrants became a focal point of Christian violence almost immediately after the Batu Merah terminal incident. Jacky Manuputty recalled that "the issue of the BBM spread to the whole Christian area." Christians "stopped public busses and *becak* as symbols of the BBM. They called upon the BBM to leave Maluku."[145] There were open calls to expel the BBM.[146] There were anti-BBM banners and slogans.¹⁴⁷ Former Ambon mayor Dicky Wattimena, who was known for his anti-BBM politics, was seen going to the market and telling the BBM to go home to their own villages. He was also seen giving orders during the violence.¹⁴⁸ The houses, shops, and market stalls burned down in Ambon city were those of the BBM; care was taken not to attack the shops of the Chinese.¹⁴⁹ The first refugees in Ambon city were the migrants. Indeed, by June 1999 the overwhelming majority of Bugis and Makassar migrants had returned to South and Southeast Sulawesi. The number of Butonese returnees alone was 107,000 people.¹⁵⁰

The BBM were targeted because they were seen as responsible for demographically shifting the balance of power in favor of the Muslims. It was feared that they would increase the vote for the Muslim parties in the upcoming elections.¹⁵¹ They were also seen as a cultural threat, diluting and undermining Ambonese *adat*.¹⁵² Moreover, there were historical grievances, including their having led the Japanese to Ambon and the fact that many of the troops that had crushed the RMS in the 1950s had been drawn from South Sulawesi. And last, but certainly not least, Ambonese Christians believed that "they would finish" the expulsion of the BBM "quickly," and that this would not affect their relations with Ambonese Muslims.¹⁵³ Indeed, many Christians thought that Ambon's Muslims would also like to see the BBM leave to reduce the economic competition but were too polite to say so.

Ambonese Muslims read the conflict as one instigated by the RMS. Nasir Rahawarin recalled that "RMS slogans were everywhere" right after the Batu Merah incident, and in his own analysis he firmly placed the RMS at the heart of the conflict.¹⁵⁴ This view was shared by the majority of Muslims at the Al-Fatah *posko*. Rustam Kastor asserted that "the mastermind is the RMS" and that the Christians were preparing the ground for an "RMS-led Muslim-cleansing operation," in order to establish a purely Christian Republic of South Maluku as part of a broader effort to separate all Christian-dominated provinces in Eastern Indonesia, which would then become a new Christian country with vast natural resources.¹⁵⁵ Similarly, Yusuf Ely explained that "this is not a religious conflict but a social conflict and behind it is the RMS. The aim is to reestablish the Republic of South Maluku."¹⁵⁶ Mohamed Atamimi, too, saw the RMS as the aggressor, stating that "the RMS used the opportunity when the government weakened with the fall of Suharto to rise up again."¹⁵⁷

Not surprisingly, when the first Kostrad soldiers arrived from Makassar on January 21, they immediately started looking for the RMS.¹⁵⁸ And by the end of January the RMS separatist narrative was firmly in place. Indeed, it was enthusiastically embraced by the Indonesian government, the Indonesian military, and Indonesian Muslim politicians as it resonated with their collective historical experience and reflected the separatist fears of the New Order.

The first wave of violence was followed by a second one that erupted in July, days after Jakarta announced the election results. The share of the former governing party Golkar had collapsed from 70 percent to 19 percent in Ambon. PDI-P had gained the majority with 53 percent of the votes and the PPP had only 14 percent. All the Muslim parties together won a mere 21 percent.[159] On July 24 fighting broke out in Poka. The following night the houses of the Muslim lecturers around Unpatti were targeted. Some escaped by boat; others were forced to swim to safety.[160] On July 27, Ambon city's commercial district was destroyed and Christian shops were looted. Two days later, the first of many "mysterious shootings" occurred. Christians attributed these to the Indonesian military, which they saw as having a range of interests in the conflict, including regaining the dominant position it had lost with the fall of Suharto.[161] The police started talking about weapons coming in from foreign countries.[162] And then the TNI stated categorically that weapons had come in from the Netherlands and hence were clearly linked to separatism.[163]

In August 1999, conflict erupted for the first time in North Maluku when fighting broke out between the Kao and Makian ethnic groups. This violence was directly linked to the government's decision to split Maluku into two provinces, but it was triggered by a pamphlet calling on Christians to convert Muslims, which had allegedly originated in Ambon but turned out to be fake.[164] In September, Muslims started targeting passenger ships leaving Ambon. In one such incident thirty-one passengers were assaulted and Edwin Nanere, the son of Unpatti's rector, was killed.[165] As a result, interisland travel and transport became segregated with Muslims traveling on ships via Makassar and disembarking at Ambon harbor, while Christians took ships via Kupang and disembarked at the Ambon naval base.[166] When the violence subsided at the end of September, it had claimed 217 lives. Some 422 people had suffered severe injuries and another 200 light injuries. More than 1,500 houses, thirteen churches, seven mosques, and four school buildings, as well as twenty-one cars, eight motorbikes, and fifty-seven three-wheeled vehicles, had been destroyed. The police had seized fifty homemade rifles and bazookas, 708 arrows, sixteen spears, eighteen machetes, 157 swords, and a large number of homemade bombs.[167] Communal segregation had become entrenched with permanent outposts and borders set up between Muslim and Christian areas.[168]

The descent into a third round of communal clashes started in December, as Christians and Muslims began arming themselves in anticipation of violence on the first anniversary of the conflict. Then on December 20, some three hundred Christians from the area around the Polytechnic attacked Kampung Peci while a separate mob from Christian Galala attacked Kampung Jawa. Six people were killed and dozens injured.[169] On the night of December 22/23, the villages of

Wayula and Batlale on the island of Buru were attacked, prompting 800 villagers to flee into the forest while another 2,750 sought refuge at the naval base as well as in churches and mosques.[170] Three days later, on December 26, a traffic accident involving a Christian and a Muslim triggered large-scale urban clashes. The subsequent burning down of Silo Church in Ambon city center resulted in the conflict spreading, first within Ambon and then to other islands. On the Tanimbar Islands, Christians attacked several mosques in retaliation.[171] By December 29, 55 civilians had been killed and 140 wounded.[172] Ambon city was enveloped in dark clouds of smoke from all the burning buildings. Power outages sent fear through whole communities as it was believed that they had been deliberately caused to provide cover for snipers. When the violence started to subside in mid-January 2000, the death toll had doubled and the number of refugees had risen to 276,446, of whom 99,572 had fled to Southeast Sulawesi.[173]

Violence also erupted in North Maluku. On December 26, "a coalition of Christian tribes in northern Halmahera around Tobelo and Galela" attacked the local Muslim population.[174] Two days later, a Christian convoy proceeded to attack the Muslim enclaves in Tobelo city, setting the houses on fire. When the inhabitants then ran out of their burning homes the men were slain.[175] Muslim women were "raped in the streets," and those who had sought refuge in the mosques of Gamsuni and Dufa-Dufa were besieged by Christian mobs who burned down the mosques with the people inside.[176] The official military report on the Tobelo violence stated that between December 26, 1999, and January 7, 2000, 907 had been killed, "while less conservative estimates reached more than 2,000."[177] The Christians who attacked Tobelo and Galela had also forced Muslims to convert, making them eat pork and dog meat as well as change their names.[178] The pictures and accounts emerging from North Maluku, according to Al Qurtuby, "served as a multiplier for the involvement of new armed militias from outside Ambon, especially Java."[179]

This third wave of violence, which took the Ambon conflict into its second year, constituted the last large-scale communal clashes in the first phase of the conflict, which Nikijuluw described as having "a mutually reinforcing circular dynamic."[180] It moved from Ambon city outward to the villages, then to neighboring islands, only to return to Ambon city and start the next convulsion of violence, which followed a similar pattern. Grievances were transferred from one area to another, often by refugees. "Revenge and vendetta" were a central driving force, fueled by the rapid spread of information and misinformation, particularly rumors of the destruction of houses of worship.[181]

Over the course of the first phase of the Ambon conflict, the military capacity of both Muslims and Christians increased. During the January–May violence traditional weapons were used. Weapons captures during the July–September violence demonstrated there had been a transition to a mixture of traditional weapons and *rakitan* (home-made weapons). The latter ranged from bombs to firearms, many of which were manufactured by the nimble fingers of the child fighters.[182] On the Muslim side, the displaced chemistry lecturers from Unpatti played a key role. As Des Alwi recounted, "The moment the lecturers left Unpatti because they had lost everything they went to Al-Fatah and produced stronger bombs. I noticed that by September stronger bombs were being used. They no longer relied on fertilizer. They had opened out-of-date mortars and used ammunition to make bombs."[183] By the third wave of violence military-grade automatic weapons had entered the picture. Some had been sold or rented out by the military and police. Others were brought in from outside Maluku. Here the Muslims benefitted from JI's connections in the Philippines, while the Christians shopped in Kupang and East Timor.[184] Christians and Muslims were also becoming more coordinated, reflected in a "visible shift from the random social clashes" of the first two waves of violence "to people being organized in frontal attacks."[185] Moreover, as Nasir Rahawarin pointed out, the Muslim community was now more "solid" and filled with "the spirit of jihad."[186] And, as Ambon's territory had become even more segregated and it was dangerous to travel, a new dynamic had emerged with the so-called speed boat shootings in Ambon Bay, which targeted those Muslims and Christians who sought to circumvent roads by crossing the sea.

Pattimura Maluku regional military commander Brigadier General Max Tamaela, who took up his post in May 1999, explained that his troops struggled to keep up with conflict as "the violence jumped from one island to another."[187] In total, Tamaela received six additional battalions during his time as Pattimura commander.[188] He closed Ambon Airport to civilian flights. He even issued shoot-on-sight orders.[189] None of this stopped the violence. Instead, the additional troops were exacerbating the conflict. Tamaela recalled that "the wrongdoings of one or two soldiers would reflect on their whole battalion and that blew up the situation."[190] The locals perceived the troops as biased.[191] And then, during the third wave of violence the local military and police fractured along religious lines, with soldiers and policemen leaving their posts to defend their own communities.[192] Any semblance of neutrality was lost when the overwhelmingly Muslim Kostrad troops were seen launching mortar attacks on Christian neighborhoods while the overwhelmingly Christian local police mobile brigades, Brimob, were seen firing into Muslim neighborhoods from hillsides and rooftops.[193]

As 1999 drew to an end, the central government's apathy, symbolized by Vice President Megawati Sukarnoputri's "shopping holiday" to Hong Kong, and the images of the massacred women and children in Tobelo resulted in the first large-scale mobilization of Muslims in Java.[194] These characterized the final months of the first phase. On January 7, 2000, some 100,000 Muslims "took to the streets of Jakarta" calling for jihad, supported by prominent politicians such as Amien Rais, Hamzah Haz, and Ahmad Sumargono.[195] Organizations such as the Indonesian Committee for Solidarity with the Islamic World (Komite Indonesia Untuk Solidaritas dengan Dunia Islam, KISDI), the Islamic Defenders Front (Front Pembela Islam, FPI), and the newly established Laskar Jihad started registering volunteers. In late January the first of these arrived in North Maluku. However, as the International Crisis Group pointed out, "these early militias were not particularly well organized or effective."[196] They had neither the military expertise of those already operating clandestinely in Ambon under the Laskar Mujahidin umbrella, nor the sheer numbers of Laskar Jihad that would arrive four months later.

Phase 2

The second phase of the Ambon conflict saw a shift in the balance of forces in favor of the Muslims. In much of the literature on the Ambon conflict this has been attributed to the arrival of Laskar Jihad in Ambon. However, Laskar Jihad was only one of five factors. The second factor was the increased military capacity of the local Muslims, whose first recruits had now graduated from the training by groups operating under the Laskar Mujahidin umbrella. The third factor was the proliferation of firearms after the attack on the Tantui arsenal. The fourth factor was the involvement of police and military as *pasukan siluman* (hidden forces). And the fifth and final factor was Christian disunity. It was the convergence of these factors that paved the way for the Muslim offensive that characterized much of the second phase of the Ambon conflict.

In April 2000, a Laskar Jihad delegation of seven arrived in Ambon. They were met by the head of the KOMPAK office in Waihaong, Abdullah Sonata, as KOMPAK had taken on the role of organizing the external humanitarian aid and mujahidin.[197] KOMPAK volunteer Ramly recalled Laskar Jihad asking for "an area" and "as they had doctors, and Galunggung had a hospital, we gave them Galunggung. We also gave them a base in Kebun Cengkeh."[198] In May, the first Laskar Jihad fighters arrived, despite orders by Indonesian president Abdurrahman Wahid to stop them going.[199] Some six hundred of them had left from Tanjung Perak port in Surabaya to Makassar, from where they then traveled on the passenger ship *Bukit Siguntang* to Ambon.[200] Laskar Jihad leader Jafar Umar Thalib and his lieutenants took commercial flights.[201] As they had arrived unarmed, they were allowed to enter Ambon.[202] They proceeded straight to the Al-Fatah *posko*, where they were met by Rustam Kastor, who became their military advisor.[203]

According to Pattimura commander Tamaela, "Three more ships came all within two weeks and they spread across the mosques."[204] They also did not remain unarmed. Nine containers appeared in Ambon harbor containing modern standard firearms. Agus Ulahaiyanan recounted that "one of them was inspected by the TNI. The soldier who saw that it contained guns was then suddenly ordered to go to the airport to meet someone. The other eight containers were not opened. When he got back from the airport, all nine had disappeared. Then after one or two weeks that soldier was rotated out of Ambon."[205] The arrival of the Laskar Jihad volunteers, followed by the nine containers of weapons, caused panic among Ambon's Christians.[206] It also raised consternation in Jakarta with Defence Minister Juwono Sudarsono publicly voicing his objections. He later asserted that "that Laskar Jihad's entry into Ambon had been facilitated by elements in the security forces and was connected to the on-going civil-military struggle in Jakarta."[207] Ambon's Muslims, however, welcomed their arrival as "until May the Muslims had limited arms and could barely hold their position."[208]

In mid-May the fourth wave of violence hit Ambon as attacks on Christian targets increased sharply.[209] Then on June 21 a loose coalition of *laskar lokal* (local Muslim fighters), Laskar Mujahidin, *pasukan siluman*, and Laskar Jihad attacked the Brimob arsenal at Tantui. According to Tamaela,

> It started when a Muslim boy was found dead behind the Brimob compound.... There were two companies of Brimob there and they were already split internally. Then the Brimob commander was killed and leadership was lost. I spoke to the Kapolda [Maluku police chief] and then sent one company of 733 to reinforce them. They were shot at by Brimob in the confusion. The situation was chaos. The radio communication with headquarters was dead and Brimob did not know 733 was coming. And in the end 733 failed to reinforce Brimob and failed to save the compound. It was plundered and burned. For days afterwards parts of Brimob uniforms appeared on the streets and in the street markets. Children and Laskar Jihad were wearing Brimob badges.[210]

The International Crisis Group (ICG) contended that the Brimob commander, who was a Muslim, was killed in a Christian attack on the police housing complex.[211] Muslims further claimed that Christians also took weapons from the Tantui arsenal.[212] The death of the Brimob commander motivated Muslim Brimob members as well as Muslim soldiers from battalions 732, 733, 303, 327, 611, and the Banteng Raiders to join with the loose coalition of mujahidin.[213] This attack was also underwritten by the popular perception that Brimob as a whole supported the Christians, and "that's why the Muslims attacked Tantui barracks and the armory."[214]

The mujahidin took as many weapons as they could carry—on foot or, as Jafar Umar Thalib did, by car. The estimates of arms seized vary greatly. Aditjondro asserted that 832 guns and eight thousand bullets were taken from Tantui, and one ICG report estimated that 700 SS-1 rifles had been seized, whereas a later ICG report provided a more detailed breakdown of 660 handguns, 217 shoulder arms, and 115 automatic rifles.[215] KOMPAK leader Sonata maintained that "from Tantui we got SKS, carbines, and old weapons. There were lots of pistols." He explained that on the one hand "many of the weapons from Tantui were not in good condition" but on the other hand, the sheer amount of them and their proliferation "changed the conflict."[216] These changes were already visible in the week following the attack, which saw Muslim attacks on Galala, Hative Kecil, Mangga Dua, Talake, Kamp Kolam, Perigilima, Mardika, Ahuru, and Nania.[217] During this week, some three hundred people were killed.[218]

On June 26, civil emergency was declared in Maluku and North Maluku. Around 1,400 "contaminated" troops were rotated out of the province and Christian Malukan Pattimura commander Tamaela was replaced by Brigadier General I Made Yasa, who as a Balinese Hindu was seen as neutral. Yet, the Muslim offensive continued unabated. On July 3, Poka-Rumahtiga was attacked and the Polytechnic burned down. The following day Unpatti was torched. As a Christian refugee from Poka recalled, "We were under siege for four days. The first two days we were able to hold out. Then the attackers took the mosque. We continued to defend the church. On the fourth day we had to surrender the church. We ran to the sea and swam to another Christian village, around 2 km away." He believed that the attackers were the mujahidin who had already been there for a while, supplemented by "soldiers because they had the same weapons as the army, but they were wearing the white jihad-gowns over their uniforms."[219] KOMPAK leader Sonata explained that Unpatti had been chosen by local Muslims as a target because of the expulsion of the Muslim lecturers and students during the first phase of the conflict. "There was a long history of discrimination against Muslim students and when the conflict erupted Unpatti gave 100 percent support to the Christian students while the Muslim students were in an emergency campus near the hospital. That was the trigger."[220] Tamaela blamed his successor's strategy: "Made had a different concept of troop deployment. He maximalized the deployment of troops in fixed positions. Unpatti was key terrain. I had a company at Unpatti and Made pulled it out. That is why it was overrun and burned."[221] The attacks on Poka-Rumahtiga and Wailela destroyed thousands of houses, nine churches, and most of Unpatti.[222] The army did not intervene and the navy did not send any ships to evacuate or rescue those who were trying to swim to safety. Indeed, the only protection the military provided was to the electricity generators in Poka.[223]

Poka-Rumahtiga was not the only Christian area attacked. Christian villages situated between Muslim villages were systematically destroyed throughout July in order to create Muslim territorial contiguity. One such attack was launched on July 5 against Waai, which was assaulted "from three sides: from the large Islamic village of Tulehu (to the South), from the Islamic village of Liang (to the North) and from the seaside (to the East). The number of attackers was estimated at several thousand warriors. They started chasing the villagers and burning the place right away, using standard weaponry, grenades, and mortars."[224] They set alight the Catholic church on its outskirts, as churches were top targets in the Muslim offensive to undermine Christian morale, but also reflecting the extent to which Muslims saw this as a religious conflict. Christian refugees from Poka-Rumahtiga estimated that between July 24 and 31 alone, seventeen churches were torched.[225]

The new territorial contiguity in rural areas was secured by Laskar Jihad's "village defence system," in which it left behind a small but highly visible number of its members in each Muslim village to protect these villages from Christian retaliation. Territorial changes also took place in Ambon city, where Laskar Mujahidin was dominant with its highly effective sniper attacks. On July 17, *Suara Maluku*, labeling Ambon city the "barbaric town," reported that Muslims had attacked the areas of Diponegoro, Airmata Cina, Urimessing, Pohon Pule and Mangga Dua, resulting in the destruction of houses, a church, an elementary school, and a pedagogic academy as well as numerous dead and wounded.[226] According to one refugee, the Christians had lost eighteen out of twenty-five neighborhoods.[227] By August, the Muslims, who in the first year of the conflict had controlled around 40 percent while the Christians controlled 60 percent of Ambon city, had reversed this ratio.[228]

The Muslim offensive, the loss of territory, and the knowledge that they were outnumbered and outgunned triggered existential fears among Ambon's Christians.[229] Many believed that the Muslims wanted "to have the whole island for themselves and wanted to wipe out any presence of the Church," and that Laskar Jihad, in particular, had a plan for "wiping out the Christians."[230] They saw their culture under attack as Unpatti, the Maluku Christian University (Universitas Kristen Indonesia di Maluku, UKIM), and the Polytechnic were destroyed. The targeting of the hitherto-spared Catholic community in Ambon, in which its churches, a hospital, and an orphanage were burned, seemed to confirm that there was a broader anti-Christian agenda.[231] This prompted the Catholic Crisis Centre to appeal to UN secretary general Kofi Annan to "send us ships and evacuate us" as the Muslims wanted to "cleanse Ambon of Christians."[232]

Fears of extinction, rumors about TNI support for Laskar Jihad, and the fact that there was no indication that the government in Jakarta even cared about the bloodshed in Maluku, gave rise to a new organization, the Maluku Sovereignty Front (Front Kedaulatan Maluku, FKM), established by a local doctor, Alex Manuputty, in July 2000. FKM's vocal presence as a "moral" movement with a separatist discourse, alongside Laskar Jihad's highly visible presence, introduced a new dynamic into the Ambon conflict in the form of an open ideological struggle. This included a press release and cyber media war.[233] It also included a campaign of psychological warfare that Laskar Jihad waged from its radio station in Ambon, the Voice of Struggle of Maluku Muslims (Suara Perjuangan Muslim Maluku, SPMM). Every evening its broadcasts evoked terror as it denounced the Christians as cruel, as *kafir*, as separatist, and as the source of *fitnah* while it encouraged jihad against them to make Maluku truly Muslim. Spyer noted that this new dimension deepened "the religious definition of the opposing parties" and crystalized the "relevant extremist discourses."[234]

As the Muslim offensive progressed, a market near the governor's office was bombed in September, speedboats in Ambon Bay attacked each other as well as ferries, fighting erupted on Haruku and Saparua, and Christian Hative Besar was assaulted, leaving thirty people dead and another two thousand displaced.[235] On September 30, Pattimura commander I Made Yasa issued shoot-on-sight orders, with little impact.[236] In October, the Christian villages of Suli, Galala, and Halong were attacked. Battles also took place in Kairatu on Seram and Sirisori on Saparua. Kairatu was attacked again in November.[237] And at the end of the month mujahidin carried out a massacre on Kesui.[238] Forced conversions also made a reappearance. Almost a year after Christians had forced Muslims to convert in North Maluku, Muslims forced Christians on Kesui, Teor, and Seram to become Muslims.[239] As Pastor Haas recalled, "conversions were forced in Salas and Pula on Seram. The *kepala kampung*'s wife and child were killed and their heads were paraded through Pula. They then said you either convert or will suffer the same fate."[240]

Christians were told that the "people of Maluku had always been Muslim and that the Dutch had made them Christian so they were just returning them to their original status."[241] These Christians were "forced by local Muslims but under pressure from some of the mujahidin." Local Muslims saw this "as a way to end the conflict. If you no longer had different religions there would no longer be conflict."[242] Christian women who later fled to Ambon recounted how they had been held down and genitally mutilated with glass shards, leaving them traumatized, in pain, and battling infection. According to church officials, some four thousand conversions had been forced across six islands.[243]

The year 2001 saw a continuation of the Muslim offensive, albeit at a reduced pace. Muslim fighters still outnumbered and outgunned Christian fighters. Where Muslims saw territorial contiguity as an issue, territorial gains were still sought. Strategically vital areas were also still fought over. However, in most areas the focus was on consolidation rather than expansion. At the same time, two notable shifts in the conflict dynamics were discernible. The first was a marked decline of large-scale communal confrontations as signs of combat fatigue at popular level set in. This was aided by the fact that most of Maluku was now split into homogenous Muslim and Christian areas with clear demarcations. The second was a shift in the attacks of the mujahidin from defending the Ambonese Muslim community to attacking the Indonesian security forces, in particular the Combined Battalion (Batalyon Gabungan, YonGab), which had arrived in August 2000 and comprised the army's Kopassus special forces, the air force's Paskhas special forces, and the marines. YonGab was seen by Ambonese Christians as a neutral and professional battalion, while Ambon's Muslims and the mujahidin saw it as anti-Muslim.

One of the worst clashes occurred on June 14, 2001, in Kebun Cengkeh as YonGab troops were sweeping the area for weapons following a Muslim attack on Gonzalo Veloso two days earlier. They were ambushed; one was killed and seven others were wounded. YonGab then attacked the building it believed the shots had been fired from. This building was used by Laskar Jihad as a medical center and for its radio station SPMM. It also, according to YonGab, contained AK47 rifles, home-made bombs, and other firearms.[244] Laskar Jihad claimed that twenty-three Muslims were killed by YonGab in a massacre of medical staff and patients, which saw twelve taken away by the military, tortured, and executed.[245] Three days after the clash, as Laskar Jihad reopened SPMM in a different location, Jafar Umar Thalib asserted that YonGab was "90 percent Christian" and issued a statement that it was obligatory for Muslims to kill Pattimura commander I Made Yasa.[246] The next day, June 18, Yasa was replaced by Brigadier General Mustopo.

Mustopo's security policy focused on "consolidating the police" and stopping "the physical conflict," for which he had five battalions. He had noted the decline in communal violence but believed that there were still extremists that needed to be dealt with, which he identified as FKM and Laskar Jihad. As he explained, "The commanders are known but not how many people support them and who they are. So I brought in one company of Kopassus and one company of intelligence. The conflict between the people is effectively over. So Kopassus are here to infiltrate the Christian and Muslim extremists and move towards taking out these organizations."[247] Mustopo's security approach, like those of his predecessors, had a mixed impact. It underwrote the absence of communal violence, but his targeting of the extremists reinforced Muslim beliefs that the RMS was an active player. It also raised renewed Christian concerns about the involvement of the Indonesian security forces. The unease over the latter was evident in the upsurge of violence in December 2001 as the second anniversary of the Ambon conflict neared. On December 11 an explosion on the motorboat *California* killed ten passengers and wounded another forty-six.[248] The next day, convinced that this had been a bomb, a crowd of Christians pelted the governor's office with stones and then proceeded to burn down the local parliament building, while another group of Christians set the Indonesian marines post in Galala on fire.[249] Then on December 19, nine more people were killed when another Christian boat was attacked in Ambon Bay. And on December 27, yet another Christian boat was attacked, this time, as the ICG pointed out, "linked to fighting between the police and marines."[250]

While the second phase of the Ambon conflict saw a clear reduction in communal violence, with the conflict being fought by more or less identifiable, yet fluid, combatant groupings, these groupings remained fragile constructions that started to fracture. Christian disunity, like Christian unity, preceded that of the Muslims and had multiple causes. It was connected to turf wars between Loupatti's Coker and Wattimena's "grassroots" organizations, which both had Kudamati as their home base. Coker asserted its control through fourteen *posko*, and at one point, Loupatti recounted, "Agus tried to conduct a sweeping of Coker." Tensions "got so bad that the synod intervened and we all prayed together."[251] These tensions were further exacerbated by the emergence of two new organizations in Kudamati: FKM and the new Black Horse gang, Kuda Hitam.

Turf wars and personal rivalries were complicated by political disagreements. Coker, which had already existed before the conflict as a gang with both Muslim and Christian members, objected to the kidnapping of Muslims. Loupatti even protected the Muslims in Benteng Atas.[252] In contrast, Wattimena declared that "when the time comes, we will wipe them [the Muslims] out."[253] Declarations such as this reflected Wattimena's belief that "the Moluccas are a sort of barometer" for the Javanese mujahidin and that "as soon as the Moluccas are subdued and its ethnic roots eradicated, the rest of Indonesia will be easy prey."[254] As the conflict progressed Wattimena grew increasingly militant, stating that "if the government won't protect us, why would we want to remain Indonesian? We'd be better off independent."[255] It was statements like this that drew FKM to look to Wattimena for support, but also increased the gap between Loupatti and Wattimena and FKM.[256] As Loupatti explained, "At the beginning of the conflict there was no RMS. Yes there were always flags raised here and there in villages on Saparua and Seram on the anniversary of the RMS proclamation but it did not mean much. RMS came later in the conflict with FKM. FKM was RMS and Alex was the local RMS leader." Loupatti disagreed with Alex Manuputty to such an extent that he decided to put Coker at the service of Kopassus: "We provided them with names of RMS members and sympathizers, their activities, who had flags, who raised flags."²⁵⁷

The greatest factor causing Christian disunity, however, was money. As Loupatti recalled,

> Money came into bank accounts. Some from the Netherlands. There was a lot of money and it changed the dynamics of the conflict. At the beginning we were all working together. And then Agus was handing out money. There were arguments. And the fighters used the money to get drunk every evening in the cafes and hang out with women. That is why Agus was killed. He was drinking a lot and had girlfriends and his wife was jealous. She shot him.²⁵⁸

After Wattimena's death on March 20, 2001, Femmy Souissa took over the leadership of the grassroots Maluku.

The intra-Muslim rift started to emerge in September 2000. After three months of joint operations and attacks, tensions started to rise between Laskar Jihad and some parts of the Malukan Muslim community as well as between Laskar Jihad and the various groups under the Laskar Mujahidin umbrella. These rifts became more and more visible as the Muslim offensive continued.

At the heart of the disagreement between Laskar Jihad and Ambon's Muslims was Laskar Jihad's religious mission, which according to Jafar Umar Thalib was the spreading of salafism as the "only scientifically correct interpretation of Islam" through "*dakwah* and social services."²⁵⁹ This mission, as he made clear during a speech at Al-Fatah on September 3, 2000, would continue until Ambon was ruled by Muslims.²⁶⁰ Laskar Jihad's preaching of salafism, however, often stood at odds with the more heterogenous Malukan Islam, which not only followed the Shafi'i *madhab* (school of jurisprudence) but was infused with local cultural practices. Ambonese Muslims soon realized "that Shafi'i and salafi don't work together."²⁶¹ While some agreed that "every Muslim is obligated to live in accordance with *syariat Islam*," they disagreed with Laskar Jihad's interpretation. They also objected to Laskar Jihad's coercive approach. As Thamrin Ely emphasized, "The salafi teachings were forced on us and that's why until now [March 2002] in Kebun Cengkeh the local community does not attend the mosque."²⁶² Others completely rejected the implementation of Islamic law in Ambon. As Muslim community leader Malik Selang explained, "First, at the time of the declaration of Indonesian independence no one in Ambon supported *syariah*. And second, Indonesia is heterogeneous and it would be difficult to implement *syariah*. The Muslims in Ambon today also don't support *syariah*. *Syariah* is not in their culture. It is against the present constitution and it is not how people here feel or think."²⁶³ On March 10, 2001, Laskar Jihad's religious mission reached its pinnacle as it proclaimed *syariat Islam* for Ambon. Muslims were forbidden to trade with Christians, three Muslims were executed by firing squad after they had been caught trading alcohol, and one Laskar Jihad member was stoned to death for having illicit relations with a local girl.[264] This marked the height of tension between Ambonese Muslims, who interpreted *syariat Islam* as only applying to Laskar Jihad members, and Laskar Jihad, who saw it as applying to everyone.[265]

A rift also quickly emerged between Laskar Jihad and Laskar Mujahidin. This was above all ideological.[266] Laskar Jihad differed from JI, DI, NII, and Mujahidin KOMPAK in that it had its roots in the Indonesian salafi movement of the 1980s, rather than the 1947–1965 Darul Islam rebellions.[267] It disapproved of political parties as divisive and did not permit or support rebellion against a Muslim government.[268] In fact, Laskar Jihad saw its role not only as helping to defend Ambon's Muslims but also as assisting the TNI in its fight against Christian separatism.[269] In contrast, the various groups under the Laskar Mujahidin umbrella saw the TNI as the enemy and were by and large not interested in fighting the RMS.

After the brief period of cautious cooperation following Laskar Jihad's arrival in May 2000, Laskar Jihad started labeling JI, DI, NII, and Mujahidin KOMPAK as *khawarij* (rebels). As KOMPAK volunteer Apud recalled, "They called us *khawarij* because we did not accept the state, political order, and leadership. And they said that all those who did not side with them did not understand Islam. It was difficult with them. On the one hand, we were Muslim brothers, on the other, they did not treat us like that."[270] Intermujahidin discord was further exacerbated by Laskar Jihad's attitude and behavior. Its "military-style hierarchy," its insistence that "they were the elite," and the constant bragging "about their relations with the military" put off the other mujahidin.[271] It seemed to confirm suspicions that Laskar Jihad was "working for [Indonesian] intelligence ... to undermine us."[272] It also stood at odds with Laskar Jihad's military performance. Both Javanese and Ambonese joked about Laskar Jihad arriving late to the battle, wearing white robes and brandishing swords, then taking credit for the victory in its press releases and radio broadcasts. Sometimes Laskar Jihad fighters simply "tagged" the battle scene with cans of spray paint, earning them the moniker *laskar pilox*—"spray paint warriors."[273] And last, but certainly not least, Laskar Jihad, being highly visible and operating openly under its own name, was often blamed for attacks it did not carry out, including the clash with YonGab in June 2001. As former JI member Jibril explained, "Those who were executed by YonGab were Laskar Jihad but it was not Laskar Jihad who attacked YonGab. YonGab was attacked in Air Kuning by the mujahidin. YonGab thought it was Laskar Jihad and the Laskar Jihad hospital was close by, so they took their revenge on it. YonGab could not differentiate between the different groups."[274] Not all that surprisingly, Laskar Jihad started taking potshots at Laskar Mujahidin. The opening salvo was Thalib's public statement "that once RMS had been dealt with Laskar Mujahidin would be next."[275] Then in September 2001, Laskar Jihad and Mujahidin KOMPAK clashed openly in Ahuru and Kebun Cengkeh.[276] Indeed, antagonism had grown to such an extent that some in JI "wanted to bomb the Laskar Jihad post in Kebun Cengkeh in response" to the Ahuru clash.[277]

Post-Malino Violence 2002–2005

The Ambon conflict was formally brought to an end with the Malino II Agreement, signed on February 12, 2002. This agreement did not, however, bring an end to the violence. The third phase of the violence, the post-Malino hostilities, started as soon as the delegates returned to Ambon. Laskar Jihad, which had been invited to the talks but declined to attend, now slipped into the quintessential spoiler role, claiming that the Muslim delegation had not been representative.[278] It denounced the delegates on its radio station, asserting they had all been paid off by the government. It labeled them an "illegal delegation" and the Malino II Agreement as "*fitnah*."[279] In its online bulletins and statements Laskar Jihad contended that the "peace" had been dictated, that it was just camouflage for the evil intentions of the Christians, and that the Muslim signatories had surrendered.[280] Joining together with Satgas Amar Ma'ruf and FPI-M, it handed out "fifty-meter banners for people to sign against Malino."[281] It also terrorized the Muslim Malino delegates by phone.[282] Some delegates had stones thrown at them, such as MUI chairman Abdul Wahab Polpoke as he was driving his car.[283] Those delegates who lived in proximity to Laskar Jihad, such as Usman Slamet who lived in Kebun Cengkeh, were "threatened every time there was news about Malino."[284] Malino delegate Thamrin Ely even had his house set on fire.

While the Christian delegates escaped violence, they too were denounced by some of their co-religionists.[285] They were accused of having become traitors because they had signed an agreement which had placed Laskar Jihad on the same level with the RMS, and because they had agreed to an independent investigation that "made the Christians look bad."[286] As Malino delegate Agus Ulahaiyanan explained, Christian opponents to Malino read the agreement as a Christian "admission of guilt."[287] FKM decried the Malino II Agreement as "a means for the Indonesian Government to wash its hands of all the wrongdoings inflicted upon the two communities in Maluku (Muslims and Christians)."[288] It particularly objected to the inclusion of Laskar Kristen and Laskar Kristus into the agreement, as neither of these organizations existed.[289]

Beyond the Malino delegation-focused threats, there were also incidents of Muslim violence against Christians, Christian violence against the local government, and bombings by both Muslims and Christians as well as shootings, bombings, and attacks by the Javanese mujahidin. Most of these occurred during 2002 and were the result of continuing distrust and local concerns but also the deliberate actions of spoilers—Christian and Muslim, local and outsider, civilian and military. On February 25, a bus with Christian government employees was shot at as it passed through the Muslim Galunggung neighborhood.[290] On March 2, a Christian motorcycle parade "celebrating" Malino had stones thrown at it as it passed Al-Fatah.[291] Amir Kiat recalled that "it was just after prayer and the worshippers were pouring out of the mosque, in front of the cavalcade and then violence broke out."[292] Some motorbikes were set on fire, some people were stabbed. In the nearby Ambon Plaza shopping area, "63 Christian shoppers, most of them women . . . were cornered by Muslims."[293] According to one foreign observer, it took five hours before they could be evacuated, raising questions about the incident, including why the motorbikes went there and why weapons had been brought. Moreover, "there were clear indications that money has been changing hands in return for actions, especially on the Christian side."[294] The ease with which these violent incidents occurred, however, also reflected the continued distrust between the two communities.

Violence against local government is best exemplified by the April 3 burning down of the governor's office by Christians who "got fed up with all the injustice done to them," particularly the governor's decision "to postpone the final date of the voluntary handing over of weaponry by civilians to April 30."[295] Moreover, this arson attack occurred within an hour after a bomb had been thrown out of a car in the Christian part of Ambon city near the Nelayan II restaurant at lunchtime, killing five and wounding fifty-seven. This left Christians angry over the lack of security.

The largest incident of post-Malino violence, however, was the attack in the early morning hours of April 28 on the Christian mountain village of Soya. Twelve villagers were killed and thirteen injured, and thirty-five houses were torched as well as the church and the *raja*'s house.[296] According to Soya village head Reuben, the electricity had suddenly gone out and then the sound of explosions woke up the villagers, many of whom rushed out of their houses into complete darkness and into a hail of bullets. The attack, Reuben explained, had come from the direction of Gunung Sirimau, where Laskar Jihad was based.[297] Some witnesses reported seeing black-clad ninjas but also white jihad robes and army uniforms. Others stated that they heard the attackers converse in Javanese.[298]

And yet others described how the attackers "went from house to house, while proclaiming Allah's Greatness, murdering anybody they could lay their hands on, not sparing women and children, including a nine-month-old baby that was killed by bullets."[299] This led them to believe that the attack had been carried out by Laskar Jihad and the military. The attack on Soya shook Ambon's Christians to the core, as they had seen Soya as a difficult-to-reach safe fortress protected by the mountains. The message was clear, no place was safe unless the Christians "knew their place" in NKRI.

After the Soya attack the violence shifted to bombings of Christian, Muslim, government, and random targets designed to instill terror. These included the July 27 bomb explosion at the alternative market of Christian Mardika, injuring fifty-two, including five small children; the September 6 bomb explosion at the Lapangan Merdeka recreation area, killing four secondary school girls and wounding several athletes who had just finished their daily training; the October 9 bomb explosion near a market stand in the Christian neighborhood of Batugantung, wounding two soldiers and two civilians; and the October 14 bomb that was lobbed from a car driving through Muslim Batumerah, injuring a four-year-old boy.[300]

By the end of 2002, the number of violent incidents had started to decline, as many of the spoilers had been neutralized. Alex Manuputty, Berthy Loupatti, and Jafar Umar Thalib had been arrested and removed from Ambon. Laskar Jihad was disbanded after the Bali bombings, and a sizeable number of Coker members had been detained and put on trial, revealing that Kopassus had paid them to plant some of the bombs.[301] There had also been concerted efforts by the security forces to reduce the proliferation of arms with regular weapons handover ceremonies and sweepings of areas where they suspected hidden caches.

Most of the subsequent post-Malino violence thus occurred on a reduced scale, manifesting in sporadic bombings and sniper shootings. These were largely perpetrated by the remnant mujahidin, who believed that Maluku's Muslims still required protection from the Christians. Two later incidents of violence stand out, the 2004 RMS anniversary clashes and the 2005 Loki attack. The former saw FKM's commemoration of the fifty-fourth anniversary of the declaration of the Republic of South Maluku on April 25 descend into ten days of Christian-Muslim violence, which reopened many of the fears and followed the familiar patterns of the Ambon conflict. Buildings were set on fire, including the UN offices and the recently rebuilt Silo Church. Attacks on the areas of Talake, Waringin, and Batugantung as well as Manga Dua prompted the Christian residents to flee as their houses were torched. In Talake, over several days of clashes, in which also soldiers had become involved, the recently rebuilt Christian University, UKIM, as well as the Nazareth Church were burned down.

Soon after the communal violence erupted additional security forces were sent in from outside Ambon. The houses of FKM supporters were searched and FKM members detained. Roadblocks were erected and shared markets vanished. Jafar Umar Thalib announced that he was ready to deploy his men to Ambon again to protect the unity and integrity of the Republic of Indonesia. Rumors of the departure of some twelve thousand Laskar Jihad from Java to Ambon sent shockwaves through Ambon's Christian community, prompting the Catholic bishop of Amboina, Monsignor Mandagi, to send urgent appeals to the Pope, the United Nations, and several Western countries.[302] By April 29, some thirty-six people had been killed, 159 wounded, and more than two hundred houses and buildings destroyed.[303] By May 3, the number of wounded had increased to 211. The situation only started to calm down after some of the FKM leadership were detained, including FKM secretary Moses Tuanakotta and Alex Manuputty's wife and daughter. This eruption of clashes clearly showed how fragile the intercommunal peace was in Ambon and how politically sensitive the issue of the RMS continued to be both at local and national level.

The second notable incident of later post-Malino violence is the 2005 Loki attack, which revealed to what extent the mujahidin had penetrated Muslim society. On May 16, a group of eight men, comprising both locals and outsiders, launched an attack on a Brimob post in the village of Loki, Seram.[304] They killed five Brimob and their cook, shooting in the head four who were ill with malaria and sleeping.[305] The Brimob post was targeted because it protected the Christians of Loki who were "the real target," but also because "its presence had disrupted jihadist training activities on the mountain behind Olas and neighboring areas."[306] The Loki attack brought the police out in full force over the execution of their own. Three days later, they discovered a large weapons cache at STAIN Islamic school in Kebun Cengkeh, which included "over a dozen rifles, 23 revolvers, thousands of rounds of ammunition and several mortars."[307] The arrests following the Loki attack disrupted the remaining mujahidin networks and marked the end of the post-Malino violence.

Alternative Narratives and National Imaginaries: From RMS to FKM

Much as in the Poso conflict, alternative national imaginaries were not advocated at the start of the violence in Ambon but emerged during the conflict from the frustration over Jakarta's lack of interest. Also, as in Poso, it was not the case that new alternative national imaginaries were constructed, but, instead, already existing ones were embraced. However, unlike Poso, where it was part of the

Muslim community that adopted the Islamist national imaginary advocated by JI, in Ambon it was part of the Christian community that dusted off the narrative of the RMS and its vision of an independent Maluku.

The RMS narrative had seen Manuhutu and Wairisal proclaim the independent Republic of South Maluku on April 25, 1950, in accordance with the "wishes and demand of the people of the South Moluccas" in response to "one of the component states, the Republic of Indonesia" starting "to liquidate and to annex the fifteen other component states by means of intimidation, infiltration and use of armed force."[308] Fear of being dominated by the Javanese was one factor underwriting this decision; fear of being a Christian minority in an overwhelmingly Muslim state was another. Indeed, Richard Chauvel in his seminal book *Nationalists, Soldiers and Separatists* stated that Soumokil in meetings before the RMS proclamation had claimed that he had seen documents that "indicated that when there was a unitary state and the TNI landed in Ambon the Christians would be forcibly converted to Islam, the churches would be destroyed."[309] Similarly, John Ruhulessin and Pieter Manoppo asserted that Soumokil had maintained that "if the TNI entered Ambon Christians would be circumcized."[310] And, a day before the proclamation Dominggus Zakarias Pesuwarissa, who would become the RMS information minister, contended that "the Indonesian Republic wants to become an Islamic state or a state based on Islam."[311]

In the RMS narrative it was clearly the Republic of Indonesia that was the aggressor, first imposing a "hunger blockade against Ambon," followed by Sukarno ordering "the conquest and annihilation of the Republic of the South Moluccas."[312] This pursuit included the "bombardment of the innocent population" of Namlea, the use of captured RMS soldiers and "a number of civilians as shields" as the TNI marched against RMS positions in Piru, Seram, "inhuman acts" by "Javanese soldiers," and "genocide committed by the Republic of Indonesia against 400 South Moluccan boys and girls between the ages of 13 and 18 while a number of Ambonese women were abducted and used by the Indonesian military for target practice."[313] What followed was what Soumokil described as "a new colonialism more savage and inhuman than the Dutch could ever have imagined!," "Javanese oppression" of the Moluccans "who are Melanesians" and "differ basically from the rest of Indonesia, both racially and historically."[314]

The RMS narrative juxtaposed the Moluccans having been granted the right to self-determination at the 1949 Round Table Conference with the Republic of Indonesia violating this agreement, the Ambonese having fought alongside the Allied Forces with the Indonesians having sided with the Japanese during the Second World War, the RMS proclamation being the product of a series of popular meetings with Indonesia having "no constitution by the will of the people, no legislation by the will of the people" and "Sukarno himself was never elected," and the Republic of South Maluku supporting "Western civilization," with Indonesia having descended into "political depravity" and communism.[315]

The national imaginary projected by the RMS was that of an anticommunist, Western-oriented Malukan republic, headed by a president and prime minister, with a parliament and a constitution, the latter modeled on that of the Netherlands and the RIS. When the RMS released its own stamps in August 1951, these depicted, among others, the United Nations headquarters at Lake Success, showing the RMS's trust in the UN to aid in the deliverance of Malukan independence. Others commemorated the fifth anniversary of the liberation of Maluku from Japanese occupation, depicting Allied Pacific commander in chief General Douglas MacArthur alongside a map of the Netherlands Indies.[316] These stamps, which were used within the RMS territory on Seram to replace the Indonesian postal service that had stopped with the blockade, were another way to assert sovereignty.[317]

The RMS national imaginary was also a Christian national imaginary. The RMS flag, which symbolizes the blue sea, the white beaches, and the green land of Maluku as well as the ancestors and the blood of the people, was based on the flag Thomas Matulessy was believed to have used in the 1817 Pattimura Uprising against the Dutch.[318] This uprising had been framed as a Christian religious war, with the Netherlands portrayed as "the wicked oppressor in Psalm XVII."[319] The national anthem of the RMS, too, invoked a distinctly Christian image in its reference to Maluku's path of suffering in the pursuit of freedom as the "via dolorosa."[320] Thus it is not all too surprising that the RMS had only a few Muslim representatives, including the raja of Tulehu, Ibrahim Ohorella, and the raja of Pelauw, Duba Latuconsina, and that relations with the Muslim community, as Chauvel phrased it, "posed particular difficulties" as the South Malukan Republic was a bastion not only against the unitary Republic of Indonesia but also against Muslim domination and Islamization.[321]

The RMS narrative and national imaginary regained relevance in the 1999 Ambon conflict not because the RMS had started the conflict, as the TNI, many Ambonese Muslims, and Laskar Jihad believed, but because of the historical parallels many Ambonese Christians saw. As in 1950, they feared Islamization and the loss of their culture; as in 1950, they felt betrayed by Jakarta. It was in this context that FKM was established in July 2000 as a "moral movement, not an armed movement" because "we could no longer stay silent" in the conflict and because "we could no longer trust the Indonesians" but also because "of the legality of the Renville agreement."[322] It was a response to humanitarian tragedy "inflicted by the state" and "the unwillingness and inability of Indonesia to protect the Alif'uru," a term FKM uses interchangeably with Malukans but also as a way to cleanse Malukan identity from the communal violence.[323]

FKM's aim was to fight "for the truth buried for 50 years," to struggle "to overcome the suffering inflicted upon the Alif'uru nation for the last 470 years," and to "restore [the] independence and the sovereignty of the RMS."[324] Its leader, Alex Manuputty, explained that "we want independence" because "the people don't agree with Indonesia's view of itself. They use their sovereignty to make people suffer and exploit our natural resources—all for the benefit of Java. And the people must pay the price."[325] In a similar vein, FKM's publications asserted sarcastically that the "gifts that Indonesia bestowed upon Maluku" were lack of development, exploitation of its resources, the weakening of its human resources, the destruction of its environment, and the slaughter of the indigenous population—the Alifuru.[326]

The Ambon conflict, Manuputty contended, had been created by "the elite, the politicians, Muslim radicals, the TNI, and terrorists." The government "here and in Java does nothing for the people." He elaborated that "for us in Maluku there is no difference between Suharto, Habibie, Gus Dur, and Megawati. The TNI wants to return to the situation as it was, to make themselves the upper class again. They want to dominate the civilians. The TNI is inside the terrorists and inside the TNI is Laskar Jihad. They let everything happen—the bombs, the shootings. They let Laskar Jihad come to the Christian villages and they let them shoot the Christians."[327] FKM's press releases further asserted that the "attacking masses are TNI in civilian clothes," that the Indonesian "government is supporting the program of militant fundamentalist Islam promoted by Laskar Jihad/Laskar Mujahidin," and that the people of Maluku were being "terrorized, murdered, interrogated, scared every day."[328] Manuputty believed that the position of Christians as a minority in Indonesia explained the lack of response from Jakarta. "We are the majority in Maluku but in Indonesia we are the minority and can do nothing. The Muslims dominate the media, politics, and the TNI."[329] Independence thus was seen as the only solution.

While FKM's narrative was, in many ways, similar to that of the RMS in its arguments for Malukan self-determination, FKM's national imaginary differed. FKM's independent Maluku was not explicitly constructed as a pro-Western, anticommunist state, although it clearly looked toward the UN to deliver independence and had a support base in the Netherlands. Nor was it explicitly a Christian state, although it suffered the same challenges as the RMS in that its leadership and representatives were predominantly Christian and it did not have the support of the Muslim community, despite Manuputty's declaration to the contrary.[330] Instead, FKM's national imaginary was an ethnic one based on a reconstructed Alifuru nation, referencing the indigenous people of Seram, but using this term for the Malukans as a whole. In its publications FKM emphasized the ethnic difference of the Alifuru compared to the Indonesians. The Alifuru are a "combination of Negroid, Melanesian," and Australoid, which in FKM's press statements became an unwieldly "the people of Maluku/Alif'uru/Ina/West Melanesia."[331]

The historical narrative FKM presented was that "Maluku was one nation which was sovereign and known under the name of the Nunusaku Kingdom."[332] Then it was colonized and Malukans have "suffered for more than 470 years decades under the Portuguese, Spanish and English," 360 of these years under the Dutch, several years under the Japanese, and 50 years under the Republic of Indonesia.[333] The latter was referred to as "the colonial state of Indonesia," "Javanese colonization," and a "wicked and evil state (filled with lies and hypocrisy)," whose rule has been "despotic and voracious."[334] An independent Maluku would "correct" this history, by restoring the status quo ante, returning Maluku to its precolonial political status, returning sovereignty to its people, and restoring Malukan culture and traditions. FKM's national imaginary also occupied a larger geo-body than that of the Republic of South Maluku, which encompassed Central, South and Southeast Maluku. As Manuputty explained, "We will start in South Maluku and then develop it to include North Maluku."[335] This larger territory did not just represent an undivided cultural unit but would also underpin the state's economic viability.

Reflecting on "Belonging" and the Ambon Conflict

The 1999–2005 Ambon conflict was rooted in the changing demographics and power balance between Christians and Muslims in Maluku resulting from Suharto's policies of transmigration, the increasing level of education of Malukan Muslims, and the erosion of local *adat* by both the Indonesian state and migrants. It was also closely tied to the shift in the Indonesian national imaginary toward a more Islamic one in the late New Order, which triggered fears among Ambonese Christians that they would become a political, social, and economic minority in Maluku. These fears were underwritten by collective historical memories dating back to Sultan Hairun and Sultan Baabullah's jihad, Hitunese Muslims' spearheading the war against Christians on Ambon during the Portuguese colonial period, and Ambonese Muslims welcoming the Japanese during the Second World War who persecuted the Christians. They also reflected the contentious belonging of Ambon's Christians.

Having had a fundamentally different historical experience during the Netherlands Indies, Ambonese Christians did not necessarily see themselves as Indonesians in the way Indonesianess was narrated and projected by Sukarno. Instead, many had seen themselves as "Black Dutchmen" and their willingness to become Indonesian had been tied to the federal Indonesian imaginary. The fragility of this Indonesianess was evident when the shift toward a unitary Indonesia in 1950 was met by an alternative Malukan national imaginary with the proclamation of the Republic of South Maluku. After the RMS rebellion was crushed, belonging remained contentious for Ambon's Christians as they continued to be stigmatized as potentially disloyal.

The alternative Malukan national imaginary haunted the Ambon conflict. The RMS rebellion, as the first revolt against the newly independent Indonesian state, had become so firmly ingrained in the minds of the Indonesian military that it actively looked for the RMS when the conflict erupted and continued to focus on rooting out the RMS after the conflict had ended. For Ambonese Muslims, too, the RMS loomed large as a collective historical memory alongside the discrimination experienced under the Dutch. This meant that when communal clashes erupted in January 1999 and Ambonese Christians targeted Muslim migrants, Ambonese Muslims quickly closed ranks with their coreligionists, fearing that the Christians would target them next. For Ambon's Christians the fears of Islamization, first by ICMI and then at the hands of Javanese mujahidin, almost inevitably resulted in the revival of the alternative Malukan national imaginary as they asked themselves what Indonesianess actually meant when the Jakarta government so obviously did not care about them. The relationship between the Indonesian Republic and the Christian Ambonese has remained complicated since the end of the Ambon conflict, evidenced by the continued annual raising of RMS flags on April 25—but also the continued lack of equality in education, development, industry, and employment between Maluku and particularly Java.

Conclusion

NATIONAL IMAGINARIES AT WAR

This is a book about violence in Indonesia, more specifically Islamist, separatist, and communal violence since 1945. It is also a history of Indonesia as seen from the periphery of the state and the periphery of the Indonesian national imaginary as defined by the political center. The Republic of Indonesia proclaimed on August 17, 1945, was conceptualized by its founding president, Sukarno, as an independent, unitary state, tied together by a shared history of 350 years of colonial repression by the Dutch. This placed anticolonialism and anti-imperialism at the heart of the political identity of the Old Order and designated the territory of the Netherlands Indies as the absolute minimum of Indonesia's geo-body. This geo-body, however, was the subject of several geographic imaginaries, including historical ones based on the Srivijaya and Majapahit empires and their tribute states as well as the archipelagic ones, stretching from the Asian mainland to Australia.

Indonesia's national identity was based on the philosophy of Pancasila and unifying values summarized in the official motto *Bhinneka Tunggal Ika*, emphasizing unity in diversity and the aspirational equality of the five recognized religions and some thirteen hundred ethnolinguistic groups. At the same time, however, the Republic of Indonesia was also quintessentially Javanese. The locus of its political center was Jakarta, the core island was Java, and state protocols had often been directly appropriated from the Kraton of Yogyakarta. Javanese culture was projected as Indonesian culture. Even the depiction of the Garuda on Indonesia's national emblem was based on the Elang Jawa, the Javanese eagle.

In Sukarno's Indonesia Islam occupied an ambiguous place. It was the religion of the majority of the population, yet it was afforded exactly the same place as Christianity, Hinduism, and Buddhism. Islamists were initially permitted to organize politically and voice their aims, as exemplified by Masyumi, yet their efforts were often unilaterally curtailed by the state, as exemplified by the fate of the Jakarta Charter, Sukarno's 1953 Amuntai speech, and the 1959 introduction of Guided Democracy, which saw the sidelining of political Islamists.

When Suharto took over the presidency in 1967, ushering in the New Order, both Pancasila and the unitary state—NKRI—were elevated to state ideology. Anticommunism was added to Indonesia's political identity, resulting in a shift to favoring the newly established ASEAN over the Nonaligned Movement and favoring the West over the East in the global Cold War. Suharto's Indonesian national imaginary was a modern, developed one, emphasizing economic prosperity and stability over political freedom and collectivity over individuality. Political parties were functionalized; Islam was depoliticized. Pancasila, by law, became the foundational basis of every social organization. At the same time, it remained very Javanese in its notions of power and harmony. In fact, during the New Order the Javanese imprint on "the Indonesian" increased as the Javanese village model was rolled out across the archipelago in line with the 1979 Law No. 5 on village governance; "the Javanese" became the norm underwriting standardization and uniformization. In the late New Order, the Indonesian national imaginary shifted toward a more Islamic one as the ageing Suharto became more religious and as he decided to court the Muslims to counterbalance the increasingly critical military. The establishment of ICMI under Vice President Habibie set the framework for a "state-controlled" Islamization, driven by Muslim intellectuals and the Muslim middle class.

The violent contestation of these national imaginaries as constructed and projected by successive Indonesian governments has been at the heart of this book on Islamist, separatist, and communal violence in Indonesia, whereby this categorization can be fluid. Antigovernment violence in Aceh evolved from anticolonial violence from 1873 to 1913, to Islamist violence from 1953 to 1959, and to separatist violence from 1976 to 2005. Violence in Ambon went the opposite direction, from separatist violence from 1950 to 1963, to communal violence from 1999 to 2005 that included Islamist, Muslim, and Christian violence. Asking *where* the violence is located not just in a geographic sense but above all in a conceptual sense, this book has argued that violence erupted particularly in those regions of Indonesia that were on the periphery of the national imaginary—geographically, ideologically, ethnically, religiously, and developmentally. Indonesian Islamists found themselves on the religious and ideological periphery of a state defined as a pluralist Pancasila state. Aceh, Ambon, and East Timor found themselves on the geographic periphery as well as the religious and ethnic periphery. Aceh, Ambon, Poso, and East Timor were also developmentally marginalized. Other conflicts not covered in this book can easily be added. Papua and West Kalimantan, too, sit on the developmental periphery of the state; they also share ethnic and religious marginalization.

The first violent challenge to Sukarno's Indonesian Republic came from militant Islamists who sought to recast Indonesia as an Islamic state. It came in the form of the Darul Islam rebellions, which erupted in 1947 in the midst of and as part of the Indonesian war of liberation against the Dutch. The rebellions lasted until 1965 when the last territory, South Sulawesi, was subdued by the Indonesian military. The end of the rebellions, however, did not spell an end to the idea of an Indonesian Islamic state. Indeed, the quest for an Islamic state continued, pursued by the various components of the DI/NII movement. This gave rise to new militant organizations, including JI in 1993, and new Islamic national imaginaries both local and global.

The idea of an Islamic Indonesia persisted, as the idea of an Islamic state is embedded in religious obligations such as implementing *syariat Islam* and in the understanding that *syariat Islam* can only be fully implemented under a truly Islamic ruler. Only an Islamic state can provide the environment for its citizens to practice Islam to its fullest. The idea also persisted because Islam was part and parcel of the early Indonesian nationalist project. Indonesian nationalism thus legitimated the Islamist narrative and placed it on an equal footing with the secular one.

The first separatist challenge came from the RMS rebellion in April 1950. This insurgency was a reaction to Sukarno's dismantling of the Dutch-imposed federal United States of Indonesia and the return to the unitary state proclaimed in 1945. It was also caused by fears that such a unitary Indonesia with a clear Muslim majority could become an Islamic state in which Christians would be second-class citizens with restricted rights. The same presence of Islam in the early Indonesian nationalism that legitimated Islamist aspirations terrified Indonesia's Christians. Thus, every time that Islamists at the local or national level tried to shift the Indonesian national imaginary in a more Islamic direction, defensive reactions were triggered. Indeed, fears of an Islamic Indonesia featured prominently in the decision by Manuhutu and Wairisal to declare the Republic of South Maluku, underwritten by the Christian Ambonese collective memory of Sultan Hairun and Sultan Baabullah's jihad. Fears of an Islamic Indonesia, alongside Indonesia's brutal invasion and occupation of East Timor, also propelled the Timorese Catholic Church into political action against the Indonesian state. Thus, Christian separatist aspirations can be understood as a defensive reaction to protect religion, culture, and identity. However, Islam also directly related to Muslim separatist aspirations, where a more Islamic imaginary underwrote ethnic nationalism, as was the case in the Aceh conflict. Additionally, separatist aspirations more broadly were the product of unequal center-periphery relations characterized by neglect, exploitation, and Javanization. The persistence of these inequalities nurtured popular grievances and ensured the endurance of separatism.

Unequal center-periphery relations and fears of an Islamic Indonesia are also important to understanding the dynamics of the communal conflicts in Ambon and Poso, alongside the opportunity for communal tensions to erupt into the open during the post-Suharto transition from authoritarianism to democracy. The establishment of ICMI in 1990, ICMI's agenda in Eastern Indonesia, and the role ICMI politicians played at a local level in pushing Christians out of local government, cannot be overstated. While communal conflicts at a local level pitted Christians against Muslims and locals against migrants, this book has demonstrated that at a national level these conflicts were related to the Indonesian national imaginary and particularly shifts in that national imaginary. The violence was thus also about the relationship between the people and the state.

The violence against the state by groups and organizations in the Islamist, separatist, and communal conflicts examined here was essentially counterhegemonic. It was also, as argued in this book, greatest and most protracted where there was a developed alternative national imaginary backed by an alternative historical narrative, as exemplified by the duration of the RMS rebellion from 1950 to 1963, the East Timor conflict from 1975 to 1999, and the Aceh insurgency from 1976 to 2005. These regions all could point to a distinctly separate history before becoming part of Indonesia. This separate history was emphasized in the narratives advanced by the RMS, GAM, and FRETILIN, where it also formed the basis for an alternative national imaginary. Here GAM emphasized the violent and contested incorporation of Aceh into the Netherlands Indies, followed by the illegal transfer of sovereignty over Aceh to the Republic of Indonesia in December 1949, and sought a return to the historic Sultanate of Aceh. The RMS pointed to the unilateral dissolution of the United States of Indonesia in 1950 and Jakarta's violation of the right to self-determination by minorities, which compelled it to proclaim the Republic of South Maluku. FRETILIN highlighted that Portuguese Timor had never been part of the Netherlands Indies, had been brutally invaded in 1975, and had been illegally incorporated into Indonesia in 1976. It aimed to establish a Timorese socialist republic.

While the separatists examined in this book had a clear alternative historical narrative and a clear alternative national imaginary, the position of the Islamists was more ambiguous. DI's historical narrative overlapped considerably with the early Indonesian national narrative but differed in its emphasis on

Islam. The same held true for JI, having evolved out of DI. That meant that a central element in the Islamist alternative narrative was how the Indonesian government had deviated from its true historical path. This was then tied to the strong alternative national imaginary of an Indonesian Islamic state, which some in JI also tied to global dynamics and aspirations.

In the communal conflicts in Ambon and Poso, only the Christians had an alternative historical narrative, with the Ambonese Christian narrative being significantly stronger and more influential than the Poso Christian narrative, as a result of the RMS rebellion. Some Christians in Ambon and some Muslims in Poso also advanced an alternative national imaginary, but these national imaginaries were not the product of the respective communal conflicts per se but the adoption of already existing national imaginaries developed by others. Some Ambonese Christians revived the alternative national imaginary of the RMS, while some Muslims in Poso embraced the national imaginary advocated by JI, both in its Indonesian and in the more globally cast version. It is notable here that neither Christians nor Muslims in Poso had their own alternative national imaginaries. This was largely due to the divided nature of both communities along ethnic lines. Moreover, unlike in Ambon, Poso Christians had never had a clear majority, nor had they been favored by the Dutch in quite the same way that provided Ambonese Christians with a privileged position and a much more distinct identity. Christians in Poso were divided by *suku* (ethnic group) while Christians in Ambon not only were one *suku* but saw themselves as a *suku-bangsa*, an ethnic group with the characteristics of a nation. Similarly, Muslims in Poso never occupied a special position in Indonesian Islamic history. That was centered on South Sulawesi.

While the case studies of Islamist, separatist, and communal violence are tied together by how they rejected the Indonesian national imaginary as conceptualized by the state, they are also tied together by how Jakarta responded. Here, the Indonesian military largely pursued a counterinsurgency strategy revolving around "decapitation"—that is, removing the intellectual and military leaders—and separating the insurgents from the people. The former were targeted in an attempt to eliminate the "ideological provocateurs" who could incite popular violence; the latter were targeted as they were seen as a vanguard that could mobilize and organize popular violence. This provides insight into how Jakarta viewed the people as easily manipulated and misled masses who were uncontrollable and dangerous if mobilized by the wrong person. The threat to the Republic of Indonesia was thus dually framed in terms of ideology and national imaginary on the one hand, and in terms of unity and integrity on the other. Indeed, it is this duality that underwrites the concept of NKRI, which is both territorial and ideological.

Territorially, in the DI rebellions, the East Timor conflict, and the Aceh insurgency, the Indonesian security forces focused on controlling urban centers and the main roads, letting the violence run its course in the rural hinterland. The RMS rebellion differed slightly as it was fought across several islands. Here, the military focused on capturing the main island, the political center, Ambon.

The Indonesian security forces also developed repertoires of violence that were implemented in most of the Islamist and separatist insurgencies but rarely in the communal conflicts, where there were fewer organized combatants. These included extreme brutality, desecration of corpses, and trophy taking. Moreover, tactics and strategy evolved over the conflicts. The clearest example is *pagar betis*. In the RMS rebellion in the 1950s there were localized incidents of TNI soldiers forcing villagers to march in front of them as human shields. This was systematically developed in 1957 under General Nasution's Rencana Dasar 21 program and widened into *pagar betis*, which became part of Indonesia's counterinsurgency strategy in 1961. It was successfully applied in subsequent years to crush the DI rebellions in West Java as well as in South Sulawesi, where there were designated "killing fields." In East Timor in the early 1980s *pagar betis* was applied on a massive scale with human chains moving across the whole province and designated killing fields on several mountains. To *pagar betis* the arsenal of modern counterinsurgency weapons was added, such as OV-Bronco planes, defoliation agents, and, according to FRETILIN, also napalm, which is disputed by Indonesia.

This book has argued that violence by the state as carried out by the Indonesian military was greatest when the insurgents had control over territory or their national imaginary contained a distinct territorial dimension. This was clearly the case in Aceh and East Timor as separatist conflicts, but this also explains why many more troops poured into Ambon compared to Poso, as Jakarta believed that it needed to send troops to defend the unity and integrity of the Indonesian state. The territorial dimension further illuminates the difference in state responses to the Darul Islam rebellions, which covered swathes of territory, and the JI bombing campaign, which had no territorial dimension.

The analysis of the six case studies of violence across the timeline of the Indonesian Republic and across its geo-body also allows for some comparative remarks. One common thread that runs through the conflicts located on the outer islands is overcentralization; another is Javanization. These were clear factors in the DI rebellions in Aceh, South Sulawesi, and South Kalimantan in the 1950s and 1960s as well as the subsequent Aceh, East Timor, Poso, and Ambon conflicts. In the violence that erupted during the New Order, transmigration was an additional factor they had in common. And in those areas with significant Christian populations the fear of Islamization was also shared.

One question that arises when looking at the Darul Islam rebellions is whether there is not a contradiction between the anti-Javanese sentiments in Aceh, South Kalimantan, and South Sulawesi and these regions joining what had hitherto been a Javanese Islamist rebellion. However, this book has demonstrated that the Darul Islam regions had considerable freedom, as exemplified by the ability of Daud Beureueh to issue a separate currency in Aceh, Ibnu Hajar to have a separate national anthem in South Kalimantan, and Kahar Muzakkar to introduce a socialist-Islamist system in South Sulawesi. While Kartosuwirjo as the imam headed the NII state, the DI regions were equal and not hierarchically subordinated, so much so that one could argue that there were in fact several connected rebellions rather than just one.

There are also important differences. In the separatist conflicts Indonesia was challenged by major insurgent militaries that used conventional forms of mobilization and had access to standard weapons, in the case of East Timor standard NATO weapons. This challenge differed greatly from that of the combatants in the post-Suharto Islamist violence, who were members of highly selective and secretive underground organizations. It also differed from that of the combatants in the communal conflicts, who were largely civilians with limited or no training, joining in communal clashes or attacks on an ad hoc basis. At the same time, in all conflicts there were core fighters who had previous military experience. In the RMS rebellion this core comprised Ambonese KNIL soldiers, in the East Timor conflict the core had been part of the Portuguese Armed Forces, and in the Aceh conflict the original core was the DI fighters from the Acehnese Darul Islam rebellion. JI, like Aceh, had a core of DI fighters but also a foundational core of those trained in Afghanistan in the 1980s. Muslims in the communal conflicts in Ambon and Poso acquired core fighters with the arrival of the Javanese mujahidin, many of whom were also Afghan alumni.

The introduction of this book asked three comparative questions: Why was Indonesia's response to the Darul Islam rebellions so much harsher than its response to the bombing campaign of JI? Why did the East Timor conflict see many more casualties than the Aceh conflict? And why were more troops sent to the communal conflict in Ambon than to Poso?

With respect to the first question, this book has demonstrated that Indonesia's response to the Darul Islam rebellions was much harsher than its response to the bombing campaign of JI for three key reasons. First, DI had control over territory in West Java, Aceh, South Sulawesi, and South Kalimantan in which it established Islamic rule. Second, the DI rebellions were a full-blown insurgency initially embedded in the war of liberation against the Dutch that involved three armies while JI's violence was a limited and sporadic campaign of terrorism carried out by a small number of Islamists. The war against the latter was thus fought by the police and intelligence services rather than the military. Third, DI's narrative that it saved the Republic of Indonesia after the withdrawal of the TNI from West Java clashed directly with the narrative advanced by the Indonesian Army, in particular that of the Siliwangi Division. This cut to the core of the army's legitimacy and political role in the state.

With respect to the second question, this book has concluded that to fully understand the violence by the Indonesian security forces in East Timor it is more useful to look at the events of 1965–1966 rather than to compare it with the Aceh conflict. The Indonesian military saw FRETILIN and its supporters as communist. And since one could not be Indonesian and communist, as the 1965–1966 violence had shown, Indonesia found itself in a position where it saw East Timor's territory as Indonesian but not the majority of the population. Moreover, once the communist label had been applied it could not be removed. It was applied to whole families across generations. It was associational, generational, and collective, explaining the killing of whole families, women, and children in the early years of the conflict. The violence in East Timor also had a higher death toll than in Aceh because East Timor was regarded as a training ground by Benny Murdani. It became the place where all weapons at the disposal of the Indonesian military, especially new acquisitions, were tried, tested, and used.

With respect to the third question, there were many more troops in the Ambon conflict than in the Poso conflict because the Indonesian military saw the conflict as separatist rather than communal. Troops upon troops were poured into Ambon to find the RMS provocateurs and to flush out its supporters. The history of the RMS rebellion ensured that in the communal conflict in Ambon both the state and the RMS were present, even if they were not. In comparison, the Poso conflict attracted little military interest and was largely characterized by the absence of the state.

This leaves the question of belonging, which has also been central to the Islamist, separatist, and communal violence examined in this book. For the people in all six case studies, belonging to Indonesia has been complicated and there have been degrees and hierarchies of belonging. In the Darul Islam rebellions there was no question about being Indonesian, but Indonesianness was defined differently, with Islam being an integral part of national and state identity. This was also true for the DI, NII, and JI members as well as some of the Muslims in the Poso conflict, for whom belonging to a "secular" Indonesia remained contentious. For the Acehnese belonging was conditional, conditional on Jakarta fulfilling the promises made to the Acehnese. It was the breaking of these promises and agreements that undermined Acehnese belonging to Indonesia. The breaking of agreements and the insecurity created as a result also made Christian

Ambonese belonging equivocal long after the RMS rebellion had been subdued. What is noticeable across the conflicts located geographically on the outer islands is the shared alienation from the center. This alienation was often accompanied by the belief that the Javanese belonged more clearly as well as uncertainty about what it actually meant to be Indonesian. At the extreme end, there were parts of the population in Aceh and Ambon that did not see themselves as Indonesian at all but only as Acehnese and Ambonese. Some of the latter even saw themselves as "Black Dutchmen." The conflict where most of the population felt little, if any, belonging was East Timor. This was the result of the extreme violence perpetrated against the East Timorese but also because for almost three decades the East Timorese felt that development had served the Indonesian military rather than the people and that their culture and customs were being trampled upon.

While belonging from the periphery of the Indonesian national imaginary was framed through notions of contentiousness and conditionality underwritten by strong feelings of alienation, belonging from the perspective of the center was equated with loyalty. Here too there were hierarchies, with the Javanese ranking the highest unless mitigated by Islamism or invalidated by communism. Thus, it was Javanese migrants who were sent specifically to regions with separatist aspirations in order to anchor the territory, as was the case in Aceh, East Timor, and Seram.

The red-and-white Indonesian flag featured prominently as a way of measuring who supported the Republic. Already Sukarno noted in his autobiography that he had "ordered 10 million red-and-white little paper flags distributed by courier to remote parts of the country," stating that this "helped those in the outlying islands feel they were part of the fight."[1] It was the failure to raise the Indonesian flag at *pesantren* Ngruki that put Abdullah Sungkar and Abu Bakar Ba'asyir on the radar of the Indonesian intelligence services in the late 1970s. In the early years of the Indonesian occupation of East Timor possessing an Indonesian flag could be a lifesaver. In the run-up to the 1999 referendum, Indonesian flags were also counted in order to ascertain East Timorese support for autonomy. The number of flags became the basis of intelligence estimates in the absence of more concrete information. In the third phase of the Aceh conflict, new red-and-white identity cards were introduced as a way to separate the loyal population from GAM. In Ambon, the new bridge built after the end of the communal conflict, which spanned Ambon Bay, was named Jembatan Merah Putih (Red-and-White Bridge), affirming the state's sovereignty over this territory.

Loyalty oaths—*ikrar kesetiaan*—were another way of the Indonesian government and security forces to ascertain loyalty. During the Darul Islam rebellions loyalty oaths were extracted from the population by both DI and the TNI, who both would also punish disloyal villages. Enforcing loyalty thus contributed to the civilian death toll. In the 1980s in East Timor, loyalty ceremonies were held for the general population, including the organization of a five-day festival in March 1984 for the people to swear loyalty to the military.[2] In the run-up to the 1999 referendum, loyalty meetings were held at district and subdistrict level where "the local population would be required to gather and affirm support for autonomy within Indonesia."[3] In the third phase of the Aceh insurgency the Indonesian military and local government also held mass loyalty oath-swearing ceremonies. Moreover, they provided *pembinaan* to guide captured GAM members and supporters back into the fold. Swearing loyalty has also become a central part of the in-prison deradicalization programs for Islamists. This usually involves raising the Indonesian flag and pledging oneself to upholding the unity and integrity of the Indonesian state, NKRI. It took the Indonesian counterterrorism force Densus 88 several attempts to get Abu Bakar Ba'asyir to take the loyalty oath that was tied to his terms of release from prison.

Lastly, concluding this book, it is interesting to note is that the Indonesian military, as the guardian of loyalty to the state, pursued a policy whereby it left a door open for rebels to return to the fold while it conducted military operations. This door, however, was not open to everyone and this, too, clearly defined who was considered to be Indonesian and who was not. It was open for DI/TII fighters during the Darul Islam rebellions. It was also open for RMS fighters who were accepted back into the fold after swearing loyalty and were even allowed to resume the prominent positions they had held in Ambon society. During the latter part of the Aceh insurgency there were incidents of GAM fighters surrendering to the military in which soldiers hugged the "repentant" GAM members, reflecting that the Acehnese were always seen as Indonesian, even if they were considered disloyal. The door, however, remained firmly shut in the early years of the East Timor conflict. Surrendering FRETILIN and FALINTIL, as communists, were often simply shot.

Notes

INTRODUCTION

1. Edward Aspinall, "Indonesia's Elections and the Return of Ideological Competition," *New Mandala*, April 22, 2019.

2. "Wiranto on Aceh Referendum: No Longer Relevant in Indonesia," *Tempo*, May 31, 2019, https://en.tempo.co/read/1211176/wiranto-on-aceh-referendum-no-longer-relevant-in-indonesia.

3. "Aceh Minta Referendum, Ikuti Sejak Timor Leste," *pokoksatu.id*, May 28, 2019.

4. Liselotte Mas, "Papuans Turn Monkey Slur into Revolutionary Symbol," *The Observers.France24*, August 23, 2019, https://observers.france24.com/en/20190823-indonesia-west-papua-papuans-demonstrations-monkey-revolutionary-symbol.

5. This book takes Sekarmadji Marijan Kartosuwirjo's call for jihad in response to the first Dutch "police action" in 1947 as the starting point of the DI rebellions and the death of Abdul Kahar Muzakkar in 1965 in South Sulawesi as the end point, rather than Kartosuwirjo's capture and execution in 1962.

6. For a more detailed discussion of the Darul Islam rebellions see Karl D. Jackson, *Traditional Authority, Islam, and Rebellion* (Berkeley: University of California Press, 1980); Kees van Dijk, *Rebellion Under the Banner of Islam: The Darul Islam Rebellions in Indonesia* (The Hague: Martinus Nijhoff, 1981); Solahudin, *The Roots of Terrorism in Indonesia: From Darul Islam to Jema'ah Islamiyah* (Sydney: New South Wales Press, 2013); and Chiara Formichi, *Islam and the Making of the Nation: Kartosuwirjo and Political Islam in Twentieth-Century Indonesia* (Leiden: KITLV, 2012).

7. Benedict Anderson, *Imagined Communities: Reflections on the Origin and Spread of Nationalism* (London: Verso, 1983); Eric Hobsbawm and Terence Ranger, eds., *The Invention of Tradition* (Cambridge: Cambridge University Press, 2012).

8. Antony Reid, *Imperial Alchemy: Nationalism and Political Identity in Southeast Asia* (Cambridge: Cambridge University Press, 2010), 8–10.

9. Thongchai Winichakul, *Siam Mapped: A History of the Geo-Body of a Nation* (Honolulu: University of Hawaii Press, 1994), 16.

10. "Dari Sabang Sampai Merauke," speech given by Sukarno on August 17, 1950. Emphasis added.

11. Sukarno, "Lahirnya Pancasila," speech given on June 1, 1945.

12. Sukarno and Cindy Adams, *Sukarno: An Autobiography—As Told to Cindy Adams* (Indianapolis: Bobbs-Merrill, 1965), 197.

13. Sukarno, "Lahirnya Pancasila."

14. Sukarno, *Autobiography*, 199.

15. For a discussion of the socialist origins of Indonesian nationalism see John T. Sidel, *Republicanism, Communism, Islam: Cosmopolitan Origins of Revolution in Southeast Asia* (Ithaca, NY: Cornell University Press, 2021), 139–145.

16. Sukarno, "The Rediscovery of Our Revolution (Political Manifesto) August 17, 1959," in Sukarno, *Toward Freedom and the Dignity of Man: A Collection of Speeches by President Sukarno of the Republic of Indonesia* (Jakarta: Department of Foreign Affairs of the Republic of Indonesia, 1961), 44.

17. Sukarno, "Rediscovery of Our Revolution," 62.

18. Sukarno, "To Build the World Anew September 30, 1960," address at the Fifteenth General Assembly of the United Nations, in Sukarno, *Toward Freedom*, 134 and 128.

19. Sukarno, "'Like an Angel that Strikes from the Skies': The March of our Revolution August 17, 1960," in Sukarno, *Toward Freedom*, 81 and 102–103.

20. "Supreme Advisory-Council Decision Respecting Specification of the Political Manifesto of the Republic of Indonesia of 17th August 1959," in Sukarno, *Toward Freedom*, 158.

21. Sukarno, "Nasionalisme, Islamisme, dan Marxisme," in Ir. Sukarno, *Dibawah Bendera Revolusi*, Jilid I (Jakarta: Yayasan Bung Karno, 2019), 1–28.

22. Sukarno, "Nasionalisme, Islamisme, dan Marxisme," 27.

23. Sidel, *Republicanism, Communism, Islam*, 146.

24. Soeharto, *My Thoughts, Words and Deeds: An Autobiography*, as told to G. Dwipayana and Ramadhan KH (Jakarta: Citra Lamtoro Gung Persada, 1991), 99 and 100.

25. Soeharto, *My Thoughts*, 101.

26. Soeharto, *My Thoughts*, 102.

27. Soeharto, *My Thoughts*, 107.

28. Soeharto, *My Thoughts*, 111.

29. Soeharto, *My Thoughts*, 113.

30. For a more detailed discussion of 1965–1966 see Geoffrey B. Robinson, *The Killing Season: A History of the Indonesian Massacres 1965–66* (Princeton, NJ: Princeton University Press, 2018).

31. Carool Kersten, *Islam in Indonesia: The Contest for Society, Ideas and Values* (London: Hurst, 2015), 16.

32. Kersten, *Islam in Indonesia*, 251.

33. Kersten, *Islam in Indonesia*, 12 and 228.

34. R. E. Elson, *The Idea of Indonesia: A History* (Cambridge: Cambridge University Press, 2008).

35. Sukarno, *Autobiography*, 241.

36. Sukarno, *Autobiography*, 224; H. Muhammad Yamin, *6000 tahun sang Merah Putih*, 2nd ed. (Jakarta: PT Balai Pustaka, 2017).

37. Sukarno, *Autobiography*, 241

38. Undang-Undang Republik Indonesia, Nomor 5 Tahun 1979 Tentang Pemerintahan Desa.

39. Ernest Gellner, *Nation and Nationalism* (Oxford: Blackwell, 1983), 7. See also John Crowley, "The Politics of Belonging: Some Theoretical Considerations" in *The Politics of Belonging: Migrants and Minorities in Contemporary Europe*, ed. Andrew Geddes and Adrian Favell (Aldershot, UK: Ashgate, 1998); 18. Montserrat Guibernau, "Antony D. Smith on Nation and National Identity: A Critical Assessment," *Nations and Nationalism* 10, nos. 1–2 (2004): 125–141; Rogers Brubaker, "Migration, Membership, and the Modern Nation-State: Internal and External Dimensions of the Politics of Belonging," *Journal of Interdisciplinary History* 41, no. 1 (2010), 61–78.

40. Michael Skey, *National Belonging and Everyday Life* (Basingstoke, UK: Palgrave Macmillan, 2011), 326.

41. Kirsten E. Schulze and Joseph Chinyong Liow, "Making Jihadis, Waging Jihad: Transnational and Local Dimensions of the ISIS Phenomenon in Indonesia and Malaysia," *Asian Security* 15, no. 2 (2019): 127.

42. Jackson, *Traditional Authority*, xx.

43. Van Dijk, *Banner of Islam*, 4; Solahudin, *Roots of Terrorism*.

44. George McTurnan Kahin, *Nationalism and Revolution in Indonesia* (Ithaca, NY: Cornell University Press, 1952), 327.

45. Pinardi, *Sekarmadji Maridjan Kartosuwirjo: Kisah lahir dan djatuhnja seorang petualang politik* (Jakarta: Aryaguna, 1964); Holk H. Dengel, *Darul Islam: Kartosuwir-*

jos Kampf um einen Islamischen Staat in Indonesien (Stuttgart: Franz Steiner Verlag Wiesbaden GMBH, 1986), 1; Formichi, *Islam and the Making of the Nation*, 2–3; C.A.O. van Nieuwenhuijze, *Aspects of Islam in Post-Colonial Indonesia: Five Essays* (The Hague: W. van Hoeve, 1958), 176; Hiroko Horikoshi, "The Dar ul-Islam Movement in West Java (1948–62): An Experience in the Historical Process," *Indonesia* 20 (1975), 60; Kevin W. Fogg, *Indonesia's Islamic Revolution* (Cambridge: Cambridge University Press, 2020), 20; Herdi Sahrasad and Al Chaidar, *Satu Guru, Tiga Ideologi: Pergulatan Ideologi HOS Tjokroaminoto dan Tiga Muridnya: Soekarno, Musso dan Kartosoewirjo* (Jakarta: Freedom Foundation & Centre for Strategic Studies—University of Indonesia, 2017), 363.

46. Rohan Gunaratna, *Inside Al Qaeda: Global Network of Terror* (New Delhi: Roli Books, 2002), 194; Zachary Abuza, *Political Islam and Violence in Indonesia* (London: Routledge, 2007), 2; Maria A. Ressa, *Seeds of Terror; An Eyewitness Account of Al-Qaeda's Newest Center of Operations in Southeast Asia* (New York: Free Press, 2004), 70; Bilveer Singh, *The Talibanization of Southeast Asia: Losing the War on Terror to Islamist Extremists* (London: Praeger Security International, 2007), 96.

47. Ken Conboy, *The Second Front: Inside Asia's Most Dangerous Terrorist Network* (*Jakarta*: Equinox Publishing, 2006), 148; Quinton Temby, "Jihadists Assemble: The Rise of Militant Islamism in Southeast Asia" (PhD diss., Australian National University, 2017).

48. Natasha Hamilton-Hart, "Terrorism in Southeast Asia: Expert Analysis, Myopia, and Fantasy," *Pacific Review*, 18, no. 3 (September 2005): 303–325; John T. Sidel, "The Islamist Threat in Southeast Asia: Much Ado about Nothing?" *Asian Affairs* 16, no. 3 (November 2008); Greg Fealy and Carlyle A. Thayer, "Al-Qaeda in Southeast Asia: Problematising 'Linkages' between Regional and International Terrorism," in *Re-Envisioning Asia-Pacific Security: A Regional-Global Nexus?*, ed. William Tow (Cambridge: Cambridge University Press, 2009), 211–227.

49. Sidney Jones, "New Order Repression and the Birth of Jemaah Islamiyah," in *Soeharto's New Order and its Legacy: Essays in Honour of Harold Crouch*, ed. Edward Aspinall and Greg Fealy (Canberra, ANU Press, 2010), 39–48; Solahudin, *Roots of Terrorism*; Julie Chernov Hwang, *Why Terrorists Quit: The Disengagement of Indonesian Jihadists* (Ithaca, NY: Cornell University Press, 2018); Andrée Feillard and Rémy Madinier, *The End of Innocence? Indonesian Islam and the Temptations of Radicalism* (Singapore: NUS Press, 2011).

50. Solahudin, *Roots of Terrorism*; Sidney Jones, "New Order Repression"; Kirsten E. Schulze and Julie Chernov Hwang, "From Afghanistan to Syria: How the Global Remains Local for Indonesian Islamist Militants," in *Exporting the Global Jihad: Critical Perspectives from Asia and North America*, ed. Tom Smith and Kirsten E. Schulze (London: IB Tauris, 2020), 15–36; Julie Chernov Hwang, "Dakwah before Jihad: Understanding the Behaviour of Jemaah Islamiyah," *Contemporary Southeast Asia*, 41, no. 1 (2019): 14–34.

51. John T. Sidel, *Riots, Pogroms, Jihad: Religious Violence in Indonesia* (Ithaca, NY: Cornell University Press, 2006), 48.

52. Noorhaidi Hassan, *Islam, Militancy, and the Quest for Identity in Post-New Order Indonesia* (Ithaca, NY: Cornell Southeast Asia Program, 2006); Birgit Bräuchler, *Cyberidentities at War: Der Molukkenkonflikt im Internet* (Bielefeld: Transcript Verlag, 2005), 57–69; Mohamed Shoelhi, *Laskar Jihad Kambing Hitam Konflik Maluku* (Jakarta: Puzam, 2002).

53. Dave McRae, *A Few Poorly Organised Men: Inter-Religious Violence in Poso, Indonesia* (Leiden: Brill Academic Publishers, 2013); Muhammad Tito Karnavian, *Explaining Islamist Insurgencies: The Case of al-Jamaah al-Islamiyyah and the Radicalisation of the Poso Conflict, 2000–2007* (London: Imperial College Press, 2015); Scott Atran, *Talking to the Enemy: Violent Extremism, Sacred Values, And What It Means to Be Human* (London: Penguin Books, 2010); Julie Chernov Hwang, Rizal Panggabean and Ihsan Ali

Fauzi, "The Disengagement of Jihadis in Poso, Indonesia," *Asian Survey*, 53, no. 4 (July/August 2013): 754–777; Badrus Sholeh, *Jihad, Conflict and Reconciliation in Ambon, Indonesia* (Saarbrücken: Lambert Academic Publishing, 2012); Julie Chernov Hwang and Kirsten E. Schulze, "Why They Join: Pathways into Indonesian Militant Islamist Organizations," *Terrorism and Political Violence* 30, no. 6 (2018): 911–932; Kirsten E. Schulze, "From Ambon to Poso: Comparative and Evolutionary Aspects of Local Jihad in Indonesia," *Contemporary Southeast Asia* 41, no. 1 (2019), 35–62.

54. Pusat Sejarah Dan Tradisi TNI, *Sejarah TNI*, Jilid II (1950–1959) (Jakarta: Markas Besar Tentara Nasional Indonesia Pusat Sejarah dan Tradisi TNI, 2000), 116–117; TNI, *Sejarah TNI*, Jilid IV (1966–1983), 134–135.

55. Wiranto, *Selamat Jalan Timor Timur: Pergulatan Menguak Kebenaran* (Jakarta: Institute for Democracy of Indonesia, 2002).

56. Kiki Syahnakri, *Timor Timur: The Untold Story* (Jakarta: Kompas, 2013), 10 and 16.

57. Tono Suratman, *Merah Putih: Pengabdian & Tanggung Jawab di Timor Timur* (Bogor: LPKN, 2000), 15.

58. Hasan di Tiro, *The Price of Freedom: The Unfinished Diary of Tengku Hasan di Tiro* (Ministry of Education and Information, State of Aceh Sumatra, 1982); José Ramos-Horta, *Funu: The Unfinished Saga of East Timor* (Trenton, NJ: The Red Sea Press, 1987); Xanana Gusmão, *To Resist Is to Win!: The Autobiography of Xanana Gusmão* (Richmond, Victoria: Aurora Books, 2000); Constancio Pinto and Matthew Jardine, *East Timor's Unfinished Struggle: Inside the Timorese Resistance* (Boston: South End Press, 1997).

59. Paul Hainsworth and Stephen McCloskey, eds., *The East Timor Question: The Struggle for Independence from Indonesia* (London: IB Tauris, 2000), 1.

60. Hamish McDonald and Richard Tanter, introduction to *Masters of Terror: Indonesia's Military and Violence in East Timor*, ed. Richard Tanter, Desmond Ball, and Gerry van Klinken (Lanham, MD: Rowman and Littlefield, 2006), 2; Carmel Budiarjo, "The Legacy of the Suharto Dictatorship," in Hainsworth and McCloskey, *East Timor Question*, 52; John Martinkus, *A Dirty Little War: An Eyewitness Account of East Timor's Descent into Hell. 1997–2000* (Sydney: Random House, 2001), xii. See also John G. Taylor, *Indonesia's Forgotten War: The Hidden History of East Timor* (London: Zed Books, 1991), 30.

61. Don Greenlees and Robert Garran, *Deliverance: The Inside Story of East Timor's Fight for Freedom* (Crows Nest, NSW: Allen & Unwin, 2002).

62. Douglas Kammen, *Three Centuries of Conflict in East Timor* (New Brunswick, NJ: Rutgers University Press, 2015), 11.

63. James Dunn, *East Timor: A Rough Passage to Independence* (Double Bay, NSW: Longueville Media, 2003); David Connery, *Crisis Policymaking: Australia and the East Timor Crisis of 1999* (Canberra: ANU Press, 2010); Bruce J. Watson, *Forgotten Island: Australia, Realism, and the Timor Crisis* (North Melbourne: Australian Scholarly, 2021).

64. Richard Chauvel, *Nationalists, Soldiers and Separatists* (Leiden: KITLV Press, 2008), xii and 395.

65. John Christian Ruhulessin and Pieter George Manoppo, *Local Political Instability in Maluku: Inspiration of the Proclamation by the Republic of South Maluku and its Implications for the Arrangement of Cultural Echo-Centric* (Chisinau: Lambert Academic Publishing, 2021), 11.

66. Ben van Kaam, *The South Moluccans: Background to the Train Hijackings* (London: C. Hurst, 1980), 2; Fridus Steijlen, *RMS Moluks Nationalisme in Nederland 1951–1994: Van ideal tot symbol* (Amsterdam: Het Spinhuis, 1996), 41; Ernst Utrecht, *Ambon: Kolonisatie, dekolonisatie en neo-kolonisatie* (Amsterdam: Van Gennep, 1972), 27.

67. Harold L. B. Lovestrand, *The President Has Been Executed* (Maitland, FL: Xulon Press, 2018).

68. Geoffrey Robinson, "Rawan Is as Rawan Does: The Origins of Disorder in New Order Aceh," *Indonesia*, no. 66 (1998), 128; Neta S. Pane, *Sejarah dan Kekuatan Gerakan Aceh Merdeka: Solusi, Harapan dan Impian* (Jakarta: Grasindo, 2001), xi.

69. Tim Kell, *The Roots of Acehnese Rebellion, 1989–1992* (Ithaca, NY: Cornell Modern Indonesia Project, 1995), 1.

70. Rizal Sukma, "The Acehnese Rebellion: Secessionist Movement in Post-Suharto Indonesia," in *Non-Traditional Security Issues in Southeast Asia*, ed. Andrew Tan and Kenneth Boutin (Singapore: Select Publishing, 2001), 377–409.

71. Damien Kingsbury and Lesley McCulloch, "Military Business in Aceh," in *Veranda of Violence: Background to the Aceh Problem*, ed. Antony Reid (Singapore: Singapore University Press, 2006), 210 and 212; Elizabeth Drexler, *Aceh, Indonesia: Securing the Insecure State* (Philadelphia: University of Pennsylvania Press, 2008), 8.

72. Edward Aspinall, *Islam and Nation: Separatist Rebellion in Aceh, Indonesia* (Stanford, CA: Stanford University Press, 2009), 8.

73. Rodd McGibbon, "Local Leadership and the Aceh Conflict," in Reid, *Veranda of Violence*, 315–316; Kirsten E. Schulze, *The Free Aceh Movement (GAM): Anatomy of a Separatist Organization* (Washington, DC: East-West Center, 2004), 1; M. Isa Sulaiman, "From Autonomy to Periphery: A Critical Evaluation of the Acehnese Nationalist Movement," in Reid, *Veranda of Violence*, 139.

74. Harold Crouch, *Political Reform in Indonesia After Soeharto* (Singapore: Institute of Southeast Asian Studies, 2010), 4.

75. Jacques Bertrand, *Nationalism and Ethnic Conflict in Indonesia* (Cambridge: Cambridge University Press, 2004), 10.

76. Jamie Davidson, *From Rebellion to Riots: Collective Violence on Indonesian Borneo* (Madison: University of Wisconsin Press, 2008), 20.

77. Gerry van Klinken, *Communal Violence and Democratisation in Indonesia: Small Town Wars* (London: Routledge, 2007), 8.

78. Lorraine Aragon, "Communal Violence in Poso, Central Sulawesi: Where People Eat Fish and Fish Eat People," *Indonesia* 72 (October 2001), 48; Martin van Bruinessen, *Contemporary Developments in Indonesian Islam: Explaining the "Conservative Turn"* (Singapore: ISEAS Publishing, 2013), 2

79. Ingrid Wessel, "The Politics of Violence in New Order Indonesia in the Last Decade of the 20th Century," in *Violence in Indonesia*, ed. Ingrid Wessel and Georgia Wimhöfer (Hamburg: Abera, 2001), 70.

80. Liem Soei Liong, "It's the Military, Stupid!" in *Roots of Violence in Indonesia*, ed. Freek Colombijn and J. Thomas Lindblad (Leiden: KITLV Press, 2002), 198; Thamrin Amal Tomagola, "Ambon Terbakar," in *Ketika Semerbak Cengkih Tergusur Asap Mesiu: Tragedi Kemanusiaan Maluku di Balik Konspirasi Militer, Kapitalis Birokrat, dan Kepentingan Elit Politik*, ed. Zairin Salambessy and Thamrin Hussain (Jakarta: Tapak Ambon, 2001), 18–23; George Junus Aditjondro, "Kerusuhan Poso dan Morowali, Akar Permasalahan dan Jalan Keluarnya," (paper presented at a conference organized by Propatria on "The Application of Emergency in Aceh, Papua and Poso?," January 7, 2004, Hotel Santika, Jakarta), 34.

81. Nancy Lee Peluso, "Passing the Red Bowl: Creating Community Identity through Violence in West Kalimantan, 1967–1997," in *Violent Conflicts in Indonesia: Analysis, Representation, Resolution*, ed. Charles A. Coppel (London: Routledge, 2006), 108.

82. Davidson, *From Rebellion to Riots*, 18.

83. Yukhi Tajima, *The Institutional Origins of Communal Violence: Indonesia's Transition from Authoritarian Rule* (Cambridge: Cambridge University Press, 2014), 4.

84. Yukhi Tajima, "Explaining Ethnic Violence in Indonesia: Demilitarizing Domestic Security," in *Collective Violence in Indonesia*, ed. Ashutosh Varshney (Boulder, CO: Lynne Rienner, 2010), 100.

85. Aragon, "Communal Violence in Poso."
86. Bertrand, *Nationalism and Ethnic Conflict*, xiv.
87. Angel Rabasa and Peter Chalk, *Indonesia's Transformation and the Stability of Southeast Asia* (Santa Monica, CA: Rand, 2001), 43; Ingrid Wessel, "The Politics of Violence in New Order Indonesia in the Last Decade of the 20th Century," in Wessel and Wimhöfer, *Violence in Indonesia*, 67.
88. Mary Somers Heidhues, "Kalimantan Barat 1967-1999: Violence on the Periphery," in Wessel and Wimhöfer, *Violence in Indonesia*, 145; Colombijn and Lindblad, *Roots of Violence in Indonesia*, 36; R. E. Elson, "In Fear of the People: Suharto and the Justification of State-Sponsored Violence under the New Order," in Colombijn and Lindblad, *Roots of Violence in Indonesia*, 173.
89. Tim Lindsay, "From Soepomo to Prabowo: Law, Violence and Corruption in the Preman State," in Coppel, *Violent Conflicts in Indonesia*, 21.
90. Lindsay, "From Soepomo to Prabowo," 23.
91. Henk Schulte Nordholt, "A Genealogy of Violence," in Colombijn and Lindblad, *Roots of Violence in Indonesia*, 37-38.
92. Sidel, *Riots, Pogroms, Jihad*, xi.
93. Sumanto Al Qurtuby, *Religious Violence and Conciliation in Indonesia: Christians and Muslims in the Moluccas* (London: Routledge, 2016), 4-5.
94. Christopher R. Duncan, *Violence and Vengeance: Religious Conflict and Its Aftermath in Eastern Indonesia* (Ithaca, NY: Cornell University Press, 2013), 7.
95. Hilmar Farid, "Political Economy of Violence and Victims in Indonesia," in Coppel, *Violent Conflicts in Indonesia*, 269.

1. THE DARUL ISLAM REBELLIONS, 1947-1965

1. For a more detailed discussion of the role of Islam in these wars see, for example, Christine Dobbin, "Islamic Revivalism in Minangkabau at the Turn of the Nineteenth Century," *Modern Asian Studies* 8, no. 3 (1974), 319-345; P.B.R. Carey, *The Power of Prophecy: Prince Dipanagara and the End of an Old Order in Java, 1785-1855* (Leiden: KITLV, 2008); Ahmed Maftuh Sujana and Saeful Iskander, "Jihad dan anti-kafir dalam geger Cilegon 1888," *Tsafoqah: Journal agama dan budaya* 17, no. 1 (June 2019), 1-15; Ibrahim Alfian, *Perang di Jalan Allah: Perang Aceh 1873-1912* (Yogyakarta: Penerbit Ombak, 2016).
2. This book takes Kartosuwirjo's call for jihad in response to the first Dutch "police action" in 1947 as the starting point of the DI rebellions and the death of Kahar Muzakkar in 1965 in South Sulawesi as the end point, rather than Kartosuwirjo's capture and execution in 1962.
3. Michael Francis Laffan, *Islamic Nationhood and Colonial Indonesia: The Umma below the Winds* (London: Routledge, 2003), 92; Deliar Noer, *The Modernist Movement in Indonesia: 1900-1942* (Singapore: Oxford University Press, 1973), 93.
4. B. J. Boland, *The Struggle for Islam in Modern Indonesia* (The Hague: Martinus Nijhoff, 1971), 12-14.
5. See, for example, Bernhard H. M. Vlekke, *Nusantara: A History of Indonesia* (The Hague: W. Van Hoeve, 1959) and M. C. Ricklefs, *A History of Modern Indonesia since c. 1200* (Basingstoke, UK: Palgrave, 2001).
6. Takashi Shiraishi, *An Age in Motion: Popular Radicalism in Java, 1912-1916* (Ithaca, NY: Cornell University Press, 1990), 43.
7. Amry Vandenbosch, "Nationalism and Religion in Indonesia," *Far Eastern Survey* 21, no. 18 December 17, 1952), 182; Justus M. van der Kroef, "The Role of Islam in Indonesian Nationalism and Politics," *Western Political Quarterly* 11, no. 1 (March 1958), 33.

8. W. F. Wertheim, *Indonesian Society in Transition: A Study of Social Change* (The Hague: Van Hoeve, 1959), 204.

9. Noer, *Modernist Movement in Indonesia*, 7; Laffan, *Islamic Nationhood and Colonial Indonesia*, 2; John T. Sidel, *Republicanism, Communism, Islam: Cosmopolitan Origins of Revolution in Southeast Asia* (Ithaca, NY: Cornell University Press, 2021), 107; Azyumardi Azra, *The Origins of Economic Reformism in Southeast Asia: Networks of Malay-Indonesian and Middle Eastern Ulama in the Seventeenth and Eighteenth Centuries* (Honolulu: University of Hawai'i Press, 2004).

10. Laffan, *Islamic Nationhood and Colonial Indonesia*, 157.

11. SI's statutes, as explained by Shiraishi, were backdated to November 1911. Thus, in some of the literature 1911 appears as the founding date for Sarekat Islam. See Shiraishi, *Age in Motion*, 42. There is also a whole body of Islamist literature that asserts that SDI was established in 1905, thus predating the protonationalist Budi Utomo. See, for example, Irfan S. Awwas, *Trilogi Kepemimpinan Negara Islam Indonesia: Menguak Perjuangan Umat Islam dan Pengkhianatan Kaum Nasionalis-Sekuler* (Yogyakarta: Uswah, 2009).

12. Shiraishi, *Age in Motion*, 47; Van der Kroef, "Role of Islam," 47.

13. Shiraishi, *Age in Motion*, 49.

14. Holk H. Dengel, *Darul Islam: Kartosuwirjos Kampf um einen Islamischen Staat in Indonesien* (Stuttgart: Franz Steiner Verlag Wiesbaden GMBH, 1986), 1; Laffan, *Islamic Nationhood and Colonial Indonesia*, 166–167.

15. Laffan, *Islamic Nationhood and Colonial Indonesia*, 187

16. Herdi Sahrasad and Al Chaidar, *Satu Guru, Tiga Ideologi: Pergulatan Ideologi HOS Tjokroaminoto dan Tiga Muridnya: Soekarno, Musso dan Kartosoewirjo* (Jakarta: Freedom Foundation & Centre for Strategic Studies—University of Indonesia, 2017), 344.

17. Van der Kroef, "Role of Islam," 47

18. Chiara Formichi, *Islam and the Making of the Nation: Kartosuwirjo and Political Islam in Twentieth-Century Indonesia* (Leiden: KITLV, 2012), 4.

19. Van der Kroef, "Role of Islam," 44.

20. Kees van Dijk, *Rebellion Under the Banner of Islam: The Darul Islam Rebellions in Indonesia* (The Hague: Martinus Nijhoff, 1981), 26

21. Van der Kroef, "Role of Islam," 48; Van Dijk, *Banner of Islam*, 38.

22. Van Dijk, *Banner of Islam*, 26.

23. Harry J. Benda, *The Crescent and the Rising Sun: Indonesian Islam under Japanese Occupation, 1942–45* (The Hague: W Van Hoeve, 1958), 150.

24. Van Dijk, *Banner of Islam*, 83.

25. Benda, *Crescent and the Rising Sun*, 187.

26. Dengel, *Darul-Islam*, 37.

27. Sahrasad and Al Chaidar, *Satu Guru*, 343.

28. Boland, *Struggle for Islam*, 55; Van Dijk, *Banner of Islam*, 28.

29. Pinardi, *Sekarmadji Maridjan Kartosuwirjo: Kisah lahir dan djatuhnja seorang petualang politik* (Jakarta: Aryaguna, 1964), 27–28.

30. Van Dijk, *Banner of Islam*, 28.

31. Karl D. Jackson, *Traditional Authority, Islam, and Rebellion* (Berkeley: University of California Press, 1980), 22; Tempo, *Kartosoewirjo: Mimpi Negara Islam* (Jakarta: KPG and Tempo Publishing, 2011), 5.

32. Hiroko Horikoshi, "The Dar ul-Islam Movement in West Java (1948–62): An Experience in the Historical Process," *Indonesia*, no. 20 (1975), 74–75.

33. Noer, *Modernist Movement in Indonesia*, 148.

34. Tempo, *Kartosoewirjo*, 3; Sahrasad and Al Chaidar, *Satu Guru*, 306.

35. Dengel, *Darul-Islam*, 177–181.

36. Dengel, *Darul-Islam*, 8.
37. S. M. Kartosoewirjo, *Sikap Hidjrah P.S.I.I.*, Bagian 2 (Malangbong, West Java, 1936), 14.
38. S. M. Kartosoewirjo, "Islamisme, Nationalisme dan Internationalisme I," *Fadjar Asia*, November 3, 1928; S. M. Kartosoewirjo, "Islamisme, Nationalisme dan Internationalisme II," *Fadjar Asia*, November 7, 1928.
39. Kartosoewirjo, "Islamisme, Nationalisme dan Internationalisme I."
40. S. M. Kartosoewirjo, "Agama dan Politiek," *Fadjar Asia*, April 3, 1928; S. M. Kartosoewirjo, "Barisan Moeda," *Fadjar Asia*, February 6, 1929.
41. Kartosoewirjo, "Agama dan Politiek."
42. Kartosoewirjo, "Islamisme, Nationalisme dan Internationalisme II."
43. S. M. Kartosoewirjo, "Keliroe Sedikit," *Fadjar Asia*, November 7, 1928.
44. S. M. Kartosoewirjo, "Rai'at dan Nasibnja," *Fadjar Asia*, February 12, 1929.
45. Kartosoewirjo, "Rai'at dan Nasibnja."
46. S. M. Kartosoewirjo, "Keberatan ra'iat," *Fadjar Asia*, April 27, 1929.
47. S. M. Kartosoewirjo, "Orang Lampung boekan monjet tetapi ialah manoesiabelaka!," *Fadjar Asia*, June 10, 1929; S. M. Kartosoewirjo, "Bahaia jang mengantjam Roeh dan Djiwa Rai'at Djajahan," *Fadjar Asia*, February 14, 1929.
48. S. M. Kartosoewirjo, "Moelai sadar akan Hak2-nja," *Fadjar Asia*, February 16, 1929.
49. Kartosoewirjo, "Rai'at dan Nasibnja"; S. M. Kartosoewirjo, "Sambil Laloe," *Fadjar Asia*, January 16, 1929; Kartosoewirjo, "Bahaia jang mengantjam Roeh."
50. Kartosoewirjo, "Rai'at dan Nasibnja."
51. S. M. Kartosoewirjo, "Agama dan Politiek," *Fadjar Asia*, April 3, 1928; S. M. Kartosoewirjo, "Memboeta toeli," *Fadjar Asia*, January 29, 1929.
52. S. M. Kartosoewirjo, "Islam terantjam Bahaja," *Fadjar Asia*, February 9, 1929; Kartosoewirjo, "Bahaja jang mengantjam Roeh dan Djiwa Rai'at Djajahan."
53. S. M. Kartosoewirjo, "Boekan memboeta toeli makahan membabi boeta," *Fadjar Asia*, March 1, 1929.
54. S. M. Kartosoewirjo, *Sikap Hidjrah P.S.I.I.*, Bagian 1 (Malangbong, West Java, 1936), 17.
55. Kartosoewirjo, *Sikap Hidjrah P.S.I.I.*, Bagian 1, 39.
56. Kartosoewirjo, *Sikap Hidjrah P.S.I.I.*, Bagian 2, 5.
57. Kartosoewirjo, *Sikap Hidjrah P.S.I.I.*, Bagian 2, 6 and 7.
58. Kartosoewirjo, *Sikap Hidjrah P.S.I.I.*, Bagian 2, 9.
59. Kartosoewirjo, *Sikap Hidjrah P.S.I.I.*, Bagian 2, 11.
60. Kartosoewirjo, *Sikap Hidjrah P.S.I.I.*, Bagian 2, 12.
61. Kartosoewirjo, *Sikap Hidjrah P.S.I.I.*, Bagian 2, 13 and 14.
62. Kartosoewirjo, *Sikap Hidjrah P.S.I.I.*, Bagian 2, 15.
63. Kartosoewirjo, *Sikap Hidjrah P.S.I.I.*, Bagian 2, 20.
64. Kartosoewirjo, *Sikap Hidjrah P.S.I.I.*, Bagian 2, 27 and 26.
65. Kartosoewirjo, *Sikap Hidjrah P.S.I.I*, Bagian 2, 28.
66. S. M. Kartosoewirjo, *Daftar—Oesaha Hijrah* (Malangbong, West Java: Poestaka Daroel-Islam, 1940), 11.
67. Kartosoewirjo, *Daftar—Oesaha Hijrah*, 3.
68. Kartosoewirjo, *Daftar—Oesaha Hijrah*, 3.
69. S. M. Kartosoewirjo, *Haluan Politik Islam: Risalah Perjuangan Menuju Darul Islam* (Bandung: Sega Arsy, 2015), 43.
70. Kholid O. Santosa, "S. M. Kartosoewirjo: Antara Pejuang dan Pemberontak," preface to Kartosoewirjo, *Haluan Politik Islam*, 40.
71. Kartosoewirjo, *Haluan Politik Islam*, 77

72. Kartosoewirjo, *Haluan Politik Islam*, 43, 59, and 108.
73. Kartosoewirjo, *Haluan Politik Islam*, 59.
74. Kartosoewirjo, *Haluan Politik Islam*, 63.
75. Kartosoewirjo, *Haluan Politik Islam*, 72 and 65.
76. Kartosoewirjo, *Haluan Politik Islam*, 79.
77. Kartosoewirjo, *Haluan Politik Islam*, 93.
78. Kartosoewirjo, *Haluan Politik Islam*, 87.
79. Kartosoewirjo, *Haluan Politik Islam*, 80.
80. Kartosoewirjo, *Haluan Politik Islam*, 106 and 107.
81. Kartosoewirjo, *Haluan Politik Islam*, 114.
82. Kartosoewirjo, *Haluan Politik Islam*, 112.
83. For example, see Boland, *Struggle for Islam*, 40; Van Dijk, *Banner of Islam*, 19; Dengel, *Darul-Islam*, 54; Solahudin, *The Roots of Terrorism in Indonesia: From Darul Islam to Jema'ah Islamiyah* (Sydney: New South Wales Press, 2013), 35; Syaukani Al-Karim, "Kepada Sekarmadji," preface to S. M. Kartosoewirjo, *Haluan Politik Islam*, 8; Sri Yanuarti, "Intelijen dan Pemberontakan Daerah: Dari Warlordism ke Integrasi," in *Intelijen Politik dan Era Soekarno*, ed. Ikrar Nusa Bhakti, Diandra Megapurti Mengko, and Sarah Nuraini Siregar (Jakarta: LIPI Press, 2018), 49.
84. B. R. Pearn, "Events in Indonesia, 1939–49," Foreign Office Research Department, 6, FO492/2 File 63825, F9324/5/62, United Kingdom National Archives (UKNA).
85. Pearn, "Events in Indonesia, 1939–49," 8.
86. Amir Sjarifuddin, "Statement by the Head of the Delegation of the Republic of Indonesia, 10 December 1947, annex II, Security Council Committee of Good Offices on the Indonesian Question, Conference with the Delegates of the Governments of the Netherlands and the Republic of Indonesia: Preliminary Cease Hostilities Order under the Truce Agreement," January 17, 1948, S/AC.10/CONF.2/8, Delegasi Indonesia 93, Arsip Nasional Republik Indonesia (ANRI).
87. Sjarifuddin, "Statement," 10 December 1947.
88. Formichi, *Making of the Nation*, 103.
89. Formichi, *Making of the Nation*, 81.
90. Boland, *Struggle for Islam*, 57; Formichi, *Making of the Nation*, 103; Santosa, "S. M. Kartosoewirjo," 41.
91. Dengel, *Darul-Islam*, 52.
92. Van Dijk, *Banner of Islam*, 84.
93. Dengel, *Dar ul-Islam*, 51; C.A.O. van Nieuwenhuijze, *Aspects of Islam in Post-Colonial Indonesia: Five Essays* (The Hague: W. van Hoeve, 1958), 172.
94. Pemerintah Negara Islam Indonesia, "Ma'lumat No. 5," Madinah 19 Sapar 1368/December 20, 1948.
95. Dengel, *Darul-Islam*, 52.
96. Formichi, *Making of the Nation*, 100.
97. Sjarif Abdullah's confession to the military, "Why I Joined Dar'ul Islam: The Way of Thinking of Sjarif Abdullah in the Past," as quoted in Jackson, *Traditional Authority*, 274.
98. Van Dijk, *Banner of Islam*, 18
99. Soeharto, *My Thoughts, Words and Deeds: An Autobiography*, as told to G. Dwipayana and Ramadhan KH (Jakarta: Citra Lamtoro Gung Persada, 1991), 67. The number of 35,000 is also given by Kahin and Van Dijk, while Dengel suggests 29,000 and Formichi 22,000; Dengel, *Darul-Islam*, 53.
100. Consul-General Shepherd to Mr Bevin, "Situation in Indonesia," September 16, 1948, FO492/2 File 63825, F13191/3/62, UKNA.
101. Van Dijk, *Banner of Islam*, 19; Dengel, *Darul-Islam*, 56.

102. Van Dijk, *Banner of Islam*, 127.
103. Van Dijk, *Banner of Islam*, 139; TNI, *Sejarah TNI*, Jilid II (1950–1959) (Jakarta: Markas Besar Tentara Nasional Indonesia, Pusat Sejarah Dan Tradisi TNI, 2000), 87.
104. TNI, *Sejarah TNI*, Jilid I (1945–1949), 268.
105. Boland, *Struggle for Islam*, 58.
106. Van Dijk, *Banner of Islam*, 20; George McTurnan Kahin, *Nationalism and Revolution in Indonesia* (Ithaca, NY: Cornell University Press, 1952), 409.
107. Boland, *Struggle for Islam*, 58–59.
108. Komandemen Tertinggi Angkatan Perang Negara Islam Indonesia, "Ma'lumat Militer No. 1," January 25, 1949.
109. John R. W. Smail, *Bandung in the Early Revolution 1945–1946* (Ithaca, NY: Cornell Modern Indonesia Project, Monograph Series, 1964), 128.
110. Dengel, *Darul-Islam*, 63.
111. NII, "Kitab Undang-Undang Hukum Pidana Negara Islam Indonesia," August 1948, paragraph 1, article 2. An English version of this penal code can be found in Jackson, *Traditional Authority*, 327–338.
112. NII, "Kitab Undang-Undang," paragraph 1, article 3.
113. Solahudin, *Roots of Terrorism*, 37
114. TNI, *Sejarah TNI*, Jilid I, 269.
115. Kahin, *Nationalism and Revolution in Indonesia*, 330
116. Van Nieuwenhuijze, *Aspects of Islam*, 165.
117. Van Nieuwenhuijze, *Aspects of Islam*, 165.
118. Dengel, *Darul-Islam*, 61; *Landjoetan Sedjara Goenoeng Tjoepoe* (Cisayong, 1948), 14 as quoted in Dengel, *Darul-Islam*, 61.
119. CIA, "Military Activities in Indonesia," Information Report, number redacted, June 16, 1949, CIA Archives online, Historical Collections, https://www.cia.gov/readingroom/docs/CIA-RDP82-00457R002800720001-5.pdf.
120. CIA, "Law and Order in West Java," Information Report, number redacted, May 31, 1949, CIA Archives online, Historical Collections, https://www.cia.gov/readingroom/docs/CIA-RDP82-00457R002800380003-1.pdf; Van Nieuwenhuijze, *Aspects of Islam*, 169.
121. Kahin, *Nationalism and Revolution in Indonesia*, 330; Horikoshi, "Dar ul-Islam Movement," 71.
122. Formichi, *Making of the Nation*, 110–111.
123. Santosa, "S. M. Kartosoewirjo," 41.
124. Boland, *Struggle for Islam*, 40 and 58.
125. Kahin, *Nationalism and Revolution in Indonesia*, 330.
126. Formichi, *Making of the Nation*, 9; Kevin W. Fogg, *Indonesia's Islamic Revolution* (Cambridge: Cambridge University Press, 2020), 116.
127. NII, "Maklumat No. 6," Madinah 20 Sapar 1368/December 21, 1948.
128. Van Dijk, *Banner of Islam*, 1.
129. Formichi, *Making of the Nation*, 11.
130. Santosa, "S. M. Kartosoewirjo," 42.
131. TNI, *Sejarah TNI*, Jilid II, 83.
132. Komandemen Tertinggi Angkatan Perang Negara Islam Indonesia, "Statemen Permerintah Negara Islam Indonesia Nomor VI/7: Perma'luman Perang Resmi Republik Indonesia (Komunis) Kepada Negara Islam Indonesia," September 3, 1953, 4, 5, and 10.
133. Komandemen Tertinggi Angkatan Perang NII, "Statemen Permerintah Negara Islam Indonesia Nomor VI/7," 6, 12.
134. Komandemen Tertinggi Angkatan Perang NII, "Statemen Permerintah Negara Islam Indonesia Nomor VI/7," 9.

135. Komandemen Tertinggi Angkatan Perang NII, "Statemen Permerintah Negara Islam Indonesia Nomor VI/7," 14.

136. Komandemen Tertinggi Angkatan Perang NII, "Statemen Permerintah Negara Islam Indonesia Nomor VI/7," 15.

137. Mr Kermode (Djakarta) to Mr Bevin (London), "Report of a Tour in Java by Mr J. E. Cable," May 8, 1950, FH 1013/21, UKNA.

138. Jackson, *Traditional Authority*, 13; TNI, *Sejarah TNI*, Jilid II, 81.

139. Jackson, *Traditional Authority*, 14; CIA, "Probable Developments in Indonesia," National Intelligence Estimate, NIE-77, June 11, 1953, CIA Archives online, Historical Collections, https://www.cia.gov/readingroom/docs/CIA-RDP79R01012A002500050001-0.pdf; CIA, "Current Intelligence Bulletin," June 22, 1952, 4, CIA Archives online, Historical Collections, https://www.cia.gov/readingroom/docs/CURRENT%20INTELLIGENCE%20BULL%5B15638355%5D.pdf.

140. TNI, *Sejarah TNI*, Jilid II, 82.

141. CIA, "The Present Situation in Indonesia," Memorandum for the Director of Central Intelligence, CIA Office of National Estimates, August 31, 1951, CIA Archives online, Historical Collections, https://www.cia.gov/readingroom/docs/CIA-RDP79R00904A000100020027-2.pdf; CIA, "Security in West Java," CIA Information Report, number redacted, September 29, 1951, CIA Archives online, Historical Collections, https://www.cia.gov/readingroom/docs/CIA-RDP82-00457R008800260011-9.pdf.

142. CIA, "Darul Islam Activity in West Java," Information Report, March 5, 1953, 1, CIA Archives online, Historical Collections, https://www.cia.gov/readingroom/docs/CIA-RDP80-00810A000300430011-9.pdf; TNI, *Sejarah TNI*, Jilid II, 82.

143. Kermode, "Report," May 8, 1950; CIA, "Current Intelligence Digest," OCI No 5178, May 12, 1952, 6, CIA Archives online, Historical Collections, https://www.cia.gov/readingroom/docs/CIA-RDP79T01146A000900300001-0.pdf.

144. Jackson, *Traditional Authority*, 14.

145. CIA, "Activities in Bantam," CIA Information Report, number redacted, January 12, 1950, CIA Archives online, Historical Collections, https://www.cia.gov/readingroom/docs/CIA-RDP82-00457R004100090025-4.pdf.

146. Kementerian Penerangan Republik Indonesia, "Keterangan dan tanggung djawab penjusun, Surat Peperiksaan," Lampiran III, Yogyakarta, September 20, 1950, Serie II/DI, ANRI.

147. CIA, "Current Intelligence Bulletin," April 8, 1952, 5, CIA Archives online, Historical collections, https://www.cia.gov/readingroom/docs/CURRENT%20INTELLIGENCE%20BULL%5B15638450%5D.pdf.

148. CIA, "Current Intelligence Digest," OCI No. 6425, June 23, 1952, 10, CIA Archives online, Historical Collections, https://www.cia.gov/readingroom/docs/CIA-RDP79T01146A001000290001-0.pdf.

149. CIA, "Current Intelligence Digest," OCI No. 6427, June 25, 1952, 6, CIA Archives online, Historical Collections, https://www.cia.gov/readingroom/docs/CIA-RDP79T01146A001100010001-9.pdf.

150. CIA, "Current Intelligence Digest," OCI No 6431, July 1, 1952, 10, CIA Archives online, Historical Collections, https://www.cia.gov/readingroom/docs/CIA-RDP79T01146A001100050001-5.pdf.

151. CIA, "Current Intelligence Digest," OCI No. 9388, September 29, 1952, 3, CIA Archives online, Historical Collections, https://www.cia.gov/readingroom/docs/CIA-RDP79T01146A001300050001-3.pdf.

152. CIA, "Current Intelligence Digest," OCI No 6460, August 12, 1952, 8, CIA Archives online, Historical Collections, https://www.cia.gov/readingroom/docs/CIA-RDP79T01146A001200030001-6.pdf.

153. CIA, "Current Intelligence Digest," June 25, 1952, 6.
154. TNI, *Sejarah TNI*, Jilid II, 83; CIA, "Darul Islam Activity in West Java," CIA Information Report, March 5, 1953, 3; CIA "Current Intelligence Bulletin," April 7, 1955, 4, CIA Archives online, Historical Collections, https://www.cia.gov/readingroom/docs/CURRENT%20INTELLIGENCE%20BULL%5B15722802%5D.pdf.
155. TNI, *Sejarah TNI*, Jilid II, 84.
156. Horikoshi, "Dar ul-Islam Movement," 76.
157. CIA, "Economic Activity in Indonesia," CIA Information Report, number redacted, April 11, 1950, CIA Archives online, Historical Collections, https://www.cia.gov/readingroom/docs/CIA-RDP82-00457R004600440005-2.pdf.
158. TNI, *Sejarah TNI*, Jilid II, 82.
159. TNI, *Sejarah TNI*, Jilid II, 83.
160. TNI, *Sejarah TNI*, Jilid II, 83.
161. TNI, *Sejarah TNI*, Jilid II, 82.
162. Solahudin, *Roots of Terrorism*, 41.
163. Dengel, *Darul-Islam*, 125.
164. Dengel, *Darul-Islam*, 125–126.
165. Horikoshi, "Dar ul-Islam Movement," 76.
166. Horikoshi, "Dar ul-Islam Movement," 75.
167. Horikoshi, "The Dar ul-Islam Movement in West Java," 84.
168. Van Dijk, *Banner of Islam*, 6
169. Van Dijk, *Banner of Islam*, 235.
170. Solahudin, *Roots of Terrorism*, 40; Boland, *Struggle for Islam*, 68; and Van Dijk, *Banner of Islam*, 155.
171. Anhar Gonggong, *Abdul Qahhar Mudzakkar: Dari Patriot hingga Pemberontak* (Jakarta: Gramedia, 1992), 104–105.
172. Boland, *Struggle for Islam*, 65.
173. CIA, "Current Intelligence Digest," OCI No. 9388, September 29, 1952, 9, CIA Archives online, Historical Collections, https://www.cia.gov/readingroom/docs/CIA-RDP79T01146A001300050001-3.pdf.
174. Muhammad Bahar Mattalioe, *Kahar Muzakkar dengan petualangannja* (Jakarta: Delegasi, 1965), 37.
175. TNI, *Sejarah TNI*, Jilid II, 101.
176. Boland, *Struggle for Islam*, 67.
177. TNI, *Sejarah TNI*, Jilid II, 99.
178. TNI, *Sejarah TNI*, Jilid II, 100.
179. Gonggong, *Abdul Qahar Mudzakkar*, 112.
180. Boland, *Struggle for Islam*, 67; Vandenbosch, "Nationalism and Religion in Indonesia," 183.
181. TNI, *Sejarah TNI*, Jilid II, 94.
182. CIA, "Current Intelligence Weekly," October 9, 1953, OCI No 0039, CIA Archives online, Historical Collections, https://www.cia.gov/readingroom/docs/CIA-RDP79-00927A000100190001-2.pdf.
183. CIA, "Current Intelligence Bulletin," September 25, 1953, 3, CIA Archives online, Historical Collections, https://www.cia.gov/readingroom/docs/CURRENT%20INTELLIGENCE%20BULL%5B15677449%5D.pdf; TNI, *Sejarah TNI*, Jilid II, 94.
184. TNI, *Sejarah TNI*, Jilid II, 94.
185. CIA, "NSC Briefing," September 24, 1953, CIA Archives online, Historical Collections, https://www.cia.gov/readingroom/docs/CIA-RDP80R01443R000100350001-3.pdf.

186. CIA, "Current Intelligence Bulletin," September 30, 1953, CIA Archives online, Historical Collections, https://www.cia.gov/readingroom/docs/CURRENT%20INTELLIGENCE%20BULL%5B15677454%5D.pdf.
187. TNI, *Sejarah TNI*, Jilid II, 96.
188. Edward Aspinall, *Islam and Nation: Separatist Rebellion in Aceh, Indonesia* (Stanford, CA: Stanford University Press, 2009), 33.
189. TNI, *Sejarah TNI*, Jilid II, 96: Van Dijk, *Banner of Islam,* 299
190. Kementerian Penerangan, *Sekitar Peristiwa Daud Beureu'eh*, vol. 1 (Jakarta: Kementerian Penerangan, n.d.), 78–79, as cited in Van Dijk, *Banner of Islam*, 299.
191. Letter from Rakjat Pembela Pantja Sila Negara R. I. to the Governor of North Sumatra, Takengon, January 22, 1955, Kabinet Presiden, Bundel IX-1-55, ANRI.
192. TNI, *Sejarah TNI*, Jilid II, 96–97.
193. TNI, *Sejarah TNI*, Jilid II, 97.
194. M. Nur El Ibrahimy, *Peranan Tgk. M. Daud Beureu-eh dalam pergolakan Aceh* (Jakarta: Media Da'wah, 2001), 324–335.
195. TNI, *Sejarah TNI*, Jilid II, 97.
196. See, for example, CIA, "Current Intelligence Bulletin," August 12, 1953, 3, CIA Archives online, Historical Collections, https://www.cia.gov/readingroom/docs/CURRENT%20INTELLIGENCE%20BULL%5B15677448%5D.pdf.
197. Yanuarti, "Intelijen dan Pemberontakan Daerah," 53.
198. TNI, *Sejarah TNI*, Jilid II, 107.
199. Van Dijk, *Banner of Islam*, 258.
200. Van Dijk, *Banner of Islam*, 261.
201. TNI, *Sejarah TNI,* Jilid II, 87; Soeharto, *My Thoughts*, 70. For a more detailed discussion of operations against Darul Islam in Central Java see Nurul Fatimah and Indriyanto, "Penumpasan Gerakan Darul Islam/Tentara Islam Indonesia Kabupaten Tegal 1949–1962," *Historiografi* 1 no. 2 (2020), 135–142.
202. Soeharto, *My Thoughts*, 71.
203. Soeharto, *My Thoughts*, 70.
204. Kermode, "Report," May 8, 1950.
205. TNI, *Sejarah TNI*, Jilid II, 101; ABRI, *Sejarah Pemberontakan dan Penumpasan DI/TII di Sulawesi Selatan dan Kalimantan Selatan* (Jakarta: Pusat Sejarah TNI, 1988), 22–23.
206. Van Dijk, *Banner of Islam*, 251.
207. Kermode, "Report," May 8, 1950.
208. CIA, "Security in West Java," September 29, 1951.
209. CIA, "Daily Digest," CIA No. 49464, December 12, 1951, 6, CIA Archives online, Historical Collections, https://www.cia.gov/readingroom/docs/CIA-RDP79T01146A000600150001-0.pdf.
210. CIA, "Daily Digest," CIA No. 49468, December 18, 1951, 4–5, CIA Archives online, Historical Collections, https://www.cia.gov/readingroom/docs/CIA-RDP79T01146A000600190001-6.pdf.
211. CIA, "Daily Digest," December 12, 1951, 6.
212. CIA, "Current Intelligence Bulletin" April 8, 1952, 5.
213. CIA, "Current Intelligence Bulletin," November 19, 1952, 4, CIA Archives online, Historical Collections, https://www.cia.gov/readingroom/docs/CURRENT%20INTELLIGENCE%20BULL%5B15653023%5D.pdf.
214. CIA, "Current Intelligence Bulletin," September 27, 1953, CIA Archives online, Historical Collections, https://www.cia.gov/readingroom/docs/CURRENT%20INTELLIGENCE%20BULL%5B15677564%5D.pdf.

215. Director of Central Intelligence, "Probable Developments in Indonesia through 1955," National Intelligence Estimate 65–55, NIE65–55, March 1, 1955, 7, CIA Archives online, Historical Collections, https://www.cia.gov/readingroom/docs/CIA-RDP79R01012 A006000030013-0.pdf.
216. Gonggong, *Abdul Qahar Mudzakkar*, 112.
217. Van Dijk, *Banner of Islam*, 243.
218. TNI, *Sejarah TNI*, Jilid II, 91.
219. Soeharto, *My Thoughts*, 67.
220. CIA, "Current Intelligence Bulletin," March 8, 1955, 4, CIA Archives online, Historical Collections, https://www.cia.gov/readingroom/docs/CURRENT%20INTELLIGENCE%20BULL%5B15722756%5D.pdf; CIA, "Probable Developments in Indonesia," June 11, 1953, 5.
221. CIA, "Probable Developments in Indonesia," June 11, 1953, 5.
222. TNI, *Sejarah TNI*, Jilid II, 82.
223. TNI, *Sejarah TNI*, Jilid II, 109.
224. CIA, "Current Intelligence Bulletin," September 1, 1955, 7, CIA Archives online, Historical Collections, https://www.cia.gov/readingroom/docs/CIA-RDP79T00975A002200010001-5.pdf.
225. J. D. Legge, "Guided Democracy and Constitutional Procedures in Indonesia," *Australian Journal of International Affairs* 13, no. 2 (1959), 98.
226. Horikoshi, "Dar ul-Islam Movement," 77; CIA, "Current Intelligence Bulletin," March 5, 1957, 4, CIA Archives online, Historical Collections, https://www.cia.gov/readingroom/docs/CURRENT%20INTELLIGENCE%20BULL%5B15755698%5D.pdf.
227. TNI, *Sejarah TNI*, Jilid II, 86.
228. TNI, *Sejarah TNI*, Jilid II, 87.
229. Yanuarti, "Intelijen dan Pemberontakan Daerah," 63. See also Tempo, *Kartosoewirjo*, 61.
230. Dengel, *Darul-Islam*, 181; Pusat Sejarah Dan Tradisi TNI, *Sejarah TNI*, Jilid III (1960–1965), (Jakarta: Markas Besar Tentara Nasional Indonesia, Pusat Sejarah Dan Tradisi TNI, 2000), 154–155.
231. Yanuarti, "Intelijen dan Pemberontakan Daerah," 65.
232. Jackson, *Traditional Authority*, 18.
233. Horikoshi, "Dar ul-Islam Movement," 77.
234. Boland, *Struggle for Islam*, 62.
235. Solahudin, *Roots of Terrorism*, 43.
236. Gonggong, *Abdul Qahar Mudzakkar*, 393.
237. Van Dijk, *Banner of Islam*, 268.
238. Kartosoewirjo, *Sikap Hidjrah P.S.I.I.*, Bagian 1, 36 and 37.
239. Kartosoewirjo, *Sikap Hidjrah P.S.I.I.*, Bagian 1, 40.
240. Kartosoewirjo, *Daftar—Oesaha Hijrah*, 12.
241. Kartosoewirjo, *Daftar—Oesaha Hijrah*, 11.
242. Kartosoewirjo, *Daftar—Oesaha Hijrah*, 12.
243. Kartosoewirjo, *Daftar—Oesaha Hijrah*, 4 and 8.
244. Jackson, *Traditional Authority*, 15.
245. Jackson, *Traditional Authority*, 16.
246. Van Dijk, *Banner of Islam*, 86; Pinardi, *Sekarmadji Maridjan Kartosoewirjo*, 94.
247. Boland, *Struggle of Islam*, 256–264; Negara Islam Indonesia, "Kanun Asasy," articles 1 and 3.
248. NII, "Kanun Asasy," article 12.
249. NII, "Kanun Asasy," articles 15, 16, 17, and 21.

250. NII, "Kanun Asasy," articles 1 and 2.
251. Jackson, *Traditional Authority*, 4.
252. Van Dijk, *Banner of Islam*, 89.
253. S. M. Kartosoewirjo, "Proclamation of the Islamic State of Indonesia," Medinah-Indonesia, 12 Syawal 1368/August 7, 1949, Appendix A: Documents of the Negara Islam Indonesia, in Jackson, *Traditional Authority*, 318–319.
254. Santosa, "S. M. Kartosoewirjo," 42.
255. NII, "Kanun Asasy," article 33.
256. Komandemen Tertinggi Angkatan Perang NII, "Ma'lumat Militer No. II," March 31, 1949.
257. Jackson, *Traditional Authority*, 16.
258. Van Dijk, *Banner of Islam*, 263.
259. Van Dijk, *Banner of Islam*, 260.
260. Van Dijk, *Banner of Islam*, 420–421.
261. Nazaruddin Sjamsuddin, *The Republican Revolt: A Study of the Acehnese Rebellion* (Singapore: ISEAS, 1985), 237–238.
262. The Acehnese NII banknotes can be found in the collection of old Indonesian banknotes held at the Indonesian Central Bank in Jakarta.
263. Van Dijk, *Banner of Islam*, 192.
264. Van Dijk, *Banner of Islam*, 191.
265. Gonggong, *Abdul Qahar Mudzakkar*, 111; Mattalioe, *Kahar Muzakkar dengan petualangannja*, 112.
266. TNI, *Sejarah TNI*, Jilid II, 100.
267. Mattalioe, *Kahar Muzakkar dengan petualangannja*, 40. See also *Sejarah TNI*, Jilid II, 100.
268. TNI, *Sejarah TNI*, Jilid II, 100.
269. Kahin, *Nationalism and Revolution in Indonesia*, 329.
270. Van Dijk, *Banner of Islam*, 191–192.
271. Van Dijk, *Banner of Islam*, 193.
272. Boland, *struggle of Islam*, 66.
273. Mattalioe, *Kahar Muzakkar dengan petualangannja*, 167.
274. Dewan Fatwa Republik Islam Indonesia Bagian Timur, Peraturan Kehakiman No: 04/P/DF/RII. Bag. T./XII/74, 15 Dzulhidjdjah 1374 (July–August 1955).
275. Peraturan Dharurat No. 4/PD/75 tentang Program Politiek Islam Revolusioner, 2/4/1375 (1955).
276. Pidato Pendjelasan Srd. Abdul Qahar Mudzakkar Dimuka Konperensi Ke (II) Pedjuang Islam Revolusioner Sewilajah Indonesia Bagian Timur Tentang Bai'atnja Untuk Menegakkan Djabatan Sebagai Pimpinan Organisasi Revolusi Islam Di Indonesia Bagian Timur (Termuat Dalam Tjatatan Bathin Djilid Ke (I), Dan Tentang Program Politek Islam Revolusioner, 2/4/1375 [1955]), 7.
277. Pidato Pendjelasan Mudzakkar.
278. Pidato Pendjelasan Mudzakkar, 10.
279. Pidato Pendjelasan Mudzakkar, 12
280. Pidato Pendjelasan Mudzakkar, 11.
281. Audio recording of speech by Abdul Kahar Muzakkar, undated (probably September 1963).
282. Muzakkar speech.
283. Jackson, *Traditional Authority*, 1 and 15.
284. Formichi, *Making of the Nation*, 114.
285. Jackson, *Traditional Authority*, 18.

286. Solahudin, *Roots of Terrorism*, 40.
287. Van Nieuwenhuijze, *Aspects of Islam*, 177; Dengel, *Darul-Islam*, 182; Boland, *Struggle of Islam*, 61; Jackson, *Traditional Authority*, 6; Solahudin, *Roots of Terrorism*, 41.

2. JEMAAH ISLAMIYAH'S JIHAD AND QUEST FOR AN ISLAMIC STATE, 1993-2019

1. Ken Conboy, *The Second Front: Inside Asia's Most Dangerous Terrorist Network* (Jakarta: Equinox Publishing, 2006), 15.
2. Solahudin, *The Roots of Terrorism in Indonesia: From Darul Islam to Jema'ah Islamiyah* (Sydney: New South Wales Press, 2013), 50.
3. Quinton Temby, "Imagining an Islamic State in Indonesia: From Darul Islam to Jemaah Islamiyah," *Indonesia*, no. 89 (2010), 7.
4. Temby, "Imagining an Islamic State," 7.
5. Solahudin, *Roots of Terrorism*, 50.
6. Conboy, *Second Front*, 15.
7. Solahudin, *Roots of Terrorism*, 74-75.
8. Tapol, *Indonesia: Muslims on Trial* (London: Tapol, 1987), 43 and 44.
9. François Raillon, "The New Order and Islam, or the Imbroglio of Faith and Politics," *Indonesia*, no. 57 (April 1993), 200.
10. Michael R. J. Vatikiotis, *Indonesian Politics under Suharto: The Rise and Fall of the New Order* (London: Routledge, 1998), 121; Conboy, *Second Front*, 14.
11. Ken Conboy, *Kopassus: Inside Indonesia's Special Forces* (Jakarta: Equinox Publishing, 2003), 148.
12. Tapol, *Muslims on Trial*, 7; Greg Fealy and Katharine McGregor, "Nahdlatul Ulama and the Killings of 1965-66: Religion, Politics, and Remembrance," *Indonesia*, no. 89 (April 2010), 59-60.
13. Tapol, *Muslims on Trial*, 13.
14. Solahudin, *Roots of Terrorism*, 49; Conboy, *Second Front*, 15.
15. Raillon, "New Order and Islam," 204.
16. Ruth McVey, "Faith as the Outsider: Islam in Indonesian Politics" in *Islam in the Political Process*, ed. James P. Piscatori (Cambridge: Cambridge University Press/Royal Institute of International Affairs, 1983), 217.
17. Tapol, *Muslims on Trial*, 8; Muhammad Natsir as quoted in Muhammad Kamal Hassan, *Muslim Intellectual Responses to "New Order" Modernization in Indonesia* (Kuala Lumpur: Dewan Bahasa dan Pustaka Kementerian Pelajaran Malaysia, 1980), 125.
18. Solahudin, *Roots of Terrorism*, 53.
19. Conboy, *Second Front*, 15.
20. Conboy, *Second Front*, 16-19.
21. Sidney Jones, "New Order Repression and the Birth of Jemaah Islamiyah," in *Soeharto's New Order and its Legacy: Essays in Honour of Harold Crouch*, ed. Edward Aspinall and Greg Fealy (Canberra, ANU Press, 2010), 40.
22. Conboy, *Second Front*, 16.
23. "NII pernah diminta dukung Golkar," *Majalah Darul Islam*, no. 10 (April-May 2001), 38.
24. Interview by Ken Conboy with Major General Himawan Soetanto as quoted in Conboy, *Second Front*, 18.
25. Solahudin, *Roots of Terrorism*, 62.
26. Solahudin, *Roots of Terrorism*, 62; Tapol, *Muslims on Trial*, 35
27. Tapol, *Muslims on Trial*, 15.
28. Vatikiotis, *Indonesian Politics under Suharto*, 128; Tapol, *Muslims on Trial*, 15.

29. Solahudin, *Roots of Terrorism*, 65.
30. Temby, "Imagining an Islamic State," 22.
31. Soeharto, *My Thoughts, Words and Deeds: An Autobiography*, as told to G. Dwipayana and Ramadhan KH (Jakarta: Citra Lamtoro Gung Persada, 1991), 198.
32. Soeharto, *My Thoughts*, 220.
33. Soeharto, *My Thoughts*, 218.
34. Soeharto, *My Thoughts*, 220.
35. McVey, "Faith as the Outsider," 208.
36. Vatikiotis, *Indonesian Politics under Suharto*, 126.
37. Conboy, *Second Front*, 30; Soeharto, *My Thoughts*, 257.
38. Jones, "New Order Repression," 41; McVey, "Faith as the Outsider," 220.
39. Raillon, "New Order and Islam," 202.
40. Vatikiotis, *Indonesian Politics under Suharto*, 121.
41. Carmel Budiardjo, "Militarism and Repression in Indonesia," *Third World Quarterly* 8, no. 4 (October 1986), 1223.
42. Soeharto, *My Thoughts*, 225.
43. Raillon, "New Order and Islam," 208.
44. Solahudin, *Roots of Terrorism*, 80.
45. McVey, "Faith as the Outsider," 203.
46. Leo Suryadinata, "Pancasila and the Challenge of Political Islam: Past and Present", *Trends in Southeast Asia* 14 (2018), 7.
47. Tapol, *Muslims on Trial*, 9.
48. Tapol, *Muslims on Trial*, 10.
49. Budiardjo, "Militarism and Repression in Indonesia," 1225.
50. Raillon, "New Order and Islam," 204.
51. Suryadinata, "Challenge of Political Islam", 6.
52. "Pernyataan Keprihatin," Jakarta, May 5, 1980, in Kelompok Kerja Petisi 50/Pernyataan Kepritatinan, *Meluruskan Perjalanan Orde Baru: Pertanggung Jawaban Petisi 50 Kepada Rakyat Indonesia*, 6, H.A.M. Fatwa Files, Lembaga Bantuan Hukum (LBH) Jakarta.
53. "Pernyataan Keprihatin," 5.
54. Interview with Ustad Akhwan, amir of Jemaah Ansharus Syariah (JAS), Malang, August 7, 2019.
55. Vatikiotis, *Indonesian Politics under Suharto*, 121.
56. Budiardjo, "Militarism and Repression in Indonesia," 1225.
57. Raillon, "New Order and Islam," 198.
58. Tapol, *Muslims on Trial*, 17.
59. Budiardjo, "Militarism and Repression in Indonesia," 1233. The number of 600 is almost certainly too high. Others, such as Michael Vatikiotis, estimated 200 as the upper limit while human rights organization Elsam counted 24 dead and 54 wounded. See Vatikiotis, *Indonesian Politics under Suharto*, 127.
60. "Testimony of Yusron bin Zainuri" at the Dharsono Trial, Appendix I, in Tapol, *Muslims on Trial*, 100.
61. Tapol, *Muslims on Trial*, 109
62. Letter from A. M. Fatwa to the Defense/Legal advisers, November 14, 1985, 3–4.
63. ELSAM, Progress Report #1 Monitoring Pengadilan HAM Tanjung Priok, 4.
64. Peter Burns, "The Post Priok Trials: Religious Principles and Legal Issues," *Indonesia*, no. 47 (April 1989), 64.
65. Tapol, *Muslims on Trial*, vii.
66. Jacques Bertrand, "Legacies of the Authoritarian Past: Religious Violence in Indonesia's Moluccan Islands," *Pacific Affairs* 75, no.1, 68.

67. Harold Crouch, *Political Reform in Indonesia after Suharto* (Singapore: Institute of Southeast Asian Studies, 2010), 245.
68. Bertrand, "Legacies of the Authoritarian Past," 68.
69. Tapol, *Muslims on Trial*, 10.
70. Solahudin, *Roots of Terrorism*, 81 and 79.
71. Interview with Abu Tholut, former head of JI Mantiqi 3, Kudus, August 8, 2017.
72. Conboy, *Second Front*, 26–27.
73. Irfan Suryahardy, *Penjalanan Hukum di Indonesia: Sebuah Gugatan* (Yogyakarta: Ar-Risalah Publishers, 1982), 96 and 129.
74. Jones, "New Order Repression," 43; Conboy, *Second Front*, 29; Suryahardy, *Penjalanan Hukum di Indonesia*, 8.
75. Conboy, *Second Front*, 29–30.
76. "Abdullah Sungkar's Defense Statement" in Suryahardy, *Penjalanan Hukum di Indonesia*, 74–75, 76, 77.
77. "Abdullah Sungkar's Defense Statement," 78; Suryahardy, *Penjalanan Hukum di Indonesia*, 5.
78. "Abdullah Sungkar's Defense Statement," 77.
79. "Abdullah Sungkar's Defense Statement," 84.
80. "Abdullah Sungkar's Defense Statement," 89–90.
81. "Abdullah Sungkar's Defense Statement," 99.
82. "Abu Bakar Ba'asyir's Defense Statement," in *Penjalanan Hukum di Indonesia*, Suryahardy, 137–138, , 145, and 146.
83. "Abdullah Sungkar's Defense Statement," 102, 85. and 87.
84. "Abu Bakar Ba'asyir's Defense Statement," 135.
85. Sermon 16 by Abdullah Sungkar, audio file "U Abdullah Sungkar 16,"n.d., ca. 1984, Internet Archive, https://archive.org/details/audio_abdullah_sungkar/U_Abdullah_Sungkar_16.mp3
86. Sermon 5 by Abdullah Sungkar, "U Abdullah Sungkar 5," n.d., ca. 1984, Internet Archive, https://archive.org/details/audio_abdullah_sungkar/U_Abdullah_Sungkar_5.mp3.
87. Sermon 5 by Abdullah Sungkar.
88. Sermon 5 by Abdullah Sungkar.
89. Sermon 7 by Abdullah Sungkar, audio file "U Abdullah Sungkar 7," n.d., ca. 1984, Internet Archive, https://archive.org/details/audio_abdullah_sungkar/U_Abdullah_Sungkar_7.mp3.
90. Jones, "New Order Repression," 46.
91. Conboy, *Second Front*, 31; Jones, "New Order Repression," 46.
92. Tapol, *Muslims on Trial*, 90.
93. Tapol, *Muslims on Trial*, 90.
94. Jones, "New Order Repression," 40.
95. Conboy, *Second Front*, 32.
96. Conboy, *Second Front*, 32.
97. Jones, "New Order Repression," 45.
98. Solahudin, *The Roots of Terrorism in Indonesia*, 143–144. See also Kirsten E. Schulze and Julie Chernov Hwang, "From Afghanistan to Syria: How the Global Remains Local for Indonesian Islamist Militants," in *Exporting the Global Jihad: "Critical" Perspectives from Asia and North America*, ed. Tom Smith and Kirsten E. Schulze (London: IB Tauris, 2020), 19.
99. Majelis Qiyadah Markaziyah Jemaah Islamiyah, *Pedoman Umum Perjuangan Al Jemaah Al Islamiyah (General Guidelines for the Struggle of Jemaah Islamiyah* (PUPJI), 1996, 12–13.

100. For a more detailed discussion of JI see International Crisis Group (ICG), "Indonesia Briefing, Al-Qaeda in Southeast Asia: The Case of the 'Ngruki Network' in Indonesia" (Jakarta and Brussels: ICG, August 8, 2002) and ICG, "Indonesia Backgrounder: How the Jemaah Islamiyah Terrorist Network Operates," Asia Report No. 43 (Jakarta and Brussels: ICG, December 11, 2002). For further reading on Mantiqi Ukhro see Shandon Harris-Hogan and Andrew Zammit, "Mantiqi IV: Al-Qaeda's Failed Co-Optation of a Jemaah Islamiyah Support Network," *Democracy and Security* 10, no. 4 (2014): 315–334.

101. Interview with Abu Rusdan, senior JI member, Kudus, August 8, 2017.

102. Solahudin, *Roots of Terrorism*, 126.

103. Schulze and Chernov Hwang, "From Afghanistan to Syria," 15.

104. Nasir Abas, *Membongkar Jamaah Islamiyah: Pengakuan Mantan Ketua JI* (Jakarta: Grafindo Khazanah Ilmu, 2005), 148–165.

105. Communication with Nasir Abas, former head of Mantiqi 3 and JI trainer, August 22, 2021; communication with Abu Tholut, former head of Mantiqi 3, August 23, 2021.

106. Interview with Syaiful, former JI member, Solo, August 19, 2015; interview with Jibril, former JI member, Jakarta, November 4, 2010; interview with Farihin, former JI member, Jakarta, August 15, 2017.

107. Interview with Abdullah Sonata, head of Kompak Ambon 2000–2001, Jakarta, December 7, 2010.

108. Interview with Zuheb, former JI member, Jakarta, December 7, 2010.

109. Interview with Abdullah Sonata, December 7, 2010.

110. For a more comprehensive discussion of the Ambon jihad see Kirsten E. Schulze, "From Ambon to Poso: Comparative and Evolutionary Aspects of Local Jihad in Indonesia," *Contemporary Southeast Asia* 41, no. 1 (2019).

111. For a more comprehensive discussion of the Poso jihad see Schulze, "From Ambon to Poso." See also Dave McRae, *A Few Poorly Organised Men: Inter-Religious Violence in Poso, Indonesia* (Leiden: Brill Academic Publishers, 2013).

112. "Indonesia Car Bomb Kills Two, Injures Philippine Ambassador," *Wall Street Journal*, August 2, 2000.

113. Interview with Farihin, August 15, 2017.

114. ICG, "Jemaah Islamiyah Terrorist Network," 7.

115. Interview with Abu Bakar Ba'asyir, cofounder of Jemaah Islamiyah, Jakarta, September 2, 2003.

116. Interview with Abu Tholut, August 8, 2017.

117. Interview with Nasir Abas, former head of JI Mantiqi 3, Jakarta, September 13, 2007.

118. ICG, "Jemaah Islamiyah Terrorist Network," 27–28.

119. Interview with Abu Bakar Ba'asyir, September 2, 2003.

120. International Istimata Battalion, "Statement," in *Voices of Islam in Southeast Asia: A Contemporary Sourcebook*, ed. Greg Fealy and Virginia Hooker (Singapore: Institute of Southeast Asian Studies, 2006), 372.

121. Imam Samudra, *Aku Melawan Teroris* (Solo: Jazera, 2004), 114.

122. Aly Ghufron bin Nurhasyim (Mukhlas), "Jihad Bom Bali: Sebuah Pembelaan. Operasi Peledakan Bom Legian dan Renon. 12 Oktober 2002," in Fealy and Hooker, *Voices of Islam in Southeast Asia*, 381.

123. Aly Ghufron, "Jihad Bom Bali," 382.

124. Aly Ghufron, "Jihad Bom Bali," 382.

125. Ali Imron, *Ali Imron Sang Pengebom* (Jakarta: Republika, 2007), 41–47.

126. For a detailed discussion of Noordin's network see ICG, "Terrorism in Indonesia: Noordin's Networks," Asia Report no. 114 (Jakarta and Brussels: ICG, August 5, 2006). See also Setya Krisna Sumargo, *Noordin M. Top & Co: The Untold Stories* (Jakarta: Kompas Gramedia, 2009).

127. Interview with Abu Rusdan, senior JI member, Kudus, April 6, 2016.
128. ICG, "Jemaah Islamiyah Terrorist Network," 4–5.
129. ICG, "Jemaah Islamiyah Terrorist Network," 5.
130. Interview with Abu Tholut, August 8, 2017.
131. Interview with Nasir Abas, former head of Mantiqi 3, Jakarta, September 13, 2007.
132. Interview with Nasir Abas, September 13, 2007; Quinton Temby, "Jihadists Assemble: The Rise of Militant Islamism in Southeast Asia" (PhD diss., Australian National University, 2017), 193; Solahudin, *Roots of Terrorism*, 171.
133. Julie Chernov Hwang, "Dakwah before Jihad: Understanding the Behaviour of Jemaah Islamiyah," *Contemporary Southeast Asia* 41, no. 1 (2019): 23.
134. See ICG, "Jihadism in Indonesia: Poso on the Edge," Asia Report no. 127 (Jakarta and Brussels: ICG, January 24, 2007).
135. For a more detailed discussion of the changes in JI see Sidney Jones, "The Changing Nature of Jemaah Islamiyah," *Australian Journal of International Affairs* 59, no. 2 (June 2005): 169–187; Gillian S. Oak, "Jemaah Islamiyah's Fifth Phase: The Many Faces of a Terrorist Organisation," *Studies in Conflict and Terrorism* 33, no. 11 (2010): 989–1018; Institute for Policy Analysis of Conflict (IPAC), "The Re-emergence of Jemaah Islamiyah," IPAC Report no. 36 (April 27, 2017).
136. Interview with Abu Rusdan, April 6, 2016.
137. Interview with Abu Rusdan, April 6, 2016.
138. Sermon 7 by Abdullah Sungkar.
139. Sermon 11 by Abdullah Sungkar, audio file "U Abdullah Sungkar 11,"n.d., ca. 1984, Internet Archive, https://archive.org/details/audio_abdullah_sungkar/U_Abdullah_Sungkar_11.mp3.
140. Abu Bakar Ba'asyir, *Demokrasi Adalah Bisikan Setan Yang Berperan Menghancurkan Tauhid & Iman*, Buku V (JAT Publishing, n.d.), 33.
141. Ba'asyir, *Demokrasi Adalah Bisikan Setan*, 46.
142. Ba'asyr, *Demokrasi Adalah Bisikan Setan*, 52; interview with Abu Bakar Ba'asyir, cofounder of Jemaah Islamiyah, Jakarta, September 2, 2003.
143. Interview with Sheikh Abdullah Sungkar, the Amir of the Islamic Group, "Soeharto's 'Detect, Deflect and Destroy' Policy Towards the Islamic Movement," *Nida'ul Islam*, no. 17 (February–March 1997), https://www.islam.org.au/articles/17/indonesia.htm.
144. Sermon 1 by Abdullah Sungkar, audio file "U Abdullah Sungkar 1," n.d., ca. 1984, Internet Archive, https://archive.org/details/audio_abdullah_sungkar/U_Abdullah_Sungkar_1.mp3; interview with Sheikh Abdullah Sungkar.
145. Sermon 5 by Abdullah Sungkar; Ba'asyir, *Demokrasi Adalah Bisikan Setan*, 40 and 53.
146. Interview with Abu Bakar Ba'asyir, cofounder of Jemaah Islamiyah, Jakarta, September 2, 2003.
147. Sungkar, interview.
148. Sungkar, interview.
149. Ba'asyir, *Demokrasi Adalah Bisikan Setan*, 54.
150. Ba'asyir, *Demokrasi Adalah Bisikan Setan*, 54, 58.
151. Ba'asyir, *Demokrasi Adalah Bisikan Setan*, 65.
152. Sungkar, interview.
153. Ba'asyir, *Demokrasi Adalah Bisikan Setan*, 41.
154. Ba'asyir, *Demokrasi Adalah Bisikan Setan*, 42.
155. Ba'asyir, *Demokrasi Adalah Bisikan Setan*, 45.
156. Interview with Abu Bakar Ba'asyir, cofounder of Jemaah Islamiyah, Jakarta, September 2, 2003.

157. Majelis Qiyadah Markaziyah JI, *PUPJI*, 29
158. Majelis Qiyadah Markaziyah JI, *PUPJI*, 12 and 14
159. Majelis Qiyadah Markaziyah JI, *PUPJI*, 15
160. Majelis Qiyadah Markaziyah JI, *PUPJI*, 22.
161. Majelis Qiyadah Markaziyah JI, *PUPJI*, 169.
162. Majelis Qiyadah Markaziyah JI, *PUPJI*, 29, 28
163. Ghufron, "Jihad Bom Bali," 379.
164. Ghufron, "Jihad Bom Bali," 379.
165. Schulze, "From Ambon to Poso."
166. Interview with Abu Rusdan, August 6, 2019.
167. Interview with Abu Rusdan, August 8, 2017.
168. Interview with Abu Rusdan, April 6, 2016.
169. Majelis Qiyadah Markaziyah JI, PUPJI, 169.
170. Majelis Qiyadah Markaziyah JI, PUPJI, 170.
171. Interview with Para Wijayanto, former JI amir, Jakarta, August 11, 2023.
172. Interview with Para Wijayanto, August 11, 2023; Markas Besar Kepolisian Republik Indonesia, Detasemen Khusus 88 Anti Teror, "Berita Acara Pemeriksaan (BAP) Ir. PARA WIJAYANTO alias ABANG alias MAS alias ABU ASKARY alias ABU FAIZ alias AJI PANGESTU alias AJI alias AHMAD ARIF alias AHMAD FAUZI UTOMO", July 19, 2019, 28.
173. Interview with Abu Rusdan, senior JI member, Kudus, March 26, 2018.
174. Ust. Abu Rusydan, "Perbedaan Pancasila dengan Islam," *An-Najah TV*, July 25, 2018, accessed September 9, 2021, youtube.com/watch?v=8E3wwqwMPNY.)
175. Interview with Para Wijayanto, August 11, 2023.
176. Interview with Para Wijayanto, August 11, 2023.
177. "BAP Para Wijayanto", 28.
178. "BAP Para Wijayanto", 28–31.
179. Interview with midlevel JI commander, August 5, 2019.
180. "BAP Para Wijayanto", 32.
181. "BAP Para Wijayanto."
182. "BAP Para Wijayanto", 45 and 55.
183. Interview with Para Wijayanto, August 11, 2023.
184. Interview with Abu Rusdan, April 6, 2016.
185. Interview with Abu Rusdan, March 26, 2018.
186. Interview with Abu Rusdan, March 26, 2018.
187. Interview with Abu Rusdan, March 26, 2018.
188. Interview with Abu Rusdan, March 26, 2018.
189. Abu Rusydan, "Dengan Inilah Islam Tegak!", *Kiblat TV*, December 8, 2017, accessed September 19, 2021, youtube.com/watch?v=cdZc9agO6n4.
190. Interview with midlevel JI commander, August 5, 2019.
191. Interview with Para Wijayanto, August 11, 2023.
192. "BAP Para Wijayanto", 48.
193. Interview with Abu Rusdan, March 26, 2018.
194. Interview with Abu Rusdan, March 26, 2018.
195. Interview with Abu Rusdan, August 8, 2017.
196. Interview with Abu Rusdan, August 6, 2019.
197. Interview with Abu Rusdan, March 26, 2018.
198. Interview with Abu Rusdan, March 26, 2018.
199. JI, "Laporan Akhir Tahun 2013 Dit Tar," Slides 22–26.
200. Interview with midlevel JI commander, August 5, 2019.

3. THE EAST TIMOR CONFLICT, 1975-1999

1. Sukarno, "Lahirnya Pancasila, speech given on June 1, 1945.
2. Sukarno, "Lahirnya Pancasila."
3. *Antara*, February 1, 1950.
4. John G. Taylor, *Indonesia's Forgotten War: The Hidden History of East Timor* (London: Zed Books, 1991), 22; Janet Gunter, "Communal Conflict in Viqueque and the 'Charged' History of '59'," *Asia Pacific Journal of Anthropology* 8, no. 1 (2007): 30.
5. James Dunn, *East Timor: A Rough Passage to Independence* (Double Bay, NSW: Longueville Media, 2003), 27-28; Taylor, *Indonesia's Forgotten War*, 22.
6. Jose Manuel Duarte, a Timorese leader of the Viqueque uprising interviewed by Jill Jolliffe on November 11, 1978, as cited in Taylor, *Indonesia's Forgotten War*, 21.
7. Gunter, "Communal Conflict in Viqueque," 35; Kiki Syahnakri, *Timor Timur: The Untold Story* (Jakarta: Kompas, 2013), 145.
8. Ruslan Abdulgani speech at protest rally on Angola, sponsored by the Afro-Asian People's Solidarity Organization, Jakarta, July 12, 1961, as cited in Donald E. Weatherbee, "Portuguese Timor: An Indonesian Dilemma," *Asian Survey* 6, no. 1 (December 1966), 689.
9. Subandrio, "Statement to the Plenary Session of the Dewan Perwakilan Rakjat," July 3, 1961.
10. Weatherbee, "Portuguese Timor," 691.
11. Dunn, *East Timor*, 87.
12. CIA, "Central Intelligence Bulletin, Daily Brief," October 25, 1962, 6, CIA Archives online, Historical Collections, https://www.cia.gov/readingroom/docs/CIA-RDP79T00975A006600460001-8.pdf.
13. CIA, "Central Intelligence Bulletin, Daily Brief," October 25, 1962, 6.
14. Taylor, *Indonesia's Forgotten War*, 21.
15. General Mokoginta interviewed in the *Washington Post*, May 10, 1963.
16. Lefo Ikhtisar, "Kilas Balik: Sesungguhnya, Dulu Timtim Masuk Ternate," *LEFO*, https://lefo.id/menulis/tulisan/98/kilas-balik-sesungguhnya-dulu-timtim-masuk-ternate.
17. Taylor, *Indonesia's Forgotten War*, 23.
18. Soeharto, *My Thoughts, Words and Deeds: An Autobiography*, as told to G. Dwipayana and Ramadhan KH (Jakarta: Citra Lamtoro Gung Persada, 1991), 273.
19. Dunn, *East Timor*, 90.
20. UDT Manifesto, Dili, May 11, 1974, as cited in Robert Lawless, "The Indonesian Takeover of East Timor," *Asian Survey* 16, no. 10 (October 1976): 949.
21. Don Greenlees and Robert Garran, *Deliverance: The Inside Story of East Timor's Fight for Freedom* (Crows Nest, NSW: Allen & Unwin, 2002), 4; Lawless, "Indonesian Takeover," 949.
22. Greenlees and Garran, *Deliverance*, 5.
23. Frente Revolucionária do Timor-Leste Independente (FRETILIN), "FRETILIN Chronology up to the Restoration of Independence," August 1, 2007, accessed January 5, 2011, www.timortruth.com/articles/FRETILIN_chronology_1970_to_2002.pdf.
24. Greenlees and Garran, *Deliverance*, 4.
25. Interview with Father Martin, SJ, Dili, East Timor, August 23, 1999; José Ramos-Horta, *Funu: The Unfinished Saga of East Timor* (Trenton, NJ: The Red Sea Press, 1987), 38.
26. Arnold S. Kohen, *From the Place of the Dead: The Epic Struggles of Bishop Belo of East Timor* (New York: St. Martin's Griffin, 1999), 72; Xanana Gusmão, *To Resist Is to Win! The Autobiography of Xanana Gusmão with Selected Letters & Speeches Edited by Sara Niner* (Kew East, Victoria: Aurora Books, David Lovell Publishing, 2000), 43.

27. "Ideological Turnaround," Message from Xanana Gusmão, FALINTIL commander-in-chief, CRRN Headquarters, East Timor, December 7, 1987, in Gusmão, *To Resist Is to Win!*, 131.

28. Annex A, Portuguese Timor, annex to Background Brief: External Relations of Indonesia for Sir Michael Palliser's visit to Indonesia 21–22 October 1975, 1, National Security Archive, George Washington University (GWU), https://nsarchive2.gwu.edu/NSAEBB/NSAEBB174/uk08.pdf.

29. Ramos-Horta, *Funu*, 35; Jacques Bertrand, *Nationalism and Ethnic Conflict in Indonesia* (Cambridge: Cambridge University Press, 2004), 137.

30. Jill Jolliffe, *East Timor: Nationalism & Colonialism* (St. Lucia: University of Queensland Press, 1978), 72.

31. Gusmão, *To Resist Is to Win!*, 66.

32. APODETI manifesto, Dili, May 27, 1974, as cited in Lawless, "Indonesian Takeover," 949.

33. Annex A, Portuguese Timor, 1.

34. Gunter, "Communal Conflict in Viqueque," 35.

35. Greenlees and Garran, *Deliverance*, 5.

36. CIA, "Staff Notes: East Asia," February 10, 1975, 1–2.

37. Ken Conboy, *Kopassus: Inside Indonesia's Special Forces* (Jakarta: Equinox Publishing, 2003), 206.

38. Memorandum to President Ford from Henry A. Kissinger, "Your Visit to Indonesia," November 21, 1975, 1, Record Group 59, Department of State Records, Executive Secretarial Briefing Books 1958–1976, box 227, President Ford's visit to the Far East—Indonesia, November–December 1975, Gerald R. Ford Library.

39. Paul M. Monk, "Secret Intelligence and Escape Clauses: Australia and the Indonesian Annexation of ET, 1963–76," *Critical Asian Studies* 33, no. 2 (2001): 187.

40. Letter from Feakes to McCredie, Canberra, June 6, 1974, document 10, in *Documents on Australian Foreign Policy: Australian and the Indonesian Incorporation of Portuguese Timor, 1974–1976*, ed. Wendy Way (Canberra: Department of Foreign Affairs and Trade, 2000), 59–60.

41. Record of Meeting between Whitlam and Soeharto, State Guest House Yogyakarta, September 6, 1974, Department of Foreign Affairs Australia, historical documents, https://www.dfat.gov.au/about-us/publications/historical-documents/Pages/volume-20/26-record-of-meeting-between-whitlam-and-soeharto.

42. CIA, "Staff Notes: Western Europe—Canada—Organizations," February 21, 1975, 5, CIA Archives, Historical Collections, https://www.cia.gov/readingroom/docs/CIA-RDP79T00865A000400150001-2.pdf.

43. Clinton Fernandes, *The Independence of East Timor: Multi-Dimensional Perspectives—Occupation, Resistance, and International Political Activism* (Brighton: Sussex Academic Press, 2011), 30; Dunn, *East Timor*, 70.

44. CIA, "Staff Notes: Western Europe—Canada—Organizations," February 21, 1975, 5.

45. United States Intelligence Board (USIB), "National Intelligence Bulletin," March 1, 1975, 11, CIA Archives, Historical Collections, https://www.cia.gov/readingroom/docs/CIA-RDP79T00975A027500010002-4.pdf.

46. USIB, "National Intelligence Bulletin," May 10, 1975, 13, CIA Archives, Historical Collections, https://www.cia.gov/readingroom/docs/CIA-RDP79T00975A0277000 10018-5.pdf.

47. CIA, "Staff Notes: Western Europe," June 11, 1975, 2, https://www.cia.gov/readingroom/docs/CIA-RDP86T00608R000500040019-4.pdf.

48. Conboy, *Kopassus*, 205.

49. Geoffrey Robinson, "People's War: Militias in East Timor and Indonesia," *South East Asia Research* 9, no. 3 (2001): 294; Conboy, *Kopassus*, 206; Australian Ambassador Woolcott, Dispatch to Willesee, June 2, 1975, document 137 in Way, *Documents on Australian Foreign Policy*, 267.

50. Conboy, *Kopassus*, 207.

51. Greenlees and Garran, *Deliverance*, 7.

52. Ramos-Horta, *Funu*, 65.

53. Ramos-Horta, *Funu*, 51.

54. Conboy, *Kopassus*, 206.

55. Conboy, *Kopassus*, 208.

56. Fernandes, *Independence of East Timor*, 34.

57. J. A. Ford, British Embassy Djakarta, to PJE Male Esq. FCO, July 14, 1975, 1, National Security Archive, GWU, https://nsarchive2.gwu.edu/NSAEBB/NSAEBB174/uk03.pdf.

58. Ford to Male, 1.

59. Greenlees and Garran, *Deliverance*, 10

60. CIA, "Weekly Summary," No. 0033/75, August 15, 1975, 13, CIA Archives, Historical Collections, https://www.cia.gov/readingroom/docs/CIA-RDP86T00608R000 300020036-9.pdf.

61. Annex A, Portuguese Timor, 2 National Security Archive, GWU.

62. Fernandes, *Independence of East Timor*, 37; Ramos-Horta, *Funu*, 55.

63. Ramos-Horta, *Funu*, 55.

64. Her Majesty's Ambassador to Jakarta to the Secretary of State for Foreign & Commonwealth Affairs, "Timor: Indonesia's Reluctant Takeover," Diplomatic Report No 182/76, March 15, 1976, FAJ 014/1, 3, National Security Archive, GWU, https://nsarchive2.gwu.edu/NSAEBB/NSAEBB174/uk25.pdf.

65. USIB, "National Intelligence Bulletin," August 22, 1975, 3, CIA Archives, Historical Collections, https://www.cia.gov/readingroom/docs/CIA-RDP79T00975A028000 010050-5.pdf.

66. Report on a visit to East Timor for the Timor Task Force of the Australian Council for Overseas Aid, October 1975, 17, File RCC/1/12/4/125 Portuguese Timor, Assistance, British Red Cross Archives.

67. Conboy, *Kopassus*, 224.

68. Greenlees and Garran, *Deliverance*, 10

69. Telex from Hocke, Director of Operations, to Geneva, October 15, 1975, File RCC/1/12/4/125 Portuguese Timor, Assistance, British Red Cross Archives. See also "Brief Report on Indonesian Red Cross Programme in East Timor Affair," 1, received January 21, 1976, File RCC/1/12/4/125 Portuguese Timor, Assistance, British Red Cross Archives.

70. J. A. Ford, British Embassy Jakarta to C. W. Squire Esq., South East Asian Department FCO, September 15, 1975, 1, National Security Archive, GWU, https://nsarchive2.gwu.edu/NSAEBB/NSAEBB174/uk05.pdf.

71. Conboy, *Kopassus*, 228.

72. Jakarta to FCO, Tel No. 394 of October 24, 1975, 1, National Security Archive, GWU, https://nsarchive2.gwu.edu/NSAEBB/NSAEBB174/uk14.pdf.

73. Lawless, "Indonesian Takeover," 953.

74. USIB, "National Intelligence Bulletin," December 2, 1975, 5, CIA Archives, Historical Collections, https://www.cia.gov/readingroom/docs/CIA-RDP79T00975A02840 0010004-2.pdf.

75. FM FCO to certain missions Tel No. Guidance 213 of December 5, 1975, "Portuguese Timor," 3, National Security Archive, GWU, https://nsarchive2.gwu.edu/NSAEBB /NSAEBB174/uk17.pdf.

76. US Embassy in Jakarta Telegram 1579 to Secretary of State, "Ford-Suharto Meeting," December 6, 1975, section 3 of 3, 1, Kissinger-Scowcroft Temporary Parallel File, box A3, Country File: Far East-Indonesia, State Department Telegrams, Gerald R. Ford Library.

77. US Embassy in Jakarta Telegram 1579 to Secretary of State, "Ford-Suharto Meeting," December 6, 1975.

78. Christopher Sweeney, "Indonesians Capture Capital in Air-Sea Invasion of Timor," *Guardian*, December 8, 1975.

79. *Hari "H": 7 Desember 1975: Reuni 40 Tahun Operasi Lintas Udara di Dili, Timor Portugis* (Jakarta: Kata Hasta Pustaka, 2015), xiv.

80. Sweeney, "Indonesians Capture Capital."

81. Conboy, *Kopassus*, 243–248; Her Majesty's Ambassador to Jakarta to the Secretary of State for Foreign & Commonwealth Affairs, "Timor: Indonesia's Reluctant Takeover," March 15, 1976.

82. Taylor, *Indonesia's Forgotten War*, 69.

83. Ramos-Horta, *Funu*, 107.

84. Conboy, *Kopassus*, 243–248; *Hari "H*," 27.

85. Her Majesty's Ambassador to Jakarta to the Secretary of State for Foreign & Commonwealth Affairs, "Timor: Indonesia's Reluctant Takeover," March 15, 1976.

86. *Hari "H*," 9.

87. Interview with Lieutenant General (ret.) Luhut Panjaitan, East Timor veteran, Jakarta, April 7, 2005.

88. *Hari "H*," 27.

89. Her Majesty's Ambassador to Jakarta to the Secretary of State for Foreign & Commonwealth Affairs, "Timor: Indonesia's Reluctant Takeover," March 15, 1976; Dunn, *East Timor*, 244.

90. "Interview with Former Bishop of East Timor," *TAPOL Bulletin No. 59*, September 1983, 3.

91. "Massacres and Torture in East Timor," *TAPOL Bulletin No. 20*, February 1977, 7. See also Dunn, *East Timor*, 244–245.

92. Jill Jolliffe, *Balibo* (Melbourne: Scribe Publications, 2009), 4; Constancio Pinto and Matthew Jardine, *East Timor's Unfinished Struggle: Inside the Timorese Resistance* (Boston: South End Press, 1997), 80.

93. Taylor, *Indonesia's Forgotten War*, 69; "East Timor; 'Catholic Priest Calls for Sanctions,'" *TAPOL Bulletin No. 36*, October 1979, 4; Greenlees and Garran, *Deliverance*, 14.

94. CIA, "The President's Daily Brief," December 18, 1975, 8, CIA Archives, Historical Collections, https://www.cia.gov/readingroom/docs/DOC_0006014982.pdf.

95. Matthew Jardine, *East Timor: Genocide in Paradise* (Monroe, ME: Odonian Press/Common Courage Press, 1995), 35.

96. Douglas Kammen, *Three Centuries of Conflict in East Timor* (New Brunswick, NJ: Rutgers University Press, 2015), 130.

97. Lawless, "Indonesian Takeover," 956.

98. *International Herald Tribune*, March 8, 1978.

99. "Pejuang Seroja yang Gugur dan Kekerasan Tahun 1974–1999," https://kisah timortimur.wordpress.com/2015/03/19/pejuang-seroja-yang-gugur-dan-kekerasan-tahaun-1975-1999/.

100. USIB, "National Intelligence Bulletin," December 8, 1975, 1, CIA Archives, Historical Collections, https://www.cia.gov/readingroom/docs/CIA-RDP79T00975A028400 010014-1.pdf.

101. Jardine, *East Timor*, 52; CIA, "The President's Daily Brief," December 18, 1975, 9.

102. *Hari "H*," 11.

103. *Hari "H,"* 38.
104. CIA, "The President's Daily Brief," December 18, 1975, 8.
105. Greenlees and Garran, *Deliverance*, 17.
106. Ramos-Horta, *Funu*, 120. See also Pinto and Jardine, *East Timor's Unfinished Struggle*, 59.
107. Reception, Truth and Reconciliation in East Timor (CAVR), *Chega! Report*, part 5: Resistance: Structure and Strategy, "FRETILIN and the Base de Apoio," 5.2 (31), presented to President of East Timor on October 31, 2005, accessed on October 21, 2021, http://www.cavr-timorleste.org/en/chegaReport.htm.
108. "East Timor; 'Catholic Priest Calls for Sanctions,'" *TAPOL Bulletin No. 36*, October 1979, 4.
109. Taylor, *Indonesia's Forgotten War*, 85.
110. Amnesty International, *East Timor: Violation of Human Rights* (London: Amnesty International, 1985), 29.
111. Taylor, *Indonesia's Forgotten War*, 85.
112. "Life during the Resistance," interview with Neobere, *TAPOL Bulletin No. 60*, November 1983, 16.
113. Pinto and Jardine, *East Timor's Unfinished Struggle*, 64.
114. *Radio Maubere* as reported in "East Timor Update," *TAPOL Bulletin No. 24*, October 1977, 8.
115. Paul Hainsworth and Stephen McCloskey, eds., *The East Timor Question: The Struggle for Independence from Indonesia* (London: IB Tauris, 2000), 5.
116. Jardine, *East Timor*, 55.
117. Bertrand, *Nationalism and Ethnic Conflict*, 138; Geoffrey Robinson, "People Power: A Comparative History of Forced Displacement in East Timor," in *Conflict, Violence and Displacement in Indonesia*, ed. Eva-Lotta E. Hedman (Ithaca, NY: Southeast Asia Program Publications, Cornell University, 2008), 97.
118. Gerry van Klinken, "Death by Deprivation in East Timor 1975–1980," World Peace Foundation, Reinventing Peace, April 17, 2012, https://sites.tufts.edu/reinventingpeace/2012/04/17/death-by-deprivation-in-east-timor-1975-1980/.
119. Robinson, "People Power," 89
120. Bertrand, *Nationalism and Ethnic Conflict*, 138.
121. Conboy, *Kopassus*, 258.
122. Greenlees and Garran, *Deliverance*, 16.
123. CAVR, Part 5: Resistance: Structure and Strategy, 5.4 (100).
124. Gusmão, *To Resist Is to Win!*, 67.
125. TNI, *Sejarah TNI*: Jilid IV (1966–1983) (Jakarta: Markas Besar Tentara Nasional Indonesia Pusat Sejarah dan Tradisi TNI, 2000), 153.
126. Syahnakri, *Timor Timur*, 73.
127. "East Timor: New Offensive, Mass Arrests," *TAPOL Bulletin No. 47*, September 1981, 1; Greenlees and Garran, *Deliverance*, 18.
128. "East Timor: New Military Offensive May Be Under Way," *TAPOL Bulletin No. 45*, May 1981, 4.
129. Syahnakri, *Timor Timur*, 92.
130. Syahnakri, *Timor Timur*, 75.
131. Syahnakri, *Timor Timur*, 85.
132. Cristiano da Costa quoted in Jardine, *East Timor*, 56.
133. Cristiano da Costa quoted in Jardine, *East Timor*, 56–57.
134. TNI, *Sejarah TNI*, Jilid IV, 153
135. Jardine, *East Timor*, 57.
136. Syahnakri, *Timor Timur*, 111–114.

137. Jardine, *East Timor*, 57–58.
138. Interview with Lieutenant General (ret.) Z. A. Maulani, former head of BAKIN, Tangerang, April 24, 2001.
139. *Age* (Melbourne), August 18, 1983.
140. Dunn, *East Timor*, 92.
141. CAVR, *Chega! Report*, "Part 6: Profile of Human Rights Violations in Timor Leste 1974 to 1999," 6.1.1 (8).
142. Robinson, "People Power," 89.
143. Taylor, *Indonesia's Forgotten War*, 71 and 80.
144. Robert Cribb, "From Total People's Defence to Massacre: Explaining Indonesia's Military Violence in ET" in *Roots of Violence in Indonesia*, ed. Freek Colombijn and J. Thomas Lindblad (Leiden: KITLV Press, 2002), 235.
145. *Hari "H,"* xi.
146. Taylor, *Indonesia's Forgotten War*, 70; Kammen, *Three Centuries of Conflict*, 133.
147. "Catholic Priest Calls for Sanctions," 4; "Massacres and Torture in East Timor," *TAPOL Bulletin No. 20*, February 1977, 7.
148. CAVR, *Chega! Report*, Part 5: Resistance: Structure and Strategy 5.2 (63).
149. CAVR, *Chega! Report*, Part 5: Resistance: Structure and Strategy 5.2 (62).
150. CAVR, *Chega! Report*, Part 5: Resistance: Structure and Strategy 5.2 (66, 67).
151. Sara Niner, *Xanana: Leader of the Struggle for an Independent Timor-Leste* (Melbourne: Australian Scholarly Publishing, 2009), 134.
152. Gusmão, *To Resist Is to Win!*, 42.
153. CAVR, *Chega! Report*, Part 5: Resistance: Structure and Strategy, 5.2 (73, 74).
154. CAVR, *Chega! Report*, Part 5: Resistance: Structure and Strategy, 5.2 (72, 76, 84).
155. Gusmão, *To Resist Is to Win!*, 50–51.
156. Gusmão, *To Resist Is to Win!*, 51.
157. CAVR, *Chega! Report*, Part 5: Resistance: Structure and Strategy, 5.2 (87).
158. Kohen, *Place of the Dead*, 84.
159. Kohen, *Place of the Dead*, 109–110.
160. "Interview with Former Bishop of East Timor," *TAPOL Bulletin No. 59*, September 1983, 3–8.
161. Kohen, *Place of the Dead*, 116.
162. "Church Refusing to Cooperate at All Levels," *TAPOL Bulletin No. 63*, May 1984, 1.
163. "Ideological Turnaround," Gusmão, in Gusmão, *To Resist Is to Win!*, 131; Gusmão, *To Resist Is to Win!*, 34; Greenlees and Garran, *Deliverance*, 18.
164. Letter by Carlos Felipe X. Belo, Apostolic Administrator, Dili, to Mgr Martinho da Costa Lopes, Lisbon, February 16, 1984, published in "Appeal to the World from the Bishop of Dili: 'Open Your Eyes to the Brutalities of Indonesia,'" *TAPOL Bulletin No. 63*, May 1984, 1.
165. Kohen, *Place of the Dead*, 122.
166. "Statement by the Head of the Catholic Church of East Timor," *TAPOL Bulletin No. 69*, May 1985, 12.
167. "Priests Boycott Pancasila Indoctrination," *TAPOL Bulletin No. 77*, September 1986, 1.
168. Pinto and Jardine, *East Timor's Unfinished Struggle*, 125.
169. "Dili Pupils Protest against Discrimination," *TAPOL Bulletin No. 83*, October 1987, 10.
170. Interview with Porfirio da Costa Oliveira, survivor of the Santa Cruz massacre, November 24, 2021.
171. Stephen Sherlock, "Political Economy of the East Timor Conflict," *Asian Survey* 36, no. 9 (September 1996): 847.

172. Pinto and Jardine, *East Timor's Unfinished Struggle*, 110.
173. Pinto and Jardine, *East Timor's Unfinished Struggle*, 116.
174. Bertrand, *Nationalism and Ethnic Conflict*, 142
175. Interview with Porfirio da Costa Oliveira, November 24, 2021.
176. Robinson, "People's War," 309.
177. Hainsworth and McCloskey, *East Timor Question*, 7
178. Transcript of the interview with Xanana Gusmão, *Democracy Now*, Pacifica Radio, March 3, 1999, www.pacifica.org/programs/democracy_now/archives/d990303a.html (accessed September 30, 1999).
179. "A Peace Plan to Resolve the Conflict in East Timor," in José Ramos-Horta, *Words of Hope in Troubled Times: Selected Speeches and Writings of José Ramos-Horta* (Haberfield, NSW: Longueville Media, 2018), 34 and 35.
180. Greenlees and Garran, *Deliverance*, 23.
181. "An Entire Village Massacred," *TAPOL Bulletin No. 78*, December 1986, 19.
182. Kohen, *Place of the Dead*, 21.
183. "Fretilin Forces Surround Soibada for Three Days," *TAPOL Bulletin No. 68/Supplement*, March 1985, 10.
184. Interview with foreign military observer, Jakarta, March 20, 2003.
185. "Fretilin Forces Surround Soibada," 10.
186. "Seminarists Write to MAWI President," *TAPOL Bulletin No. 65*, September 1984, 15.
187. "Priests Boycott Pancasila Indoctrination," 1; "Letters Tell of New Atrocities," *TAPOL Bulletin No. 63*, May 1984, 2.
188. "Appeal to the World," 1.
189. "Life during the Resistance," 15.
190. "Indonesian Church Leaders Pave the Way for 'Second Integration,'" *TAPOL Bulletin No. 81*, June 1987, 6.
191. Interview with Brigadier General Tono Suratman, East Timor Commander June 1998–July 1999, Jakarta, June 13, 2001.
192. Robinson, "People's War," 306.
193. Robinson, "People's War," 310.
194. Peter Carey, "A Personal Journey through ET," in Hainsworth and McCloskey, *East Timor Question*, 21.
195. Sherlock, "Political Economy," 841.
196. Interview with Joseph Naseriman and Thomas Tongge, Florinese migrants, Dili, East Timor, August 22, 1999; interview with Father Herman, Kupang, West Timor, August 25, 1999; interview with Sister Alfonsa, Kupang, West Timor, August 26, 1999.
197. Sherlock, "Political Economy," 840 and 842.
198. For a more in-depth discussion of the church burnings see John T. Sidel, *Riots, Pogroms, Jihad: Religious Violence in Indonesia* (Ithaca, NY: Cornell University Press, 2006), 68–105.
199. Carey, "Personal Journey," 23.
200. USIB, "National Intelligence Bulletin," December 8, 1975, 1,; CIA, "The President's Daily Brief," December 18, 1975, 8.
201. *East Timor: Building for the Future: Issues and Perspectives* (Jakarta: Department of Foreign Affairs, 1992), 10.
202. Taylor, *Indonesia's Forgotten War*, 73; Sekretariat Jenderal Dewan Perwakilan Republik Indonesia, "Dewan Perwakilan Rakyat Republik Indonesia Periode 1971–1977," 136, accessed on November 1, 2021, http://repositori.dpr.go.id/82/1/DPR%20RI%20PERIODE%201971-1977.pdf.

203. A. M. Simons, South East Asia Department, "Invitation to Attend Second Stage of 'Self-Determination' by the People of East Timor," 1, National Security Archive, GWU, https://nsarchive2.gwu.edu/NSAEBB/NSAEBB174/uk30.pdf.

204. Sekretariat Jenderal DPR Republik Indonesia, "Dewan Perwakilan Rakyat Republik Indonesia Periode 1971-1977," 136.

205. On transmigration see J. M. Hardjono, *Transmigration in Indonesia* (Kuala Lumpur and London: Oxford University Press, 1977); Timothy Babcock, "Transmigration: The Regional Impact of a Miracle Cure," in *Central Government and Local Development in Indonesia*, ed. Colin MacAndrews (Singapore: OUP, 1986); and Riwanto Titosudarmono, *Transmigration Policy and National Development Plans in Indonesia (1969-1988)*, Working Paper No. 90/10 (Canberra: National Centre for Development Studies, ANU, 1990), 1–30.

206. *East Timor: Building for the Future*, 14; *East Timor Develops* (Dili: The Regional Government of East Timor Province, 1984), 27–28.

207. *East Timor Develops*, 29.

208. *Building for the Future*, 13.

209. *East Timor Develops*, 37.

210. *East Timor Develops*, 37.

211. *Building for the Future*, 13.

212. *Indonesia Membangun*, Jilid IV (Jakarta: PT Dumas Sari Warna, January 1988), 584.

213. *East Timor Develops*, 38.

214. *East Timor Develops*, 38.

215. *Indonesia Membangun*, Jilid IV, 569; *East Timor Develops*, 12.

216. *Building for the Future*, 12.

217. Sherlock, "Political Economy," 836.

218. Interview with Lieutenant General Luhut Panjaitan, April 7, 2005; Interview with Lieutenant General (ret.) Z. A. Maulani, April 24, 2001.

219. Alberto Arenas, "Education and Nationalism in East Timor," *Social Justice* 25, no. 2 (Summer 1998): 141.

220. Pinto and Jardine, *East Timor's Unfinished Struggle*, 87.

221. *East Timor Develops*, 35.

222. Pinto and Jardine, *East Timor's Unfinished Struggle*, 87.

223. *East Timor Develops*, 32.

224. Arenas, "Education and Nationalism," 139.

225. Helene van Klinken, *Making Them Indonesians: Child Transfers out of East Timor* (Clayton, Victoria: Monash University Publishing, 2012), 17.

226. CAVR, *Chega! Report*, Part 7: Violations of the Rights of the Child, 7.8.1 (353); Van Klinken, *Making Them Indonesians*, 40.

227. Van Klinken, *Making Them Indonesians*, 116.

228. Bertrand, *Nationalism and Ethnic Conflict*, 93.

229. R. E. Elson, *Suharto: A Political Biography* (Cambridge: Cambridge University Press, 2001), 254–255.

230. Interview with Lieutenant General Kiki Syahnakri, East Timor veteran, Jakarta, April 9, 2003.

231. Interview with Lieutenant General Kiki Syahnakri, April 9, 2003.

232. Interview with J. Kristiadi, MPR delegate for East Timor 1987–1992, Jakarta, April 18, 2001.

233. Interview with J. Kristiadi, April 18, 2001.

234. Jardine, *East Timor*, 65.

235. Interview with Father Rolando and Father Andrew Wong, Dili, East Timor, August 23, 1999.
236. Pinto and Jardine, *East Timor's Unfinished Struggle*, 83; interview with Father Rolando and Father Andrew Wong, August 23, 1999.
237. Interview with J. Kristiadi, April 18, 2001; Van Klinken, *Making Them Indonesians*, 17.
238. Interview with Porfirio da Costa Oliveira, November 24, 2021.
239. Mubyarto et al., *East Timor: The Impact of Integration, An Indonesian Socio-anthropological Study* (Northcote, Victoria: Indonesia Resources and Information Program, 1991), 53–60.
240. Pinto and Jardine, *East Timor's Unfinished Struggle*, 91.
241. Van Klinken, *Making Them Indonesians*, 90–91.
242. Bishop Belo as quoted in Sherlock, "Political Economy," 837; Elson, *Suharto*, 254–255.
243. Greenlees and Garran, *Deliverance*, 21.
244. Sherlock, "Political Economy," 838. See also Carey, "Personal Journey," 26.
245. Hainsworth and McCloskey, *East Timor Question*, 4; Interview with Lieutenant General Kiki Syahnakri, April 9, 2003.
246. Bertrand, *Nationalism and Ethnic Conflict*, 139
247. East Timor Regional People's Representative Assembly (DPRD), "Situation Report on the Progress on the government of East Timor," 102/DPRD/VII/1981, enclosure in letter by the East Timor DPRD to President Suharto, June 3, 1981, translated and published in *TAPOL Bulletin No. 47*, 5.
248. "Frente Revolucionara de Timor Leste Independente"—Manifesto, Appendix A in Jolliffe, *East Timor*, 327 and 328.
249. "Frente Revolucionara de Timor Leste Independente"—Manifesto, 328.
250. "Frente Revolucionara de Timor Leste Independente"—Manifesto, 329.
251. CAVR, *Chega! Report*, Part 5: Resistance: Structure and Strategy, 5.1 (4) and 5.2 (56).
252. Ramos-Horta, *Funu*, 35.
253. "Programme of the Revolutionary Front of East Timor," Appendix A in Jolliffe, *East Timor*, 333.
254. "Programme," 333–335.
255. Jolliffe, *East Timor*, 100.
256. Bertrand, *Nationalism and Ethnic Conflict*, 137.
257. Ramos-Horta, *Funu*, 37.
258. CAVR, *Chega! Report*, Part 5: Resistance: Structure and Strategy 5.2 (60).
259. Pinto and Jardine, *East Timor's Unfinished Struggle*, 47.
260. Taylor, *Indonesia's Forgotten War*, 56.
261. Taylor, *Indonesia's Forgotten War*, 46.
262. "Patria," national anthem of East Timor, lyrics written by Francisco Borja da Costa.
263. Jolliffe, *East Timor*, 336.
264. Kohen, *Place of the Dead*, 84
265. Jolliffe, *East Timor*, 335.
266. Jolliffe, *East Timor*, 329.
267. Catherine Arthur, "From Fretilin to Freedom: The Evolution of the Symbolism of Timor-Leste's National Flag," *Journal of Southeast Asian Studies* 49, No. 2 (June 2018): 234.
268. Arthur, "From Fretilin to Freedom," 235–236.
269. Ramos-Horta, *Funu*, 18.
270. "A History that Beats in the Maubere Soul, Message to Catholic Youth in East Timor and Students in Indonesia," May 20, 1986, in Gusmão, *To Resist Is to Win!*, 88.

271. Ramos-Horta, *Funu*, 49.
272. Ramos-Horta, *Funu*, 186.
273. Jolliffe, *East Timor*, 78; Ramos-Horta, *Funu*, 186.
274. Gusmão, *To Resist Is to Win!*, 19; Ramos-Horta, *Funu*, 32.
275. Ramos-Horta, *Funu*, 62 and 84.
276. Ramos-Horta, *Funu*, 62 and 188.
277. Ramos-Horta, *Funu*, 43.
278. "Message to the 37th United Nations General Assembly," October 14, 1982, in Gusmão, *To Resist Is to Win!*, 79; Paulino Gama [Mauk Muruk], "The War in the Hills, 1975–85: A Fretilin Commander Remembers," in *East Timor at the Crossroads: The Forging of a Nation*, ed. Peter Carey and G. Carter Bentley (Honolulu: University of Hawaii Press, 1995), 100; "CRRN Salute, The National Council of Revolutionary Resistance Salutes the Fretilin Delegation of External Services," October 13, 1982, in Gusmão, *To Resist Is to Win!*, 72; "Message to the 37th United Nations General Assembly," 81 and 74.
279. "Message to the 37th United Nations General Assembly," 77.
280. "Message to the 37th United Nations General Assembly," 74.
281. Pinto and Jardine, *East Timor's Unfinished Struggle*, 240.
282. "Peace Plan for East Timor," October 5, 1989, in Gusmão, *To Resist is to Win!*, 139; Gama, "The War in the Hills," 99.
283. "Defence Plea of Xanana Gusmão," May 17, 1993, in Gusmão, *To Resist Is to Win!*, 187.
284. Ramos-Horta, *Funu*, 175.
285. Ramos-Horta, *Funu*, 175.
286. "CRRN Salute," 71.
287. "Message to the 37th United Nations General Assembly," 76; "Defence Plea of Xanana Gusmão," 185.
288. Ramos-Horta, *Funu*, 22, 3.
289. Ramos-Horta, *Funu*, 76, 87; "Message to the 37th United Nations General Assembly," 83.
290. CAVR, *Chega! Report*, Part 5: Resistance: Structure and Strategy, 5.2 (66, 67).
291. "'Catholic Priest Calls for Sanctions,'" 4.
292. Taylor, *Indonesia's Forgotten War*, 82.
293. CAVR, *Chega! Report*, Part 5: Resistance: Structure and Strategy, 5.2 (45–46).
294. "History that Beats," 97.
295. "From the Dreams of the Mountains, Message to Strategic Development Conference," May 5, 1999, in Gusmão, *To Resist Is to Win!*, 240.
296. Jose "Kay Rala Xanana" Gusmão, "Reconciliation, Unity and National Development in the Framework of the Transition to Independence," in *Guns and Ballot Boxes: East Timor's Vote for Independence*, ed. Damien Kingsbury (Clayton, Victoria: Monash Asia Institute, 2000), 2 and 3.
297. Gusmão, "Reconciliation, Unity and National Development," 5–6.
298. Ian Martin, *Self-Determination in East Timor: The United Nations, the Ballot, and International Intervention* (Boulder, CO and London: Lynne Rienner, International Peace Academy Occasional Paper Series, 2001), 19.
299. Bacharuddin Jusuf Habibie, *517 Tage—Indonesien: Geburt einer Demokratie* (München: Herbert Utz, 2009), 141–142.
300. Habibie, *517 Tage*, 144.
301. Interview with Lieutenant General (ret.) Z. A. Maulani, April 24, 2001.
302. Habibie, *517 Tage*, 140.
303. Habibie, *517 Tage*, 60.
304. Habibie, *517 Tage*, 251.

305. Habibie, *517 Tage*, 12 and 228.
306. Habibie, *517 Tage*, 242.
307. Greenlees and Garran, *Deliverance*, 99.
308. Interview with Juwono Sudarsono, first civilian defense minister, Jakarta, June 5, 2001.
309. Lela E. Madjiah, *Timor Timur: Perginya Si Anak Hilang* (Antara Pustaka Utama, 2002), 11.
310. "Letter from Australian Prime Minister John Howard to Indonesian President BJ Habibie," December 19, 1998, in *East Timor in Transition 1998-2000: An Australian Policy Challenge* (Canberra: Department of Foreign Affairs and Trade, 2001), 181–182.
311. Interview with Dewi Fortuna Anwar, Jakarta, June 13, 2001.
312. Interview with Dewi Fortuna Anwar, June 13, 2001. See also Martin, *Self-Determination in East Timor*, 21.
313. Greenlees and Garran, *Deliverance*, 94.
314. Interview with Dewi Fortuna Anwar, June 13, 2001.
315. Interview with Dewi Fortuna Anwar, June 13, 2001.
316. Martin, *Self-Determination in East Timor*, 23.
317. Interview with Lieutenant General Luhut Panjaitan, April 7, 2005.
318. Menteri Pertahanan Keamanan/Panglima Tentara Nasional Indonesia Kepada Menko Polkam, "Kegiatan TNI dan Polri dalam rangka mempersiapkan kegiatan Jajak Pendapat di Timtim, K/362/P/VI/1999, Konfidensial," Jakarta, June 15, 1999, *Dokumen Tertulis Sebagai Pelengkap Terhadap Keterangan Yang Telah Disampaikan Oleh Jenderal TNI Wiranto Di Hadapkan KPP HAM Timtim Pada Tanggal 24 Desember 1999*, 2.
319. Bob Lowry, "East Timor: An Overview of Political Developments," in *Indonesia in Transition: Social Aspects of Reformasi and Crisis*, ed. Chris Manning and Peter van Diermen (London: Zed Books, 2000), 93.
320. Tono Suratman, *Merah Putih: Dedication & Duty in East Timor* (Bogor: Lembaga Pengkajian Kebudayaan Nusantara, 2001), 37.
321. Samuel Moore, "The Indonesian Military's Last Years in ET: An Analysis of Its Secret Documents," *Indonesia*, no. 72 (October 2001), 13.
322. Suratman, *Merah Putih*, 34.
323. Madjiah, *Timor Timur*, 38–39.
324. Greenlees and Garran, *Deliverance*, 44.
325. Robinson, "People Power," 106.
326. Lowry, "East Timor," 98.
327. Tentara Nasional Indonesia Markas Besar, "Rencana Tindakan Menghadapi Kontinjensi Purna Penentuan Pendapat di Timtim Opsi-1 Gagal," Jakarta, August 1999, 4 (document obtained by the author).
328. Suratman, *Merah Putih*, 13.
329. Greenlees and Garran, *Deliverance*, 139; Moore, "Indonesian Military's Last Years" 30; Robinson, "People's War," 302.
330. Interview with Monsignor Belo, Bishop of Dili, Dili, East Timor, August 23, 1999.
331. Interview with Father Albrecht, SJ, Dili, East Timor, August 21, 1999.
332. Damien Kingsbury, "The TNI and the Militias," in Kingsbury, *Guns and Ballot Boxes*, 72.
333. Martin, *Self-Determination in East Timor*, 75.
334. Report of the International Commission of Inquiry on East Timor, A/54/726, S/2000/59, January 31, 2000, 10, https://www.securitycouncilreport.org/atf/cf/%7B65BF CF9B-6D27-4E9C-8CD3-CF6E4FF96FF9%7D/TL%20S2000%2059.pdf.
335. *Agence France Presse*, April 17, 1999.
336. Martin, *Self-Determination in East Timor*, 92.

337. Martin, *Self-Determination in East Timor*, 94–95.
338. Martin, *Self-Determination in East Timor*, 95.
339. Report of the International Commission of Inquiry on East Timor, 17.
340. International Crisis Group (ICG), "The Implications of the Timor Trials," *ICG Report No. 6* (Jakarta and Brussels: ICG, May 8, 2002), 7.
341. Martin, *Self-Determination in East Timor*, 95.
342. Greenlees and Garran, *Deliverance*, 221.
343. James J. Fox, "The UN Popular Consultation and its Aftermath in East Timor: An Account by One International Observer," in Manning and Van Diermen, *Indonesia in Transition*, 117.
344. *Suara Pembaruan*, September 11, 1999.
345. Report of the International Commission of Inquiry on East Timor, 13.
346. Greenlees and Garran, *Deliverance*, 221.
347. Greenlees and Garran, *Deliverance*, 221.
348. Report of the International Commission of Inquiry on East Timor, 13
349. Madjiah, *Timor Timur*, 128.
350. Report of the International Commission of Inquiry on East Timor, 13.
351. *Jakarta Post*, December 28, 1999.
352. "Wiranto: Tawaran Dunia International Penting Dipertimbangkan," *Suara Pembaruan*, September 12, 1999.
353. Interview with General (ret) Wiranto, former armed forces commander, Jakarta, June 5, 2001.
354. Interview with General (ret) Wiranto, June 5, 2001.
355. Suratman, *Merah Putih*, 25; Madjiah, *Timor Timur*, 86.
356. TNI Markas Besar, "Rencana Tindakan Menghadapi Kontinjensi Purna Penentuan Pendapat di Timtim Opsi-1 Gagal," 2.
357. Greenlees and Garran, *Deliverance*, 258.
358. Geoffrey Robinson, "The Fruitless Search for a Smoking Gun: Tracing the Origins of Violence in East Timor," in Colombijn and Lindblad, *Roots of Violence in Indonesia*, 227.
359. Lowry, "East Timor," 100.
360. Interview with Eurico Guterres, Aitarak commander, Dili, August 23, 1999.
361. Madjiah, *Timor Timur*, 100.
362. TNI Markas Besar, "Rencana Tindakan Menghadapi Kontinjensi Purna Penentuan Pendapat di Timtim Opsi-1 Gagal," 5.
363. Greenlees and Garran, *Deliverance*, 201.
364. Greenlees and Garran, *Deliverance*, 201.
365. Interview with Lieutenant General (ret.) Z. A. Maulani, April 24, 2001.
366. Interview with Lieutenant General (ret.) Z. A. Maulani, April 24, 2001.
367. KPP-HAM, *Laporan Akhir Penyelidikan Pelanggaran Hak Asasi Manusia di Timor Timur*, Jakarta, January 31, 2000.

4. THE ACEH CONFLICT, 1976–2005

1. Paul van't Veer, *De Atjeh-oorloog* (Amsterdam: De Arbeiderspers, 1969). Van't Veer divides this period into four Aceh wars: the first in 1873, the second from 1874 to 1880, the third from 1881 to 1886, and the fourth from 1897 to 1942. See also Anthony Reid, *An Indonesian Frontier: Acehnese and Other Histories of Sumatra* (Singapore: University of Singapore Press, 2005), 339; and Edward Aspinall, *Islam and Nation: Separatist Rebellion in Aceh, Indonesia* (Stanford, CA: Stanford University Press, 2009), 35, 47.
2. Aspinall, *Islam and Nation*, 20.

3. Hasan Basri, "Islam in Aceh: Institutions, Scholarly Traditions, and Relations between the Ulama and Umara," in *Aceh: History, Politics, Culture*, ed. Arndt Graf, Susanne Schröter, and Edwin Wiering (Singapore: ISEAS, 2010), 183; Geoff Wade, "Early Muslim Expansion in South-East Asia, Eighth to Fifteenth Centuries" in *The New Cambridge History of Islam*, vol. 3: *The Eastern Islamic World, Eleventh to Eighteenth Centuries*, ed. David O. Morgan and Anthony Reid (Cambridge: Cambridge University Press, 2011). See also Anthony Reid, "Islam in Southeast Asia and the Indian Ocean Littoral, 1500–1800: Expansion, Polarization, Synthesis," in Morgan and Reid, *New Cambridge History of Islam*, vol. 3.

4. Basri, "Islam in Aceh," 188.

5. Peter G. Riddell, "Aceh in the Sixteenth and Seventeenth Centuries: 'Serambi Mekkah' and Identity," in *Veranda of Violence: Background to the Aceh Problem*, ed. Antony Reid (Singapore: Singapore University Press, 2006), 38–51.

6. Teuku Ibrahim Alfian, "Aceh and the Holy War," in Reid, *Verandah of Violence*, 109–120. See also Basri, "Islam in Aceh," 186.

7. Anthony Reid, *The Contest for North Sumatra: Acheh, the Netherlands, and Britain, 1858–1898* (Kuala Lumpur: Oxford University Press, 1969), 282.

8. Anthony Reid, *The Blood of the People: Revolution and the End of Traditional Rule in Northern Sumatra* (Kuala Lumpur: Oxford University Press, 1979), 9–10.

9. Kees van Dijk, *Rebellion under the Banner of Islam: The Darul Islam Rebellions in Indonesia* (The Hague: Martinus Nijhoff, 1981), 270.

10. Abdullah Arif, ed., *Bingkisan kenang2an kongres besar PUSA dan P PUSA* (Kutaradja: Seksi Penerangan/Penjiaran Raya Kongres besar PUSA/P.PUSA, ca. 1951), 18.

11. Aspinall, *Islam and Nation*, 28; Isa Sulaiman, *Sejarah Aceh: Sebuah gugatan terhadap tradisi* (Jakarta: Pustaka Sinar Harapan, 1997), 54–55.

12. Van Dijk, *Banner of Islam*, 272.

13. Sulaiman, *Sejarah Aceh*, 114–164; Reid, *Blood of the People*, 185–217.

14. Pusat Sejarah Dan Tradisi TNI, *Sejarah TNI*, Jilid II (1950–1959) (Jakarta: Markas Besar Tentara Nasional Indonesia Pusat Sejarah dan Tradisi TNI, 2000), 94; B. J. Boland, *The Struggle for Islam in Modern Indonesia* (The Hague: Martinus Nijhoff, 1971), 70.

15. Pemerintah R. I. Daerah Aceh, *Revolusi Desember '45 di Atjeh atau Pembasmian Penchianat Tanah Air* (n.d.); TNI, *Sejarah TNI*, Jilid II, 94.

16. Van Dijk, *Banner of Islam*, 281.

17. Irna H. N. Hadi Soewito, Nana Nurliana Suyono, and Soedarini Suhartono, *Awal Kedirgantaraan di Indonesia: Perjuangan AURI 1945–1950* (Jakarta: Yayasan Pustaka Obor, 2008), 192–193.

18. TNI, *Sejarah TNI*, Jilid II, 94.

19. M. Nur El Ibrahimy, *Peranan Tgk. M. Daud Beureu-eh dalam pergolakan Aceh* (Jakarta: Media Da'wah, 2001), 78.

20. Van Dijk, *Banner of Islam*, 286–287.

21. Van Dijk, *Banner of Islam*, 288.

22. Peraturan Wakil Menteri Pengganti Peraturan Pemerintah No. 8/1949.

23. Peraturan Pemerintah No. 21/1950.

24. Van Dijk, *Banner of Islam*, 291.

25. Van Dijk, *Banner of Islam*, 298.

26. TNI, *Sejarah TNI*, Jilid II, 94.

27. TNI, *Sejarah TNI*, Jilid II, 94.

28. Van Dijk, *Banner of Islam*, 292.

29. A. H. Gelanggang, *Rahasia pemberontakan Atjeh dan kegalan politik Mr. S.M. Amin* (Kutaradja: Pustaka Murnihati, 1956), 17; Nazaruddin Sjamsuddin, *The Republican Revolt: A Study of the Acehnese Rebellion* (Singapore: ISEAS, 1985), 63–76.

30. Van Dijk, *Banner of Islam*, 299.

31. Van Dijk, *Banner of Islam*, 294.
32. Van Dijk, *Banner of Islam*, 294: Kementerian Penerangan, *Sekitar Peristiwa Daud Beureu'eh* (Jakarta: Kementerian Penerangan, n.d.), 1:240, 3:83, as cited in Van Dijk, *Banner of Islam*, 295.
33. TNI, *Sejarah TNI*, Jilid II, 97.
34. Herbert Feith, "Repressive-Developmentalist Regimes in Asia: Old Strengths, New Vulnerabilities," *Prisma*, no. 19 (1980), 39–55.
35. Edward Aspinall, "Place and Displacement in the Aceh Conflict," in *Conflict, Violence and Displacement in Indonesia*, ed. Eva-Lotta E. Hedman (Ithaca, NY: Southeast Asia Program Publications, Cornell University, 2008), 124.
36. Dayan Dawood and Sjafrizal, "Aceh: The LNG Boom and Enclave Development," in *Unity and Diversity: Regional Economic Development in Indonesia since 1970*, ed. Hal Hill (Singapore: Oxford University Press, 1989), 115.
37. Interview with Azwar Abubakar, vice governor, Banda Aceh, June 27, 2001.
38. Interview with Azwar Abubakar, June 27, 2001.
39. Basri, "Islam in Aceh," 194.
40. Basri, "Islam in Aceh," 194.
41. Interview with Malik Musa, head of Pemuda Muhammadiyah, Banda Aceh, June 26, 2001.
42. Interview with Malik Musa, June 26, 2001.
43. Dawood and Sjafrizal, "Aceh," 6.
44. Michael L. Ross, "Resources and Rebellion in Aceh, Indonesia," Yale World Bank project on "The Economics of Political Violence," (unpublished manuscript 2003), 14.
45. Tim Kell, *The Roots of Acehnese Rebellion, 1989–1992* (Ithaca, NY: Cornell Modern Indonesia Project, 1995), 26.
46. Kirsten E. Schulze, "The Conflict in Aceh: Struggle over Oil?" in *Oil Wars*, ed. Mary Kaldor, Terry Lynn Karl, and Yahyia Said (London: Pluto Press, 2007), 190.
47. Interview with Lieutenant General (ret.) Sofian Effendi, former Nanggala unit commander, Jakarta, September 25, 2003.
48. Schulze, "The Struggle over Oil?," 191.
49. Ross, "Resources and Rebellion in Aceh," 15.
50. Amnesty International, "Shock Therapy: Restoring Order in Aceh, 1989–1993" (London: Amnesty International, 1993), 4.
51. Kell, *Roots of Acehnese Rebellion*, 17.
52. M. C. Riklefs, *A History of Modern Indonesia since c.1200* (Basingstoke: Palgrave, 2001), 388.
53. Schulze, "The Struggle over Oil?," 194.
54. Hasan di Tiro, *The Price of Freedom: The Unfinished Diary of Tengku Hasan di Tiro* (Ministry of Education and Information, State of Aceh Sumatra, 1982), 84; interview with Hasan di Tiro, leader and Wali Negara of GAM, Norsborg, Sweden, February 22, 2002.
55. Interview with Hasan di Tiro, February 22, 2002.
56. Ross, "Resources and Rebellion in Aceh," 12.
57. Di Tiro, *Price of Freedom*, 8.
58. See ANSLF, "Aims of the ASNLF," accessed June 20, 2001, www.asnlf.org.
59. Edward Aspinall, "Modernity, History, Ethnicity: Indonesian and Achenese Nationalism in Conflict," *Review of Indonesian Malaysian Affairs* 36, no. 1 (2002): 22.
60. Interview with Malik Mahmud, GAM minister of state, Norsborg, Sweden, February 22, 2002.
61. Interview with Amri bin Abdul Wahab, GAM Tiro field commander, Banda Aceh, April 22, 2003.

62. Interview with Hasan di Tiro, February 22, 2002; data obtained from Indonesian Military Intelligence (SGI), Lhokseumawe, April 2003.
63. Interview with humanitarian aid worker A, Aceh, June 25, 2001.
64. Interview with humanitarian aid worker B, Aceh, June 29, 2001.
65. Interview with Malik Mahmud, February 22, 2002.
66. Data obtained from Indonesian Military Intelligence (SGI), Lhokseumawe, April 2003.
67. International Crisis Group (ICG), "Why Military Force Won't Bring Lasting Peace," *ICG Report No. 17* (Jakarta and Brussels: ICG, June 12, 2001), 3.
68. ICG, "Military Force," 7.
69. *Tempo*, November 17, 2003.
70. Interview with Sofyan Ibrahim Tiba, senior GAM negotiator, Banda Aceh, April 21, 2003.
71. Interview with Sofyan Dawod, GAM Pasè commander, Nisam, North Aceh, April 19, 2003.
72. Interview with Sofyan Dawod, April 19, 2003.
73. Interview with Rizal Sukma, Aceh expert, Center for Strategic and International Studies, Jakarta, April 24, 2001.
74. *Joyo Indonesian News*, June 9, 2002. See also *Jakarta Post*, June 10, 2002, and *Jakarta Post*, June 15, 2002.
75. *Joyo Indonesian News*, May 28, 2002.
76. *Associated Press*, August 29, 2001.
77. *Dow Jones Newswires*, May 6, 2002.
78. *Agence France Presse*, July 2, 2002.
79. Di Tiro, *Price of Freedom*, 30.
80. Di Tiro, *Price of Freedom*, 70.
81. Ken Conboy, *Kopassus: Inside Indonesia's Special Forces* (Jakarta: Equinox Publishing, 2003), 262.
82. Interview with Major General Sjafrie Sjamsoedin, former Nanggala unit commander in Aceh, Cilangkap, September 4, 2003.
83. Interview with Major General Bambang Dharmono, Commander of Operasi Terpadu, Lhokseumawe, via telephone, October 19, 2003. See also Rizal Sukma, *Security Operations in Aceh: Goals, Consequences, and Lessons*, Policy Paper 3 (Washington, DC: East-West Center, 2004), 6; and Isa Sulaiman, *Aceh Merdeka: Ideologi, Kepimpinan dan Gerakan* (Jakarta: Al-Kautsar, 2000), 79–80.
84. Conboy, *Kopassus*, 263
85. Interview with Amni Ahmad bin Marzuki, GAM negotiator, Banda Aceh, June 24, 2001.
86. Interview with Malik Mahmud, February 23, 2002.
87. Asia Watch, "Continuing Human Rights Violations in Aceh," June 19, 1991, 6.
88. Interview with Malik Mahmud, February 22, 2002.
89. Interview with Malik Mahmud, February 22, 2002.
90. Interview with Hasan di Tiro, February 22, 2002.
91. Interview with Amni Ahmad bin Marzuki, June 24, 2001.
92. Executive Council of the Free Acheh Movement—MP GAM, "Why Acheh Wants Independence from the Colonialism of the Republic of Indonesia," August 1999, 4.
93. Richard Barber, ed., *Aceh: The Untold Story* (Bangkok: Asian Forum for Human Rights and Development, 2000), 32.
94. Anthony L. Smith, "Aceh: Democratic Times, Authoritarian Solutions," *New Zealand Journal of Asian Studies* 4, no. 2 (December 2002): 77; Kell, *Roots of Acehnese Rebel-*

lion, 74; Amnesty International, "Shock Therapy," 6; Geoffrey Robinson, "Rawan Is as Rawan Does: The Origins of Disorder in New Order Aceh," *Indonesia*, no. 66 (1998), 229.

95. Amnesty International, "Shock Therapy," 6.

96. Human Rights Watch (HRW), "Indonesia: The War in Aceh," vol. 13, no. 4 (August 2002, 8; Amnesty International, "Shock Therapy," 8; Kontras data as cited in Samsul Bahri, "Aceh: A Land of Silenced and Marginalized voices," paper presented at the World Social Forum, Mumbai, India, January 2004, 3.

97. *Suara Pembaruan*, November 26, 1999; data gathered by Forum Peduli HAM as cited in Barber, *Aceh: The Untold Story*, 47.

98. Press release, Aceh-Sumatra National Liberation Front, Central Bureau for Information, June 4, 2001, 1.

99. Press release, Aceh-Sumatra National Liberation Front, 2.

100. For a comprehensive discussion of Indonesia's autonomy policies in Aceh see Michelle Ann Miller, *Rebellion and Reform in Indonesia: Jakarta's Security and Autonomy Policies in Aceh* (London: Routledge, 2010).

101. For a full discussion see Kirsten E. Schulze, "Insurgency and Counter-Insurgency: Strategy and the Aceh Conflict, October 1976–May 2004," in Reid, *Verandah of Violence*, 225–271.

102. Interview with General Endriatono Sutarto, TNI headquarters, Cilangkap, May 5, 2004.

103. *Straits Times*, January 10, 2005.

104. Interview with Malik Mahmud, February 23, 2002.

105. Interview with Jusuf Kalla, coordinating minister for people's welfare, Jakarta, April 11, 2003.

106. Di Tiro, *Price of Freedom*, 65–66.
107. Di Tiro, *Price of Freedom*, 89–90.
108. Di Tiro, *Price of Freedom*, 17 and 197.
109. Di Tiro, *Price of Freedom*, 199.
110. Di Tiro, *Price of Freedom*, 121.
111. Di Tiro, *Price of Freedom*, 74.
112. Di Tiro, *Price of Freedom*, 74.
113. Di Tiro, *Price of Freedom*, 74.
114. Di Tiro, *Price of Freedom*, 66.
115. Di Tiro, *Price of Freedom*, 145.
116. Di Tiro, *Price of Freedom*, 32 and 39.
117. Di Tiro, *Price of Freedom*, 17.
118. Di Tiro, *Price of Freedom*, 199.
119. Di Tiro, *Price of Freedom*, 21.
120. Di Tiro, *Price of Freedom*, 47.
121. Di Tiro, *Price of Freedom*, 127.
122. Di Tiro, *Price of Freedom*, 93.
123. Di Tiro, *Price of Freedom*, 93.
124. Di Tiro, *Price of Freedom*, 94.
125. Di Tiro, *Price of Freedom*, 95.
126. Di Tiro, *Price of Freedom*, 22.
127. Di Tiro, *Price of Freedom*, 98.
128. Di Tiro, *Price of Freedom*, 209.
129. Husaini M. Hassan, *Dari Rimba Aceh ke Stockholm* (Jakarta: Batavia Publishing, 2015), 95.
130. Di Tiro, *Price of Freedom*, 53.

131. Interview with Amni Ahmad bin Marzuki, June 24, 2001.
132. Interview with Malik Mahmud, February 22, 2002.
133. Interview with Malik Mahmud, February 22, 2002.
134. ASNLF, "Stavanger Declaration," July 21, 2002.
135. Kirsten E. Schulze, "From the Battlefield to the Negotiating Table: GAM and the Indonesian Government, 1999–2005," *Asian Security* 3, no. 2 (2007): 82.
136. *Jakarta Post*, June 3, 2003.
137. Testimony of Sidney Jones, Indonesia Project Director, International Crisis Group, before the Subcommittee on East Asia and the Pacific, House International Relations Committee, *Hearing on Recent Developments in Southeast Asia* US House of Representatives, June 10, 2003.
138. *Agence France Presse*, June 5, 2001.
139. Press statement, ASNLF military spokesman, January 26, 2002.
140. Press release, ASNLF Central Military Command, January 23, 2002.
141. Press statement issued by Tgk. Sofyan Dawod, military spokesman of the Aceh-Sumatra National Liberation Front, January 4, 2002.
142. *Jakarta Post*, June 1, 2003.
143. *Agence France Presse*, June 10, 2003.
144. General Endriatono Sutarto, press conference, TNI headquarters, Cilangkap, May 5, 2004.
145. Interview with Malik Mahmud, February 23, 2002.
146. *Jakarta Post*, October 29, 2002.
147. ICG, "Aceh: How to Lose Hearts and Minds," *Indonesia Briefing* (Jakarta and Brussels: ICG, 2003), 1.
148. *Kompas*, June 19, 2002.
149. *Jakarta Post*, September 13, 2002; September 16, 2002; May 4, 2004.
150. *Waspada*, September 19, 1975.
151. Luth Ari Linge, *Malapetaka di Bumi Sumatra* (Medan: PT Kemalasari Enterprise, 1993), 5–6.
152. Barber, *Aceh: The Untold Story*, 32.
153. Amnesty International, "Shock Therapy," 5.
154. *Jakarta Post*, September 9, 1999.
155. Schulze, "Insurgency and Counter-Insurgency," 234.
156. Smith, "Democratic Times, Authoritarian Solutions," 76.
157. ICG, "Aceh: A Slim Chance for Peace," *Asia Briefing Paper* (Jakarta and Brussels: ICG, January 30, 2002), 7.
158. Interview with resident of Kresek, Aceh, August 20, 2002.
159. Staffan Bodemar, "Conflict in Aceh, Indonesia: Background, Current Situation and Future Prospects" (unpublished paper, March 2004), 24.
160. Di Tiro, *Price of Freedom*, 78.
161. Di Tiro, *Price of Freedom*, 107.
162. GAM leaflet quoted in di Tiro, *Price of Freedom*, 108–109.
163. Di Tiro, *Price of Freedom*, 125–126.
164. Interview with Lieutenant General (ret.) Sofian Effendi, September 25, 2003.
165. *Sydney Morning Herald*, April 3, 2001.
166. Interview with Bill Cummings, public affairs manager, ExxonMobil Oil Indonesia, Jakarta, March 19, 2003.
167. Interview with Isnander al-Pase, GAM spokesman, Nisam, North Aceh, April 19, 2003.
168. Robinson, "Rawan Is as Rawan Does," 217; Ross, "Resources and Rebellion in Aceh," 18.

169. Interview with Lieutenant General (ret.), Sofian Effendi, September 25, 2003.
170. Schulze, "Insurgency and Counter-Insurgency," 250.
171. Robinson, "Rawan Is as Rawan Does," 226.
172. Interview with Major General Djali Yusuf, Pangdam Iskandar Muda, Banda Aceh, April 18, 2003.
173. *Kompas*, May 20, 2003.
174. HRW, "Aceh Under Martial Law: Inside the Secret War," vol.15, no. 10 (December 2003): 16.
175. General Endriatono Sutarto, press conference, TNI headquarters, Cilangkap, May 5, 2004.
176. Ross, "Resources and Rebellion in Aceh," 13; Robinson, "Rawan Is as Rawan Does," 227.
177. Ross, "Resources and Rebellion in Aceh," 13.
178. Robinson, "Rawan Is as Rawan Does," 227.
179. Schulze, "Insurgency and Counter-Insurgency," 252.
180. Schulze, "Insurgency and Counter-Insurgency," 252.
181. *Acehkita*, July 16, 2004. Reports from Aceh, Acehnese Community of Australia, July 14, 2004.
182. *Acehkita*, July 16, 2004. Reports from Aceh, Acehnese Community of Australia, July 14, 2004.
183. "GAM Families Targeted May/April," Aceh Human Rights Online, July 27, 2004.
184. Schulze, "Insurgency and Counter-Insurgency," 254.
185. Interview with Major Edi Sulistiadi, Satgaspen, Korem 012, Banda Aceh, June 26, 2001.
186. HRW, "Indonesia: The War in Aceh," 20.
187. Interview with Mohamad Nazar, SIRA chairman, Banda Aceh, December 26, 2001.
188. HRW, "Indonesia: The War in Aceh," 33.
189. Interview with Colonel Endang Suwarya, Danrem Teuku Umar 012, Banda Aceh, June 28, 2001.
190. Schulze, "Insurgency and Counter-Insurgency," 254.
191. Interview with General Ryamizard Ryacudu, Army chief of staff, Jakarta, April 5, 2003.
192. *Jakarta Post*, May 27, 2003.
193. *Agence France Presse*, January 26, 2004; *World Press Review*, February 9, 2004; *Jakarta Post*, June 9, 2003.
194. *Analisa*, July 12, 2004.
195. Kell, *Roots of Acehnese Rebellion*, 74.
196. Amnesty International, "Shock Therapy," 6.
197. Robinson, "Rawan Is as Rawan Does," 227.
198. *Time*, April 23, 2001. See also HRW, "Indonesia: The War in Aceh," 12–13 and 18.
199. Schulze, "From the Battlefield," 9
200. Interview with Colonel Endang Suwarya, December 26, 2001.
201. ICG, "How to Lose Hearts and Minds," 4.
202. *Straits Times*, May 31, 2003.
203. Indonesia Consolidated Situation Report No. 132, Office for the Coordination of Humanitarian Affairs, June 7–13, 2003.
204. *Jakarta Post*, June 13, 2003.
205. *Jakarta Post*, May 28, 2003.
206. Schulze, "From the Battlefield," 9.
207. Interview with Major Prasetyo, Lhokseumawe, February 21, 2004.

208. Interview with Major Prasetyo, February 21, 2004.
209. Di Tiro, *Price of Freedom*, 47
210. Di Tiro, *Price of Freedom*, 18.
211. Interview with Teuku Kamal S, NGO representative in Banda Aceh, Jakarta, April 7, 2003.
212. Interview with Malik Musa, June 26, 2001.
213. Interview with Yusny Saby, Institut Agama Islam Negeri (IAIN) Ar-Raniry Darussalam, Banda Aceh, June 24, 2001.
214. Interview with Yusny Saby, June 24, 2001.
215. Interview with Yusny Saby, June 24, 2001.
216. Interview with Abdullah Puteh, February 17, 2004.
217. Interview with Imam Suja, Muhammadiya chairman, Banda Aceh, June 27, 2001.
218. Interview with Alyasa Abubakar, Kepala Dinas Syariat Islam, NAD, Banda Aceh, April 12, 2002.
219. Interview with Malik Musa, June 26, 2001.
220. Interview with Teuku Kamal S, April 7, 2003.
221. Interview with Azwar Abubakar, June 27, 2001.
222. Interview with Yusny Saby, June 24, 2001.
223. Interview with Abdullah Puteh, February 17, 2004.
224. Interview with Nasrullah Dahlawy, Monitoring Team on Security Matters, Peace through Dialogue, Banda Aceh, June 24, 2001.
225. Interview with Mohammed Nazar, December 26, 2001.
226. Interview with Yusny Saby, June 24, 2001.
227. Memorandum of Understanding between the Government of the Republic of Indonesia and the Free Aceh Movement, https://www.europarl.europa.eu/meetdocs/2004_2009/documents/dv/mou_aceh/mou_acehen.pdf.
228. Memorandum of Understanding between the Government of the Republic of Indonesia and the Free Aceh Movement.

5. THE POSO CONFLICT, 1998–2007

1. Interview with Reverend Irianto Kongkoli, Palu, January 8, 2003.
2. Graham Brown and Yukhi Tajima with Suprayoga Hadi, *Overcoming Violent Conflict*, vol. 3: *Peace and Development Analysis in Central Sulawesi* (Jakarta: Indonesia Printer, 2003), 10.
3. Interview with Reverend Irianto Kongkoli, January 8, 2003; Gerry van Klinken, *Communal Violence and Democratisation in Indonesia: Small Town Wars* (London: Routledge, 2007), 73.
4. Lorraine Aragon, "Communal Violence in Poso, Central Sulawesi: Where People Eat Fish and Fish Eat People," *Indonesia* 72 (October 2001), 52.
5. Interview with Reverend Tarau, Partai Kristen, DPRD, Palu, January 8, 2003.
6. For a comprehensive discussion of the Permesta rebellions see Barbara S. Harvey, *Permesta—Half a Rebellion* (Ithaca, NY: Cornell Modern Indonesia Project, Cornell University Press, 1977).
7. Aragon, "Communal Violence in Poso," 53; Brown and Tajima, *Overcoming Violent Conflict*, 12.
8. Van Klinken, *Communal Violence and Democratization*, 78.
9. Interview with Reverend Tarau, January 8, 2003.
10. Interview with Reverend Tarau, January 8, 2003.
11. Jacques Bertrand, *Nationalism and Ethnic Conflict in Indonesia* (Cambridge: Cambridge University Press, 2004), 93.

12. Interview with Jusuf Kalla, coordinating minister for people's welfare, Jakarta, April 11, 2003.
13. Human Rights Watch (HRW), "Breakdown: Four Years of Communal Violence in Central Sulawesi," vol. 14, no. 9 (December 2002): 6.
14. Rinaldy Damanik, *Tragedi Kemanusiaan Poso: Menggapai surya pagi melalui kegelapan malam* (Palu: PBHI & LPS-HAM, 2003), 44.
15. Interview with Reverend Irianto Kongkoli, January 8, 2003.
16. Damanik, *Tragedi Kemanusiaan Poso*, xxi.
17. Forum Cheq and Recheq, "Tragedi Kemanusiaan di Poso: Kerusuhan Bernuansa SARA di Kota 'Citra' Poso dan Sekitarnya," report (n.d.), 2.
18. Damanik, *Tragedi Kemanusiaan Poso*, 44.
19. Aragon, "Communal Violence in Poso," 56.
20. HRW, "Four Years of Communal Violence," 6.
21. Interview with Albert Tumimor, district attorney, Tentena, January 13, 2003.
22. Interview with Albert Bisalemba, Lucas und Rasip Ley, Kelompok Merah, Tentena, January 13, 2003; Damanik, *Tragedi Kemanusiaan Poso*, 43.
23. Damanik, *Tragedi Kemanusiaan Poso*, 43.
24. HRW, "Four Years of Communal Violence," 6. See also Brown and Tajima, *Overcoming Violent Conflict*, 13.
25. Interview with Jusuf Kalla, April 11, 2003.
26. Interview with Mohamed Daeng Raja, Poso, January 10, 2003.
27. Interview with Albert Bisalemba, Lucas und Rasip Ley, January 13, 2003.
28. Aragon, "Communal Violence in Poso," 53.
29. Interview with Reverend Tobundo, GKST Synod Head, Tentena, January 12, 2003.
30. Damanik, *Tragedi Kemanusiaan Poso*, xl.
31. Appendix 2, "Balance of Strategic Posts in Poso District, 1989-1999" in *Respon Militer Terhadap Konflik Sosial di Poso*, ed. Suriadi Mappangara (Palu: Yayasan Bina Warga, 2001).
32. Damanik, *Tragedi Kemanusiaan Poso*, xxxvii.
33. Interview with Albert Bisalemba, Lucas und Rasip Ley, January 13, 2003.
34. Van Klinken, *Communal Violence and Democratization*, 87.
35. John T. Sidel, *Riots, Pogroms, Jihad: Religious Violence in Indonesia* (Ithaca, NY: Cornell University Press, 2006),101.
36. Interview with Albert Bisalemba, Lucas und Rasip Ley, January 13, 2003.
37. Yukhi Tajima, "Explaining Ethnic Violence in Indonesia: Demilitarizing Domestic Security," in *Collective Violence in Indonesia*, ed. Ashutosh Varshney (Boulder, CO: Lynne Rienner, 2010), 111.
38. Damanik, *Tragedi Kemanusiaan Poso*, xxxvii.
39. Aragon, "Communal Violence in Poso," 62.
40. David Gregory McRae, *The Escalation and Decline of Violent Conflict in Poso, Central Sulawesi, 1998-2007* (PhD diss., Australian National University, 2008), 6.
41. Aragon, "Communal Violence in Poso," 78.
42. Interview with Kombes Errol Theodorus Rahakbaw, police intelligence Central Sulawesi, Palu, January 9, 2003.
43. Damanik, *Tragedi Kemanusiaan Poso*, 14-15.
44. Interview with Samsu Mohamed, former lurah of Kayamanya, Poso, January 11, 2003.
45. McRae, *Escalation and Decline of Violent Conflict*, 41.
46. Aragon, "Communal Violence in Poso," 60.
47. Forum Cheq and Recheq, "Tragedi Kemanusiaan di Poso," 3.
48. Interview with Reverend Nelly, Silanca village, January 11, 2003.

49. Interview with Adnan Arsal, Poso, January 11, 2003. See also McRae, *Escalation and Decline of Violent Conflict*, 49; interview with Dion Djon, S.H., VERITAS, Jakarta, May 16, 2001; interview with Reverend Irianto Konkoli, January 8, 2003; interview with Adnan Arsal, January 11, 2003.

50. Interview with Dolfi Monding, rector of English school in Poso, Tentena, January 13, 2003.

51. McRae, *Escalation and Decline of Violent Conflict*, 46.

52. McRae, *Escalation and Decline of Violent Conflict*, 44

53. Interview with Reverend Irianto Kongkoli, January 8, 2003.

54. Aragon, "Communal Violence in Poso," 61.

55. Tajima, "Explaining Ethnic Violence in Indonesia," 111.

56. McRae, *Escalation and Decline of Violent Conflict*, 40.

57. *Managing Communal Conflict in Sampit, Poso and Maluku* (Jakarta: Coordinating Ministry for Political and Security Affairs, 2003), 9; interview with Herry Sarumpaet, deputy head of the DPRD (Golkar), Poso, January 11, 2003.

58. Interview with Adnan Arsal, January 11, 2003; interview with Samsu Mohamed, January 11, 2003; interview with Daeng Raja, January 10, 2003.

59. Interview with Samsu Mohamed, January 11, 2003.

60. "Poso Bakal Rusuh Kembali," *Mercusuar*, April 15, 2000.

61. Damanik, *Tragedi Kemanusiaan Poso*, 25.

62. Damanik, *Tragedi Kemanusiaan Poso*, 24.

63. Forum Cheq and Recheq, *Tragedi Kemanusiaan di Poso*, 4–5.

64. Forum Cheq and Recheq, *Tragedi Kemanusiaan di Poso*, 5.

65. Interview with Syarifuddin Lukman, *Morowali Pos*, April 25, 2000, as quoted in Damanik, *Tragedi Kemanusiaan Poso*, 27.

66. McRae, *Escalation and Decline of Violent Conflict*, 50.

67. McRae, *Escalation and Decline of Violent Conflict*, 50. Later Dedi admitted that he had lied about the wound. He was sentenced to three years in prison.

68. Aragon, "Communal Violence in Poso," 64.

69. Forum Cheq and Recheq, "Tragedi Kemanusiaan di Poso," 6.

70. Interview with Samsu Mohamed, January 11, 2003.

71. Tajima, "Explaining Ethnic Violence in Indonesia," 112. See also McRae, *Escalation and Decline of Violent Conflict*, 51.

72. Interview with Herry Sarumpaet, January 11, 2003.

73. Interview with Hajji Umar Nanya, deputy head of MUI, Poso, January 11, 2003; McRae, *Escalation of Violent Conflict*, 56.

74. HRW, "Four Years of Communal Violence," 16.

75. McRae, *Escalation and Decline of Violent Conflict*, 58.

76. Aragon, "Communal Violence in Poso," 64.

77. McRae, *Escalation and Decline of Violent Conflict*, 60.

78. HRW, "Four Years of Communal Violence," 16; Aragon, "Communal Violence in Poso," 64.

79. Interview with Reverend Nelly, January 11, 2003.

80. McRae, *Escalation and Decline of Violent Conflict*, 61.

81. McRae, *Escalation and Decline of Violent Conflict*, 70.

82. HRW, "Four Years of Communal Violence," 15.

83. Brown and Tajima, *Overcoming Violent Conflict*, 14.

84. George Junus Aditjondro, "Kerusuhan Poso dan Morowali, Akar Permasalahan dan Jalan Keluarnya" (paper presented at a conference organised by Propatria on "The Application of Emergency in Aceh, Papua and Poso?," January 7, 2004, Hotel Santika, Jakarta), 57.

85. Tajima, "Explaining Ethnic Violence in Indonesia," 112; Aragon, "Communal Violence in Poso," 63; Interview with Dolfi Monding, January 13, 2003. Damanik, *Tragedi Kemanusiaan Poso*, 61.
86. Interview with Dion Djon, May 16, 2001.
87. Interview with Reverend Tarau, January 8, 2003.
88. Interview with Dolfi Monding, January 13, 2003.
89. Interview with Albert Tumimor, January 13, 2003.
90. Interview with Albert Tumimor, January 13, 2003.
91. McRae, *Escalation and Decline of Violent Conflict*, 121.
92. McRae, *Escalation and Decline of Violent Conflict*, 75.
93. Aragon, "Communal Violence in Poso," 67.
94. HRW, "Four Years of Communal Violence," 16.
95. McRae, *Escalation and Decline of Violent Conflict*, 78.
96. Damanik, *Tragedi Kemanusiaan Poso*, 161.
97. "Poso Rioters Got Supply of Guns," *Jakarta Post*, January 30, 2001. See also Aragon, "Communal Violence in Poso," 72.
98. HRW, "Four Years of Communal Violence," 40.
99. McRae, *Escalation and Decline of Violent Conflict*, 74.
100. McRae, *Escalation and Decline of Violent Conflict*, 117; interview with Dolfi Monding, January 13, 2003.
101. "Kelompok Merah akan Turun Poso," *Mercusuar*, June 10, 2000.
102. Interview with Letkol Dewantara, Commander Kodim 1307, Poso, January 10, 2003.
103. Aragon, "Communal Violence in Poso," 66.
104. Interview with Samsu Mohamed, January 11, 2003; interview with Adnan Arsal, January 11, 2003; interview with Hajji Umar Nanya, January 11, 2003.
105. "Kami Hanya Mencari Provokator," *Formasi*, July 2000, 10.
106. Interview with Samsu Mohamed, January 11, 2003.
107. Interview with BR, Mujahidin Tanah Runtuh, Palu, August 6, 2017.
108. Interview with Adnan Arsal, January 11, 2003.
109. HRW, "Four Years of Communal Violence," 17; interview with Samsu Mohamed, January 11, 2003.
110. Interview with Samsu Mohamed, January 11, 2003.
111. McRae interview with Fabianus Tibo in July 2003, *Escalation and Decline of Violent Conflict*, 95.
112. Interview with Dolfi Monding, January 13, 2003.
113. Drs. M. Tito Karnavian, *Indonesian Top Secret: Membongkar Konflik Poso* (Jakarta: PT Gramedia Pustaka Utama, 2008), 63.
114. McRae, *Escalation and Decline of Violent Conflict*, 101–102.
115. Interview with Reverend Nelly, January 11, 2003.
116. McRae, *Escalation of Violent Conflict*, 104.
117. Interview with Reverend Tobundo, January 12, 2003.
118. McRae, *Escalation and Decline of Violent Conflict*, 104.
119. McRae, *Escalation and Decline of Violent Conflict*, 104–105.
120. Interview with Reverend Nelly, January 11, 2003.
121. Interview with Reverend Tobundo, January 12, 2003; Aragon, "Communal Violence in Poso," 68.
122. Interview with Reverend Tobundo, January 12, 2003; interview with Reverend Nelly, January 11, 2003.
123. McRae, *Escalation and Decline of Violent Conflict*, 103.
124. Aragon, "Communal Violence in Poso," 68.

125. Aragon suggests that they were held in Tagolu village hall.
126. McRae, *Escalation and Decline of Violent Conflict*, 107–108.
127. Interview with Reverend Tobundo, January 12, 2003.
128. Aragon, "Communal Violence in Poso," 70.
129. McRae, *Escalation and Decline of Violent Conflict*, 103 and 107; interview with Adnan Arsal, January 11, 2003.
130. HRW, "Four Years of Communal Violence," 18; interview with Hajji Nuhun, former village head, Tangkura, January 10, 2003.
131. HRW, "Four Years of Communal Violence," 19.
132. McRae, *Escalation and Decline of Violent Conflict*, 111.
133. HRW, "Four Years of Communal Violence," 19.
134. "Kodam Kirim 1500 Tentara ke Poso," *Detik.com*, May 30, 2000.
135. Damanik, *Tragedi Kemanusiaan Poso*, 29.
136. Aragon, "Communal Violence in Poso," 68.
137. Aragon, "Communal Violence in Poso," 69.
138. Damanik, *Tragedi Kemanusiaan Poso*, 30.
139. "Amanat Lateka," Letter to Komnas HAM, as reproduced in McRae, *Escalation and Decline of Violent Conflict*, 80–81.
140. *Mercusuar*, June 7, 2000, and June 5, 2000.
141. Karnavian, *Indonesian Top Secret*, 86.
142. Aragon, "Communal Violence in Poso," 47.
143. *Managing Communal Conflict*, 11–12.
144. Interview with Adnan Arsal, January 11, 2003.
145. Interview with Iwan Ambo, Mujahidin Tanah Runtuh, Palu, August 5, 2017.
146. Interview with Adnan Arsal, January 11, 2003.
147. Interview with Adnan Arsal, January 11, 2003.
148. Interview with Iwan Ambo, August 5, 2017.
149. Interview with Aris Munandar, head of KOMPAK Solo, Solo, August 19, 2015.
150. International Crisis Group (ICG), "Weakening Indonesia's Mujahidin Networks: Lessons from Maluku and Poso," Asia Report No. 103 (Jakarta and Brussels: ICG, October 13, 2005), 7.
151. ICG, "Indonesia Backgrounder: Jihad in Central Sulawesi," Asia Report No. 74 (Jakarta and Brussels: ICG, February 3, 2004), 7.
152. ICG, "Jihad in Central Sulawesi," 8.
153. Interview with Abu Tholut, former head of JI Mantiqi 3, Kudus, August 8, 2017.
154. Interview with Abu Hakam, Palu, January 9, 2003.
155. ICG, "Jihad in Central Sulawesi," 9.
156. "Adnan Arsal (panglima mujahidin Poso): Mereka Mau Menang Sendiri," *BU NYAN*, January 2002, 22.
157. ICG, "Jihad in Central Sulawesi," 9.
158. Interview with Yahyia Abdel Malik, Laskar Jihad, Jakarta, April 17, 2001.
159. Interview with Jafar Umar Thalib, Laskar Jihad leader, Kaliurang, April 5, 2002.
160. Interview with Alam, LPS-HAM, Palu, January 9, 2003; Damanik, *Tragedi Kemanusiaan Poso*, 148.
161. Kirsten E. Schulze, "From Ambon to Poso: Comparative and Evolutionary Aspects of Local Jihad in Indonesia," *Contemporary Southeast Asia*, 41, no. 1 (2019): 54.
162. Julie Chernov Hwang and Kirsten E. Schulze, "Why They Join: Pathways into Indonesian Militant Islamist Organizations," *Terrorism and Political Violence*, 30, no. 6 (2018): 911–932.
163. ICG, "Jihad in Central Sulawesi," 9.
164. Interview with Cecep, Mujahidin Tanah Runtuh, Palu, August 5, 2017.

165. McRae, *Escalation and Decline of Violent Conflict*, 139.
166. Interview with Cecep, August 5, 2017.
167. Interview with BR, August 6, 2017.
168. Interview with BR, August 6, 2017. For a more detailed discussion of the joining process see Chernov Hwang and Schulze, "Why They Join."
169. HRW, "Four Years of Communal Violence," 12.
170. Ayip Syafruddin, "Mengapa Laskar Jihad ke Poso," *Mercusuar*, August 7–8, 2001; interview with Yahyia Abdel Malik, April 17, 2001.
171. Interview with Kombes Errol Theodorus Rahakbaw, January 9, 2003.
172. HRW, "Four Years of Communal Violence," 23.
173. LPS-HAM, "Rekapitulasi Korban Konflik Poso Januari s/d 10 December 2001."
174. HRW, "Four Years of Communal Violence," 21
175. Lasahido et al., *Suara dari Poso: Kerusuhan, Konflik dan Resolusi* (Jakarta: Yappika, 2003), 57.
176. "Kekejaman atas Muslimin Poso Ditutp-tutupi," September 1, 2001, accessed October 17, 2011, apakabar@saltmine.radix.net; HRW, "Four Years of Communal Violence," 21.
177. McRae, *Escalation and Decline of Violent Conflict*, 154.
178. Interview with Mohamed Daeng Raja, January 10, 2003.
179. "Kekejaman atas Muslimin Poso Ditutp-tutupi," September 1, 2001.
180. McRae, *Escalation and Decline of Violent Conflict*, 143.
181. HRW, "Four Years of Communal Violence," 22.
182. Aragon, "Communal Violence in Poso," 45–79.
183. *Mercusuar*, July 19, 2001.
184. Interview with Reverend Irianto Konkoli, January 8, 2003.
185. HRW, "Four Years of Communal Violence," 23.
186. Brown and Tajima, *Overcoming Violent Conflict*, 15–16.
187. HRW, "Four Years of Communal Violence," 25.
188. *Berita Laskar Jihad*, November 18, 2001.
189. "Kronologi Poso Membara," laskarjihad.or.id, accessed December 5, 2001; "Kronologi Direbutnya Kembali Desa-Desa Muslim Poso," *BUNYAN*, January 2002, 19–20.
190. Interview with Deki Molilo, Tangkura, January 10, 2003.
191. HRW, "Four Years of Communal Violence," 26–27.
192. Interview with Reverend Nelly, January 11, 2003.
193. "Napak Tilas Jihad di Bulan Suci," *BUNYAN*, December 2001, 11–16.
194. Interview with Samsu Mohamed, January 11, 2003.
195. Damanik, *Tragedi Kemanusiaan Poso*, 78.
196. Brown and Tajima, *Overcoming Violent Conflict*, 17.
197. *Report on Poso Conflict Reconciliation*, Report II (Jakarta: Coordinating Ministry for People's Welfare, 2002), 47.
198. McRae, *Escalation and Decline of Violent Conflict*, 247; ICG, "Weakening Indonesia's Mujahidin Networks," 11.
199. ICG, "Jihadism in Indonesia: Poso on the Edge," Asia Report no. 127 (Jakarta and Brussels: ICG, January 24, 2007), 18.
200. McRae, *Escalation and Decline of Violent Conflict*, 200.
201. Interview with Reverend Nelly, January 11, 2003.
202. McRae, *Escalation and Decline of Violent Conflict*, 199.
203. Interview with Reverend Nelly, January 11, 2003.
204. Damanik, *Tragedi Kemanusiaan Poso*, 162.
205. McRae, *Escalation and Decline of Violent Conflict*, 201.
206. ICG, "Jihad in Central Sulawesi," 19–22.

207. *Report on Poso Conflict Reconciliation*, 47.
208. ICG, "Jihad in Central Sulawesi," 21.
209. Brown and Tajima, *Overcoming Violent Conflict*, 36.
210. McRae, *Escalation and Decline of Violent Conflict*, 201.
211. "Sulawesi Christian Priest Killed," *BBC News*, October 16, 2006, http://news.bbc.co.uk/go/pr/fr/-/2/hi/asia-pacific/6054152.stm.
212. "Pembunuhan Irianto Kongkoli: Pemerintah Harus Ambil Lankah Extra," press release, *Kontras*, October 16, 2006, http://www.kontras.org/index.php?hal=siaran_pers&id=415; .
213. Markas Kepolisian Negara Republik Indonesia, Detasemen Khusus 88 Anti Terror, "Berita Acara Pemeriksaan (BAP) Anang Muhtadin alias Papa Enal," Jakarta, June 12, 2011, 5; interview with Iwan Ambo, August 5, 2017.
214. Karnavian, *Indonesian Top Secret*, 92.
215. "Basri," *Indonesia Matters*, February 4, 2007, http://www.indonesiamatters.com/1078/basri/.
216. *Report on Poso Conflict Reconciliation*, 47.
217. Karnavian, *Indonesian Top Secret*, 109–115.
218. ICG, "Weakening Indonesia's Mujahidin Networks," 10.
219. Interview with Iwan Ambo, August 5, 2017.
220. "Beheadings Trial," *Indonesia Matters*, March 21, 2007, http://www.indonesiamatters.com/804/beheadings-trial/.
221. For full wording of the note see McRae, *Escalation and Decline of Violent Conflict*, 221–222.
222. "Basri," *Indonesia Matters*.
223. For full wording of the note see McRae, *Escalation and Decline of Violent Conflict*, 221–222.
224. Karnavian, *Indonesian Top Secret*, 26.
225. "Napak Tilas Jihad di Bulan Suci," 11–16.
226. "Beheadings Trial," *Indonesia Matters*.
227. "Abu Dujana: Saya Marah Kepada Noor Din," *Tempo*, June 24, 2007; interview with Abu Rusdan, senior JI member, Kudus, August 6, 2019.
228. ICG, "Poso on the Edge," 2; Karnavian, *Indonesian Top Secret*, xiv.
229. ICG, "Poso on the Edge," 15.
230. ICG, "Indonesia: Tackling Radicalism in Poso," Asia Briefing No. 57 (Jakarta and Brussels: ICG, January 22, 2008), 2.
231. Interview with Adnan Arsal, January 11, 2003
232. ICG, "Jihad in Central Sulawesi," 17.
233. Interview with Abu Tholut, August 8, 2017.
234. Interview with Abu Tholut, August 4, 2019.
235. Interview with Abu Tholut, August 8, 2017.
236. Conversation with Nasir Abas, former head of JI Mantiqi 3, Semarang, August 6, 2019.
237. Interview with Nasir Abas, Jakarta, October 15, 2010.
238. Interview with Nasir Abas, October 15, 2010.
239. Interview with Nasir Abas, Jakarta, April 3, 2017.
240. Interview with Nasir Abas, April 3, 2017.
241. Interview with BR, August 6, 2017.
242. Kirsten E. Schulze and Joseph Chinyong Liow, "Making Jihadis, Waging Jihad: Transnational and Local Dimensions of the ISIS Phenomenon in Indonesia and Malaysia," *Asian Security*, 15, no. 2 (2019): 13.

243. Interview with Reverend Irianto Konkoli, January 8, 2003.
244. Conversation with Basri, member of Mujahidin Tanah Runtuh and MIT, Jakarta, August 2, 2017.
245. Conversation with Basri, August 2, 2017.

6. THE AMBON CONFLICT, 1999-2005

1. Human Rights Watch (HRW), "Indonesia: The Violence in Ambon, IV. The Conflict," March 1999, http://www.hrw.org/reports/1999/ambon/amron-03.htm.
2. *The Maluku Crisis: Report of the Joint Assessment Mission* (Jakarta: Government of Indonesia, February 6, 2000), 8, 17 states that 4,000 people were killed and 123,000–370,000 displaced. Patricia Spyer, in her article "Fire without Smoke and Other Phantoms of Ambon's Violence: Media Effects, Agency, and the Work of Imagination," *Indonesia*, no. 74 (October 2002), 24, asserts that a minimum of 5,000, possibly as many as 10,000 people, were killed and close to 700,000 internally displaced. George Junus Aditjondro, "Guns, Pamphlets, and Handie-Talkies: How the Military Exploited Local Ethno-Religious Tensions in Maluku to Preserve Their Political and Economic Privileges," in *Violence in Indonesia*, ed. Ingrid Wessel and Georgia Wimhöfer (Hamburg: Abera, 2001), 100 claims that 4,000–10,000 were killed and 860,000 displaced.
3. Manuel Lobato, "The Moluccan Archipelago and Eastern Indonesia in the Second Half of the 16th Century in the Light of Portuguese and Spanish Accounts," in *The Portuguese and the Pacific*, ed. Francis A. Dutra and Joao Camilo dos Santos (Santa Barbara: Center for Portuguese Studies, University of California, 1995), 47.
4. Leonard Y. Andaya, *The World of Maluku: Eastern Indonesia in the Early Modern Period* (Honolulu: University of Hawaii Press, 1993), 3; A. H. de Oliveira Marques, *History of Portugal*, vol. 1, *From Lusitania to Empire* (New York and London: Columbia University Press, 1972), 336.
5. Adolf Heuken, SJ, *"Be My Witness to the Ends of the Earth": The Catholic Church in Indonesia before the 19th Century* (Jakarta: Yayasan Cipta Loka Caraka, 2002).
6. Lobato, "Moluccan Archipelago," 43.
7. Lobato, "Moluccan Archipelago," 47–48.
8. Andaya, *World of Maluku*, 132; Heuken, *"Be My Witness*, 40.
9. Interview with Monsignor Sol, Bishop Emeritus of Amboina, Ambon, May 8, 2001.
10. Bernhard H. M. Vlekke, *Nusantara: A History of Indonesia* (The Hague: W. Van Hoeve, 1959), 87.
11. G. J. Knaap, *Kruidnagelen en Christenen: De Vereenigde Oost-Indische Compagnie en de bevolking van Ambon 1656–1696* (Dordrecht and Providence: Foris, 1987), 83.
12. Richard Chauvel, *Nationalists, Soldiers and Separatists* (Leiden: KITLV, 2008), 20.
13. Chauvel, *Nationalists, Soldiers and Separatists*, 4.
14. Chauvel, *Nationalists, Soldiers and Separatists*, 7. For a full discussion of *pela* alliances see Dieter Bartels, "Guarding the Invisible Mountain: Intervillage Alliances, Religious Syncretism and Ethnic Identity among Ambonese Christians and Muslims in the Moluccas," PhD thesis, Cornell University, 1977. See also Dieter Bartels, "The Evolution of God in the Spice Islands: The Converging and Diverging of Protestant Christianity and Islam in the Colonial and Post-colonial Periods," in *Christianity in Indonesia*, ed. Susanne Schröter (Berlin: Dr. W. Hopf, 2010), 225–258.
15. Interview with Monsignor Sol, May 8, 2001.
16. M. C. Ricklefs, *A History of Modern Indonesia since c. 1200* (Basingstoke, UK: Palgrave, 2001), 76.
17. Ricklefs, *History of Modern Indonesia*, 76.

18. Thamrin Ely quoted in Daniel Wattimanela, "Perjumpaan Islam dan Kristen di Maluku Tengah: Suatu Pendeklatan Sosiologi Historis," MA Thesis, Universitas Kristen Satya Wacana, 2003, 95.

19. Amry Vandenbosch, *The Dutch East Indies: Its Government, Problems, and Politics* (Berkeley: University of California Press, 1942), 53.

20. Ben van Kaam, *The South Moluccans: Background to the Train Hijackings* (London: C. Hurst, 1980), 42.

21. Richard Chauvel, "The Rising Sun in the Spice Islands: A History of Ambon during the Japanese Occupation," Working Paper No. 37 (Clayton, Victoria: The Centre for Southeast Asian Studies, Monash University, 1985), 3.

22. Interview with Ali Fawzi, Badan Imarah Muslim Maluku (BIMM), Ambon, December 20, 2001.

23. Sasamu Tozuka, *Ambon and Timor Invasion Operations*, Japanese Monograph Series No. 16 (Washington, DC: Office of the Chief of Military History, Department of the Army, 1953), 11.

24. Chauvel, "Rising Sun," 15–16.

25. Chauvel, *Nationalists, Soldiers and Separatists*, 70.

26. Chauvel, "Rising Sun," 3.

27. Frank Leonard Cooley, "Altar and Throne in Central Moluccan Societies: A Study of the Relationship between Institutions of Religion and the Institutions of Local Government in a Traditional Society undergoing Rapid Social Change," PhD thesis, Yale University, 1962, 367.

28. Chauvel, "Rising Sun," 21.

29. Chauvel, "Rising Sun," 6.

30. Chauvel, "Rising Sun the Spice Islands," 16–17.

31. Interview with John Ruhulessin, Ambon, May 4, 2001.

32. As cited in Van Kaam, *South Moluccans*, 26.

33. Van Kaam, *South Moluccans*, 7.

34. Chauvel, *Nationalists, Soldiers and Separatists*, 52.

35. Special Commissioner in South-East Asia Lord Killearn (Singapore) to Foreign Office, May 3, 1946, PREM8/1224, UKNA, 4.

36. "Helfrich to the Minister of the Navy," December 2, 1945, in *Officiële bescheiden betreffende de Nederlands-Indonesische betrekkingen 1945–1950*, vol. 2, ed. S. L. van der Wal, P. J. Drooglever, and M.J.B. Schouten (The Hague: Nijhoff, 1981), 272.

37. Anthony Reid, *The Indonesian National Revolution 1945–1950* (Westport, CT: Greenwood, 1974), 45; Benedict R. O'G. Anderson, *Java in a Time of Revolution: Occupation and Resistance, 1944–1946* (Jakarta: Equinox, 2006), 198.

38. Reid, *Indonesian National Revolution*, 29; Chauvel, *Nationalists, Soldiers and Separatists*, 201.

39. Anderson, *Java*, 190.

40. "Extract from a letter from Maj. J. C. Hoekendijk," PAPWI Headquarters, Batavia, Java, October 23, 1945, "Report by A. Anderson," November 28, 1945, FO371/46401, 1.

41. Telegram from Supreme Allied Command South-East Asia to Foreign Office, November 29, 1945, FO371/46402, UKNA.

42. Mr. Stewart to Mr. Bevin, "Indonesia: Annual Review for 1949," Djakarta, January 26, 1950, in *British Documents on Foreign Affairs: Reports and Papers from the Foreign Office Confidential Print*, Series E, Vol. 11, January–December 1950, ed. Antony Best (Bethesda, MD: University Publications of America, 2003), 148.

43. Sukarno, *Toward Freedom and the Dignity of Man: A Collection of Speeches by President Sukarno of the Republic of Indonesia* (Jakarta: Department of Foreign Affairs of the Republic of Indonesia, 1961), 42.

44. Ir. Sukarno, *Dibawah Bendera Revolusi*, Jilid II (Yogyakarta: Yayasan Bung Karno/Penerbit Media Pressindo, 2019), 67; Sukarno, *Toward Freedom*, 42; *Algemeen Handelsblad*, March 3, 1950.

45. Dr. J. Leimena, *The Ambon Question: Facts and Appeal* (Jakarta, October 1950), 6.

46. Leimena, *Ambon Question*, 7.

47. Leimena, *Ambon Question*, 7.

48. Leimena, *Ambon Question*, 13–14.

49. Dr. A. H. Nasution, Djenderal TNI, *Sedjarah Perdjuangan Nasional dibidang Bersendjata* (Jakarta: Mega Bookstore, 1965), 172.

50. TNI, *Sejarah TNI*, Jilid II (1950–1959) (Jakarta: Markas Besar Tentara Nasional Indonesia Pusat Sejarah dan Tradisi TNI, 2000), 117–118.

51. TNI, *Sejarah TNI*, Jilid II, 119.

52. Chauvel, *Nationalists, Soldiers and Separatists*, 391.

53. Mr. Morland to Mr. Eden, "Mr. Heath's Tour of the Moluccas and Celebes," February 8, 1954, in Best, *British Documents on Foreign Affairs*, 11:288.

54. Lieutenant Muir, Imperial War Graves Commission Ambon, "Report on Amboina Operations," December 1950, Series A4357.252/9, Australian War Memorial Archives, Canberra.

55. Mr. Mohamed Roem, minister of foreign affairs, Djakarta, to the chairman of the United Nations Commission for Indonesia, Hotel des Indes, Djakarta, "Letter Dated 30 September 1950 from the Indonesian Minister for Foreign Affairs in Reply to the Commission's Letter of 25 September 1950 with regard to the Commission's Offer Assistance in the South Moluccas Affair," S-0681-0015-02-0001, United Nations Archives (UNA), 1; Sukarno, "'Dari Sabang Sampai Merauke' Pidato Bung Karno pada perayaan HUT ke 5 Republik Indonesia," August 17, 1950.

56. Mr. Mohamed Roem, minister of foreign affairs, Djakarta, to the chairman of the United Nations Commission for Indonesia, Hotel des Indes, Djakarta, "Letter Dated 23 September 1950 from the Indonesian Minister for Foreign Affairs in Reply to the Commission's Letter of 4 August 1950 Offering the Commission's Assistance with regard to the South Moluccas Affair," S-0681-0015-02-0001, UNA, 2.

57. Letter from Rochmuljati Wirjohatmodjo, press officer of the Indonesian Delegation to the United Nations, *New York Times*, February 21, 1957; Letter from A. Kamil, press and public relations officer, Indonesian Permanent Mission to the United Nations, *New York Times*, April 26, 1958; Sukarno, *Dibawah Bendera Revolusi*, Jilid II, 175; Letter from A. Kamil, press and public relations officer, Indonesian Permanent Mission to the United Nations, *New York Times*, April 26, 1958.

58. Roem, "Letter Dated 23 September 1950," 1.

59. Nasution, *Sedjarah Perdjuangan Nasional dibidang Bersendjata*, 171; *Lintasan Sejarah: Kodam XVI Pattimura* (Ambon: Kodam Pattimura, 2002), 58; Sukarno, *Dibawah Bendera Revolusi*, Jilid II, 175; "Rebels Attack in South Moluccas; Jakarta Aide Discounts Incidents," *New York Times*, December 10, 1954.

60. Republik Indonesia Serikat, Kementerian Penerangan, AI/AE293, Djakarta, May 22, 1950, S-0681-0015-02-00002, UNA.

61. Morland, "Mr. Heath's Tour," February 8, 1954, in Best, *British Documents on Foreign Affairs*, 288.

62. Jacques Bertrand, *Nationalism and Ethnic Conflict in Indonesia* (Cambridge: Cambridge University Press, 2004), 116.

63. TNI, *Sejarah TNI*, Jilid III (1960–1965), 164.

64. Robert B. Baowollo, "Konfliktresolution als Konfliktprävention," Langgur, March 14–18, 2001, The Go East Institute (now Center for East Indonesian Affairs [CEIA]) Muslim-Christian Dialogue, 4.

65. S. Yunanto, "Militant Islam in the Ambon Conflict," in *Militant Islamic Movements in Indonesia and South-East Asia*, ed. S. Yunanto et al. (Jakarta: Friederich Ebert Stiftung, 2003), 133; International Crisis Group (ICG), "Overcoming Murder and Chaos in Maluku," Asia Report No. 10 (Jakarta and Brussels: ICG, December 19, 2000), 2; Harold Crouch, *Political Reform in Indonesia after Soeharto* (Singapore: Institute of Southeast Asian Studies, 2010), 244.

66. Gerry Van Klinken, "The Maluku Wars: Bringing Society Back In," *Indonesia*, no. 71 (April 2001), 12.

67. ICG, "Indonesia: The Search for Peace in Maluku," Asia Report No. 31 (Jakarta and Brussels: ICG, February 8, 2002), 1.

68. Jubilee Campaign UK, "Analysis of the Sectarian Conflict in Maluku and Its Role in the Islamicisation of Indonesia," Report, December 1999, 4.accessed on June 10, 2002, http://www.jubileecampaign.co.uk/world/asia.htm#Indonesia.

69. Crouch, *Political Reform in Indonesia*, 244.

70. Interview with Tony Pariela, University of Pattimura, Ambon, May 8, 2001.

71. Interview with Ignatius Ismartono, SJ, Indonesian Bishops Conference, Jakarta, May 17, 2001.

72. Milob Team 9 to Milex Board, "Special Report on Visit to South Moluccas," April 22, 1950, S-0681-0015-02-00002, UNA, 7.

73. A. Halim M. A. Tuasikal, "De Islam in de Molukken," *Cultureel Nieuws Indonesië* 2, no. 20 (1952): 385–386.

74. Interview with Ali Fawzi, December 20, 2001.

75. Interview with Jusuf Kalla, coordinating minister for people's welfare, Jakarta, April 11, 2003.

76. Interview with Des Alwi, "raja of Banda," Jakarta, June 18, 2001.

77. Interview with Des Alwi, June 18, 2001.

78. Interview with Reverend Jacky Manuputty, Gereja Protestant Maluku, Ambon, April 1, 2005.

79. Interview with Amir Kiat, Pemuda Batu Merah, delegate to Malino, Ambon, March 27, 2002.

80. Jacques Bertrand, "Legacies of the Authoritarian Past: Religious Violence in Indonesia's Moluccan Islands," *Pacific Affairs* 75, no.1 (2002): 73.

81. Interview with Des Alwi, June 18, 2001; interview with John Ruhulessin, May 4, 2001; Bertrand, "Legacies of the Authoritarian Past," 73.

82. Aditjondro, "Guns, Pamphlets, and Handie-Talkies," 104.

83. Interview with Jusuf Kalla, April 11, 2003.

84. Interview with Reverend Jacky Manuputty, April 1, 2005.

85. Tony Pariella, "Social Transformation in Soya Atas Village," in *Remaking Maluku: Social Transformation in Eastern Indonesia*, ed. David Mearns and Chris Healy, Special Monograph No. 1 (Darwin: Centre for Southeast Asian Studies, Northern Territory University, 1996), 116.

86. Interview with P. M. Laksono, Gajah Mada University, Yogyakarta, April 30, 2001.

87. Interview with Steve Gasperz, UKIM, Ambon, March 28, 2017.

88. Interview with Reverend Jacky Manuputty, April 1, 2005.

89. Crouch, *Political Reform in Indonesia*, 245.

90. Van Klinken, "Maluku Wars," 19; interview with Reverend Jacky Manuputty, April 1, 2005.

91. Sumanto Al Qurtuby, *Religious Violence and Conciliation in Indonesia: Christians and Muslims in the Moluccas* (London: Routledge, 2016), 37.

92. Bertrand, *Nationalism and Ethnic Conflict*, 118.

93. Bertrand, *Nationalism and Ethnic Conflict*, 118.
94. Van Klinken, "Maluku Wars," 19.
95. Interview with Jusuf Kalla, April 11, 2003.
96. Bertrand, *Nationalism and Ethnic Conflict*, 119.
97. Interview with Jusuf Kalla, April 11, 2003.
98. Interview with Reverend Broeri Hendriks, Protestant Synod, GPM, Ambon, May 4, 2001; Aditjondro, "Guns, Pamphlets, and Handie-Talkies," 104; interview with Reverend Jacky Manuputty, April 1, 2005.
99. Interview with Monsignor Sol, May 8, 2001.
100. Van Klinken, "Maluku Wars," 21.
101. Spyer, "Fire without Smoke," 27.
102. Interview with humanitarian aid worker, Ambon, February 24, 2011.
103. Interview with Pastor C. J. Böhm, Crisis Centre of the Diocese of Amboina, Ambon, May 4, 2001.
104. Interview with Reverend Jacky Manuputty, April 1, 2005.
105. Interview with a Muslim humanitarian aid worker, February 24, 2011.
106. Interview with Reverend Jacky Manuputty, April 1, 2005.
107. Interview with Emang Nikijuluw, Christian "grassroots" leader, Ambon, February 22, 2011.
108. Interview with Berthy Loupatti, leader of Coker, November 10, 2010.
109. Interview with George Siahaja, senior police sergeant when the conflict erupted, Ambon, August 3, 2012.
110. Interview with Berthy Loupatti, November 10, 2010.
111. Interview with Reverend Jacky Manuputty, Maluku Protestant Church (GPM), Ambon, July 31, 2012.
112. Des Alwi, "Operatornya Preman Eks Ketapang," *DëTAK*, March 9–15, 1999. (Alwi was a member of the investigative team formed by President Habibie.)
113. Interview with Pastor C. J. Böhm, May 4, 2001.
114. HRW, "Indonesia: The Violence in Ambon, IV. The Conflict."
115. HRW, "The Violence in Ambon," IV. The Conflict.
116. HRW, "The Violence in Ambon," IV. The Conflict.
117. *Gatra*, January 30, 1999.
118. Badrus Sholeh, *Jihad, Conflict and Reconciliation in Ambon, Indonesia* (Saarbrücken: Lambert Academic Publishing, 2012), 30; *Gatra*, January 30, 1999.
119. Interview with Yusuf Ely, Satgas MUI coordinator, April 3, 2005.
120. Interview with Yusuf Ely, April 3, 2005.
121. Interview with humanitarian aid worker, February 24, 2011.
122. Interview with Reverend Jacky Manuputty, July 31, 2012.
123. Al Qurtuby, *Religious Violence and Conciliation*, 78–79.
124. Interview with Emang Nikijuluw, February 22, 2011.
125. Interview with Berthy Loupatti, November 10, 2010.
126. Interview with Emang Nikijuluw, February 22, 2011.
127. Interview with Mahfud, member of Sam's group, Ambon, February 23, 2011; interview with Ronal, former *agas* member, Ambon, February 24, 2011.
128. Aditjondro, "Guns, Pamphlets, and Handie-Talkies," 101. See also *AP*, February 24, 2000, and *Tempo*, January 23, 2000, 23.
129. Interview with Sam's parents, Kebun Cengkeh, February 22, 2011; interview with Mahfud, February 23, 2011.
130. Interview with Ronal, February 24, 2011.
131. For a more detailed discussion of the entry and roles of Jemaah Islamiyah and KOMPAK in the Ambon conflict see Kirsten E. Schulze, "From Ambon to Poso:

Comparative and Evolutionary Aspects of Local Jihad in Indonesia," *Contemporary Southeast Asia*, 41, no. 1 (2019): 35–62.

132. Interview with Zulkarnaen, former JI top military commander, Jakarta, August 11, 2023.

133. Interview with Ali Imron, former member of Jemaah Islamiyah, Jakarta, December 6, 2010.

134. Interview with Zulkarnaen, August 11, 2023.

135. Interview with Ali Imron, December 6, 2010.

136. Interview with Jibril, former member of Jemaah Islamiyah, Jakarta, November 4, 2010.

137. Schulze, "From Ambon to Poso," 42; interview with Aris Munandar, leader of KOMPAK, Dewan Dakwah, Solo, August 19, 2015.

138. Bertrand, *Nationalism and Ethnic Conflict*, 125.

139. Bertrand, *Nationalism and Ethnic Conflict*, 125.

140. "Kerusuhan Pulau Haruku, Menguji Solidaritas Kita," *Merdeka*, February 17, 1999.

141. For a discussion of the conflict in the Kei Islands see Craig Thorburn, "Musibah: Governance, Intercommunal Violence and Reinventing Tradition in the Kei Islands, Southeast Maluku," Working Paper 125 (Clayton, Victoria: Monash Asia Institute, 2005); Phillip Winn, "Banda Burns," *Inside Indonesia*, no. 61, January–March 2000, accessed October 7, 2002, http://www.insideindonesia.org/edit60/winn1.htm.

142. Interview with Karel Ralahalu, Maluku governor, Ambon, February 25, 2011.

143. Kirsten E. Schulze, "The 'Ethnic' in Indonesia's Communal Conflicts: Violence in Poso, Ambon and West Kalimantan," *Ethnic and Racial Studies* 40, no. 12 (2017): 2096–2114.

144. Interview with Emang Nikijuluw, February 22, 2011.

145. Interview with Reverend Jacky Manuputty, April 1, 2005.

146. M. Nasir Rahawarin, "Konflik Maluku Dan Solusinya," Ambon, October 2000, paper obtained by the author, 3–4.

147. "Kemarin Ambon, kine Seram," *Ummat*, February 15, 1999.

148. "Kemarin Ambon, kine Seram," *Ummat*, February 15, 1999.

149. Rahawarin, "Konflik Maluku Dan Solusinya," 3–4.

150. *Jawa Pos,* June 16, 2000; *Antara,* May 17, 2000.

151. Van Klinken, "Maluku Wars," 22.

152. Interview with Reverend Jacky Manuputty, July 31, 2012.

153. Interview with a humanitarian aid worker, Ambon, May 7, 2001.

154. Interview with Nasir Rahawarin, Badan Imarah Muslim Maluku (BIMM), Ambon, December 20, 2001; Rahawarin, "Konflik Maluku Dan Solusinya," 1.

155. "Dua Kapal berisi Preman masuk ke Ambon," *Media Indonesia*, February 1, 1999; Rustam Kastor, *Fakta, data dan analisa conspiracy RMS dan Kristen menhancurkan umat Islam di Ambon—Maluku* (Yogyakarta: Wihdah Press, 2000), 33–34, 185, 197–207, and 108.

156. Interview with Yusuf Ely, April 3, 2005.

157. Interview with Mohamed Atamimi, head of the State Islamic High School (STAIN), Kebun Cengkeh, April 4, 2005.

158. Interview with Emang Nikijuluw, February 22, 2011.

159. Van Klinken, "Maluku Wars," 22.

160. Interview with Des Alwi, June 18, 2001.

161. Interview with Reverend Broeri Hendriks, May 4, 2001; interview with Alex Manuputty, leader of the Maluku Sovereignty Front, Kudamati, Ambon, December 18,

2001; interview with Pastor Agus Ulahaiyanan, Crisis Centre of the Diocese of Amboina, Gonzalo Veloso, December 19, 2001.

162. "Penembak Misterius Berkeliaran di Ambon," *Suara Karya*, July 30, 1999.

163. "Senjata Gelap Masuk ke Ambon," *Media Indonesia*, August 10, 1999.

164. ICG, "Overcoming Murder and Chaos," 6; Smith Alhadar, "The Forgotten War in North Maluku," *Inside Indonesia*, no. 63 (July–September 2000), accessed on October 7, 2002, www.insideindonesia.org/edit63/alhadar.htm(). For a more detailed discussion of the North Maluku conflict see Jan Nanere, ed., *Halmahera Berdarah: Suatu Upaya Menungkap Kebenaran* (Ambon: Yayasan Bina Masyarakat Sejahtera dan Pelestarian Alam, 2000); Chris Wilson, *Ethno-Religious Violence in Indonesia: From Soil to God* (London: Routledge, 2008); and Christopher R. Duncan, *Violence and Vengeance: Religious Conflict and Its Aftermath in Eastern Indonesia* (Ithaca, NY: Cornell University Press, 2013).

165. "Bomber Killed, Travellers Beaten in Ambon Violence," *Jakarta Post*, September 20, 1999.

166. Van Klinken, "Maluku Wars," 5.

167. "Maluku Communal Clashes Claim at Least 217 Lives," *Jakarta Post*, September 29, 1999.

168. Bertrand, *Nationalism and Ethnic Conflict*, 129

169. "Ambon Bentrok Lagi, 6 tewas, puluhan luka luka," *Republika*, December 20, 1999.

170. "Some 800 Missing on Buru Island," *Jakarta Post*, January 12, 2000.

171. Bertrand, "Legacies of the Authoritarian Past," 83.

172. "Ambon Terus Bergolak, Pejabat TK1 Diusulkan Diganti," *Suara Karya*, December 29, 1999.

173. *Kompas*, January 14, 2000.

174. ICG, "Search for Peace in Maluku," 3.

175. *Republika*, January 4, 2000.

176. *Republika*, January 4, 2000.

177. Bertrand, *Nationalism and Ethnic Conflict*, 129.

178. ICG, "Search for Peace in Maluku," 10; interview with Ignatius Ismartono, SJ, May 17, 2001.

179. Al Qurtuby, *Religious Violence and Conciliation*, 27.

180. Interview with Emang Nikijuluw, February 22, 2011.

181. Interview with Saleh Latuconsina, Maluku governor, Ambon, December 20, 2001.

182. Interview with Pastor Agus Ulahaiyanan, December 19, 2001.

183. Interview with Des Alwi, June 18, 2001.

184. Interview with Ali Imron, December 6, 2010; interview with Mubarok, former member of Jemaah Islamiyah, Jakarta, December 7, 2010; interview with Pastor C. J. Böhm, May 4, 2001; interview with Pastor Agus Ulahaiyanan, December 19, 2001.

185. Interview with Des Alwi, June 18, 2001.

186. Rahawarin, "Konflik Maluku Dan Solusinya," 6.

187. Interview with Major General Max Tamaela, Pattimura Military Commander, May 1999 to July 2000, Jakarta, January 8, 2002.

188. Interview with Major General Max Tamaela, January 8, 2002.

189. ICG, "Overcoming Murder and Chaos," 5.

190. Interview with Major General Max Tamaela, January 8, 2002.

191. Interview with Major General Max Tamaela, January 8, 2002.

192. "Lima TNI dibunuh, Pangdam bersembunyi," *Republika*, December 29, 1999.

193. ICG, "Overcoming Murder and Chaos," 8.

194. "Ambon berdarah, Wapres Berlibur ke Hong Kong," *Republika*, December 29, 1999.
195. ICG, "Overcoming Murder and Chaos," 7.
196. ICG, "Overcoming Murder and Chaos," 8.
197. Schulze, "From Ambon to Poso," 46.
198. Interview with Ramly, Mujahidin KOMPAK, Jakarta, April 10, 2017.
199. ICG, "Overcoming Murder and Chaos," 13.
200. Tracy Dahlby, "Religious Zealots and Regional Separatists Force the Issue: Can This Far-Flung Nation Hold Together?," *National Geographic*, March 2001, 92.
201. ICG, "Overcoming Murder and Chaos," 13.
202. Interview with Indonesian military intelligence officer, Jakarta, June 20, 2001; interview with Major General Max Tamaela, January 8, 2002.
203. Interview with Major General Max Tamaela, January 8, 2002; Yunanto, "Militant Islam," 145.
204. Interview with Major General Max Tamaela, January 8, 2002.
205. Interview with Pastor Agus Ulahaiyanan, December 19, 2001.
206. Interview with Major General Max Tamaela, January 8, 2002.
207. Interview with Juwono Sudarsono, Indonesian defense minister, Jakarta, June 5, 2001.
208. Interview with Ali Fawzi, December 20, 2001.
209. Crouch, *Political Reform in Indonesia*, 254.
210. Interview with Major General Max Tamaela, January 8, 2002.
211. ICG, "Illicit Arms in Indonesia," Asia Briefing No. 109 (Jakarta and Brussels: ICG, September 6, 2010), 10.
212. Interview with Des Alwi, June 18, 2001; interview with Abdullah Sonata, head of KOMPAK Ambon 2000–2001, Jakarta, December 7, 2010.
213. Crouch, *Political Reform in Indonesia*, 254.
214. Interview with Yusuf Ely, April 3, 2005.
215. Aditjondro, "Guns, Pamphlets and Handie-Talkies," 117; ICG, "Search for Peace in Maluku," 5; ICG, "Illicit Arms in Indonesia," 10.
216. Interview with Abdullah Sonata, December 7, 2010.
217. TAPAK Ambon, "Notes on Weaknesses in the Implementation of the State of Civil Emergency in Maluku," October 2000, 4.
218. ICG, "Search for Peace in Maluku," 3.
219. Interview with a group of Christian Ambonese refugees, Sorong, September 14, 2000.
220. Interview with Abdullah Sonata, December 7, 2010.
221. Interview with Major General Max Tamaela, January 8, 2002.
222. "Report No. 12," July 6, 2000, in C. J. Böhm, *Brief Chronicle of the Unrest in the Moluccas 1999–2005* (Ambon: Crisis Centre Diocese of Amboina, 2005), 37.
223. "Report No. 12," July 6, 2000, in Böhm, *Brief Chronicle*, 37.
224. "Report No. 13," July 7, 2000, in Böhm, *Brief Chronicle*, 39.
225. Interview with a group of Christian Ambonese refugees, September 14, 2000.
226. "Report No. 20," July 17, 2000, in Böhm, *Brief Chronicle*, 46.
227. Interview with a group of Christian Ambonese refugees, September 14, 2000.
228. Interview with Pastor C. J. Böhm, May 4, 2001.
229. Interview with Pastor C. J. Böhm, May 4, 2001.
230. Interview with Christian Ambonese refugees, September 14, 2000; interview with Pastor Agus Ulahaiyanan, December 19, 2001.
231. Interview with Monsigneur Sol, May 8, 2001.
232. "Letter to Mr Kofi Annan, Secretary General United Nations, Ambon, 9 July 2000," in Böhm, *Brief Chronicle*, 39.

233. For a more detailed discussion see Birgit Bräuchler, "Cyber Identities at War: Religion, Identity and the Internet in the Moluccan Conflict," *Indonesia*, no. 75 (2003): 123–151.
234. Spyer, "Fire without Smoke," 26.
235. ICG, "Overcoming Murder and Chaos," 11–12.
236. "Military Issues Shoot on Sight Orders in Maluku," *Jakarta Post*, October 2, 2000.
237. ICG, "Overcoming Murder and Chaos," 19.
238. ICG, "Overcoming Murder and Chaos," 12.
239. Interview with Ignatius Ismartono, SJ, May 17, 2001.
240. Interview with Pastor Haas, Ambon, May 8, 2001.
241. Interview with Monsignor Sol, May 8, 2001.
242. Interview with Jibril, November 4, 2010.
243. ICG, "Search for Peace in Maluku," 10.
244. ICG, "Search for Peace," 13.
245. "Kronologis Pembantaian Muslimin oleh Yon Gab: Tawanan Disiksa Lalu Titembak," June 16, 2001, accessed on June 16, 2001, www.Laskarjihad.or.id.
246. "90 persen Anggota Yon Gab Beragama Kristen," June 17, 2001, accessed on June 17, 2001, www.Laskarjihad.or.id.
247. Interview with Brig. Gen. Mustopo, Pattimura Military Commander, Ambon, December 19, 2001.
248. ICG, "Search for Peace in Maluku," 20.
249. "Report No. 213," December 11, 2001, in Böhm, *Brief Chronicle*, 204.
250. ICG, "Search for Peace in Maluku," 20.
251. Interview with Berthy Loupatti, November 10, 2010.
252. Interview with Berthy Loupatti, November 10, 2010.
253. Wattimena quoted in ICG, "Overcoming Murder and Chaos," 15.
254. "Report No. 102," December 6, 2000, in Böhm, *Brief Chronicle*, 113.
255. Wattimena quoted in ICG, "Overcoming Murder and Chaos," 15.
256. Crouch, *Political Reform in Indonesia*, 255.
257. Interview with Berthy Loupatti, November 10, 2010.
258. Interview with Berthy Loupatti, November 10, 2010.
259. Interview with Jafar Umar Thalib, Laskar Jihad leader, Kaliurang, April 5, 2002.
260. *Jakarta Post*, September 11, 2000.
261. Interview with Nasir Rahawarin, December 20, 2001.
262. Interview with Thamrin Ely, Muslim delegate to the Malino talks, Ambon, March 28, 2002.
263. Interview with Malik Selang, Muslim community leader, MUI, Ambon, May 7, 2001.
264. Interview with Pastor C. J. Böhm, May 4, 2001; Kirsten E. Schulze, "Laskar Jihad and the Ambon Conflict," *Brown Journal of World Affairs* 9, No. 1 (Spring 2002): 67.
265. Interview with Ali Fawzi, December 20, 2001.
266. Schulze, "From Ambon to Poso," 52
267. For a comprehensive discussion of Laskar Jihad see Noorhaidi Hassan, *Islam, Militancy, and the Quest for Identity in Post–New Order Indonesia* (Ithaca, NY: Cornell Southeast Asia Program, 2006).
268. Interview with Jafar Umar Thalib, April 5, 2002.
269. Schulze, "Laskar Jihad," 63.
270. Interview with Apud, former member of Mujahidin KOMPAK in Ambon, Bekasi, 8 January 2014.
271. Interview with Ramly, April 10, 2017; interview with Apud, January 8, 2014.
272. Interview with Ramly, April 10, 2017.

273. Interview with Jibril, November 4, 2010.
274. Interview with Jibril, November 4, 2010.
275. ICG, "Jihad in Central Sulawesi," 6.
276. ICG, "Jihad in Central Sulawesi," 6.
277. Interview with Ramly, April 10, 2017.
278. Interview with Thamrin Ely, March 28, 2002.
279. Interview with Amir Kiat, March 27, 2002.
280. *Bulletin Laskar Jihad*, edition 6, as cited in "Report No. 236," February 14, 2002, in Böhm, *Brief Chronicle*, 216–217.
281. Interview with Thamrin Ely, March 28, 2002.
282. Interview with Amir Kiat, March 27, 2002.
283. "Report No. 237," February 15, 2002, in Böhm, *Brief Chronicle*, 217.
284. Interview with Amir Kiat, March 27, 2002.
285. Interview with Saleh Latuconsina, March 26, 2002.
286. Interview with Pastor Agus Ulahaiyanan, Gonzalo Veloso, Ambon, March 25, 2002.
287. Interview with Pastor Agus Ulahaiyanan, March 25, 2002.
288. Front Kedaulatan Maluku (FKM), press statement No. 102/DPP.FKM/II/2002, "Pernyataan Sikap terhadap Hasil Perjanjian Malino Untuk Maluku," February 15, 2002.
289. FKM, "Seruan Terbuka, Seputar Kesepakatan Malino II," February 22, 2002.
290. "Report No. 242," February 25, 2002, in Böhm, *Brief Chronicle*, 221.
291. "Report No. 245," March 2, 2002, in Böhm, *Brief Chronicle*, 223.
292. Interview with Amir Kiat, March 27, 2002.
293. "Report No. 245," March 2, 2002, in Böhm, *Brief Chronicle*, 223.
294. Interview with foreign observer, March 26, 2002.
295. "Report No. 254," April 3, 2002, in Böhm, *Brief Chronicle*, 228.
296. "Report No. 294," June 12, 2002, in Böhm, *Brief Chronicle*, 259.
297. "Rusuh Lagi, 13 Orang Tewas di Ambon," *Tempo*, April 28, 2002, https://nasional.tempo.co/read/8786/rusuh-lagi-13-orang-tewas-di-ambon.
298. *Siwalima*, April 29, 2002.
299. "Report No. 271," April 29, 2002, in Böhm, *Brief Chronicle*, 238.
300. "Report No. 304," July 27, 2002, 267; "Report No. 314," September 6, 2002, 172; "Report No. 321," October 20, 2002, 276, in Böhm, *Brief Chronicle*.
301. "Berty Loupaty: Kopassus Dalang Kerusuhan di Ambon," *Tempo*, August 25, 2003, https://nasional.tempo.co/read/383/berty-kopassus-dalang-kerusuhan-di-ambon.
302. Msgr. P. C. Mandagi, "SOS Message from the Bishop of Amboina," "Report No. 426," April 30, 2004, in Böhm, *Brief Chronicle*, 338–339.
303. "Report No. 425," April 29, 2004, in Böhm, *Brief Chronicle*, 337.
304. ICG, "Weakening Indonesia's Mujahidin Networks: Lessons from Maluku and Poso," Asia Report No. 103 (Jakarta and Brussels: ICG, October 13, 2005), 1.
305. ICG, "Weakening Indonesia's Mujahidin Networks," 4.
306. ICG, "Weakening Indonesia's Mujahidin Networks," 5. See also "Pos Brimob Diserang karena Ganggu Latihan Para Teroris," *Sinar Harapan*, June 14, 2005.
307. ICG, "Weakening Indonesia's Mujahidin Networks," 5.
308. Radio Ambon, April 25, 1950; "Dr. Chr. R. S. Soumokil, President of the Republic of the South Moluccas, Appeal from Ceram to the Geneva Conference, 2 April 1954," in *Republik Maluku Selatan—Der Selbstbestimmungskampf der Ambonesen: Untersuchungen und Dokumente zum Selbstbestimmungsrecht der Ambonesen, zum Föderalismus und Kolonialismus in Indonesien*, ed. Günter Decker (Göttingen: Verlag Otto Schwarz, 1957), 149.
309. Chauvel, *Nationalists, Soldiers and Separatists*, 360.

310. John Christian Ruhulessin and Pieter George Manoppo, *Local Political Instability in Maluku: Inspiration of the Proclamation by the Republic of South Maluku and its Implications for the Arrangement of Cultural Echo-Centric* (Chisinau: Lambert Academic Publishing, 2021), 11.

311. Radio Ambon, April 24, 1950.

312. "UNCI Secretariat, Text of Telegram received from Sgravenhage [The Hague] 28 July 1950," from Dr. Nikijuluw, Chargé d'Affaires of the Republic of South Moluccas in the Hague, S-0681-0015-02-00002, UNA; *The Forgotten War: An Appeal from the Republic of the South Moluccas*, No 11A (Department of Public Information of the Republic of the South Moluccas, Pocketbook Edition No. 2, n.d.), 1.

313. "Radiogram from Soumokil, Foreign Office, Republic of the South Moluccas to Dr. Nikijuluw, Charge d'Affaires of the Republic of the South Moluccas," forwarded to the UNCI by Dr. J. P. Nikijuluw, Representative of the Republic of the South Moluccas, Rotterdam, June 15, 1950, S-0681-0015-02-00001, UNA; "Text of Telegram received from Sgravenhage," from Dr. Nikijuluw, Representative of South Moluccas, Rotterdam to UNCI Secretariat, August 1, 1950, S-0681-0015-02-00002, UNA; "Cable from Mr. Nikijuluw," October 5, 1950, S-0681-0015-02-00001, UNA; letter by Charles J. V. Nikijuluw, chairman of the South Moluccas Delegation New York, in *New York Times*, November 16, 1950.

314. Harold L. B. Lovestrand, *The President Has Been Executed* (Maitland, FL: Xulon Press), 107 and 137; *Forgotten War*, 4.

315. *Forgotten War*, 3-4 and 10; "Ambon Wishes to Support the United Nations," Dr. J. P. Nikijuluw, Representative of the Republic of South Moluccas, The Hague, to the General Assembly of the United Nations, Lake Success, January 23, 1951, S-0681-0015-02-00003, UNA, 3; "Dr. J. P. Nikijuluw, Representative of the Republic of the South Moluccas to UNCI," Rotterdam, June 15, 1950, S-0681-0015-02-00001, UNA.

316. "The Stamps of the South Moluccas Republic and the Forgotten War," D. J. Hansen Ltd., Philatelic Services and Universal Stamp Co, Eastrington, Goole, Yorkshire. In 1952, 1953, and 1954 further RMS stamps were released depicting diamonds, animals, and flowers. Some of these are believed to be overprints, stamps of the Netherlands Indies with Republik Maluku Selatan printed on them. Further "RMS" stamps were released in 1955 by Henry Stolow, including the triangular ones, generally considered to be fakes or forgeries.

317. "News of the World of Stamps: South Moluccas, Fighting for Independence, Put Out First Issue," *New York Times*, August 12, 1951.

318. Chauvel, *Nationalists, Soldiers and Separatists*, 369.

319. Van Kaam, *South Moluccas*, 7.

320. "Maluku Tanah Airku," RMS anthem, written by Chris Soumokil and O. Sahalessy.

321. Chauvel, *Nationalists, Soldiers and Separatists*, 370.

322. Interview with Alex Manuputty, leader of the Maluku Sovereignty Front, Kudamati, Ambon, December 18, 2001.

323. FKM, *Keabsahan Bangsa Alif'uru (Maluku) Sebagai Bangsa Yang Merdeka dan Berdaulat Penuh Sejak Awal* (Ambon: FKM, 2001), 40.

324. FKM, *Keabsahan Bangsa Alif'uru*, 39, 41.

325. Interview with Alex Manuputty, December 18, 2001.

326. FKM, *Keabsahan Bangsa Alif'uru*, 30.

327. Interview with Alex Manuputty, December 18, 2001.

328. FKM, press statement No. 90/DPP.FKM/I/2002, January 17, 2002; FKM, "Seruan Terbuka, Seputar Kesepakatan Malino II," February 22, 2002; FKM, press statement No. 137/DPP.FKM/IV/2002, "Requesting International Attention and Protection," April 17, 2002.

329. Interview with Alex Manuputty, December 18, 2001.
330. Interview with Alex Manuputty, December 18, 2001.
331. FKM, *Keabsahan Bangsa Alif'uru*, 17; FKM, press statement No, 155/DPP.FKM/IV/2002, "TNI Tortured and Slaughtered People at Waisarissa, Ceram Island," April 30, 2002.
332. FKM, press statement No. 109/DPP.FKM/II/2002, "Mohon Dukungan Bagi Suksesnya Pelaksanaan Hari Ulang Tahun (HUT) Proklamasi Kemerdekaan Republik Maluku Selatan (RMS) ke-52 Tanggal 25 April 2002," February 22, 2002
333. FKM, *Keabsahan Bangsa Alif'uru*, 18.
334. Letter from MOZART to FKM representatives in Jakarta, Amboina, November 6, 2002; FKM, "Seruan Terbuka, Seputar Kesepakatan Malino II," February 22, 2002; FKM press statement No. 176/DPP.FKM/VIII/2002; "Rencana 'Operasi' Sera Oleh Penguasa Darurat Sipil Daerah Maluku (PDSDM) Terhadap Pengibar Bendera RMS Tanggal 25 April 2002."
335. Interview with Alex Manuputty, December 18, 2001.

CONCLUSION

1. Sukarno and Cindy Adams, *Sukarno: An Autobiography—As Told to Cindy Adams* (Indianapolis: Bobbs-Merrill, 1965), 224.
2. "Letters Tell of New Atrocities," *TAPOL Bulletin No. 63*, May 1984, 2.
3. Ian Martin, *Self-Determination in East Timor: The United Nations, the Ballot, and International Intervention* (Boulder, CO, and London: Lynne Rienner Publishers, International Peace Academy Occasional Paper Series, 2001), 43.

Index

Abas, Nasir, 70, 185, 186–87
Abdulgani, Ruslan, 86
Abubakar, Alyasa, 151
Abubakar, Azwar, 129, 152
Abu Hakam, 174
Abu Rusdan: arrest, 81; on JI organization and aims, 67, 71, 78–79, 80; on Pancasila, 75, 76; in Poso conflict, 175, 184, 185
Abu Tholut, 62–63, 70, 174, 185–86
Aceh: centralization policies for, 128–30; colonial experience, 12, 24, 124–26, 138–40; DI rebellions in, 2, 39–40, 41–42, 45, 47, 53, 128, 151; Islamic administration, 49–50, 52, 233; status over time, 126–28, 137, 151; *syariat* Islam in, 42, 125, 126, 128, 129, 137, 141, 151; tsunami (2004), 138
Aceh conflict (1976–2005): ceasefire, 154; civilian and NGO targets, 143–45, 147–50, 152–53; competing nationalist imaginaries, 124, 138–43, 150–54, 230, 234; DI veterans in, 52, 130–31, 233; generally, 5, 16–17, 123–24; independence referendum call, 1, 122, 152–53; loyalty tests for citizens, 12, 149–50, 235, 236; origins, 39, 124–30, 150–51; phases, 134–38. *See also* GAM
Ahok, 1, 77
Albrecht, Karl, 118, 119
Ali, Hasan, 42
Ali Sastroamidjojo, 37
Almeida Santos, Antonio de, 89–90
Alwi, Des, 202, 208
AM (Aceh Merdeka). *See* GAM
Amaral, Xavier do, 88, 95, 99, 109
Ambo, Iwan, 173, 182, 183
Ambon conflict (1999–2005): competing national imaginaries, 190, 221–26, 230, 231, 234–35; generally, 4, 5–6, 19, 67–68, 68–69, 189–90; origins, 193–200, 222–23, 226, 230; phase 1 (1999–2000), 201–9; phase 2 (2000–02), 209–18; phase 3 (2002–05), 218–21. *See also* RMS (Republic of South Maluku) rebellion
Ambon Island, Maluku: colonial experience, 11, 190–94, 225; Red-and-White bridge, 12,
235; RMS rebellion on, 190, 195–96, 232; transmigration to, 197–98, 199, 204–5
Annan, Kofi, 118, 212
anticentrist movements: Aceh conflict as, 39, 127–30, 143–45, 150–51; "Javanization" of Indonesia concern, 11, 39–40, 112, 230; PRRI/Permesta rebellions (1957–61), 2, 46, 82. *See also* communal violence; separatist movements
anticommunist policies: FRETILIN targeted, 15, 88, 89, 97–98, 111; Islamists seen as ally, 45, 56; origins, 9, 85, 87, 121, 228; US view of, 89
anti-imperial narratives: in Aceh, 6, 138–41, 142–43, 154; in East Timor, 6, 109–10, 111–13; generally, 6, 11–12, 19; of Indonesian national imaginary, 6–7, 85–87, 121; of Islamists, 26–28, 30, 31–32, 49
Anwar, Dewi Fortuna, 115–16
APODETI (political party), 88–89, 90, 91, 92, 111
archipelagic principle, 7, 85–87, 121
Arsal, Adnan, 165, 170, 172–73, 174, 175, 184, 185
ASDT (political party), 88, 109
ASEAN (Association of Southeast Asian Nations), 114, 228
Asian financial crisis (1997), 4, 10, 114, 159
Atamimi, Mohamed, 205
Ataturk, Mustafa Kemal, 30
Australia: East Timor conflict role, 89, 113, 115; JI activity in, 67, 70, 71
Aziz, Andi, 44
Azzam, Abdullah, 66, 71, 74, 78

Baabullah, Sultan of Ternate, 191
Ba'asyir, Abu Bakar: civil disobedience, 3, 63, 235; ideology, 64–65, 68–69, 70, 72–73, 236; JI establishment, 65–67
BAKIN (intelligence agency), 55, 56, 57, 58, 84, 87
Balibo Declaration (1975), 92
Bali bombings (2002), 69–71, 78, 82
Banten Jihad (1888), 24
Basri, Hassan, 129, 188

"BBM" (Sulawesi migrants to Maluku), 197–98, 199, 204–5
Belo, Carlos Felipe Ximenes, 100–101, 102, 103, 114, 118, 119
"belonging" concept: Aceh conflict and, 124, 150–53, 234; of Christian groups, 13, 188, 190, 193–94, 226, 234–35; East Timor conflict and, 110, 121, 235; generally, 4, 11–13; of Islamic groups, 13, 82–83, 234. *See also* Indonesian national imaginary
Beureueh, Daud: Aceh's Islamic administration by, 49–50, 52, 233; as Aceh's military governor, then governor, 126, 127, 140; in DI rebellions, 40, 41, 42, 43, 47, 53, 54, 128
Bin Laden, Osama, 68, 70–71, 78
Bisalemba, Roy, 163, 164
bombing campaigns, Islamist, 68–71, 78, 82, 182–83
Brimob (mobile police brigade): attacks against, 173, 210, 221; violence by, 148, 164, 166, 180, 208
Buyung Katedo massacre (2001), 173, 176, 183

Caday, Leonides, 68
Carrascalão, Mario, 87–88
Central Java, 4, 34, 37, 43–44, 56
Central Sulawesi, 156–60. *See also* Poso conflict
Christian groups: "belonging" of, 13, 188, 190, 193–94, 234–35; East Timorese Catholic Church, 99–101, 102, 103, 229; political marginalization, 5–6, 10, 157–63, 196–200, 231. *See also* religious conflicts
Coker (Ambon gang), 201, 203, 215–16, 220
colonial resistance. *See* anti-imperial narratives
communal violence: generally, 4, 10, 17–20, 233; Indonesian national imaginary and, 4–6, 228–29, 230. *See also* Ambon conflict; anticentrist movements; Poso conflict; religious conflicts
Conceição, José da, 97
Costa, Cristiano da, 96
Costa Gomes, Francisco da, 89
Costa Lopes, Martinho da, 93, 100, 103
Costa Oliveira, Porfirio da, 101, 108
counterinsurgency tactics: against DI, 46–47, 53, 232, 233–34; differing intensity levels, 6, 44, 232, 233–34; against FRETILIN, 96–97, 103, 121, 232, 234; against GAM, 134–35, 135–36, 137–38, 145–50, 152–53; *pagar betis*, 46–47, 53, 96–97, 121, 232
Cumbok Incident/War, Aceh (1945–46), 125
Cummings, Bill, 145

Damanik, Rinaldy, 160, 161, 165, 172, 177, 180, 182
Darul Islam (DI) rebellions (1947–65): in Aceh, 2, 39–40, 41–42, 45, 47, 53, 128, 151; generally, 2, 3–4, 13, 24–25, 53, 140, 229, 233; ideology, 28–32, 35, 37, 47–48, 52, 230–31; Islamic state imaginary (*See* NII); JI's emergence from, 54, 57, 66, 81, 233; origins, 25–28, 52; phase 1 (1947–49), 32–36; phase 2 (1950–57), 36–43; phase 3 (1957–65), 43–47, 82; tactics against, 46–47, 53, 232, 233–34, 235–36. *See also* Jemaah Islamiyah (JI)
Dawod, Sofyan, 133
DDII (Dewan Dakwah Islamiyah Indonesia), 56, 62, 107
Dedi, 165–66
democracy: Guided Democracy policy of Sukarno, 8–9, 36, 45–46, 228; in Habibie era, 10–11, 85, 114–15; Islamist denunciations of, 51, 72, 73, 76, 78. *See also* Pancasila
Densus 88 (counterterrorist unit), 78, 82, 184, 236
Djaelani, Adah, 54
Djaelani, Ateng, 58
Duarte, José Manuel, 86
Dutch "police action" (1947), 32–34, 48

East Timor conflict (1975–99): Catholic Church's role, 99–101, 102, 103, 229; generally, 2, 5, 12, 15, 84–85; human rights violations, 122, 136–37, 142; national imaginary and "belonging" concept, 85–87, 108–14, 121, 230, 235; phase 1 (1975–84), 92–99; phase 2 (1984–98), 99–104; phase 3 (1998–99), 116–21; Portuguese Timor invasion (1975), 7, 15, 84, 92–93, 111; preliminary events, 87–92; referendum (1999), 114–16, 118, 121, 122, 136. *See also* FRETILIN
education programs: in Aceh, 12, 125, 143, 149–50; in East Timor, 101, 106–7, 108, 109; of Islamist organizations, 3–4, 49, 54, 65–66, 81, 175; in Maluku, 198–99; in Poso, 159–60, 161
Effendi, Sofian, 129–30, 145
Ely, Thamrin, 192, 201, 216, 218
Ely, Yusuf, 201, 203, 205
Endang, 34
Endriatono Sutarto, 138, 143

Farihin, 68, 174
Fatah, Amir, 34
Fatwa, A. M., 60, 61
Fauzi, Ihsan Ali, 14, 174, 192–93, 201, 204

Fernandes, Alarico, 88
FKM (Maluku Sovereignty Front), 190, 212–13, 215, 218, 220–21, 223–25
flag of Indonesia, 11, 12, 106, 149, 235
Ford, Gerald, 92
Free Aceh Movement. *See* GAM
FRETILIN (Revolutionary Front for an Independent East Timor): in civil war and invasion (1975), 91–93; communist sympathies, 15, 88, 89, 97–98, 111; establishment and organization, 88, 96, 99, 109; FALINTIL (military wing), 94, 95, 96, 98, 102–3, 116, 236; internal divisions and arrest of leaders, 95, 98–99, 102; national imaginary, 109–14, 230; tactics against, 96–97, 103, 121, 232, 234. *See also* East Timor conflict
Front Pembela Islam (Islamist organization), 77, 209

Gaharu, Syamaun, 42
GAM (Free Aceh Movement): civilian targets, 143–45; demobilization, 154, 236; establishment, organization and funding, 130–34; guerrilla forces, 132–33, 134–35; independence declaration and referendum call, 1, 2, 122, 140; national imaginary, 124, 131, 138–43, 150, 154, 230; tactics against, 134–35, 135–36, 137–38, 145–50, 152–53. *See also* Aceh conflict
Gani, Ayah, 42
Greenstock, Sir Jeremy, 120
Guided Democracy policy, 8–9, 36, 45–46, 228
Gusmão, José Alexandre. *See* Xanana
Guterres, Eurico, 118, 120

Habibie, Bacharuddin Jusuf, 10–11, 62, 85, 114–16, 162, 228
Hairun, Sultan of Ternate, 191
Hambali, 69, 70
Hasan, Danu Muhammad, 38, 56, 57, 58
Hasanudin, 183–84
Hatta, Mohammed, 2, 25, 126
Heath, Edward, 196–97
Hispran, 57, 58, 63
Hizbullah (paramilitary organization), 32, 33, 34
Howard, John, 115
Husin, Azahari, 71

Ibnu Hajar: in DI rebellions, 40, 42–43, 45, 47, 53; South Kalimantan, Islamic kingdom vision for, 49, 52, 233

ICMI (Indonesian Association of Muslim Intellectuals): establishment and mission, 10, 62, 104, 228, 230; influence on conflicts, 115, 156, 161, 162, 185, 200
Imron, Ali, 69–70, 204
Indonesian national imaginary: Acehnese rival, 124, 138–43, 150, 153–54, 230; anti-imperial narrative, 6–7, 85–87, 121; archipelagic principle, 7, 85–87, 121; conflicts and, 4–6, 228–36; East Timorese rival, 108–14, 121, 230; in Habibie era, 10–11, 85, 114–15; ideology (*See* NKRI; Pancasila); Islamic rival (*See* Islamic state imaginary); in Suharto era (*See* New Order regime); in Sukarno era, 6–9, 11, 25–26, 36–37, 39, 85–86, 194, 227–28; symbols of Indonesia, 11, 12, 106, 149, 227, 235. *See also* "belonging" concept
Indonesian Revolution (1945–49), 19, 31–36, 120, 126, 194
Irian (West New Guinea) annexation, 2, 44, 86, 90, 111
Irsya, M., 42
Islam. *See* political Islam; *syariat* Islam
Islamic Defenders Front (Islamist organization), 77, 209
Islamic state imaginary: Ambon Christians' fear of, 222; of DI leaders (*See* NII); of JI, 66, 68, 71–77, 80–81, 83, 231; of Masyumi, 27, 45; Poso "secure base" aim, 68, 75, 82, 156, 185–87. *See also* political Islam; *syariat* Islam
Islamic State/ISIS, 13, 80, 83, 187
Islamist movements: education programs, 3–4, 49, 54, 65–66, 81, 175; GAM as, 131; generally, 2–4, 13–15; internationalization, 13, 54, 66, 77–80, 83, 187; Pancasila denounced by, 51–52, 63–65, 72, 75, 76. *See also* Darul Islam (DI) rebellions; Islamic state imaginary; Jemaah Islamiyah (JI); mujahidin; political Islam; religious conflicts; *syariat* Islam

Jakarta: communal violence in, 1, 4, 77; JI bombing attacks, 69, 70; Tanjung Priok massacre (1984), 61–62, 63, 102
Jakarta Charter (1945), 8, 28, 56, 185, 228
Javanese village model, 11, 105, 128–29, 158, 199, 228
"Javanization" of Indonesia, 11, 39–40, 112, 230
Java War (1825–30), 24
Jemaah Islamiyah (JI): in Ambon conflict, 67–68, 204; generally, 3–4, 13–14, 54–55; global jihad aim, 70–71, 77–80, 83; Islamic state imaginary, 66, 68, 71–77, 80–81, 83,

Jemaah Islamiyah (JI) *(continued)* 231; jihadi training by, 67, 78, 79, 83, 233; origins and establishment, 54, 58–59, 60–67, 81–82, 83, 233; in Poso conflict, 174, 179–80, 183–84, 185–86; regional *(mantiqi)* structure and internal divisions, 66–67, 68, 70–71, 74–76, 81, 82

jihadis. *See* mujahidin

jilbab (Islamic headscarf) rules, 10, 60, 62, 73, 187

John Paul II, Pope, 101, 103

Kalla, Jusuf, 138, 158
Kamal, Teuku, 150, 151
Kamran, 34, 48
Kartosuwirjo, Dodo Mohammad Darda, 47, 54, 58
Kartosuwirjo, Sekarmadji Marijan: capture and execution, 43, 47, 53, 197; DI jihad declaration, 33–34, 37, 48; ideology, 28–32, 36–37, 47–48, 52; as military commander, 34–35; NII presidency, 43, 45, 48–49, 233
Kastor, Rustam, 205, 209
Kelompok Merah (Christian militants in Poso), 168–70, 176
Kiat, Amir, 219
Komando Jihad (mujahidin), 57–58, 62, 204
KOMPAK (mujahidin), 14, 173–74, 175, 178, 179, 209, 217
Konfrontasi (Indonesia-Malaysia confrontation, 1963–66), 7
Kongkoli, Rev. Irianto, 158, 164, 177, 182
KOPKAMTIB (national security force), 55, 64
Kraemer, Hendrik, 193
Kraras massacre (1983), 97
Kristiadi, J., 107
Kurnia, Aceng, 54

Ladjalani, Damsyik, 162, 165, 166
Lamusu, Nani, 170
Laskar Jihad (mujahidin): in Ambon conflict, 14, 209–11, 212–14, 216–18, 220, 221; in Poso conflict, 173, 174, 175–76, 177–78, 180
Laskar Jundullah (mujahidin), 173, 175, 180, 204
Laskar Khos (mujahidin), 204
Laskar Mujahidin (mujahidin umbrella group), 204, 209, 210, 212, 216, 217–18
Lateka, A. L., 168, 170, 172, 177
Latuconsina, Akib, 200
Latuconsina, Saleh, 200
Latuharhary, Johannes, 196–97
Leimena, Johannes, 195
Lemos Pires, Mario, 89, 91

Leuhery, Jacob, 189
Lim Bian Kie, 89
Loki attack (2005), 221
Lopez da Cruz, Francisco Xavier, 90, 91, 94
Loupatti, Berthy, 201, 203, 215–16, 220
loyalty tests, 12, 149–50, 235–36
Lukman, Syarifuddin, 165

Madiun uprising (1948), 56
Mahmud, Malik, 131, 132, 133, 135, 138, 142
Majlis Mujahidin Indonesia, 70
Malino Agreement (2001), 179, 186, 188
Malino II Agreement (2002), 218–19
Malukan separatism. *See* Ambon conflict; RMS (Republic of South Maluku) rebellion
Maluku Sovereignty Front (FKM), 190, 212–13, 215, 218, 220–21, 223–25
Manaf, Muzakir, 1, 147
Mandagi, Petrus Canisius, 221
Manuhutu, Johannes Hermanus, 195
Manuputty, Alex, 213, 215, 220, 224, 225
Manuputty, Jacky, 201, 204
Mao Klao, 86
Marzuki, Amni Ahmad bin, 142
Mashudi, Srie Handono, 174
Masyumi (Islamic party): bans on, 9, 46, 56; in conflicts, 82, 128, 199–200; Islamic state imaginary, 27, 45; Kartosuwirjo in, 28, 31, 33, 48
Maulani, Z. A., 106, 114
MIT (mujahidin), 187, 188
Mohamed, Samsu, 165, 170, 172–73
Mokoginta, 86
Molilo, Deki, 178
Monding, Dolfi, 164
Monjo, John Cameron, 101
Muhammadiyah (Islamic group), 27, 77, 78, 82, 151, 160, 199–200
Muis, Abdul, 182
Al Mujahid, Amir Hussein, 42
mujahidin: in Ambon conflict, 67, 173, 204, 209–11, 212–14, 216–18, 221; generally, 14, 21; overseas training, 67, 78, 79, 83, 233; in Poso conflict, 173–76, 177–78, 179–84, 187, 188. *See also* Islamist movements; names of mujahidin groups
Mukhlas, 69, 70, 74
Munandar, Aris, 204
Murdani, Benny, 61, 62, 97, 234
Murtopo, Ali, 56, 57, 58, 89, 90
Musa, Malik, 129, 150–51
Muslim groups. *See* Islamist movements; political Islam

Mustopha (Abu Tholut), 62–63, 70, 174, 185
Mustopo, 214
Muzakkar, Abdul Kahar: in DI rebellions, 40, 41, 43, 47, 53; Pancasila denunciation, 51–52; South Sulawesi's Islamic administration by, 50–51, 233

Nahdlatul Ulama (NU) (Islamic group), 27, 56, 59, 60, 82
Naro, John, 87
NASAKOM (national ideology), 9
Nasution, A. H., 46, 232
Nasution, A. Y., 148–49
Nasution, Mohamed Amin, 126
national imaginary. *See* Indonesian national imaginary
Natsir, Mohammad, 27, 56, 60, 127
Nazar, Muhammad, 148, 152–53
Negara Islam Indonesia. *See* NII
Negara Kesatuan Republik Indonesia. *See* NKRI
Nelly, Rev., 163, 178, 180
New Order regime (1967-98): Aceh policies, 128–30; communal violence attributed to, 16, 19, 197–200; downfall, 4, 10, 17–18; East Timor policies, 104–8, 121; Pancasila policies, 9–10, 58–59, 60–65; political Islam "courted" (1990s), 6, 10, 62, 156, 159–61, 198–200, 228; political Islam repressed, 9, 55–62, 62–66, 83; village governance policy, 11, 105, 128–29, 158, 199, 228. *See also* anticommunist policies; transmigration policy
NII (Negara Islam Indonesia): declaration, 33, 36, 37, 48–49; DI leaders' imaginaries of, 5, 27, 34, 36, 47–52, 83, 229, 233; expansion, 39–43; government appointments, 43, 48, 49, 52; in JI thought, 73, 75; Sukarno's denunciation of, 8, 37, 43, 228. *See also* Darul Islam (DI) rebellions; Islamic state imaginary
Nikijuluw, Emang, 201, 203, 204, 207
NKRI (unitary state idea): adoption, 10, 228; Islamist denunciations of, 75, 83; loyalty tests, 12, 149–50, 235–36; motto of Indonesia ("unity in diversity"), 11, 227; separatist movements seen as enemy to, 105, 137, 146, 149–50, 231; violence to uphold, 6, 44, 232. *See also* Pancasila
North Sumatra, 4, 57
Notodihardjo, 28
NU (Islamic group), 27, 56, 59, 60, 82

Oni, 34, 48

Padri War (1803–37), 24
pagar betis (counterinsurgency tactic), 46–47, 53, 96–97, 121, 232
Pahe, Mandor, 165, 170
Paliudju, 166, 172
Pancasila (pluralism): Aceh, opposition in, 124–25, 126, 151; five principles, 7–8; Islamist denunciations of, 51–52, 63–65, 72, 75, 76; Poso Christians' support for, 156; resistance to generally, 1–6; in Suharto era, 9–10, 58–59, 60–65, 228. *See also* democracy; NKRI; *syariat* Islam
Panjaitan, Luhut, 93, 116
Papuan separatism, 1, 2, 229
Parimo, Herman, 163–64, 168
Parmusi (political party), 56
al-Pasè, Isnander, 145
Patanga, Agfar, 165, 166, 167, 170
Patanga, Arief, 161, 162, 164, 165
Patiro, Yahya, 162
PDI (political party), 59
Pesuwarissa, Dominggus Zakarias, 222
Pinto, Constancio, 15, 108
pluralism. *See* Pancasila
political Islam: anti-imperial narrative, 26–28, 30, 31–32, 49; in colonial era, 25, 26–28, 52; "courted" by Suharto, 6, 10, 62, 156, 159–61, 198–200, 228; repressed by Suharto, 9, 55–62, 62–66, 83; in Sukarno era, 8, 9, 25–26, 228. *See also* Islamist movements; names of Islamic groups
Portuguese Timor: annexation preparations, 87–92; in Indonesian national imaginary, 85–87, 121; invasion (1975), 7, 15, 84, 92–93, 111. *See also* East Timor conflict
Poso conflict (1998–2007): competing national imaginaries, 184–88, 231; generally, 4, 15, 18, 155–56; Islamic "secure base" aim, 68, 75, 82, 156, 185–87; origins, 5–6, 156–63, 231; phases 1 and 2 (1998–2000), 163–67; phase 3 (May-June 2000), 68, 156, 167–73, 183, 185; phase 4 (2000–01), 172–79; phase 5 (2002–07), 179–84; revival (2012), 188
PPP (political party), 59, 60
Pranoto, Haji Ismail (Hispran), 57, 58, 63
Prawiranegara, Sjafruddin, 60, 127
PRRI/Permesta rebellions (1957–61), 2, 46, 82
PSII (political party), 27, 28, 31
Purnama, Basuki Tjahaja (Ahok), 1, 77
Purwanto, Gatot, 97
PUSA (All-Aceh Ulama Association), 40, 41, 125, 126, 127

Pusadan, Abdul Muin, 161, 177
Puteh, Abdullah, 143, 151, 152

Al-Qaeda, 14, 67, 69, 71, 74, 137, 187

Rahawarin, Nasir, 205, 208
Raja, Mohamed Daeng, 160, 165, 170, 176
Ramly, 209
Ramos-Horta, José, 15, 99, 102, 110, 111, 112–13
Red Group (Christian militants in Poso), 168–70, 176
Rego, Leoneto do, 94
Reis Araujo, Arnaldo dos, 104, 105
religious conflicts: attributed to colonialism, 19, 30, 192–93; during DI rebellions, 41; in East Timor, 104, 118, 119. *See also* Ambon conflict; Christian groups; Islamist movements; Poso conflict; RMS (Republic of South Maluku) rebellion
Renville Agreement (1948), 32, 34
research methodology and resources, 20–21
Revolutionary Front for an Independent East Timor. *See* FRETILIN
Ribeiro, José Joaquim, 99
Ridwan, 57
Riwu, Marinus, 168, 169, 177, 182
RMS Movement, 202–3, 205, 215–16, 230
RMS (Republic of South Maluku) rebellion (1950–63): Ambon conflict and, 196–97, 222–23, 226, 230; on Ambon Island, 190, 195–96, 232; generally, 15, 16, 44, 229, 232, 233; on Seram Island, 2, 196. *See also* Ambon conflict
Roem, Mohammad, 27, 196
Ruhulessin, John, 222
Ryacudu, Ryamizard, 148

Sabilillah (paramilitary organization), 32, 33, 34
Saby, Yusny, 151, 152, 153
Said, Firman (Dedi), 165–66
Saleh, Hasan, 41, 42
Salim, Agus, 27, 28
Samanhudi, 26
Samudra, Imam, 69, 70
Santa Cruz massacre (1991), 101–2, 142
Santos Goncalves, Vasco dos, 89
Sarekat Islam (Islamic group), 26–27, 29
Sarumpaet, Herry, 166
Selang, Malik, 216
separatist movements: generally, 2–3, 16–17, 122; Indonesian national imaginary and, 4–6, 228–29, 229–30; Papuan separatism, 1, 2, 229. *See also* Aceh conflict; Ambon conflict; anticentrist movements; East Timor conflict; NKRI; RMS (Republic of South Maluku) rebellion
Shultz, George, 100
Silalahi, Hari Tjan, 89
Silva, Dominggus da, 168, 170, 171, 172, 177, 182
Silva Tavares, Joao da, 117
SIRA (Aceh Referendum Information Center), 147–48, 152–53
Siyono, 78
Sjarifuddin, Amir, 27, 33
Slamet, Usman, 218
Soares, Mario, 89
socialism, 8–9
Soetanto, Himawan, 57
Sol, Andreas Peter Cornelius, 200
Solihat, Kadar, 54
Sonata, Abdullah, 173, 209, 211
Souissa, Femmy, 216
Soumokil, Chris, 2, 15, 16, 195, 196, 197, 222
South Kalimantan: DI rebellions in, 2, 39–40, 42–43, 44, 45, 53; Islamic kingdom vision for, 49, 52, 233
South Sulawesi: DI rebellions in, 2, 39–41, 44, 45, 53; Islamic administration, 50–51, 233
Stahl, Max, 102
Suai massacre (1999), 119
Subandrio, 86
Sudarsono, Juwono, 210
Sudjadi, Djaja, 54
Sugito, 119
Suharto: in DI rebellions, 43; Pasar Klewer speech (1971), 58–59; Portuguese Timor invasion (1975), 7, 15, 84, 92–93, 111; rise to power, 9, 55–56. *See also* New Order regime
Suja, Imam, 151
Sukarno: Aceh visits, 126, 128; Ambonese Christians, view of, 194, 196–97; DI attacks on, 38; Guided Democracy policy, 8–9, 36, 45–46, 228; Indonesian independence declared by, 2, 5, 126; Indonesian national imaginary of, 6–9, 11, 25–26, 36–37, 39, 85–86, 194, 227–28; Islamism denunciation, 8, 37, 43, 228; RMS rebellion response, 195, 196
Sukarnoputri, Megawati, 137, 208
Suleiman (Nasir Abas), 70, 185, 186
Sumarto, Sutikno P., 41–42
Sungkar, Abdullah: civil disobedience, 3, 63, 235; death, 70, 71; ideology, 64–65, 72–73, 80; JI establishment, 65–67, 81
Suratman, Tono, 15, 103, 116
Suwarya, Endang, 148

INDEX   301

Syahnakri, Kiki, 15, 96, 107
syariat Islam (Islamic law): in Aceh, 42, 125, 126, 128, 129, 137, 141, 151; in Ambon, 216–17; "belonging" concept and, 13, 82, 83, 234; Islamist views on, 72, 73, 76, 78–79, 80–81, 185, 187, 229; Jakarta Charter safeguarding, 8, 28, 56, 185, 228; *jilbab* (headscarf) rules, 10, 60, 62, 73, 187; in Poso, 185; in South Sulawesi, 50–51; *takfiri* (declaring Muslims apostates), 35, 39, 48, 77. *See also* Islamic state imaginary; Pancasila
symbols of Indonesia, 11, 12, 106, 149, 227, 235

Tadi, Lorenzo, 181
Talangsari massacre (1989), 3
Tamaela, Max, 208, 210, 211
Tanjung, Feisal, 115, 116
Tanjung Priok massacre (1984), 61–62, 63, 102
Tarau, Rev., 157
Tarcisius, Dewanto, 119
Taufik, Gaos, 54, 58
Taur Matan Ruak, 116
Tauziri, Kiyai Jusuf, 28, 39
Thalib, Jafar Umar, 174, 209, 211, 214, 216, 218, 220
Tiba, Sofyan Ibrahim, 133, 146
Tibo, Fabianus: ceasefire demands, 172; in Poso conflict violence, 168, 169, 170, 171; reprisals against, 177, 178, 181, 182
Tinulele, Rev. Susianti, 181, 182
Tiro, Hasan di: Aceh conflict narrative, 15, 132, 134, 138–42, 144, 150, 145, 154; Acehnese independence declaration, 2, 140; GAM establishment, 130–31; NII role, 52
Tjokroaminoto, Omar Said, 26, 27, 28
Tobundo, Rev., 161
Tompo, Aliansyah (Maro), 165, 166, 167, 170
Top, Noordin Mohammad, 70, 71
transmigration policy: Aceh, effect in, 130, 135, 144; Ambon, effect in, 197–98, 199, 204–5; East Timor, effect in, 105, 107; generally, 19, 232, 235; Poso, effect in, 157–60. *See also* New Order regime
Tumimor, Albert, 159, 167–68
Tungkanan, Paulus, 168

UDT (political party), 87–88, 90, 91, 111
Ulahaiyanan, Agus, 210, 218
unitary state idea. *See* NKRI
United Development Party (PPP), 59, 60
United States: denunciations of, 70, 72–73, 113; views on Indonesian policies, 15, 89, 92

Vasconcellos, Sancho de, 191
village governance policy, 11, 105, 128–29, 158, 199, 228
Viqueque Revolt (1959), 85–86

Wahdah Islamiyah (Salafi organization), 173
Wahid, Abdurrahman, 137, 156, 172, 188, 209
Wahid Hasjim, Abdul, 27
Wairisal, Albert, 195
Walad, Muzzakir, 129
Walisongo massacre (2000), 68, 156, 171, 173, 183, 185
Wanandi, Jusuf, 89
Wattimena, Agus, 201, 202, 203, 215, 216
Wattimena, Dicky, 201, 205
Westerling, Raymond, 44
West Java: communal violence in, 4, 19, 57, 120; DI rebellions in, 34–36, 37–39, 44–45, 47, 53; Dutch "police action" in, 32–34, 48; Islamic administration, 48
West Kalimantan, 4, 17, 18, 229
West New Guinea (Irian) annexation, 2, 44, 86, 90, 111
West Timor: East Timorese exiles in, 91, 111, 119, 120; other mentions, 86, 104, 106
Whitlam, Gough, 89, 113
Widodo, Joko, 76
Wijayanto, Para, 76–78, 79–80, 81
Wirananggati, Abdul Fatah, 52
Wiranto, 15, 115–16, 119–20, 136
women: DI rebellions role, 41; *jilbab* (Islamic headscarf) rules, 10, 60, 62, 73, 187; New Order policies focused on, 59, 60; victimized in conflicts, 93, 147, 171, 176, 183–84, 213

Xanana: attempts to capture, 97–98, 102; East Timor conflict narrative, 15, 88, 94, 100, 102, 111, 112, 113–14; FRETILIN presidency, 96

Yamin, Muhammad, 11, 85
Yasa, I Made, 211, 213, 214
Yeimo, Victor, 1
Yogyakarta Special Region, 126
Yopi, 189
Yudhoyono, Susilo Bambang, 138
Yusuf, Djali, 147
Yusuf, Mohammad, 97

Zarkasih, 76
Zulkarnaen, 204